AFTER THE VIRUS

Why was the UK so unprepared for the pandemic, suffering one of the highest death rates and worst economic contractions of the major world economies in 2020? Hilary Cooper and Simon Szreter reveal the deep roots of our vulnerability and set out a powerful manifesto for change post-COVID-19. They argue that our commitment to a flawed neoliberal model and the associated disinvestment in our social fabric left the UK dangerously exposed and unable to mount an effective response. This is not at all what made Britain great. The long history of the highly innovative universal welfare system established by Elizabeth I facilitated both the industrial revolution and, when revived after 1945, the post-war Golden Age of rising prosperity. Only by learning from that past can we create the fairer, nurturing and empowering society necessary to tackle the global challenges that lie ahead: climate change, biodiversity collapse and global inequality.

Hilary Cooper is a former government economist and senior policy maker with expertise in labour markets, children's services and local development. Her current freelance work examines the challenges of ageing. She was the joint winner of the 2019 IPPR Economics Prize for the essay 'Incentivising an Ethical Economics', with Simon Szreter and Ben Szreter.

Simon Szreter is Professor of History and Public Policy at Cambridge University, researching economic, social and public health history. His publications include *Health and Wealth*, which won the American Public Health Association's Viseltear Prize, and, with Kate Fisher, *Sex before the Sexual Revolution*, longlisted for the Samuel Johnson Prize. He is co-founder and editor of *History & Policy*.

After the Virus

Lessons from the Past for a Better Future

HILARY COOPER AND SIMON SZRETER

CAMBRIDGE
UNIVERSITY PRESS

University Printing House, Cambridge CB2 8BS, United Kingdom

One Liberty Plaza, 20th Floor, New York, NY 10006, USA

477 Williamstown Road, Port Melbourne, VIC 3207, Australia

314–321, 3rd Floor, Plot 3, Splendor Forum, Jasola District Centre,
New Delhi – 110025, India

103 Penang Road, #05–06/07, Visioncrest Commercial, Singapore 238467

Cambridge University Press is part of the University of Cambridge.

It furthers the University's mission by disseminating knowledge in the pursuit of
education, learning, and research at the highest international levels of excellence.

www.cambridge.org
Information on this title: www.cambridge.org/9781009005203
DOI: 10.1017/9781009036412

First published 2021

Printed in the United Kingdom by TJ Books Limited, Padstow Cornwall

A catalogue record for this publication is available from the British Library.

ISBN 978-1-009-00520-3 Paperback

Let today embrace the past with remembrance and the future with longing.

Kahil Gibran, *The Prophet*

For Iridium, Ben and Zack

CONTENTS

List of Figures and Images   *Page* xii
Preface   xvii

INTRODUCTION   1

What This Book Is   1
Why Read This Book?   4
Quick Guide to the Book   11

**Part I COVID-19 Was Always a Matter of
'When' Not 'If'**   19

**1 THE EXTRAORDINARY HISTORY OF
PANDEMIC CONTROL**   21

An Ever-Present Threat   21
The Myth of Progress   22
How Pandemics Spread   29
Pandemics and the Role of the State: From
    Divine to Human Responsibility   32
A Plague on All Our Houses: Learning to Control
    Pandemics   36

**2 PANDEMICS ARE NOT RANDOM 'BLACK
SWANS'**   44

We Were Expecting a Pandemic, So Why Was
    the UK So Unprepared?   44
Your Money or Your Life   51
Light at the End of the Tunnel   59

Part II Why COVID-19 Was a Perfect Storm 67

3 THE FRAGILITY OF THE NEOLIBERAL STATE 69

The Neoliberal Project 69
The Capture of Democracy 75
How COVID-19 Was Able to Wreak Havoc 80
   A 'Just in Time' Health Service 81
   A 'Cinderella' Social Care Service 87
A Dysfunctional State 91

4 INEQUALITY SAPS RESILIENCE 99

Inequality and the Laissez-Faire State 99
'This Is Not an Easy Life Any More, Chum' 105
Are We Bothered? 113
It's the Economy, Stupid 119
The 'Burning Injustices' 122

5 THE PANDEMIC ONSLAUGHT 128

Those Who Lived and Those Who Died 128
The Tattered Safety Net 133
The COVID Generation 138
Where's Next? 141
Looking to the Future 143

Part III How COVID-19 Challenges Us To Change 145

6 'TOO BIG TO FAIL?' WE NEED A PAYBACK THIS TIME 147

Lessons from the 2007–8 Financial Crash 147
What Does All This Have to Do with the 2020 Pandemic? 153
A First Look at the Winners and Losers 155

Securing the Pandemic Payback: How Are Things
    Looking This Time?   162
Is the Old Order Beginning to Crack?   168

7 NO TIME FOR AUSTERITY NOW   **174**

So We Found the Magic Money Tree   174
When Austerity Was in Vogue   176
Let's Just Put It on the Tab   180
Storm Clouds Ahead?   187

8 WHO HAS THE DEEPEST POCKETS?   **193**

A Better Future and a Proactive State   193
Will We Find the Pot of Gold?   197

9 RETHINKING WELFARE   **208**

Is It Time for a No-Strings Attached Universal
    Basic Income?   208
'Dignity and Security'   212
Universal Services   222
Who Cares?   226
What of Later Life?   232

**Part IV After the Virus: Who Do We Want
    to Be?**   **235**

10 CASTING ASIDE THE NEOLIBERAL STATE   **237**

Homo Economicus and the Myth of Rationality   237
History and Morality   241

**11 THE BIRTH OF A COLLECTIVIST
    INDIVIDUALISM**   **251**

How Elizabeth I Gave Us the World's First
    Welfare State   251
The Poor Laws and Local Communities   253

'Crowding-in Charity': The Charitable Uses Act 256
The Poor Laws and Economic Growth 258
The Turn Away from Collectivist Individualism
    after 1834 266
The Boer War and the 'New Liberal' Reforms 271
The 'Golden Age': 1945–73 275
Wealth, Redistribution and Progressive Taxation 278
What Lessons Can We Take from History? 281

12 A NURTURING AND EMPOWERING STATE 286

What Does It Mean to Have a Nurturing and
    Empowering State? 286
Freedom and the State 287
Building Collective Commitment 291
The Case for Fair and Progressive Contributions 295
Democratic Participation and Devolved Power 301
The Nurturing State and Our Natural
    Environment 309

13 SEVEN PILLARS OF EMPOWERMENT 318

1. A Nurturing State: Respect and Inclusive
    Support for All 319
2. Ethical Capitalism: Working with Business to
    Redefine Our Values 322
3. Fair Contributions: Full Participation by the
    Prosperous 326
4. Open Public Discourse: Enabling All Voices to
    Have an Equal Hearing 329
5. Measuring What We Value: Signalling the
    Changes We Need 332
6. A Sustainable Future: Responsible Stewardship
    of Our Planet's Resources 335
7. Participatory Politics: Reviving Democracy and
    Civic Engagement 338

14 GREATER EVEN THAN A PANDEMIC **341**

Conclusion 345

Acknowledgements 347
Notes 351
References 372
Index 403

FIGURES AND IMAGES

Figures

Figure 1   The Gini Coefficient of income inequality
            in Great Britain, 1961 to 2018–19   100
Figure 2   Percentage of children living in relative
            poverty (after housing costs), 1961 to 2019–20 110
Figure 3   Trends in UK education spending,
            1955–56 to 2019–20   116
Figure 4   Average percentage change in council
            service spending per person by local area
            deprivation, 2009–10 to 2017–18   118
Figure 5   Deaths by local area deprivation, 1 March
            to 31 July 2020   129
Figure 6   Children's daily learning time: gaps in
            educational activity   140
Figure 7   National debt as a percentage of GDP,
            1693–2019   181
Figure 8   Debt interest payments as percentage of
            total annual revenue 1680–2020 (and
            forecast 2021–25)   183
Figure 9   Attitudes to differences in wealth   198
Figure 10   Total household wealth and amount of
            wealth taxed, each as a percentage of Gross
            Domestic Product in Great Britain, 1965–2017   201
Figure 11   Urban growth in England, France and the
            Netherlands, 1600 to 1850   260
Figure 12   Gross Domestic Product, year on year
            growth, 1949–2019   277

Figure 13 Comparison of top marginal income tax
           rates, 1900–2013 in the USA, UK, France and
           Germany   279
Figure 14 Seven Pillars of Empowerment   319

Images

Image 1   A seventeenth-century illustration of a
          physician wearing protective clothing,
          including a mask, as a defence against the
          plague   26
Image 2   Warehouses were converted during the
          1918–20 influenza to keep infected people
          quarantined   28
Image 3   Painting depicting a couple suffering from
          the Black Death. From the Swiss manuscript
          the Toggenburg Bible, 1411   33
Image 4   The title page of a 1665 compilation of the
          London Bills of Mortality   36
Image 5   Number 10 special adviser Dominic
          Cummings on 25 May 2020, after giving a
          press conference to answer allegations that
          he and his family broke the rules when they
          travelled from London to Durham while the
          nation was under full lockdown   48
Image 6   Medical workers take a patient into a newly
          built temporary hospital, Rome, 16 March
          2020   50
Image 7   Margaret Keenan, the first person in the
          world to be vaccinated, is applauded by
          staff after being vaccinated at University
          Hospital, Coventry   60
Image 8   Socially distanced shoppers outside
          Debenhams   73
Image 9   A medical professional wearing a face mask

and flimsy plastic apron at the entrance of the
A&E department at Frimley Park
Hospital, Surrey, 22 May 2020   84

Image 10   Care home visit during the coronavirus
pandemic   88

Image 11   Dido Harding outside Downing Street, 16
September 2020   93

Image 12   A woman walks past a homeless tent in
Bradford City Centre, 12 February 2021   112

Image 13   NHS nurses protest outside the entrance to
Downing Street, 3 June 2020   132

Image 14   Greater Manchester mayor Andy Burnham
speaks to the media on 20 October 2020
after the failure to agree a financial package
to help those whose jobs were threatened by
a tier-three lockdown   142

Image 15   Worker leaving Lehman Brothers' European
headquarters, Canary Wharf, 15 September
2008   148

Image 16   Klaus Schwab (right) with staff at the World
Economic Forum, Switzerland, 20 January
2020   171

Image 17   Finding the magic money tree   176

Image 18   The 'Eat Out to Help Out' subsidy, August
2020   190

Image 19   Mural of footballer Marcus Rashford, MBE,
with pizza boxes celebrating his campaign
on child hunger   216

Image 20   William Beveridge's five Giants: Want,
Ignorance, Disease, Squalor and Idleness   222

Image 21   Mother combining work and childcare
during the coronavirus pandemic   228

Image 22   Cartoon depicting the 1878 Birmingham

municipal election: the Liberal caucus led
by Joseph Chamberlain with his trademark
monocle defending the newly constructed
Council House building behind them, with
their cannons proclaiming their
achievements of Gas, Water and Health   244

Image 23   Greta Thunberg, speaking at the UN Climate
Action Summit   248

Image 24   The 'Pelican' portrait of Elizabeth I, c.1575 by
Nicholas Hilliard. The pelican symbolised her
sacrificial devotion to her 'children' – the
nation   252

Image 25   Distress in Ireland: collecting limpets and
seaweed for food   268

Image 26   Protest marchers on the Jarrow Crusade,
March–October 1936   273

Image 27   Members of the British Youth Council and
Youth Parliament hold a live debate on the
film set of *The Iron Lady* at Wimbledon
Studios, to debate the role of women in
politics on 10 April 2012   304

Image 28   Extinction Rebellion protest in Leeds, 15 July
2019   312

Image 29   The tsunami ahead   342

PREFACE

The COVID-19 virus has starkly exposed just how vulnerable Britain's highly unequal society has become. The new decade of the 2020s has begun with an important moment of reckoning. We need to face up to the fact that this may well turn out not to be a one-off, but a dress rehearsal. As things stand there are going to be many more global-scale crises heading our way in the twenty-first century. Humankind has inadvertently become trapped within an unsustainable high-carbon, high-inequality, globalised economy that worships growth. This is now placing an intolerable pressure on the planet and our relationship with other species, right down to micro-organisms like the coronavirus.

This means that it is imperative that we take stock and learn all the lessons that we can to address the coming century's urgent problems. Science can be an important resource but equally important is a critical reappraisal of our society and our values. This book argues that history can play a vital role in enabling us to do this because history can emancipate us to think differently – about the future economy, our future society, how we govern ourselves and who we want to be.

Revisiting Britain's modern history, going right back to the reign of Elizabeth I, can enable us to see that Britain's undoubted success as a global economic leader by the beginning of the nineteenth century was not, in fact, based on today's unrestrained individualist, free-market economics. This only emerged later, becoming British government policy during the course of the nineteenth century – and it caused terrible problems both domestically and globally. Ultimately, expansion of this ideological virus of voracious self-enrichment went global, leading eventually to the First World War, fascism in Europe and the Second World War. Temporarily set aside after the cataclysm of that second war, since 1980 the siren song of self-interest has returned once again in the form of neoliberal government policies that have pared back the public sphere, bringing the rising inequalities and weakened democracy that left us so exposed when COVID-19 struck.

It is well-known that the story of the industrial revolution and modern economic growth began in Britain. What is far less well-known is that two centuries before the first factory steam-engines began to be heard, Britain innovated something just as significant, a treasure that has lain buried and forgotten until the most recent generation of historians revealed it. This was the world's first ever welfare state, the universal social security system of the 'Elizabethan' Poor Law, first put in place in 1601. Its principles were those of a collectivist individualism, a unique English creation. Individuals were empowered and their independent capacities to take economic risks encouraged, but within a supportive framework. This was possible because every individual had a statutory entitlement to support from their community, which was funded by a compulsory, progressive local tax on land – the main source of wealth.

After 200 years of expansion in response to need, this empowering and nurturing welfare system had brought British society and its highly mobile workforce to its industrial revolution. But it was then abandoned in 1834 and the New Poor Law was born. Collectivist individualism was replaced by a harsher outright individualism. The poor were no longer viewed as deserving of assistance but as lazy, deserving only the discipline of the workhouse. But this new economic orthodoxy did not deliver. No longer investing in the well-being of the wider population as it previously had, slowly but surely, under the New Poor Law the economy's leadership in international productivity ebbed away.

A tumultuous century later a national policy of collectivist individualism had to be reinvented by William Beveridge as the post-war welfare state and its iconic National Health Service. For the first time in seventy years the productivity of the national economy once again lifted after 1945 as the British people 'never had it so good', with secondary education, decent housing and secure employment increasingly available to all.

It was this same ethos of unconditional commitment to the support of others, encapsulated by the selfless workers of the NHS, which got British society through the darkest days of the coronavirus crisis. As this book shows, this was despite the repeated ineptitudes during 2020 of a shockingly unprepared administration in Westminster, reluctant to engage with the nation's provincial public health or local government services and instead spending the nation's money lavishly on private sector contracts, many of which, notably in the case of the highly expensive test and trace system, failed ignominiously. The government's principal success, the vaccination programme, was a classic and heroic creation of the public sector and the non-profit ethos.

This book argues that the most valuable lessons of British history – both throughout the last forty and the last 400 years – are that we need to rediscover our nation's long-proven capacity to prioritise collective commitment to support each other – especially the most vulnerable – and that this fosters a responsible, not a reckless individualism. Far from state support being the enemy of

individualism, initiative-taking by individuals has flourished most widely in this country's history – and has been
of the greatest economic benefit to all – when society has
committed itself to generous collective support and security for all. The late Chief Rabbi Jonathan Sacks argued
that 'a nation is strong when it cares for the weak … it becomes rich when it cares for the poor'. As Britain's history
shows, it is not just a moral but an economic argument,
too. Welfare's focus on nurturing human and social capital
is a promoter of economic prosperity and well-being, not
a burden on it.

We conclude our book by offering seven pillars of empowerment that describe the principles and practical
policies required once again to build a nurturing society,
empowering of all individuals, to face the oncoming challenges of the twenty-first century. Informed by our own
history, this should rightly start here across the nations of
the UK. We should once again take up the mantle, not wait
for others to do the work for us.

INTRODUCTION

What This Book Is

This is a book about history and policy. It is about how public policy can be designed for the future. But it is also about how that policy can best be framed with a full understanding of some extremely important lessons from our own history – to enable that policy to succeed.

We start with an analysis of the reasons for the devastating impact of the COVID-19 pandemic in the UK. A commitment from 1979 onwards to neoliberalism – a doctrine that advocates the expansion of 'free markets' and reduced investment by the state in our social fabric – left us dangerously exposed. We had neither the capacity to respond effectively when COVID-19 arrived nor the flexibility in our institutions to turn this situation around quickly as the crisis developed. At the same time, we had let social and racial inequalities and health challenges multiply for decades – to such an extent that our resilience to infection risk and severe disease was compromised, not least among people of colour.[1]

COVID-19 has laid bare the underlying stresses in our society, stresses that resulted in a pandemic that was polarising in its impact. With the exception of the older population, those most at risk of dying were the poor, many with pre-existing health problems, who were nevertheless frequently working in exposed front-line roles providing essential health, care or transport services, while others stayed safely inside. COVID-19 was not simply a pandemic, but a syndemic. In other words what we faced was not just an infectious disease that had to be controlled by cutting the lines of transmission. It was a super-toxic coming together of a deadly respiratory illness, with latent, non-communicable health conditions (such as heart disease, diabetes, obesity and asthma) that interacted with embedded social inequality. A syndemic occurs when these risk factors intertwine and reinforce each other to exacerbate and magnify the overall burden that the population experiences during a pandemic disease.[2]

This book will contrast the last forty years with two previous eras in which our welfare state was nurturing and inclusive, beginning this story by looking at the original Elizabethan Poor Law inaugurated in 1601, the first of its kind in the world. The unique provisions of that first universal social security system protected England from the scourge of famine – that other devastator of populations – to the extent that the English were free of large-scale famine more than 150 years earlier than the rest of Europe. We show that the Old Poor Law (1601–1834) also helped power England's exceptional economic growth as it enabled a mobile workforce to develop, secure in the knowledge that they would be supported if times were hard. When the Poor Law was retrenched after 1834 into a deterrent workhouse system, the UK's economic performance subsequently fell back. It was this retreat into a minimised laissez-faire state that left the UK unable to cope with a different microbial threat – in this case the potato blight. In the province of Ireland the new workhouse system proved completely inadequate to the task and millions fell prey to starvation or destitution between 1845 and 1851 in Ireland's tragic Great Famine.

There are many other publications about the COVID-19 pandemic that offer insights by focusing on comparisons between the UK and other countries. What this book does is different. It firstly provides an historically informed analysis of how we arrived in the dysfunctional state in which we found ourselves in 2020, and secondly it draws heavily on our own longer-term history to show how this vitally assists us to chart a way out of it. We will not of course be suggesting the same policies as in the past – times have changed. The principles we derive from our history are not dated or backward-looking – they are fresh and surprising insights into the best of our past and the optimism it can supply for our future.

Politicians and policy makers are always looking over the fence at attractive alternatives elsewhere in the world, but they often overlook the policy resources to be found in our own country's history. Drawing on England's unique history as the cradle of a universal welfare approach, we will show how previous periods of investment in the population's welfare, security and health supported inclusive economic participation and initiative-taking by the maximum proportion of the population. This happened firstly in the long lead-in to industrialisation, c.1600–1800, and then again in the high growth decades of the Golden Age after the Second World War when productivity growth reached historic highs and inequality reached historic lows.

Our policy contribution starts from an analysis of the risks that decades of public disinvestment have exposed us to. It will argue that even now the way that we are structuring our economic response to the pandemic and its aftermath could well simply act to enrich further those with property and assets, exactly as happened after the 2008 financial crisis. It will propose new policies, institutional arrangements and incentive structures to inform the way we rebuild UK society and our economy after the pandemic, ensuring that we do not default to tired and failed old formulae such as austerity.

It will set out proposals for replacing a disempowering state with a fully empowering state focused on nurturing the rising generation and promoting population well-being. It will provide proposals showing how a new more ethical capitalism, supporting this change to a nurturing society, can be created. It will also set these policy proposals in the context of the future destabilising risks of climate change and biodiversity collapse, arguing that we urgently need to embrace these changes because we simply cannot address the even greater challenges that we face in the near future if we stick with the neoliberal framework that has prevailed for the last four decades.

Why Read This Book?

Events such as revolutions and pandemics reveal for us – like an X-ray – what is going on beneath the surface in a particular society at a particular time. The huge stresses they cause suddenly make starkly visible the damaging effects of the power relationships and the embedded inequalities, which were all already there, but which had been too often ignored as people got on with their busy lives.

We are living in the UK – and across the world – at such a moment of revelation. It is a point of historical contingency, when people's political imagination can be engaged in new directions. It has been dawning on increasing numbers of people for some time that radical change is necessary. Ecological activists, starting as long as fifty years ago (Friends of the Earth and Greenpeace), have now grown in numbers – Extinction Rebellion is the most recent manifestation. Alongside the ecological movement, we saw the 'Occupy Wall Street' and 'We are the 99%' movements protesting against threatening increases in inequality made painfully visible after the

2008 financial crash; and in 2013 Black Lives Matter revived the longest-running anti-inequality civil protest campaign of all, dating back to eighteenth-century Abolitionism against racial slavery. In the summer of 2020 Black Lives Matter demonstrations erupted across the globe like a cultural pandemic, sparked by the capture on mobile phones in Minneapolis on 25th May of a white policeman deliberately kneeling on the neck of a local black man – George Floyd – squeezing his last breath out of him over nine agonising minutes.

Greta Thunberg, the talismanic figurehead of the mass movement of striking school children, has made explicit the direct connection between an extreme form of inequality-generating capitalism and the carnage being wreaked on the natural environment. And in late 2019 the world's economic leaders came forward with a statement on the need for a 'stakeholder capitalism' to replace relentless 'shareholder value', published in the 2020 Davos Manifesto on the purpose of the company.[3] Even the investment behemoth Blackrock appeared to announce a cautious shift away from the most carbon-intensive of its vast portfolio of energy investments.[4] But many of the world's powerful institutions – banks based in the City of London and Wall Street, transnational corporations headquartered wherever they pay least tax, and governments in hock to their wealth elites, such as those of the UK, USA and Brazil – were nevertheless continuing despite the Davos statement to pursue business as usual, maximising shareholder value at the expense of environmental destruction and rising inequality.

That, however, was until the COVID-19 coronavirus struck, rapidly reaching right across the globe and even infecting the leaders of these three countries – UK prime minister Boris Johnson, US president Donald Trump and Brazil's president Jair Bolsonaro – each of whom had initially refused to take it seriously. The coronavirus has now profoundly disrupted the global economic system, built on sourcing everything from the cheapest possible location, which often tends to be those countries where 'costly' protections for workers and natural environments are weak or non-existent. It is certainly a crisis in the economies of all the world's countries, including that of the UK.

The fact that the conventional global 'free-market' economics of the last four decades is being turned upside down by the coronavirus is, therefore, a moment of historical opportunity when there can be a fair and proper hearing at the bar of public opinion for new approaches that have been fighting for attention for some time.

This book contributes to this growing chorus. As will be shown in the chapters below, all the following recommendations for an alternative way of conducting ourselves in the future come with the knowledge that they are adaptations for our new and different times of policies and arrangements that have already served British society well in the past – in fact for most of the last 400 years. In its analysis of history this book argues that, above all, we need to start our re-evaluation by directly confronting the issue of morality. We should not be shy of using this word. It is powerful.

History teaches that no society lives without a collective notion of its morality. The policies originating in the reign of Elizabeth I show us that both British society and its economy have worked best when laws and institutions have been implemented that engender a public morality committed to providing collectively funded support for all individuals to thrive and flourish as independent agents. This is *collectivist individualism*, a peculiarly British innovation of enormous social and economic value.[5] A similar morality of collectivist individualism was also clearly evident in 1945 in Britain after the devastation of two world wars, when what is sometimes described as a new 'social contract' recognised the valid expectations of the newly democratic population for a welfare state that delivered employment, and health, education and housing for each citizen according to need, not ability to pay.

Many people may find 'morality' a quaint word. It's 'live and let live' today, isn't it? Apart from the religious, aren't most of us just pragmatic and rational? And shouldn't public policy be judged mainly by the criteria of reason, evidence and science, not morality? But the self-consciousness we all have in common does not just give us reason. As has been said, 'we are the moral animal'.[6] Furthermore, as research clearly shows, our moral intuitions, imbibed from childhood, come first, our reasoning second.[7]

A society that does not actively deliberate on and choose its morality has its morality supplied for it. It is there in the way we do things. And since 1979 there has been a powerful set of economic, cultural and media-owning forces determined to ensure that the way we do things maximises the opportunity for finance and commerce to derive as much profit as it can from our social and economic system, including through deregulation and tax cuts, while ignoring the damage that this might be doing. This way of doing things has its own morality.

The arguments that have been made in public by our political class to justify all this and persuade voters of its value have not usually been explicitly moral ones, though they have occasionally talked of 'scroungers' in their rush to promote the interests of one group over another. They have instead been about the virtues of efficiency, competition, privatisation, national GDP growth, consumer choice and shareholder value. There is an implicit 'morality of the market' in all of this. Lying behind it and supporting it are propositions asserting that everything of importance in economics can be priced and that individual self-interest is the only dependable and certain basis for determining the rules, not only of the economy, but of society. As Michael Sandel puts it, 'market reasoning smuggles in certain moral judgements despite its claim to be value neutral'.[8] But we don't have to accept this morality by proxy. As the late Chief Rabbi Jonathan Sacks observed: if we lose respect for people in our commercial activities, 'we lose freedom, trust and decency, the things that have a value, not a price'.[9] So we need to rouse ourselves, to change this default morality, recognising that it has become a problem for us – a moral problem, a social problem, an environmental problem.

There is no reason, in principle, why we can't democratically decide on what our explicit moral goals truly are. We can redesign the laws governing how our businesses operate so they are legally bound to play by rules that reflect those moral values. If all companies wanting to trade in the UK are subject to the same rules, this does not interfere with the healthy aspect of competition, which is to promote efficiency. But it does prevent the unhealthy aspects of competition, which are the cutting of corners and preparedness to exploit weaknesses in worker and environmental protections around the world to boost profits. This kind of exploitative capitalism must be called-out for the immorality it rests on. If we want an ethical economy, it is within our power to create it.

Furthermore, this book argues that in order to bring this into being we, the citizens, need to vote for an empowering state. We have endured decades of the neoliberal state. This is the disempowering state that has systematically worked to weaken the many forms of civic organisation, local representative government, employee representation and protection that might interfere with commercial freedoms to maximise profits.

The empowering state is not a controlling state. Nor is it a nannying state telling people how to live their lives. It is about setting people free to take control of their lives.

It is quite the opposite of the strong-arm bullying state that tells you how many children you can expect to have supported if you are poor. The claim at the heart of the 'free-market' ideology is that the 'small state' is an adjunct to freedom. But whose freedom? While the neoliberal state makes little effort to prevent large corporations and rich individuals from using their freedom to whisk away their wealth and their profits to avoid tax, it comes down like a ton of bricks on the weak and the poor, freezing their benefits and taking away their right to a single spare bedroom.

In order for the poor to be able to buy-in – literally – to the new set of ethical economic practices we propose here, they need to be assured of the basic decencies of life, such as an adequate income, food on the table and satisfactory, secure housing. We need a state that actively nurtures every individual, empowering them with an equal start in life. All citizens should be provided with high-quality universal public services that are delivered on the principle of proportionate need. That means those from the most underprivileged communities or in the most disadvantaged circumstances receive proportionately more support to access and benefit from the services on offer. All this must be combined with a restored safety net for those who find themselves facing hardship for whatever reason.

In this book we show how the nurturing state can draw on the principles of a new green and pro-social morality of collective responsibility to create a new architecture of incentives for rich and poor alike. The innovative financing of the range of public services that will be needed to promote a more empowered and socially connected citizenry, and the investment needed to build back a stronger economy, must be based on the effective taxation of wealth and on fully progressive taxation of income. These are not measures provoked by envy. They are necessary to ensure that everyone is seen to be contributing fairly. We need to bring the nation together in the life-and-death struggle we have ahead of us to avert the impending environmental catastrophe. The wealthy should now stand up and be counted in making the fullest contributions from their greater resources in leading this battle.

In our empowered society we also need to build up and revive all the institutions that can promote full democratic participation and voices from all quarters of the national community, including the voice of workers and trade unions. This should also extend to empowering local government, something that is very simply done. Discretionary power needs to be statutorily granted to manage more of their affairs responsively and accountably to their local electorates; and the centre needs to concede significantly greater revenue streams to local authorities so that they have the resources to take initiatives, which their local electorates can be the judge of.

An equally important dimension of ensuring full and fair democratic participation is to expunge the cancer of corruption and cronyism from central government, which the COVID-19 crisis has revealed to have reached alarming proportions after forty years during which the state has increasingly become dependent on large corporate interests. In the teeth of a deadly national crisis we have had almost weekly revelations of a state that is in danger of approaching a kleptocracy and that, in the case of the absolutely vital test, track and trace system, has presented a record of dismal incompetence, which will no doubt be shown in due course to have tragically cost many, many lives. At the same time, the lobbying firms and pseudo-think tanks drip feeding into government must be made to come clean on who is paying them for their advocacy work. We can no longer afford to tolerate this in a society needing to ensure, as its highest priority, that its economy is to become morally green, transparent and inclusive so that all can prosper and share in its rewards.

Finally, this book will show how all of this empowerment of ourselves and the step-change into much greater social equity (there will still be rich and poor but rather fewer individuals hoarding hundreds of times the wealth of the average citizen) relates to the green economy. Far greater equity, both within the UK and globally, is necessary for us all to find acceptable the more moderate form of growth – kinder to the environment – that is necessary to save the planet.

This does not in any way mean the end of dynamic economic growth, which will remain the source of important further progress, but it does mean defining it and measuring its value in a completely different way as so many economists, environmentalists and politicians are now proposing.

Quick Guide to the Book

Part I begins by looking back at more than 650 years of history to see how governments have tried to protect their populations from pandemic diseases. It will show how the role of the state – initially Italian city-states and then the British and other nation-states – changed radically after plague first became endemic in Europe after 1347. Where previously they had appealed to divine intervention for help, governments instead began to intervene directly, protecting and controlling their citizens at the most minute level. Across Europe and elsewhere the full range of tools of pandemic control from surveillance, tracking, quarantine and border patrols to economic support for those unable to work have in fact existed for hundreds of years.

This historic perspective will then be used to review and critique the comparable responses to COVID-19 and to question why, with the clear warnings of SARS, MERS and Ebola, the UK was apparently so extraordinarily unprepared for an event that had been anticipated for so long. It will explore the deficiencies of leadership and strategy in the lead-in to and especially during the response to COVID-19 in 2020, looking at whether decisions over lockdown were dangerously delayed and examining failures that ranged from the provision of personal protective equipment (PPE) to the inadequacy of the test, track and trace infrastructure. It will examine the U-turns, the loss of authority over the stay safe messaging and the panicked decisions that contributed to further misery and confusion.

It will end by reviewing the astonishing achievement of the scientists who were able to compress the time for development of an effective vaccine against COVID-19 from several years down to just a few months. By 15 February 2021 the UK had met its target to vaccinate 15 million of its most vulnerable citizens, thanks to the efficiency of the NHS and supportive networks of community volunteers. It will show the desperate race against time as the vaccination roll out, taking place during a third national lockdown, coincided with escalating infections and deaths. Still at the end of January 2021 the UK was in the top five countries in the world for both total deaths and deaths per million people.

Part II will ask why the UK, one of the richest countries in the world, had become so fragile and lacking in resilience by the time COVID-19 struck. It will look firstly at the corrosive narrative of neoliberalism, which has held sway for much of the last forty years portraying the state as an unwelcome intrusion into people's lives and especially into the workings of the economy. It will look at how this led to economically damaging deregulation and financialisation of the economy from the 1980s onwards. This fed a wealth oligarchy that sought to bolster its political influence, such that an ominous relationship of mutual dependence between politicians and the wealthy began to intensify. Nowhere was this more obvious than in the contracts that were let with minimal scrutiny during the pandemic to close contacts of ministers, racking up enormous bills but in too many cases simply failing to deliver.

It will then focus on the cuts to public spending that went with this neoliberal philosophy and the condition that this had put our public services in by 2020. It will argue that the reorganisation of the NHS and swingeing cuts to public health functions after 2012, combined with the cuts in bed capacity, staff shortages and 'just in time' procurement, had left the sector unable to prepare for or effectively respond to the pandemic as it hit. With so many of its scarce beds occupied by elderly patients, over 25,000 of them were peremptorily discharged into care homes with an instruction that negative COVID-19 tests were 'not required'. Deaths in care homes in the first weeks of the pandemic became a national scandal, especially when it emerged that on top of COVID-19 deaths many other 'unexpected' deaths of care home residents had been the result of what appeared to be a systematic withdrawal of normal medical care.

There were longer-run causes of our society's weakness when it came to be tested by the virus. Steep increases in wealth and income inequality went directly alongside a doubling of child poverty, both occurring during the Thatcher decade, 1979–90, when neoliberalism rapidly rose to ascendancy. Less obvious but equally pervasive inequalities of health and economic opportunity emerged alongside this, accentuated by the severe cuts to public services – education, public health and adult social care – ratcheted up during the post-2010 decade of austerity. At the same time, those who needed to fall back on the social safety net to claim Universal Credit and its predecessor benefits were subjected to relentless cuts, which are set out in detail, and a five-week waiting period that pushed people into reliance on food banks and plunged many into permanent debt.

The section will conclude by looking in further depth at why, in the light of all of this, COVID-19 was anything but levelling in its impact, as so many people had little or no savings to cushion them and were unable to afford to take time off sick or to self-isolate. The pattern of deaths from COVID-19 is shown to be clearly linked to deprivation and ethnicity due to greater exposure to the risk of catching COVID-19 in front-line roles compounded by greater health vulnerabilities once sick. Alongside this, we are now seeing the emergence of a 'COVID generation' scarred not only by the loss of education and work but also carrying a mental health burden into the future.

Part III will introduce the idea that businesses, especially companies of significant size, who receive government funding, should expect there to be conditionality attached to their support. It will show how other European countries have, unlike the UK, built in to their COVID-19 support packages requirements for environmental targets and protections for jobs and have put caps on the interest rates banks can charge when they make loans that are backed by a government guarantee. It will discuss the missed opportunity to secure a proper payback during and after the 2008 banking crisis and describe how large-scale bailouts and the loosening of monetary policy, both then and now, will, if not managed properly, continue to funnel money to the rich.

It will look at proposals for how we might learn from past mistakes to secure a pandemic payback. There is the potential for the government to take advantage of historically low interest rates to purchase equity stakes in businesses that are facing challenges but are fundamentally sound. It will look at other voices calling for a fundamental change in how companies are governed and who they are set up to serve, including changes to the law to make it the duty of directors to promote the long-term success of a company in place of short-term shareholder interest.

There will then be a refutation of the argument that austerity is an appropriate response to the unprecedented costs of the lockdown – that it has to be 'paid for' and the reckoning must come soon. Using detailed historical comparisons and arguments about the peculiar opportunity that negative real interest rates provide, it will show that we can accommodate a rise in the national debt without yet more austerity cuts to public services. The costs of the pandemic response can and should be treated in the same way that the one-off costs of war were in the past – paid off over the long term.

It will argue, though, that there urgently needs to be a national conversation about our future spending requirements as we build back from the pandemic, address the much discussed 'levelling up' of our country and face up finally to the costs of an ageing population. There is a clear appetite for a more active state, spending more on public investment and services. The case is put for a radically revised approach to wealth taxation to support this investment, building on newly published research that shows this can raise money just as effectively as increases in income tax or VAT.

The section will conclude by considering the nature of the welfare state we need in the post-pandemic world, arguing that, despite the current interest in it, a Universal Basic Income is *not* the right way forward. It will expose the risks of this as a panacea for economic and social ills and argue that we need to focus instead both on devising a fit-for-purpose safety net and restoring high-quality universal public services. It will put the case for renewed ambitious investment in education and training, health, housing and digital access and argue that care – both childcare and care of the elderly – must now be integrated into our welfare state, reversing the historic 'male breadwinner' model of welfare support.

Part IV then moves on from the preceding analysis of the underlying weaknesses of our pre-pandemic state and the urgent need to reset the power relationships that underpinned it. Its focus is on bringing out the lessons of history to chart a way forward. It starts by challenging the idea that there is a natural human condition of selfishness, as personified by the figure that has dominated the ab-

stract realm of economic theory for so long – 'rational economic man'. It shows how the calculations and trade-offs
that this sort of thinking promotes jar with our socially
produced instincts and are entirely inappropriate morally.
It presents evidence that refutes any such easy correspond-
ence between this abstract *Homo economicus* and our actual
motivations and behaviours.

It then looks back at our history to show that it has been
moral narratives about who we are and want to be that have
driven transformational changes in our economy and society. It shows what can happen if we choose now to move
away from an over-dominant individualist approach and
towards more balanced thinking and policy. It sets out in
detail how Elizabeth I's extraordinary Poor Laws brought
into being the world's first collectivist-individualist society, a unique English political and moral achievement that
mandated community support for orphans, widows, the
infirm and sick, the old, the involuntary unemployed and
single mothers and their children.

However, these Poor Law provisions were misguided-
ly overturned in 1834 by the new, more exclusively individualist economics and utilitarianism of the nineteenth
century before returning, over a century later, with the
founding of the post-war Beveridge welfare state. This
saw a collectivist-individualist balance restored in full all
across society, establishing a comprehensive welfare system funded by progressive taxation and with the leaders of
enterprise incentivised to consider long-term returns that
would be set alongside the welfare of their workforces and
communities.

Part IV goes on to further elucidate the idea of an empowering and nurturing state – one that provides its citizens with positive freedoms through protection from
vulnerabilities, resources to achieve their potential, and
access to full participation in democratic institutions
and decision making. It explores how and why we should

aspire to create such an empowering state to replace the disempowering state of the last forty years when many were excluded by poverty and lack of opportunity, while for others active citizenship and participation were stifled. It contrasts the negative liberty of a neoliberal state, in which wealthy people and corporations are accorded freedom from interference and regulation, with the positive freedoms of a nurturing state where everyone is furnished with the wherewithal to fulfil their diverse potential.

It argues that British society is indeed an individualist society but that it is a very special fusion of collectivism with individualism that has enabled this country and its citizens to prosper most during the last four centuries. Achieving this dynamic balance has provided a nurturing environment for its families and communities that has facilitated the economic independence of its people. Unfortunately, there is a tendency also clearly visible in British history for its collectivist form of individualism periodically to become corrupted into an unbalanced ideology of outright individualism, which results instead in a disempowering state focused only on negative freedom. This is what happened during the mid-nineteenth century and has happened once again during the last forty years.

We see the COVID-19 pandemic as a warning shot across our bows, alerting us to the seriousness of the imminent challenge of climate change and the escalating and interlocking crises of nature, the economy and social inequality. These cannot be addressed without a fundamental change that begins with discarding the neoliberal straightjacket so that we can embrace a new vision of a nurturing state and a nurtured planet. The book concludes by proposing seven pillars of empowerment to achieve this. These draw together our arguments into a holistic set of values, behaviours and practical policies to revitalise and rebuild our society as we emerge into the post-COVID world.

PART I
COVID-19 WAS ALWAYS A MATTER OF 'WHEN' NOT 'IF'

1 THE EXTRAORDINARY HISTORY OF PANDEMIC CONTROL

Everyone who has lived through the COVID-19 pandemic will have had their life changed in some way by it. Certainly, few of us will ever forget it. If COVID-19 has posed existential questions for many at a personal level, how much more powerful are those questions magnified on a global scale? Why did it happen? Had we prepared sufficiently for something like this? Was it our fault? Or someone's fault? Did we do the right things? Should we have done something different? How do we recover from it? What do we need to change? And, before we let down our guard, what new disaster might be round the corner?

An Ever-Present Threat

In this first section of *After the Virus* we will begin by looking back to the time *before* the virus to see what answers there might be to some of these questions. In early 2020 we found ourselves on the eve of the greatest threat to public health and the economy in our lifetimes, but in fact what we were facing was what our forebears had grappled with for centuries. Drawing on the rich resources of the past, we will look at just how much we can discover from hundreds of years during which people every bit as clever and ingenious as we are used every possible means they could think of to deal with repeated pandemics, most notoriously plague, that threatened to ravage their populations and for which there was no prevention or cure. We may have better science and technologies today but what we will find is that the basic principles of isolation and containment until a pandemic infection is overcome remain the same now as they always have been.

We will show, too, that what happened was not random bad luck. COVID-19 was indeed always a matter of 'when' not 'if'. By 2020, we had, in our quest for ever-expanding global commerce and trade, created the perfect breeding ground for a new pandemic to emerge as we increasingly disturbed the habitats of other species. And we had also provided it with the perfect conditions to spread. In 2015 Bill Gates – with no special knowledge beyond his own reading of works such as David Quammen's *Spillover* – but with a keen appreciation of the global economic implications, tried his best to warn that a catastrophic pandemic was an imminent global threat, and that it would most likely originate in a food market in China. With deadly precision, Gates predicted that with 'the continual emergence of new pathogens ... and the ever-increasing connectedness of our world, there is a significant probability that a large and lethal ... pandemic will occur in our lifetime'.[1]

Before we consider our lack of preparedness for the tests and challenges of the pandemic, this opening chapter takes us back through history to reveal the fascinating and at times surprising methods our ancestors deployed to protect and control their populations in the face of otherwise uncontrollable disease.

The Myth of Progress

The British Isles have not experienced plague on a serious scale since the self-sacrificial village of Eyam in Derbyshire allowed themselves to be walled in for months to snuff out the last embers of the 1665–66 outbreak that terrorised London, as graphically recorded in Samuel Pepys' famous diary. Plague had travelled to Eyam in cloth sent from London to the village tailor.[2] Two hundred and sixty souls died, about a third of Eyam's population, including eighteen alone named Moreton, the ill-fated family that supplied the last ever recorded death from plague in England on 1 November 1666.

The reason for the absence of plague in the UK after that date is not happy-go-lucky chance. It is – at least in part – because the whole of western Europe set up a heavily resourced apparatus of control against it. There is a continuous history of governments and their agents scanning the horizon for signs of approaching disease that in Europe goes back to fifteenth and sixteenth-century Italy.[3] It involved information scouts stationed in the Ottoman empire and further east, where plague was endemic. It involved quarantine procedures at all Mediterranean ports to stop sailors and goods disembarking from potentially infected ships.[4] It even led to the first 'iron curtain' in Europe, the *Militärgrenze*. This militarised land barrier over 1,000 miles long operated through most of the eighteenth and nineteenth centuries, built by the Austro-Hungarian empire to close off trade and travel whenever there was news of infection in the Ottoman empire.[5]

With that barrier long since gone, one of the most abiding and comforting myths of modern life until the opening weeks of 2020, at least for the richer half of the world's population, was that human progress had all but vanquished epidemics and pandemics. Economic growth and all the plentiful food, extraordinary science and medicine that goes with it had, so the story went, extinguished – or at least enabled us to control – all the nasty infectious diseases that used to dispatch so many of us to early graves.

This victory over the perilous past is symbolised by the complete eradication in 1980 of smallpox, a prolific killer, especially of children. And who hears today of rampaging deaths from the plague, which used to kill whole families lying in their agony; or uncontrollable cholera, capable of almost dissolving a person in the street, as their bodily fluids suddenly convulsively evacuated? *Little Women* can be read safe in the knowledge that a favourite sister is not going to succumb to scarlet fever, which was raging at its epidemic height on both sides of the Atlantic when Louisa May Alcott first published her novel in 1868.

If we appeared, too, to have vastly reduced the frequency with which the appearance of novel infections become pandemic global killers, this is in large part because we have both national and global institutions continually monitoring all signals of a possible new disease. As the World Health Organization (WHO) and informed analysts know, the potential for pandemics has been growing as the world economy grows.[6] The definition of a pandemic now offered by the celebrated immunologist Anthony Fauci is of a global disease, with movement from place to place, high attack rates and explosiveness, novelty along with minimal population immunity, severity and lethality of the disease and transmissibility between people.[7]

SARS, MERS and Ebola could each have become twenty-first-century pandemics were it not for the painstaking efforts to control and contain them as they emerged. In the case of Ebola, active surveillance and control remain very much in force today. On 1 June 2020, even as the world was battling COVID-19, the Democratic Republic of Congo reported its eleventh outbreak of Ebola, with four out of six patients having already died. The World Health Organization was on the ground immediately overseeing the response. But this efficiency meant that it hardly made the news in the West. Thinking we are protected by science, public opinion has become complacent, content to judge their national governments by their economic growth rates, while leaving global safety to experts working for acronyms: WHO, MSF (Médecins Sans Frontières), CDC (Centers for Disease Control).

Economic progress has without doubt given us a large arsenal of weapons against pandemics, but we should not lose sight of the fact that commerce and trade are also a large part of the reason they happen in the first place. Spectacular pandemics are not spontaneous natural events. Unlike earthquakes, meteor strikes or total eclipses, pandemics are to a significant degree manmade. Though involving terrible amounts of suffering and death, pandemic events are – unintentionally, of course – produced by human, purposeful activity. A virus, like COVID-19, or a bacterium, like *Yersinia pestis*, which causes plague, is a necessary element in each pandemic, often as well as intermediary species, such as rats, fleas, bats or wildfowl. But it is large-scale human societies and their economic, trading or military activity that have always created the conditions for pandemic events to occur.

The Black Death of the fourteenth century – a bubonic plague – was the most devastating pandemic to hit Europe in nearly 800 years. Not since Justinian's Plague, which may have killed up to half of those it infected in AD 541–49 – and from which the emperor himself had a narrow escape – had there been anything like it. The eight-century gap reflects the absence, after the fall of the Roman empire, of the population density and long-distance trading conditions required for a pandemic while Europe was living through its subsistence 'Dark Ages'.

But from the eleventh century onwards an era of agrarian prosperity and urban growth began to dawn, its wealth symbolised in that age's great cathedrals. There was a rising trade with the Middle and Far East via Constantinople and the silk road. It was from this direction, as a result of military clashes with the Mongol Golden Horde, that the Black Death came west in 1347 from its endemic homeland in central Asia. It used to be claimed that this was the result of a ruthless case of bio-terrorism when infected corpses were catapulted into the besieged Black Sea port of Caffa. The latest research has established that it was in fact a temporary outbreak of peace between the two sides that allowed the resumption of trade across the Black Sea to Constantinople in 1347 and that the plague arrived unwittingly in grain cargoes accompanied by infected rats and fleas.[8] The subsequent outbreak of the Black Death killed between a third and a half of the populations it ravaged across Europe.[9]

Image 1. A seventeenth-century illustration of a physician wearing protective clothing, including a mask, as a defence against the plague. Source: Bettmann / Getty Images

Thereafter, from 1348 right through until 1680 there would be a plague epidemic in one European city or another in every single year. London, alone, experienced twenty-two separate plague visitations between 1485 and 1665 – an average of once every eight years. No wonder, then, that those tending to plague victims clothed themselves in such elaborate protective garments (see Image 1).

In 1564, the year that Shakespeare was born, his hometown of Stratford-upon-Avon recorded 200 deaths from plague, around one sixth of the population, with four children dying on Shakespeare's street alone. Holy Trinity Church's parish register contains the record of Shakespeare's baptism, while its burial register at almost exactly the same time notes *hic incipit pestis* – here begins the plague. Throughout his life Shakespeare would have to contend with the disruption of theatre closures due to new outbreaks of plague and the threat this posed to his livelihood. Shakespeare's son, Hamnet, who died at the age of eleven, may even have succumbed to the deadly disease. Not long afterwards, Shakespeare produced one of his greatest tragedies, *Hamlet*, a masterpiece of reflection on grief.

Plague was a hard taskmaster for European national and civic governments. Although early microscopes date from 1590, it was to take almost another three centuries before germ theory was developed. The top medical authorities of the day simply could not pin down its cause, though, as time wore on, the most perspicacious of them, such as Charles I's physician, Sir Theodore de Mayerne, strongly suspected the transmission role of rodents, unwelcome stowaways on the trading ships of the time.[10]

While plague was eventually vanquished, the global expansion of trade in the eighteenth and nineteenth centuries soon brought other intensive exchanges of disease. Four successive cholera epidemics, each originating in India, the 'jewel' in Britain's imperial and commercial crown, reached Britain for the first time, one outbreak in each decade from the 1830s to the 1860s. They provoked fear and panic, including among the property-owning section of society, who increasingly fled with their families to the suburbs and beyond, away from the filth and poverty of the overcrowded urban centres where their wealth was manufactured.[11]

A few decades later an epoch-making conflict would once again become the merciless facilitator of disease on a pandemic scale. The 'Spanish' flu of 1918–20, estimated to have killed 50 to 100 million people worldwide, was believed to have at least in part been spread by troop movements in the final phase of the First World War.

Fast-forward to the present and we have created a far more globally connected economy than ever before in history. It is therefore now also a more globally connected microbial environment. We bring exotic fruit and vegetables from around the world to our tables, hop on planes for recreational breaks (when not in lockdown) and have been permitting deforestation on an unprecedented scale

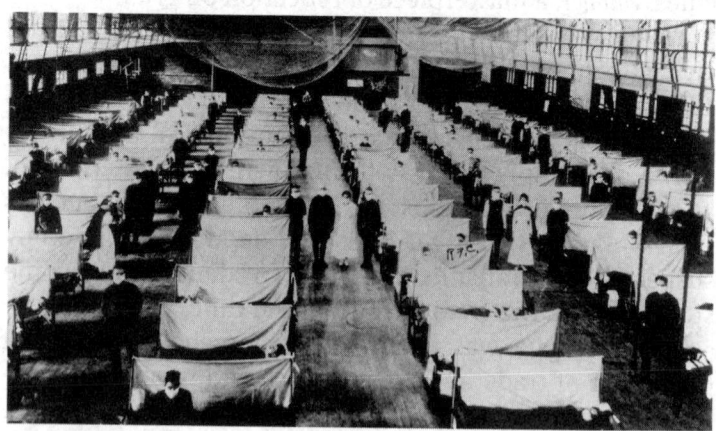

Image 2. Warehouses were converted during the 1918–20 influenza to keep infected people quarantined.
Source: Universal History Archive / Getty Images

to feed an insatiable demand for meat, soya and palm oil. What we perhaps forget is that the other species on the planet do not simply stand still while we humans create our civilisations, multiply in numbers and density and alter the environment in so many ways to suit our needs.[12] While we are changing and putting pressure on our environment, other species are adapting and evolving, as they always have, and we humans are part of their environment, too.[13] Our twenty-first-century nexus of trade, travel and dense urban living is theirs too – viruses, bacteria and parasites can move as rapidly and as far as we can.[14]

Bill Gates knew this when he made his prediction of a new lethal pandemic. World health bodies and individual governments knew this, too. COVID-19 was no surprise and nor should it have been: SARS, MERS and Ebola had been the heralds. Despite this, the WHO issued a report in 2019, *A World At Risk*, warning that most countries were simply not making appropriate preparations for this near certain event.

How Pandemics Spread

Dramatic and deadly diseases threaten most where a population has not previously encountered the infecting organism. The most extraordinary of sudden, mass death events in history are closely associated with moments of contact between two previously separated civilisations, where each plays host to a range of endemic pathogens to which they have adapted over generations. As two such civilisations come into contact, one population's endemic micro-organism may assume epidemic lethality when it encounters the other 'virgin' human population for the first time.

The classic and well-documented example is that of the Spanish *conquistadors* arriving in the Americas in the late fifteenth century.[15] The smallpox virus, in particular, was new to the Incas and Aztecs and indeed to all indigenous peoples in South and North America. The invading and settling Europeans hailed the devastation wrought as novel diseases felled those opposing their incursion as their Christian God's handiwork. Less celebrated in their history books of course is that the Europeans in turn took back with them the spirochaete *Treponema pallidum pallidum*, the source of the scourge of syphilis that spread across Europe in the sixteenth century and which European travellers then introduced to the rest of the planet.[16]

Pandemic diseases are an eclectic mix, some caused by bacteria, like *Yersinia pestis* (the plague), *Vibrio cholerae* (cholera) and *Mycobacterium tuberculosis* (TB); others by viruses, as with influenza, smallpox, coronavirus and HIV/ AIDS; and still others by tiny animal parasites, such as the *Plasmodium* protozoa injected into the human bloodstream by the mosquito bites that produce malaria. Many of these diseases, most notably malaria, cholera and tuberculosis, can still today be considered global pandemics, regularly killing tens of millions of people each year.

These latter three, though, are not diseases that are new to populations, and for many there are effective treatments or vaccinations that would protect those such as babies and children who are most at risk. They spread in conditions of poor sanitation and overcrowding, and in the last half-century have formed an unholy alliance in the world's poorest populations with HIV/AIDS and the other bacterial STIs of syphilis and drug-resistant gonorrhoea. Their heavy mortality burden is not the result of medical incapacity to deal with them. Rather it is the unavailability of that medical care to those afflicted. This should be a source of persistent shame for us all: many of the world's poorest countries had incipient free and universal primary health care systems that were degraded in the 1980s and 1990s by the conditions imposed on their governments by the IMF and the World Bank's market-oriented structural and sectoral adjustment loans, which insisted that health care users should pay fees.[17]

When an entirely new pathogen such as COVID-19 arrives on the scene, there is of course no vaccination, no immediate treatment beyond palliative care and no previously acquired immunity. While scientists across the world jumped into action to analyse its genetic code and modus operandi, we did not know for sure at the start how rapidly COVID-19 would spread, what its case fatality rate would be and who would be most vulnerable. What we did know is that if each infected person infected more than one other, the pandemic would start to spread exponentially. This infection rate – known as the R rate – measures the onward transmission of a disease from each initial case. The higher the R, the more rapidly cases multiply. Only with R below 1 does the disease go into retreat.

In the UK in early to mid-March 2020 the R for COVID-19 was estimated to be potentially as high as 3, with infections doubling around every three days. If you were to start with just fifty-six infected people, the official UK figure on 10th March, that exponential rate of increase would, if left unchecked, produce 896 cases within twelve days, 57,344 within thirty days and getting on for 59 million within sixty days! Worse still for the R rate, scientists found that while a small percentage of the population was highly susceptible to the disease, large numbers, especially young people, were infected asymptomatically, so could be transmitting a potentially lethal disease to their parents and grandparents entirely unwittingly.

The most dangerous of carriers in this situation – and one or two were identified at the start – are the superspreaders, the 'Typhoid Marys' who infect large numbers of other people without knowing it. The reference is to Mary Mallon, a cook to several of New York's most affluent families in the early years of the twentieth century. Her alleged poor hand hygiene and much sought-after signature dessert – ice cream and frozen peaches – were believed to have been the conduit for her infecting scores of people, a handful of whom died, with the disease that she herself denied ever having had.

The WHO declared the outbreak of COVID-19 a Public Health Emergency of International Concern on 30 January 2020. On 11th March it was declared a pandemic, meaning that it had spread worldwide. The only safe initial assumption for authorities to make with such a novel disease was that both its transmissibility and its case fatality could be extremely high. The topmost priority in that scenario would be to identify all those affected and to detain or quarantine them and their contacts as quickly as possible. It was a race against time, for which some countries were better prepared than others. COVID-19 was to test our twenty-first-century governments every bit as severely as plague had tested those of the past, holding up a mirror to the capacity and resilience of individual states and their leaders.

Pandemics and the Role of the State: From Divine to Human Responsibility

Along with famine and war, disease, plague and pestilence have challenged rulers from time immemorial. In most early historic civilisations, such as those of Egypt, Mesopotamia and China, the ruling dynasty was considered to have divine dispensation. All major turns of fortune, good or bad, were explained in terms of religious favour and disfavour, and this could redound menacingly on the ruling dynasty. China's 'Mandate of Heaven' meant that so long as the emperor appeared able to protect his people from natural disasters, just as from foreign invaders, he was confirming his divine status. If he failed, he was demonstrating that he lacked divinity and must be replaced.

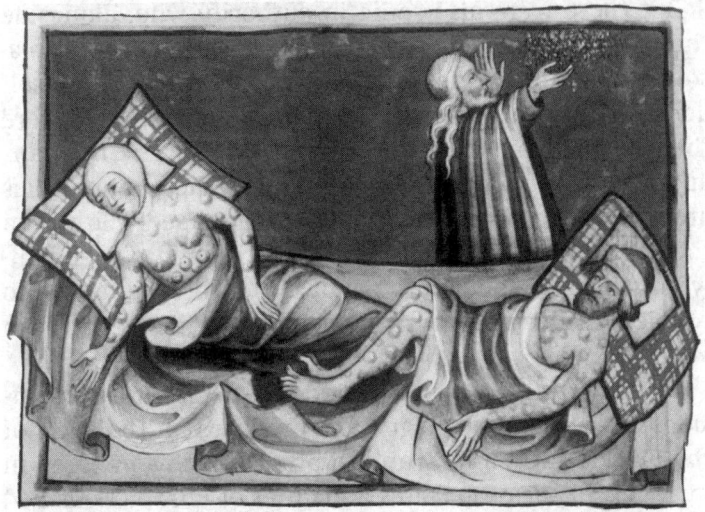

Image 3. Painting depicting a couple suffering from the Black Death.
From the Swiss manuscript the Toggenburg Bible, 1411.
Source: Bettmann / Getty Images

These kinds of religious or superstitious understandings of what was happening when pandemics struck continued pretty much unabated until the resurgence of plague in Europe in the fourteenth century. The Black Death was a cosmology-shattering event, which at the beginning had seen an upsurge in calls to prayer and self-mortification among the faithful across Christendom to assuage divine wrath.

In the climate of fear and dread there were equally those who sought astrological explanations for their distress. Notoriously it also resulted in an escalation of religious intolerance and paranoia with appalling and brutal persecution visited on Jewish communities. This was despite Pope Clement VI (1291–1352) issuing two decrees in 1348 threatening excommunication, the highest spiritual penalty, for those harming a Jew.

But there were also some in authority who, alongside the confusion and heightened emotion, began to apply reason and to interrogate evidence. Pope Clement VI himself deployed such arguments. He pointed out that Jews were themselves dying from the plague as well as Christians and that Jews were absent in many of the communities around the known world where plague raged. With even the Pope emboldened to reason publicly and independently, organised responses to pandemic outbreaks started to rely less exclusively on ritual acts of religious contrition and penance.

Faced with incessant, repeated threats of further incursions of the bubonic plague, coming hard on the heels of the Black Death, a new philosophy gradually emerged in many of the western states and cities of Europe. This had its roots in humanist, Renaissance Italy. Civil authorities began to talk of a duty to direct fellow citizens to protect their lives. Rather than leaving everything to prayer, humanist teaching on epidemics and pestilence stressed that, since reason was a divine gift, it should be actively deployed to overcome such calamities.

It was not in the least surprising that Europe's urban authorities should have cast round in desperation for new ideas to protect themselves from further plague visitations in the centuries following the Black Death. In the space of just a year or two the Black Death had wiped out 30–40 per cent of the entire population across Europe. In England, 42 per cent of its 4.8 million inhabitants were cut down, half of them in three short summer months in 1349. Almost 50 per cent of London's populace perished.[18]

The near contemporary chronicle of Henry Knighton of Leicester records that 'throughout the land … sheep and cattle perished in out-of-the-way places amongst the furrows and under hedges from want of a keeper, in numbers beyond reckoning … for there was such a shortage of hands and servants that no one knew what ought to be done'.[19]

Numbers buried and wills registered tell a similar story in Siena, Arezzo, Perugia, Pisa; and in Florence, Italy's third largest city after Milan and Venice, it is estimated that 50,000 died, fully 60 per cent of the city's inhabitants.[20] In response, over the next half-century, with plague 'after-shocks' still repeatedly rearing their ugly heads, Italian civic authorities set about developing a new range of countermeasures, many of which provided the model for plague responses across Europe. As Paul Slack has put it, 'Europeans came to accept policies and practices for the control of plague which managed to reconcile secular prudence with religious piety … that combination was peculiar to Christian Europe.'[21]

Innovative and comprehensive, their solutions included just about everything we saw once again put into operation around the world to combat COVID-19 in 2020: isolation; quarantine; surveillance; identifying, recording, compiling and publicising death rates; tracing contacts; disinfecting; rules and sanctions to govern behaviour and social distancing. This willingness to begin to engage in human plans to thwart what had previously been seen as the will of God is the origin of where we stand today in our relationship with erupting pandemics.

As Italian city-states and then many other urban authorities in Germany, France, the Low Countries and, finally, the national government in Britain began to enforce what were often draconian measures, it challenged and changed the relationship between governors and governed. Enacted with the force of law, these policies deeply challenged emotional links and support between members of the same community. Measures needed to contain disease also placed local livelihoods under severe strain, requiring authorities to devise forms of charity and taxation to support the afflicted, raising funds from the wider community, even as those communities were themselves often under significant pressure.

A Plague on All Our Houses: Learning to Control Pandemics

The first requirement in controlling a pandemic is to know what you are up against. Soon after the Black Death many Italian towns began the practice of both international and internal surveillance. City authorities were keen to receive information from merchants and others of plague

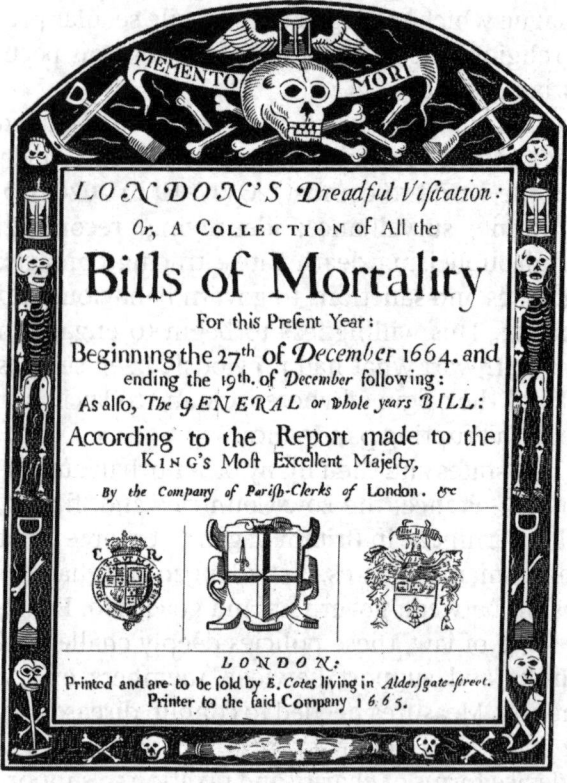

Image 4. The title page of a 1665 compilation of the London Bills of Mortality.
Source: Oxford Science Archive / Getty Images

outbreaks and would then quarantine ships accordingly. Internally, recording of deaths began to be used to give early warning of unusual mortality patterns. In 1399, the dukes of Milan established a system of notification for all illnesses and deaths to facilitate this, moving to put death registration on a continuous basis from 1452.[22]

Similarly, in Britain, from 1518 the Crown ordered weekly counts in London when plague threatened, with parishes listing burials and attributing those due to plague separately. These were printed and publicly displayed for the first time during the 1592 epidemic.[23] From 1603 London's Bills of Mortality could also be compared with those of other towns such as Bristol, Norwich, Chester, Oxford, York and Newcastle.[24] A forerunner of the late-nineteenth-century Notification of Diseases Acts, these listings provided the intelligence that authorities needed to stay on the front foot in controlling the disease, just as COVID-19 testing does today. But that intelligence depended on knowing who had actually died from plague.

Elizabeth I's Book of Plague Orders, issued to all local magistrates in 1578, created the new occupation 'Searcher of the Dead'. As Kevin Siena has aptly remarked, 'If there was an "essential worker" during a sixteenth- or seventeenth-century epidemic, surely this was it. Authorities needed to know whether a death was caused by plague or something more mundane. It was the single most important piece of information for managing the crisis.'[25] Rather than doctors, as one might expect, it was frequently impoverished elderly women who went out to inspect the corpses, sometimes under threat of financial sanction if they didn't carry out the work, and of course always under threat of losing their life to infection.

The Italian cities were the first to set up designated authorities – secular health commissions – to take active steps to control infection. They set about removing infected persons from their city, even at times burning their goods and bedding, stopping entry by those from infected areas, and in some cities restricting the numbers allowed to attend funerals. Venice's colony Ragusa (now the city of Dubrovnik) was the first – as early as 1377 – to institute a thirty-day detention on travellers.[26] Milan's hospitals were ordered to manage the sick outside the city, a similar precaution to the later provisions in English Plague Orders for designated pesthouses for the sick.

Where an outbreak of plague was starting to escalate, the next stage would be the full-scale isolation of infected (or suspected) individuals or, in extremis, quarantining of a whole community. The word 'quarantine' itself comes from the Italian for forty days – *quaranta giorni*. In the absence of precise medical evidence this became the accepted period of isolation. No doubt this was in part because it was seen to be effective, but it was certainly also because of its broader biblical and symbolic significance as a period of retreat and self-denial.

The authorities recognised full well that isolation and quarantine could not succeed without providing for the basic material needs of those they wished to contain. When the health board of Florence shut the city down for forty days in early 1631, they brought free food and drink each day to over 30,000 people. This apparently included two loaves of bread, half a litre of wine, regular portions of meat, rice and cheese, and fresh salad on Fridays, adding up of course to a significant economic burden on the city-state.[27]

The English Plague Orders dealt with the issue even more directly, placing local responsibility on each community for the welfare of the afflicted. Household quarantines in England were particularly strictly enforced and the 1604 Plague Act made it a felony to be found wandering with an open plague sore. Houses were singled out with a painted red cross and watchmen were paid to guard the shut-up household day and night, with locals even bringing the watchers food to sustain them.[28] To make all this feasible economically, the Act insisted that compulsory taxes be raised locally in the parish or more widely in the county to meet all necessary costs and to feed those confined in their households cut off from their livelihoods. This was a bold fiscal innovation by the British state, the scale of the compulsion going beyond anything attempted in Italy.[29]

Such compulsory local responsibilities were so novel that they could initially also engender complaints, such as when poor rural parishes in the county of Lancashire were called on to support the normally wealthier parish of Preston in 1631, which had as many as 756 of its 887 inhabitants in isolation and needing relief.[30] In another wealthy city, Cambridge, financial assistance extended in 1625 to its voluntarily paying money to the adjacent infected parish of Trumpington purely to keep their residents from coming into Cambridge to work or sell their wares.[31]

During the quarantine in Florence in 1631, citizens were given a little more latitude than the English, being allowed to stand on their balconies and terraces to take the air (and perhaps to sing) and even to hear Mass from a distance at portable street altars. But then some were discovered having used the rooftops to climb across to party with friends. Although it didn't happen in Florence or Bologna, in both Milan and Rome punishments for serious infringements of this kind could extend to execution![32]

Over the centuries, as more was understood about water and airborne transmission of disease, authorities began to tackle issues of sanitation and hygiene. Expensive and large-scale sanitation measures in English cities to deal with sewage-contaminated water were critical in containing outbreaks of cholera.[33] Hamburg, by contrast, was disinclined to go to the expense of upgrading its sanitation system. Consequently, the city was the last significant European casualty of cholera in 1892, when its failure to invest in a modernised sand-filtration system resulted in its population being, in effect, centrally supplied with cholera-contaminated water into their homes.[34]

In a similar vein, attempts to protect populations during the 1918–20 flu pandemic and all subsequent winter flu outbreaks have required basic public health measures. Rules prohibiting public spitting were in place in many US states (and there were still warning notices against spitting on public transport in the UK in the 1970s and 80s), as was public education on basic hygiene techniques such as hand washing and appropriate ways of containing coughs and sneezes.

From the late nineteenth century onwards a sequence of important scientific developments produced major advances in the control of pandemic diseases. Anti-toxins (diphtheria sufferers were the first beneficiaries in the 1890s), chemotherapies (the first was neo-salvarsan to treat syphilis in the 1910s), antibiotics (penicillin from the 1940s) and vaccinations (in fact the first one was for smallpox from as early as 1796) have all played their part. Preventative vaccination of course remains the Holy Grail. It has led to the total eradication of smallpox and continues to control cholera, typhoid, yellow fever, TB, diphtheria, measles and polio, among others. Each year new vaccines are produced to combat the annual mutations of the influenza virus, still a significant killer and one that is monitored and reported weekly in the UK in its official statistics on deaths.

However, as with all forms of pandemic disease control, vaccination has been treated with distrust and resistance by some right from the outset. The increasingly stringent British Vaccination Acts of 1853, 1867, 1871, 1874, which fined or imprisoned parents who didn't vaccinate their children against smallpox, provoked many protests, with about 100,000 people involved in the biggest demonstration, in Leicester in 1885.[35] By 1898, the British government had relented under the pressure, permitting 'conscientious objectors' to vaccines an exemption from the law.

For many people the 'Spanish' flu is now viewed as the last catastrophic global pandemic before COVID-19, killing, as it did, 50 to 100 million people. It is only just out of living memory, as we learned when the UK's oldest victim of COVID-19 at the time, Hilda Churchill, died in a care home in March 2020, days before her 109th birthday. Hilda herself survived the Spanish flu but vividly remembered the day it killed her baby sister.[36]

Coming towards the end of the First World War (whose end it may well have hastened), the misattributed 'Spanish' flu is believed in fact to have originated in the USA and to have been initially carried to Europe by American troops. As waves of infection hit the USA, state, county and local authorities were at the forefront of the response. Measures including bans on large gatherings, restrictions on weddings and funerals and economic lockdowns of all but essential businesses were variously imposed. Unsurprisingly, there was a fair amount of resistance to the hardship that this caused. Just as in past plague outbreaks – when the presumed contamination of cloth robbed textile workers of employment and put a stop to the widespread trade in second-hand clothes – so in the USA businesses railed against closures. Indeed, several theatre owners went so far as to pursue legal action against their state governors.

Using data published at the time, the state-by-state response to the flu pandemic across the USA can give us some pretty clear insights into the effects of different approaches to social distancing and lockdown. The findings of researchers today looking back at these data are unequivocal: early and sustained intervention reduced subsequent deaths.[37] Seattle was meticulous in restricting business activity, closing schools and churches and public entertainment and requiring masks to be worn in public. It had one of the lowest death rates on the west coast. Philadelphia, by contrast, suffered one of America's highest death rates when it took little action to prepare for the approaching infection and allowed flu cases to escalate dangerously by permitting a large public parade to go ahead without heeding the risks.[38]

Despite its place in popular memory as the last great pandemic, the hundred years since the Spanish flu have in fact seen many other disastrous global infections, not least from HIV/AIDs. National and international public health institutions now assiduously monitor global signs of new disease, with better-resourced countries springing into action to support local responses, as they did to great effect with Ebola. Meanwhile across the world public surveillance and control of disease extends to highly developed and, usually, localised systems for catching and stamping out infections before they spread. South Africa, for instance, with its experience in dealing with transmissible diseases such as TB and HIV/AIDs, has sophisticated track and trace systems. These countries deploy armies of health workers on the ground who are trained in identifying local outbreaks of infection and managing the response. In Asia, the SARS and MERS coronavirus outbreaks of the early 2000s were aggressively contained using these same techniques, a vital learning exercise that countries such as South Korea, Taiwan and Singapore used to great effect in the control of COVID-19.

It would be fair to say that the toolkit for managing pandemic disease continues to encroach ever further into the most intimate areas of life, as the authorities seek to change or modify behaviour. During the Second World War, soldiers were routinely issued with condoms as part of their daily rations, in order to protect them from STIs. In the 1980s, as the HIV/AIDs epidemic began to be better understood, urgent public health campaigns on condom use were promulgated worldwide in an effort to contain the disease's spread. Delicate interventions in the burial practices of West African communities, which were quickly recognised as contributing to the lethal spread of Ebola from the corpses of the dead, have had to be brokered. And traditional etiquettes of greeting – the Gallic kiss and even the British handshake – were banished by the social distancing rules of COVID-19. There is, it seems, nowhere the state will not go in the quest to stop the spread of disease.

What all of this history shows us, then, is that before the first vaccinations against COVID-19 were administered in December 2020, all the initial efforts to control the spread and lethality of the new virus – in Britain and everywhere else – drew from exactly the same repertoire of measures developed originally in the fight against the plague and then applied in subsequent outbreaks of pandemic diseases. Over 600 years of medicine later we were still pretty much in the same position as the rulers of Florence and Milan.

But how well did we remember and implement all these hard-won lessons of history? What would our forebears have thought of the world's response? How would they have judged the world's surveillance systems, containment rigour, pursuit of infected cases, support for those confined and border controls once the COVID-19 pandemic broke? History should have taught us, too, that to engage in ever more active and intense trading, travelling and commercial activity is to require more, not less, protective and preventative public health infrastructure and personnel. Did we also forget this lesson, lulled into the false notion that we have somehow found a costless, risk-free way of organising our economy and society across porous international borders?

2 PANDEMICS ARE NOT RANDOM 'BLACK SWANS'

It should be clear by now that pandemics are indeed an ever-present threat. The most disingenuous reaction to the eruption of COVID-19 has come from those who have labelled it a 'Black Swan' event. This is a term re-coined by the statistician Nassim Taleb for something so rare as to be entirely unpredictable and only capable of rational analysis with hindsight.[1] To the contrary, pandemics demand foresight to prepare, not hindsight to bemoan what could have been.

We Were Expecting a Pandemic, So Why Was the UK So Unprepared?

By the time COVID-19 arrived most countries should have had a novel pandemic at the top of their list of risks. Mindful of the lessons of the recent SARS, MERS and Ebola outbreaks, some would have been using wargaming exercises to rehearse pandemic preparedness. The UK used to have a reputation for being good at all this, its expertise on disease and pandemic control much sought after by the WHO and indeed many individual countries.

Why, then, was the UK seemingly not prepared for COVID-19? It is well-known that the government had been warned in no uncertain terms about deficiencies in its pandemic preparedness following Exercise Cygnus in 2016 – a large-scale simulation of what would happen in a fictitious 'swan flu' pandemic – intended to test how well our systems would cope.[2] How far the Cygnus recommendations were acted on is unclear, but what *is* clear is that by the time COVID-19 was approaching our shores, there were serious and pressing concerns over personal protective equipment (PPE), testing capability, availability of ventilators for the sick and nursing skills to operate them and intensive care bed capacity for very ill patients.

It's not hard to understand why. Two years after Cygnus the Department of Health and Social Care had outsourced its procurement function to a new company that it had tasked with delivering £2.4 billion of savings in the space of four years. The company, apparently, had been given '[no] targets related to the resilience of its supplies to the NHS'. No surprise, then, that government stockpiles of PPE in early 2020 amounted to only around two weeks' worth of the PPE needed during a pandemic.[3] And there were reports that the haphazard quarter-mastering of stores meant that by the time it was needed in 2020 even this limited stock of PPE included items already past their safe use date.

We now know, too, from leaked documents that the UK government's national security risk register, signed off by the government's chief scientific adviser, was flashing red in 2019 in the box marked pandemic, as it had been for years.[4] A red risk is the highest alert level, signifying a major threat to the nation both because of its extremely high likelihood and its extremely high impact should it materialise. One can only conclude, then, that the actions taken to mitigate that real and present risk were simply not up to the task. Nor apparently had there been any thought given to conducting an economic equivalent of Exercise Cygnus. A report in July 2020 by the Public Accounts Committee showed MPs to be incredulous at the failure to plan for the economic impact of a large-scale pandemic-induced health crisis.[5]

As news arrived in early 2020 of a hitherto unknown coronavirus circulating in the Wuhan province of China, new alarm bells started to ring as influential voices close to government began, ominously, to warn that the substantially privatised care home sector, already in crisis, would struggle to cope if there were a fully-fledged pandemic, as now looked increasingly likely.[6]

There can be no doubt that the government had taken its eye off the ball in the lead-up to COVID-19. A determination since 2016 to pursue Brexit at any cost had diverted ministers away from the big policy challenges, many of which were put on the backburner for years. While resources were ploughed into preparing for a no-deal Brexit, pandemic planning took a back seat, with capacity pared back in any case by austerity cuts. In late 2019, health chiefs, up against tens of thousands of staff vacancies – many directly or indirectly linked to Brexit – were mainly worried about how an overstretched NHS would cope with a severe flu outbreak that winter. The threat of a pandemic – coronavirus or something else – was simply not on their radar, and in fact many health leaders believed, as they had for years, that a SARS-type coronavirus could not reach the UK.

Matters were made worse by the fact that the initial arrival of COVID-19 coincided with mass flooding across the Midlands and North of the country, while the prime minister inexplicably went off on a twelve-day holiday. Everyone knows emergencies have a nasty habit of hitting at a bad time, but that is precisely when clear and dedicated leadership is most at a premium, its absence most keenly felt. Already on the back foot, with no apparent strategic plan emerging, a series of logistical errors compounded the problems even as nonchalant public pronouncements continued. Johnson missed five COBRA national emergency planning meetings in January and February, yet at the beginning of March announced that 'this country is very, very, well prepared'.[7]

The government was, as we now know, unable to protect health and care workers adequately for weeks on end, with their families believing that many paid for that with their lives. UK supply chains for key equipment were so diffuse and dependent on such a multiplicity of private UK and overseas suppliers as to have no resilience in a pandemic. With testing for COVID-19 infection at risible levels, agency workers were moving between care homes with insufficient protective clothing and under the threat of sub-subsistence sick pay if they couldn't work.[8] Care homes had been shut to visitors but in the period up to mid-April 25,060 patients were simply discharged from hospital into these facilities without mandatory testing for COVID-19 in the rush to free up hospital beds.[9]

The litany of errors continued. The failure to restrict or monitor passengers from incoming flights, the poor handling of communications by inexperienced ministers in charge when Boris Johnson was hospitalised, the dangerously slow ramping up of PPE and testing capacity, the botched announcements around the lifting of lockdown in the summer of June 2020, including a schools reopening that had to be reversed. All this was only further compounded by highly confused messaging after the initial pretty clear 'stay home' slogan was replaced with 'stay alert', with little attempt made at that point to promote the wearing of masks as other countries had done.

The debacle of the prime minister's chief political adviser's alleged breach of the lockdown rules when he travelled from London to Durham with his sick wife and child in the car was, for many, the final straw. His appearance in the Downing Street rose garden to claim he had driven to Barnard Castle, a tourist destination, to 'test his eyesight' before driving back to London was met with widespread ridicule. With no punitive action taken against Dominic Cummings the government's grip on the public health message on lockdown and social distancing began ebbing away.

Meanwhile, withering assessments of the government's 'guided by the science' policy came from all directions. Richard Horton, the editor-in-chief of *The Lancet*, didn't

Image 5. Number 10 special adviser Dominic Cummings on 25 May 2020, after giving a press conference to answer allegations that he and his family broke the rules when they travelled from London to Durham while the nation was under full lockdown.
Source: TOLGA AKMEN / Getty Images

mince his words in an interview with the *Observer* on 14th June, declaring that 'The UK response to coronavirus is the greatest science policy failure for a generation.' *The Sunday Times* newspaper's Insight team produced a forensic analysis on 24th May of '22 days of dither and delay … that cost thousands of British lives'. Even the normally dependably pro-Conservative *Daily Mail* piled in, its headline on 19th June, 'How many more Corona fiascos? After PPE and testing shambles, Minister scraps his own virus testing app … and new version may not even be ready by winter!'

Were there, though, more systematic forces at work during this period than just this apparent veneer of lazy or shambolic leadership? By the end of the first major wave of pandemic deaths in late May 2020, the UK had one of the highest rates of excess deaths per million people of any leading world economy.[10] It also had some of the worst outcomes for deaths of key workers and of deaths in care homes – at the peak care home deaths were running at close to half of all deaths. It is hard to think that, with the unwelcome distinction of being at or near the top of these grisly league tables, a public inquiry will not follow.

But was there evidence already, as *The Sunday Times*' report suggested, that we locked down too late? As early as 10th June 2020 the leading scientist Neil Ferguson told the House of Commons' Science and Technology Committee that the death toll from COVID-19 would have been reduced 'by at least a half' if the government had acted just one week earlier than it did to impose full lockdown.[11] This view was supported by others, given what was known about the reproduction rate of the disease in those crucial weeks in mid-March. In an interview with *The Times Magazine* published on 27th June 2020 the former chief scientific adviser, David King, was unequivocal: 'It was very clear that we should have gone into lockdown weeks earlier … [i]f we had even gone … a week earlier, then we would have probably had a quarter of the deaths we have now.'

The *Financial Times*, too, highlighted what looked like a strong correlation between late lockdown and high levels of excess deaths in the first wave of the pandemic. The UK, Spain and Italy all delayed lockdown until infections were running at very high rates, and, as the *Financial Times* analysis showed, all three countries went on to record significantly higher deaths than those who locked down in the early stages of the virus, notably Germany, Denmark and Norway.

Italy of course had the misfortune to be the trailblazer of the virus in Europe. By the time they had seen its impact, the Italians were begging other countries to act faster than they themselves had. The *Financial Times* article concluded, completely in line with the scientists quoted above, that 'locking down in the early stages of the virus is linked to a reduced excess death toll'.[12] The message of history, it seems, has not changed.

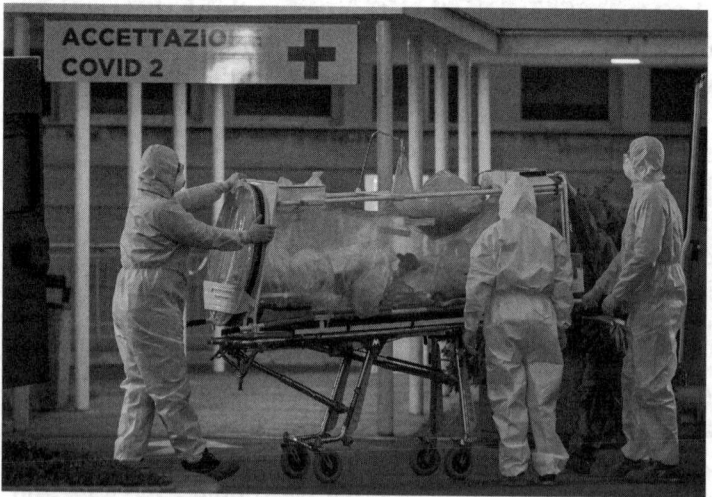

Image 6. Medical workers take a patient into a newly built temporary hospital, Rome, 16 March 2020.
Source: ANDREAS SOLARO / AFP / Getty Images

Your Money or Your Life

What was going on in ministers' minds as this all played out? In a characteristically flamboyant speech on 3rd February 2020, Boris Johnson had signalled his intention to keep the economy going. The great risk, as he saw it, was that 'coronavirus will trigger a panic ... beyond what is medically rational ... doing real and unnecessary economic damage'. The UK could, though, he proposed, turn this to its advantage and, Clark Kent-like, 'leap into the phone booth and emerge with its cloak flowing as the supercharged champion of the right of the populations of the earth to buy and sell freely'.[13]

On 12th March he therefore told the nation that we must accept that many will 'lose loved ones before their time'.[14] While governments such as Germany's and New Zealand's moved fast, the UK government remained unwilling to countenance a full lockdown, apparently hoping that if the most vulnerable were protected things could carry on as normal for everyone else. Even as infections were rising Boris Johnson was making his point, ostentatiously shaking hands with hospital patients with COVID-19. If, as some commentators thought, this was a resort to a 'herd immunity' strategy, potentially a reasonable response to a flu virus, it was in no way appropriate to a coronavirus of significantly greater severity. As the Greek journalist Georgios Skafidas wrote, the policy looked from the outside as if it were 'essentially ask[ing] Britons ... to accept death'.[15]

It was, though, an approach that seems in fact to have been rooted in earlier pandemic planning going back more than a decade and evident in documents first produced in 2005 and then updated in 2011. According to a meticulous analysis prepared for the *New Statesman*, the possibility of a national lockdown was apparently simply 'not contemplated' as a potential response in these blueprints for pandemic control. As the article argues, 'If a pandemic such as

COVID-19 struck, the UK intended only to mitigate rather than suppress the impact.' The result was that 'strict social distancing of the kind Britain has now enforced does not underpin any of its planning documents'.[16]

It took a biblical forecast of the likely deaths that would result from this approach – anything between a quarter and a half a million – to start to focus Boris Johnson's (or perhaps Dominic Cummings') mind. But still events such as the Cheltenham race festival were allowed to go ahead on 10–13th March, with a quarter of a million people attending. The Irish government, by contrast, had cancelled the Ireland v. Italy Six Nations rugby match in Dublin the previous weekend and was to forbid all St Patrick's Day festivities from proceeding on 17th March.

With a total economic shutdown against all of his instincts, and those of much of his party, and no prior planning for that eventuality, Johnson carried on wavering. Policy was still being framed in terms of the NHS's ability to care for the ill and dying, rather than as an all-out assault on COVID-19. Ministers opined that we needed to 'flatten the curve' or, in Johnson's more colourful language, 'squash the sombrero', meaning that infection rates needed to be kept within the limit of our health service capacity. They had acted quickly in respect of expanding that capacity with the building of the Nightingale hospitals and the calls for retired health professionals to return to service. But this was a strategy that still spoke of managing rather than suppressing the disease, of keeping the disruption to normal life to a minimum. The *Telegraph*'s Charles Moore at one point rather oddly suggested that a 'lumbering' NHS was somehow to blame for what came next, implying that more efficient hospitals might have enabled us to simply keep the economy going through an escalating pandemic.[17]

Finally, on 23rd March, with infections estimated to be in the hundreds of thousands, Boris Johnson accepted what should have been obvious days or weeks earlier. The UK population was ordered to isolate at home and all non-essential businesses that could not be conducted away from the workplace were closed. A few days later and un-surprisingly, given his behaviour, Boris Johnson did, in-deed, by his own admission come very close to 'accepting death', having caught COVID-19 along with his political adviser, health secretary and chief medical officer.

With lockdown in place, infections and deaths fell over the ensuing weeks and the R rate dropped below 1, although not by very much. As voices from his party began to call for the lockdown to be lifted, Johnson announced plans to do this for England from mid-June, taking action faster than the more cautious leaders in Scotland, Wales and Northern Ireland believed safe. The move was also against the advice of David King's independent Scientific Advisory Group of Ex-perts (SAGE), set up in exasperation at the lack of transpar-ency over the government's scientific evidence. Independent SAGE argued in its 12th May communiqué that

> *The government should take all necessary measures to control the virus through suppression and not simply managing its spread. Evidence must show that COVID-19 transmission is con-trolled before [lockdown] measures are relaxed.*[18]

That the government went ahead regardless was another sign of the primacy of the economic argument. In a move that may have raised a few eyebrows, Roula Khalaf, the ed-itor of the *Financial Times*, tweeted on 31st May, 'What the government will not say: we're not at the stage where we should ease the lockdown, but we're doing it anyway to save the economy.'[19]

This was a risky strategy. What it needed at the very least was an effective test and trace system behind it, of the sort that other democracies like Germany, South Korea and New Zealand had in place from early on. This should have been a community-based system, making use of local authorities' contact tracing and public health expertise, with vast experience built up since the original 1889 and 1899 Notification of Diseases Acts required local authorities to isolate those with infections.[20]

A locally based approach was repeatedly called for by public health specialists on Independent SAGE and elsewhere. Instead, the government ignored the nation's valuable historic public sector endowment and outsourced the contact tracing role to a private contractor with no relevant expertise. Serco, with £108 million in its pocket for a three-month contract, simply recruited large numbers of poorly trained call centre staff who, unsurprisingly, struggled to deliver and indeed many sat idle.[21] It is hard to conclude that this was driven by anything other than the dogma of the free market and its well-established gravy train of government contracts let to private sector contacts. But it was a policy choice that was to have massive health and economic consequences.

All this was going on while the government was actively encouraging a 'return to normal' by offering subsidies for pub and restaurant meals during August ('Eat Out to Help Out') and urging people working from home to get back to their workplace to save the lunchtime economy (and, it was implied, potentially their own jobs). It was no wonder that people no longer understood the already confused public health messaging and no surprise, in view of that, that vast numbers celebrated the end of lockdown by booking last-minute trips abroad. Completely inadequate controls on returning passengers – no COVID-19 tests, no temperature checks, no procedures for monitoring quarantine where required – undoubtedly aided the renewed spread of infection. This was confirmed when a mutated Spanish strain of COVID-19 was found to be spreading in the UK over the summer months.

If this cocktail of unseemly haste to release lockdown, of mixed messaging on safety and social distancing over the summer months, and of wing and a prayer tracking of infections had proved a successful strategy, it would have been more through luck than design. In the event a second wave of infections was already taking hold in early September, with the R rate having risen to 1.2 even before schools and universities had fully returned. As infections continued to multiply, the scientists on SAGE (the official scientific body advising government) warned on 21st September of the risk of a 'very large epidemic with catastrophic consequences', pointing out that it would disproportionately impact the frail, the poor and people of colour.[22] They argued for an urgent two-week 'circuit-breaker' lockdown that could lead into the half-term school holiday, advice followed in Wales and Northern Ireland but ignored in Westminster for the best part of six weeks. A government that had previously insisted it would be 'guided by the science' was to dither again until, 'humbled by nature', and a lot of very scary charts, Boris Johnson had no choice but to act, announcing a new lockdown to begin on 5th November.

The government's reluctance to act earlier was no doubt driven by the belief that the economic costs of a new national lockdown were too high and that the more localised restrictions that had already been imposed on high infection areas in parts of the North and Midlands would suffice. But it was a false dichotomy. There is no trade-off that says you must choose between protecting lives and protecting the economy. The truth is that those countries that acted decisively to stop the spread of infection did better on both counts – a lower economic hit and a lower death toll. That is for the very simple reason that the sooner you bring a pandemic under control the fewer curbs are needed on what people can do and the sooner and more secure your economic recovery will be. That was clear in many East and South East Asian countries – South Korea, Vietnam, Taiwan, Singapore – from early on, as it was also in New Zealand and Australia. The UK, by contrast, had by the end of 2020 suffered one of the world's highest COVID-19 death rates per head of population *and* close to the largest fall in economic output of the OECD countries.

The foot-dragging before bringing in a full autumn lockdown across England inevitably meant that, once imposed, it was going to have to be longer – four weeks instead of the two originally advised by SAGE – because there was that much further to go to bring infections down to a safe level. It had been a self-defeating decision to delay. The following March, the Office for Budget Responsibility gave this assessment of the self-inflicted double whammy in their budget report,

> *The primary reason that the UK has suffered a greater economic hit from the pandemic is simply that the UK has experienced higher rates of infection, hospitalisation, and deaths from the virus than other countries … [and] spent longer in stricter lockdowns than other advanced economies.*[23]

Lockdown was in any case a blunt and brutal instrument. It was as if we had resorted to a position where, after a lockdown, we would turn the economic taps back on when we thought the R – the infection rate – had fallen below 1. Then we'd let people go on holiday, travel to see family at Christmas, or whatever it was that was thought necessary to restore morale, and give the economy a boost, and see what happened. If that meant we overshot and the R went back over 1, then, reluctantly, and far too slowly, we would undo all the weeks or months of sacrifice – the missed weddings and funerals, the insensitive last-minute cancellation of Eid celebrations – and, after the brief respite, slam on the brakes. The longer we waited to do it, the longer and harsher the eventual lockdown would be, and the more lives unnecessarily lost as a result of the delay.

The inevitable third lockdown came hot on the heels of Christmas, although the festivities had already been summarily curtailed for some in a panicked reversal of the seasonal relaxation. A new mutation of COVID-19, which had a far greater level of infectiousness, was producing soaring infections in London and the South East in mid-December. By early January COVID-19 cases were threatening to overwhelm hospital and mortuary capacity around the country and by the end of January hospitalisations in just that one month had exceeded 100,000, one third of the total since the pandemic began.

Bad luck for the Brits to be the ones to get this rogue 'Kent' mutation. The rest of the world had, as soon as it had got a whiff of the new variant, lost no time in shutting their borders to the UK. The response by the French government was particularly harsh as thousands of truck drivers were left stranded at British ports in the lead-in to Christmas, unable to travel back via France to their country of origin until they could access negative COVID tests.

What was the alternative to these painful stop–start lockdowns? After the summer lockdown, there was pretty much universal agreement that the absolute key priority was for children to return to school in September after nearly six months of absence. Those advising the government were clear that this would add significantly to the R rate if nothing else changed. Given that we knew that we had to keep R below 1, this was the point at which we needed to think hard about how to achieve that. Remember R was already topping 1 when schools went back. So, we had to think in terms of having an 'R budget' and work out quickly what we needed to do to stay within that budget – in other words what was going to have to stop when schools went back?

The data showed that we could get a good bit off the R by asking people to stop going back into workplaces if they could possibly work from home, although it took weeks for this to find its way into official advice. To the contrary, one of the government's own agencies, the Driver and

Vehicle Licensing Agency (DVLA) based in Swansea, was revealed in January 2021 to have brought large numbers of staff back to work after the first lockdown, in what were alleged by workers to have been crowded and unsafe conditions, such that this single workplace had by that point recorded 535 infections.[24]

Workplace distancing aside, reducing household mixing either in private homes or hospitality venues was obviously also one of the main chances we had to economise on our R budget. But the messages given out and the measures put in place to curtail social mixing and back it up with widespread mask wearing in public places were either not introduced early enough or not pursued systematically enough to do the job. And without an all-out assault on the drivers of the R, and with schools open, too, it was simply inevitable that we would bust the R budget and go back to exponentially rising infections and all the deaths that would follow when winter pushed the population and the virus back indoors, as the government had indeed been advised by its own SAGE scientists weeks before.[25]

The real culprit though was the failure to use the summer lull in infections to sort out the test, track, trace and isolate strategy. If we had been able to do that, to find local flare-ups of infection and stamp them out quickly then we might have had a chance of controlling things into the autumn. Everyone, from government to scientists and the population at large, understood the importance of this. As one member of SAGE had wearily put it in a late-night TV interview, he 'couldn't care less' whether we had the 'world-beating' system that ministers had boasted of, he just wanted us to have a 'virus-beating' one.[26]

And yet we seemed to be incapable of even delivering that. The insistence on setting up a centralised outfit instead of drawing on our world-leading local public health infrastructure was equivalent, as public health expert Allyson Pollock pointed out at the start, to calling a fire engine from Westminster, when you have a fire – and plenty of fire engines – in Blackpool or Cumbria or the Isle of Wight.[27] The privatised system lacked capacity and leadership, so that testing delays and failures continued through the autumn, the tracing hit rate was sporadic and frequently insufficient to be effective and there was no strategy to support or even monitor those required to isolate, with the result that adherence was inevitably compromised.

Yet an effective system to suppress the virus would have limited the scope for dangerous new mutations of COVID-19 to emerge over the autumn months. Mutations occur more readily when there are high levels of transmission and that means that the most effective way to prevent new mutations is to reduce the spread of the virus.[28] In other words it might not just have been bad luck that was behind our escalating numbers of deaths as we went into 2021 with a mutant strain tightening its grip.

The UK's failure over so many months to tackle its dysfunctional test, track and trace system so that we could contain not just levels of infection but also the risk of more transmissible mutations occurring was, then, arguably, one of the biggest and most expensive fiascos of the whole sorry story of the pandemic response. It is where a great deal of soul-searching is going to be called for.

Light at the End of the Tunnel

Of course, we have something not available to our predecessors in the fight to overcome a deadly new pathogen. In the end COVID-19's hall of fame was always going to be reserved for the scientists who produced the vaccine that could stop it in its tracks or, failing that, the treatment that could render it less lethal.

The first 'game-changing' vaccine to hit the headlines in mid-November 2020 came from a research team at BioNTech, working with Pfizer in Germany. Astonishing in its rapidity – vaccines are normally years in development – it was soon followed by vaccines produced by Moderna in the USA and an Oxford University team collaborating with the Cambridge-based company AstraZeneca.[29] International attention then quickly turned to how we would administer the many candidate vaccines that would most likely come forward over the course of 2021 and beyond, and how we would prioritise who would be in line to get them first.

When on 8 December 2020, ninety-year-old Margaret Keenan made history as the first person in the world outside of trials to be vaccinated against COVID-19 in University Hospital, Coventry, the world began to look forward to what might be a return to something possibly recognisable as 'normal'. Ministers sought to extract maximum political capital from the fact that the UK's fleet-footed

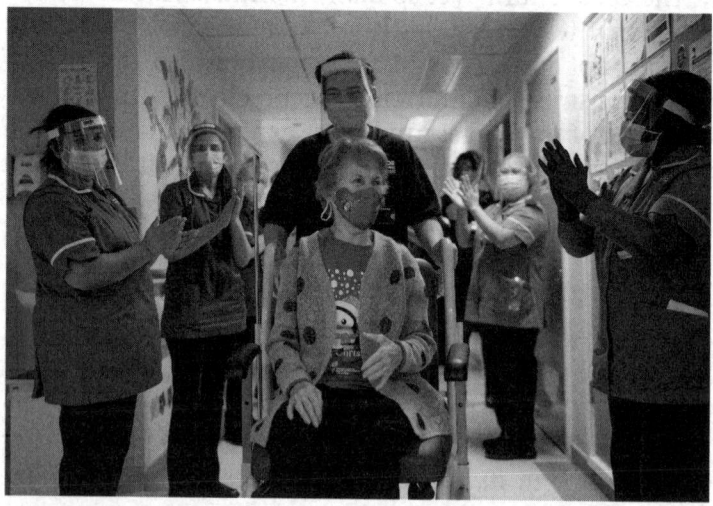

Image 7. Margaret Keenan, the first person in the world to be vaccinated, is applauded by staff after being vaccinated at University Hospital, Coventry.
Source: JACOB KING / AFP / Getty Images

medicines regulator had been the first to approve a vaccine against COVID-19 – the Pfizer one administered to Keenan. The mood in the country gradually began to pick up and, as more needles went into arms over the next few weeks, political fortunes started to revive, too.

While the EU struggled to get its vaccination programme up and running, bogged down by slow procurement and ponderous regulatory approval, the UK's programme powered ahead. Boris Johnson's approval ratings bounced back as the UK met its target to vaccinate four key priority groups by 15 February 2021. More than 15 million first vaccinations had been delivered by that date to care home residents, health and care workers, the over seventies and the clinically extremely vulnerable.

It was certainly an impressive performance and one that was in stark contrast to the lacklustre handling of most other aspects of the pandemic up to that point. The UK's strength in life sciences, the product of long-term government investment, had paid off as Oxford University's vaccine emerged as one of the world leaders. The UK had implemented an early and smart procurement strategy via the government Vaccine Taskforce, which, courtesy of a very large government cheque book, had set about ordering vaccines significantly over requirement from all the likely candidate producers, as well as investing at speed in home-grown manufacturing capacity. Crucial also to its success was the fact that the vaccination programme was rolled out using the existing, efficient NHS infrastructure and community-minded volunteers across the country. A task on this scale and requiring this level of professionalism, mercifully, could not be outsourced.

Mass vaccination, then, was potentially the light at the end of the tunnel. But in the early months of 2021 that tunnel still seemed very long and very dark. In the ten weeks between the start of the vaccination roll out and the date in February when the first target of 15 million vaccinations had been reached, the UK saw 55,000 more COVID-19 deaths – very nearly half of all pandemic deaths up to that point.[30] It was a tragedy that in all likelihood would have been averted had lessons been learned, attributable in no small part to a second disastrously delayed lockdown and its premature release for Christmas, a celebration that turned out for many to be their last.

On 26 January 2021 the prime minister was forced to announce that the grim milestone of 100,000 deaths had been passed, our numbers of dead and our death rate both in the top five in the world. When he addressed the nation that day, Johnson declared himself 'deeply sorry', but nevertheless insisted that his government had done 'everything we could'.[31]

It was not long before chinks in the vaccination armour began to appear, as questions were raised about its efficacy against several new COVID-19 variants. The South African government suspended its entire programme on 7th February amid fears that its new variant was resistant to the Oxford/AstraZeneca vaccine it had bulk purchased. As alarm grew over new potentially resistant strains of COVID-19 the UK for the first time implemented stronger border controls with mandated, hotel quarantine for arrivals from some high-risk countries, although still leaving too many gaps that the virus could slip through.

Accusations of 'vaccine nationalism' also began to materialise, with richer countries in particular being accused of trying to monopolise supplies, leaving poorer countries high and dry. The UK and EU became embroiled in an ugly spat over restrictions in the supply of the AstraZeneca vaccine to the EU. Brussels threatened in retaliation to ban exports of the Pfizer vaccine to Northern Ireland, using an emergency clause in the Brexit agreement on which the ink had only just dried, before the quarrel was eventually papered over. Ironically, many EU citizens and their political leaders started to refuse the AstraZeneca vaccine over the ensuing weeks, despite an adequacy of supply, amid claims that its efficacy and safety were in doubt.

The path out of the pandemic would see many such twists and turns. Researchers appeared confident in early 2021 that vaccines could be adapted – 'tweaked' – to deal with important COVID-19 mutations, and that regular booster vaccinations could be provided at speed. The science also suggested that even where protection was not at its maximum the vaccines would nearly always prevent serious disease developing. But with much of the world unable to access sufficient vaccines, and some countries, notably Brazil and India, continuing to experience escalating cases of infection and death, there was certainly a continuing concern that 'no one is safe until everyone is safe'. The risk was not just from transmission between countries but from the opportunity that uncontrolled infection in some parts of the world would provide for new mutations of COVID-19 to get established. If variants were to emerge that rendered current vaccines ineffective, the need for mass revaccination, even assuming new vaccines were developed as fast as hoped for, would again put us in a race against time with the virus.

Maintaining confidence in the vaccines was absolutely critical. Vaccine scepticism, already being fuelled by social media disinformation, would damage the programme's effectiveness if take-up was not at sufficiently high levels. Young people's attitudes would be crucial. With less personal benefit from vaccination they would need to be persuaded of the wider benefit to others.

A further challenge for the vaccination roll out in the UK was that vulnerable individuals and some more deprived communities and particular ethnic groups were recording lower rates of vaccine take-up.[32] Some were finding it difficult to travel to vaccination centres but there was also an issue of trust and what seemed to be a disengagement from a system that many did not feel was serving their needs.

Unless addressed this carries the real risk that COVID-19 will persist as a disease of poverty in isolated areas of deprivation and among certain communities, further widening disparities in health and life outcomes.

It was impossible at the time of writing, as the first anniversary of the March 2020 lockdown passed, to say if and when we could realistically expect the cloud of COVID-19 to be lifted. The economy would be unlocked, there would be at least a temporary lull in infections and no doubt a surge of pent-up spending and partying. Beyond that, whether there would be further waves of infections and how lethal they would be, and how much that depended not just on vaccines but also on keeping up the sanitising and social distancing, were still unclear.

But at the point – whether sooner or later – at which we do eventually take off our face masks and reach out to hug our relatives and friends in celebration we should also pause to reflect on the warning shot that COVID-19 has given us.

When deaths in the UK exceeded the 100,000 mark in January 2021, Richard Murray, chief executive of the health think tank the King's Fund, expressed what so many were feeling:

> *This time last year, it would be almost impossible to believe that a wealthy island nation with a universal healthcare system would go on to have one of the highest death tolls from the … coronavirus pandemic.*[33]

If we are serious as a country that we must never again find ourselves in this position that must mean, in the right time and the right way, holding to account those shown to be culpable through their actions or inactions.

But we also need to ask why. How was it that COVID-19 hit some of our communities so much harder than others? Why were we, one of the richest countries in the world, so fragile and lacking in resilience that we could not withstand its devastating impact? What had happened to our institutions and economic governance that had left us so ill-prepared? What does that mean for our capacity to be ready for future, potentially even more devastating, challenges?

These are the deeper questions we now address, drawing on our own rich history for inspiration and answers.

PART II
WHY COVID-19 WAS
A PERFECT STORM

3 THE FRAGILITY OF THE NEOLIBERAL STATE

This chapter focuses on one of the most socially corrosive narratives in existence today, yet one which has gained significant currency over the last forty years: namely that the state is an unwelcome intrusion into people's lives and the workings of the economy that needs to be kept at arm's length as much as possible. It will show how the type of government we pursued and the choices we made in the name of this dogma critically weakened our capacity to mount an effective response when, as was all but inevitable, the neoliberal state came up against one of history's ultimate tests – a novel pathogen.

The Neoliberal Project

The post-war welfare state with its steeply progressive taxation had seen occupational and social mobility expand in the UK and productivity positively soaring as decent employment, housing, education and health care were opened up to all. With the country's first majority Labour government elected with the backing of enhanced union power, the key social and economic policies of this period produced a dramatic uplift in the income security of working-class families, ushering in an era of widely shared rising living standards. It was a nurturing, facilitating state that delivered a National Health Service based on need, not ability to pay, full employment and, although it is rarely celebrated, twenty-five years of uninterrupted growth from 1948 to 1973.

But the 'Golden Age', as it was known, eventually began to tarnish. By the 1970s the economy had taken a nosedive in the face of two massive oil price shocks and it seems many thought the pendulum had swung too far. Amid fears that union practices had damaged our competitiveness and that strikes were holding business and the nation to ransom, the electorate turned to the right, embracing Thatcherism and her promise of policies to quash inflation and curtail union power. Thatcher, making a virtue of being a grocer's daughter, crafted a new narrative of the household economy in which she argued that governments, like 'housewives', should not spend more than they have. Harking back to Victorian values she repudiated the principles of collective social responsibility of the post-war era along with what her secretary of state Peter Lilley was later to call 'the something for nothing society'.

It was the beginning of a forty-year period of what has come to be termed 'neoliberalism', so called because it propounded similar free-market, small-state policies to those first advocated by the classical liberal economist Adam Smith in his celebrated book *The Wealth of Nations*, published in 1776. By the 1990s neoliberalism had spread like a virus, its global influence such that it had been branded the 'Washington Consensus'.[1] It offered a formula that would refashion the post-war welfare states of many Western governments and international institutions into something significantly more hard-edged than ever envisaged by their founders. What, then, does this nebulous term 'neoliberalism' actually mean?

In a nutshell, the central tenet of neoliberalism can be summarised as a requirement that the state should retreat.[2] Privatisation, globalisation, free flows of capital, deregulation, low tax, curbs on public spending, welfare cutbacks and deficit reduction are all part of the mix, driven by the claim that the market is always more efficient than the state. Regulations are seen as 'red tape' that inhibit business freedoms, and the public sphere is something to be minimised to avoid crowding out private enterprise. But the measures introduced in the name of neoliberalism in the 1980s and 90s were also, as argued by David Garland in his analysis of welfare state dynamics, 'expressions of sectional interests'. They marked a shift in power 'away from organised labour towards corporate and finance capital, weakening the public sector and empowering market forces'.[3] Let's explore what this meant in the UK.

It was financial deregulation that formed the hallmark of the early period of neoliberalism. The growth of the City of London, the UK's financial centre, and its liberation from previous controls, including, of course, on international capital flows, from the 1970s onwards was hailed as a victory for the free market against the controlling state.[4] The finance sector became ever more important to the UK economy, its increasing dominance celebrated and indeed actively encouraged by successive governments. Yet there is a school of thought that argues that, far from benefiting the economy, it began to act as a drain on other sectors as it grew in size, attracting the best talent and permanently diverting resources from areas of potentially more productive investment as well as from scientific research and innovation.[5]

Financial deregulation was a dogma founded in the belief that individuals' self-interest should be allowed to take centre stage as the force that would deliver efficient market outcomes. Yet as Nicholas Morris and David Vines argue in their book *Capital Failure: Rebuilding Trust in Financial Services*, the pursuit of self-interest instead led the sector to behave in untrustworthy ways. Encouraged by inappropriate compensation schemes, institutions and the people who worked in them 'sold unsuitable products, loaded their clients with unacceptable risk and debt, extracted excessive fees, rigged markets and defrauded clients'. All this, Morris and Vines argue, is the result of a selfish system that lacked adequate regard for the interests of clients.[6]

Where the financial sector led, others followed. The ideological shift of neoliberalism with its aggressive free-market mentality changed the focus of many managers and business leaders towards short-term returns. Gone was the broader vision of the post-war era, laid out in Peter Drucker's influential 1946 study *The Concept of the Corporation*, that the purpose of corporations went beyond just the narrow focus on creating profit to embrace the broader aims of providing good jobs, good products, taxes and healthy communities.[7] Instead a new mantra, maximising 'shareholder value', began to replace a more considered and long-term view of business interest or social value as the driver of decisions. As tax rates were repeatedly cut for the highest earners the effect was to create incentives to seek lucrative bonuses as the reward for short-term risk-taking. Institutions became increasingly controlled by people primarily interested in making short-term returns to maximise shareholder rewards (and their own bonus-laden pay-packets) above any other objectives.[8]

All of this was bound up with the phenomenon of financialisation, where many corporate bosses stopped being concerned with creating wealth *for* the economy, the unglamorous hard work of investing to boost productivity and inject genuine entrepreneurship, as the traditional textbooks would have us believe they do. Instead, they would be seeking out ways to extract wealth *from* the economy and its businesses, which they are able to do through the use of elaborate financial arrangements designed for the benefit of shareholders. It delivers, as Nicholas Shaxson describes in his book *The Finance Curse*, 'the more profitable sugar rush of financial engineering to tease out more profit for the owners'.[9] More often than not the proceeds from these activities find their way into complex and opaque legal and financial vehicles that funnel the money offshore and away from the legitimate demands of the tax authorities.[10]

The UK department store Debenhams, which collapsed at the end of 2020, was considered by retail analysts to have been a victim of just this sort of aggressive financial engineering. Founded in 1778 when George III was on the throne, and by 1950 the UK's largest department store group, Debenhams was taken over in 2003 by a private equity consortium. The group made huge returns from its £600 million investment, paying its owners £1.2 billion in dividends in less than three years. But this came at a terrible cost: in the short period that the private equity owners were in charge Debenhams' debt rose from £100 million to over £1 billion, which is where it stood when it was off-loaded by the consortium and refloated in 2006. Many of its stores had by then been remortgaged and twenty-three had been sold by the equity consortium, with the business then having to pay rent to continue to occupy them. As one analyst commented, at the time that Debenhams most needed to invest in its future to stay ahead of the game, its

Image 8. Socially distanced shoppers outside Debenhams.
Source: Mike Kemp / Getty Images

'wherewithal to react, i.e. money, was removed. It was removed into the bank accounts of private equity investors. That is the truth of it.'[11] Debenhams never recovered from that speculative intervention.

Alongside this predatory financial culture, other forces were compounding the diversion of investment into non-productive uses, especially housing and commercial real estate. The relaxation of regulations on mortgage lending that had been part of the liberalisation agenda was producing a misallocation of capital resources as money chased real estate. Rent seeking through housing wealth, dubbed 'residential capitalism', because housing was becoming so dominant in investors' financial portfolios, accelerated after the 1980s. It was a development that dampened economic growth as other parts of the economy lost out on this investment and helped fuel a hike in house prices in the UK that now threatens to shut upcoming generations out of home ownership.[12]

All of this matters because, as Shaxson and others argue, the siphoning of wealth away from the productive economy as a result of the massive expansion and deregulation of the financial sector has taken a huge toll on growth, on investment and on productivity. Shaxson cites research suggesting that an oversized City of London may have cost the British economy the equivalent of £4.5 trillion in the period 1995–2015 once the impact of the financial crash, which the sector brought upon itself through its excessive risk-taking, is included.[13] That is about two and a half years of economic output, quite a hefty Danegeld paid to these new Viking invaders. He contrasts this with the earlier era of high tax, broadly drawn corporate purpose and tightly controlled financial flows across borders, noting that 'the fastest economic growth in world history came in the roughly quarter of a century after the Second World War, when finance was savagely suppressed'![14]

The Capture of Democracy

There is also a much darker side to the economic liberal-isation of the neoliberal era that we cannot afford to shy away from. The world-famous economist Thomas Piketty has documented the damage that is done when wealth becomes ever more concentrated, as has happened once again in the last forty years. He shows that when the returns that can be made from owning capital (wealth) grow more rapidly than the rest of the economy and these returns are not sufficiently dampened by taxation or regulation, then a destabilising spiral of ever-rising inequality in wealth holdings inevitably follows. Ultimately, he argues, this becomes a threat to democracy as an effective oligarchy of wealth concentrates not just economic power but also begins to wield disproportionate political power.[15]

Unfortunately, this is clearly visible in the UK today. An oligarchy of wealthy individuals use their money to buy political influence in order to shore up their position and block policies – wealth taxation or the ending of offshore havens, for instance – that might deny them the ability to continue amassing their fortunes. The amounts that wealthy individuals and corporations are prepared to spend on political lobbying reveal just how much this is worth to them, as do the cosy deals done so often behind the scenes.

Robert Jenrick, the Conservative Secretary of State for Housing, Communities and Local Government, was caught out early in 2020 when one such episode, in which he fast-tracked a £1 billion planning application for billionaire ex-publisher of pornography and the *Daily Express*, Richard Desmond, came to light. After sitting next to Jenrick at a Conservative fundraising dinner, which Desmond paid £12,000 to attend, Desmond repeatedly pressed Jenrick for the application to be advanced quickly. Desmond made no secret of the fact that this was so that he could get out of paying the local council a new community charge of £45 million on the development – or, as Desmond put it in a text message to Jenrick, avoid 'giv[ing] the Marxists loads of doe [sic] for nothing'. Jenrick approved the application with only hours to go, despite later admitting he had acted illegally in doing so.[16]

Of course, as political coffers are filled with the donations of the wealthy the relationship becomes symbiotic. The politicians can no more do without the wealthy than the wealthy can do without politicians.[17] This further compromises democracy and ethical governance. Contracts are put out to private sector contractors to deliver public services, with controls and due diligence not always at the forefront of the commissioning minister's mind. Justified by the mantra 'private sector good, public sector bad' this soon becomes second nature. How else could a £13.8 million contract have been given to a 'ferry' company in 2018 to provide emergency cross channel transportation in the event of a no-deal Brexit, despite the company never having run a ferry service and not having any ships?[18]

Private Finance Initiative (PFI) contracts are another example of this symbiotic political coexistence. Once hailed as the solution to public investment financing, they have now been exposed as vehicles that leeched money from public funds into the coffers of private corporations. The many complex layers of beneficiaries and intermediaries, each requiring a cut of the profits, hoovered up money to the extent that one respected analyst characterised the operation of PFIs as tantamount to delivering 'one hospital for the price of two'.[19]

There are shocking examples of major corporations securing public contracts only to fail dismally, leaving the taxpayer high and dry. Worst of these was the construction company Carillion, which went into insolvency in January 2018 while holding contracts for huge public construction projects and government services ranging from school meals to prison maintenance and NHS cleaning. Carillion's chairman had been an adviser to David Cameron for five years while at the helm of the company.

A report by two parliamentary select committees in the months after its collapse found that Carillion had deliberately misrepresented its financial position with 'increasingly fantastical figures',[20] enabling the company to continue paying out bonuses and lavish dividends even as the firm neared collapse on the back of these same payments. Frank Field, chair of one of the committees, said of the debacle, 'Same old story. Same old greed. A board of directors too busy stuffing their mouths with gold to show any concern for the welfare of their workforce or their pensioners.' The committees' harshest judgement was reserved for the auditors who had picked up massive fees while being 'complicit' in rubber-stamping Carillion's accounts and neglecting to flag 'failings that proved terminal'.[21] Amid calls for the competition regulator to break up the big four accountancy firms to increase competition, Rachel Reeves, the other committee chair, slammed these firms' 'parasitical' relationship with the companies whose books they were supposed to scrutinise.[22]

If neoliberalism delivers what many commentators now describe as a 'rigged' capitalism, it is also an ideology that can engender a dangerously fragile and corrupt state. It was the neoliberal state that tore up regulations and left the financial sector with inadequate supervision, ignoring rampant risk-taking until it had got so out of control that it triggered the biggest economic crash since the 1930s, at which point the kitchen sink was thrown at the banks to save them. This, too, was the state that failed to stop flammable cladding that had been banned for years in Germany and the USA from being added to tower blocks purely to cut costs for profit-hungry developers. It was the state that apparently knew in 2018 that garment factories in Leicester were operating in breach of the law under pressure to service the online clothing industry, but somehow appeared to be taken by surprise in 2020 when conditions in these same factories came under the spotlight during a local COVID-19 outbreak.[23] It was also, of course, the state that by late 2020 seemed prepared to risk a no-deal Brexit happening by default, with hedge funds that were claimed to have close political ties to the government said to have been gambling billions on just such an outcome.[24]

As Brexit approached, the UK government was showing itself to be prepared to engage in undemocratic, authoritarian expedients, so determined was it to get its way. In September 2019 Boris Johnson attempted an illegal prorogation of parliament in a bid to stop opposition to his hard Brexit policy. The following autumn, once again backed into a corner, his government openly and brazenly brought forward the Internal Market Bill, a piece of UK law that ministers admitted would break international law by subverting the obligations in the Brexit withdrawal agreement over Northern Ireland trading arrangements that the government had signed only a few months earlier.[25] It was a slippery slope, in which the ideology and power base of economic neoliberalism was now threatening to undermine the rule of law and democracy. This is the kind of unprincipled behaviour that reminded some less of Winston Churchill, Boris Johnson's declared idol, than of the regime he was fighting against.

By the time that COVID-19 arrived, it seemed as if much of the pretence had already evaporated. Contracts amounting to billions of pounds of public money went to contacts and supporters of ministers for anything from PR services to PPE to testing capacity, with the government freed by emergency procurement regulations from normal expectations over open and transparent tendering.[26] Nor did anyone seem particularly troubled by the need to set parameters over quality, performance or prior expertise in awarding contracts. It was no wonder things went wrong.

At one point 50 million face masks bought for the NHS were rejected as unsafe because they had been manufactured with ear loops instead of head loops.[27]

All of this was the visible side of the so-called 'chumocracy' of democratic capture that no one was by this point even attempting to deny. To the contrary, Serco chief executive Rupert Soames (grandson of Winston Churchill) had told staff early on in a leaked – and then retracted – email of his hope that the contracts that the business had secured during the pandemic would 'go a long way in cementing the position of the private sector companies in the public sector supply chain'.[28]

And behind the scenes, as Peter Geoghegan has documented, there was also the 'dark money' – the financial largesse that had for years been coming into the political process through shady funding vehicles and 'think tanks', many with charitable status, who will not reveal who their financial backers are.[29] In nearly all cases those organisations whose funding is most secretive espouse neoliberal policies and most enjoy close connections to the Conservative Party: the Adam Smith Institute, Policy Exchange Network, Institute of Economic Affairs, Centre for Policy Studies, Taxpayers' Alliance and Civitas.[30] Indeed, so cosy are their relationships with the Conservative government that health secretary Matt Hancock used the Policy Exchange Network (co-founder Michael Gove) as the forum to announce the abolition of an official body, Public Health England, in August 2020 and its replacement by a new agency headed by a Conservative peer.[31]

In the autumn of 2020, as serious questions were being asked about the country's future direction, these anonymously funded organisations ratcheted up their activities. The right-wing Centre for Policy Studies, which was founded in 1974 by Keith Joseph and Margaret Thatcher, and whose funding is one of those deemed highly opaque, put out press releases and briefings against policies that might undermine the privileged status of wealth. Their attack on any reform of Capital Gains Tax was entirely predictable. Less savoury was their salvo against the annual uprating of the minimum wage and their lobbying for a three-year public sector pay freeze. Their messages were picked up and parroted by the right-wing press as planned at precisely the moment when ministers were meeting to consider their options.[32]

When Richard Sharp was made chairman of the BBC in January 2021, the Centre for Policy Studies was quick to congratulate its board member of eighteen years on this influential appointment. Influential in many ways. Sharp had been Chancellor Rishi Sunak's boss at Goldman Sachs and had stepped in to advise him in 2020 on the government's pandemic response. He has also donated more than £400,000 to the Conservative Party since 2001. Certainly, then, a man from the heart of the neoliberal establishment was now heading up one of our most important democratic institutions.[33]

Boris Johnson, of course, had his own solution to any inconvenient accusations of cronyism, able to call on the aid of one of his MPs, John Penrose, as his anti-corruption 'champion'. Might not be a problem, but probably worth mentioning that Penrose is married to Dido Harding. Her stint at the helm of the privatised test and trace system, which consistently failed to deliver on its promises, had, it would be fair to say, been one of the most controversial of all the pandemic appointments.

How COVID-19 Was Able to Wreak Havoc

The UK government was certainly tested and found wanting by COVID-19. Many of the decisions made and the actions taken – or not taken – as the pandemic escalated will be endlessly revisited and scrutinised. But scratch the surface and it will quickly be evident that what happened in 2020 was in fact shaped by the many prior decades of state retreat. The health and care set-up that we found ourselves with on the eve of the pandemic is in many ways a case study of the neoliberal project. It brought together the ramifications of marketisation, privatisation and austerity with a dysfunctional, diminished democracy into a microcosm of the bigger story of the times.

A 'Just in Time' Health Service

After New Labour lost the 2010 election, the Conservatives, with their Liberal Democrat coalition partner, ramped up the rhetoric on neoliberalism. They asserted that the debts racked up as a result of the financial crash could only be dealt with by a period of belt-tightening austerity, with public services the first line of attack.

In 2012 – the year in which the National Health Service had been celebrated at the London Olympics' opening ceremony as our most cherished institution – legislation was passed to break it up. The 2012 Health and Social Care Act was designed to inject more USA-style free-market capitalism and marketisation. There was to be an 'internal market' of clinical commissioners (or GPs as they are more commonly known) who were to buy health services from competing providers. There would no longer be any strategic overview of future health needs by regional health authorities as these were jettisoned – as indeed was the health secretary's statutory responsibility for the quality and performance of the system.

Rather than just stick to one change, the 2012 Act also threw in a reorganisation of public health structures for good measure. Public Health Observatories and the disease control and rapid response teams required by government pandemic plans were moved, with their shrinking budgets, out of the NHS and into local authorities. The independent Health Protection Agency, which provided specialist support on the threat of emerging disease, was hived off into a new body – Public Health England – whose operational budget was cut by 40 per cent in real terms between 2013 and 2019.[34]

An impressive array of 400 health professionals, led by a past president of the British Medical Association, Michael Marmot, had begged the House of Lords to reject the reforms in an open letter published in the *Daily Telegraph* in October 2011, which presciently predicted that the new legislation would:

> widen health inequalities; waste much money on attempts to regulate and manage competition; and undermine the ability of the health system to respond effectively and efficiently to communicable disease outbreaks and other public health emergencies.

It was hardly an endorsement of a shake-up that was trumpeted as a market-driven revolution in the efficiency and economy of health provision. Indeed, it was not long before senior Conservatives themselves began to regret what they had done. Former minister Stephen Dorrell told the *Observer* in 2015 that the reforms were his party's biggest mistake in government and others privately accepted that it had been a disaster to proceed with them.[35]

In the event, the wanton destruction of the UK's public health infrastructure, whittled away by cuts and reorganisation, did indeed prove disastrous. Nowhere was this more evident than in its impact on test and trace capacity as the pandemic took hold. According to a *Guardian* investigation, Public Health England, the body with lead responsibility at that time, had only 210 people working in its contact tracing operation in the two months leading up to 12 March 2020. That was the date that large-scale testing and contact tracing was controversially – but presumably necessarily given the capacity issues – abandoned against World Health Organization advice. It was a situation that

William Hanage, a professor of infectious disease epidemiology at Harvard University described to *The Guardian* as 'shocking', saying that it 'beggars belief to see these numbers held up as adequate'.[36] It was a circus of test and trace failures that was to continue for months, ironically in the country that was once the world leader in preventative public health, including the control of communicable diseases.

Back within the NHS, managers trying to deal with the cuts of the austerity years began to ape market practices, embracing 'just in time' procurement – buying only what you need when you need it – along with the bizarrely named principle of 'running hot'. This latter is the practice of operating with only the usual number of beds or services needed – with little capacity to expand should there be an unpredicted surge in demand. Even in a business this can be a risky practice, but it is presumably justified by the overall savings it produces. You just take a hit once in a while when things don't quite work out as planned. In a health service 'not quite working out as planned' can be of greater consequence, given that it is human lives that are on the line.

In June 2020, the National Audit Office (NAO) laid bare what had been happening. Despite being advised in June 2019 by the snappily named New and Emerging Respiratory Virus Threats Advisory Group (Nervtag) to stockpile gowns and get in full-face visors instead of glasses in preparation for a future emergency, they found that this had not been acted on. Far from endorsing such forward planning, the NAO investigation reported that 'The department [of Health and Social Care] told us that the manufacture and supply of PPE has for many years been based on "just in time" procurement and manufacturing principles.' Incredibly the department also admitted to the auditors that procurement had stuck rigidly to buying only exactly what was needed at the time right up until April 2020![37]

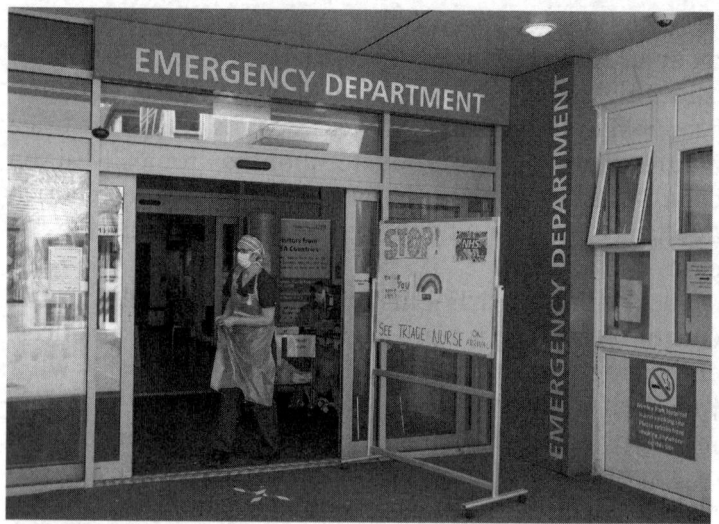

Image 9. A medical professional wearing a face mask and flimsy plastic apron at the entrance of the A&E department at Frimley Park Hospital, Surrey, 22 May 2020.
Source: STEVE PARSONS / AFP / Getty Images

As was then discovered, trying to procure extra equipment when the emergency is on you – and international supply chains are seizing up – is the stuff of nightmares. In the scramble to access supplies, an extra £10 billion had to be spent to cover a 400 per cent increase in the cost of vital PPE.[38] Yet we should have known that in a globalised world where resilience to disease transmission is compromised, there needs to be a plan for the right level of health sector resilience *before*, not after, a global crisis hits you. Imagine if the entire world had been embracing neoliberal 'just in time', 'running hot' principles – how much worse the scramble for the few supplies available might have been!

It was no better elsewhere in the system. Austerity had taken funding from the NHS by stealth. Politicians could stand up and announce that the NHS budget was ring-fenced and increasing year on year but in practice it had started to fall as a percentage of GDP after 2010 and had for years been too little to keep pace with the combined demands of higher costs and the expanding health needs of an ageing population, something successive governments had failed to address.[39] A major comparative study long before COVID-19 showed the UK ranked 24th in Europe for critical care bed capacity with just 6.6 beds for every 100,000 people. Germany, with its much higher per capita health spending, had 29.2 critical care beds per 100,000.[40] When COVID-19 arrived, normal overnight bed capacity was also at its limits, having fallen by around 32,000 in just over a decade as every possible corner was cut.[41]

This had disastrous consequences. The government already knew that the NHS would be hard-pressed to cope with a big flu outbreak, let alone a full-blown pandemic. In February 2020 shocking footage from northern Italy, where COVID-19 first took hold in Europe, began to reach TV screens. Images of overflowing hospitals, patients languishing in outdoor tents and tearful doctors recounting choices about who could access life-saving ventilators and who was of 'lower priority' would certainly have hammered home the message, if nothing else did. 'Save the NHS' was much more than a slogan. It was an imperative. It meant ramping up capacity for COVID-19 patients by something like 33,000 beds[42] (that 'slack' that we used to have) but it also meant putting lots of other day-to-day stuff – routine operations but also cancer diagnostics and treatment – on ice. This urgency to free things up for the onslaught of COVID-19 in an under-resourced service will inevitably add to the final human toll of the pandemic. It will be found in the figures for 'excess deaths' sitting alongside those from COVID-19.

But it was the beds occupied by the elderly that became key to unlocking capacity. On 19th March new guidance was issued announcing that the new default would be 'discharge home today', presumably replacing the old default of 'stick around because we don't yet have a care plan for you'. NHS England and the government suddenly now had an all too clear plan for the elderly, which was to expedite the 'safe discharge of patients from acute hospital beds'.[43] Such was their haste that they advised that negative COVID-19 tests for patients transferred into care homes were 'not required'.[44]

NHS England data show that between 17th March and 15th April, when the guidance on testing was revised, 25,060 hospital patients were moved to care homes.[45] One in three care homes – and remember these were institutions that had mostly been closed to visitors since mid-March and certainly since lockdown – suffered COVID-19 outbreaks. Around 12,000 care home residents died from COVID-19 in April 2020 alone, nearly half of all coronavirus deaths in that cruellest of months.[46] Jeremy Hunt was later to issue a statement in his capacity as Conservative Chair of the Health and Social Care Committee, in which he said, 'It seems extraordinary that no one appeared to consider the clinical risk to care homes despite widespread knowledge that the virus could be carried asymptomatically.'[47] One might add and 'despite overwhelming evidence that age is the biggest single factor in mortality from this disease'.

If there was a rationale – albeit a flawed one if it was based on saving lives – for the way in which patients were precipitously discharged from hospital without testing, what happened next is nothing short of scandalous. The Labour leader Keir Starmer had already brought his forensic questioning over care home deaths to parliament on 13th May, asking why there were 10,000 unexplained excess deaths in care homes in April on top of those officially attributed to COVID-19.[48] Starmer may not have got an answer on that occasion, but we now know from a study by the health care consultancy LaingBuisson that much of the explanation for these unaccounted-for extra deaths is likely to lie in a quite shocking withdrawal of medical care from care homes in those early frenetic weeks.[49]

William Laing, who compiled the report, writes of ambulances not turning up to care homes for emergencies because hospitals had to be kept clear for COVID-19 patients, of medical support simply being withdrawn and of care home residents in some cases being asked to consider signing DNR (Do Not Resuscitate) notices to be applied in the event of serious illness. There is substantial evidence within the professional literature that this did indeed happen and it is corroborated by testimony from Martin Green, chief executive of Care England, who said, 'I saw letters from GPs sent to care homes, saying "we will not be doing consultations, we will not be sending people to hospital".'[50] Laing goes on in his report to attribute the 'concentration of collateral damage' – his euphemism for the spike in non-COVID deaths in care homes – to this absence of normal medical attention.[51] If he is right, it is quite some indictment of our post-austerity, minimised state that we could not in the early twenty-first century protect our most vulnerable citizens from disease; or even care for them properly in the last days and weeks of their lives before affording them the most cursory funerals.

A 'Cinderella' Social Care Service

It is commonplace these days to talk about social care as the Cinderella service, but perhaps it is worth delving into this a bit more, given what has happened in our care homes. Why was the welfare of their residents so below the radar that care home deaths were not even identified in official statistics for several weeks into the pandemic? That in itself may have added to the death toll. One can imagine no one in government was going to act to remedy a problem that early warning systems weren't picking up,

Image 10. Care home visit during the coronavirus pandemic.
Source: Hugh R. Hastings / Getty Images

especially when they'd been told by the health secretary
Matt Hancock that he'd already done what was needed to
put a 'protective ring' around care homes.

Social care sits separately from the NHS, and at present
there is only patchy integration of health and social care
provision in the UK. Adult social care is a local authority
responsibility to be met from budgets that have seen severe
austerity cuts since 2010. But that is not the only way in
which social care sits apart. Up until the Thatcher years residential care homes were in the main directly run by local
authorities. Today 85 per cent of the UK's 22,000 care homes
are owned by private companies, the rest by charitable or
non-profit organisations.[52] Many are large outfits – in effect
chains running multiple facilities over which local authorities have little control. Three of the four biggest providers
of care homes in terms of revenue have parent companies
registered offshore. All four are also distinguished by their
poor inspection records for safety.[53]

Social care provision is one of the hidden scandals of the neoliberal project. Austerity brought chronic under-investment in the sector with none of the public noise about ring-fencing funding that the health sector received. No doubt privatisation to deliver greater 'efficiency' and supposedly offload 'costs' was seen as an alternative to addressing underfunding. But in practice the fragmentation of our care infrastructure into the thousands of small companies who were sending carers into people's homes, alongside the proliferation of the big privatised residential facilities, has done much to weaken regulation and the enforcement of care standards. In 2018–19, one in forty adults over the age of eighty-five was the subject of a safeguarding enquiry, meaning that there is an indication of abuse or neglect that needs investigating.[54] 'Efficiency' can come with a heavy price it seems.

The most shocking aspect of this lies in the financialisation of the sector, the sorry hallmark of the last forty years of loosened control. Ian Birrell, writing for the journal *Tortoise*, talks of a sector exploited by corporate giants who were 'using offshore tax havens hidden behind opaque corporate structures [and] the world of corporate finance' to siphon off money overseas. He exposes a world in which, as he says, 'some of the country's most vulnerable citizens have become a source of profit for billionaire owners, hedge fund operators and private equity barons'.[55] Many of these institutional purchasers buying up care homes in the good years had mortgaged the properties with the primary aim of extracting money to be used for the benefit of shareholders. The plan was that the resulting debt would be paid back from the future fees charged to care home residents. These debt payments are now estimated to swallow up 16 per cent of the fee income received by the largest private equity-owned care providers.[56] The consequences of all this financial engineering have 'left the largest operators teetering on the brink of bankruptcy for years' because in practice they can no longer afford to pay back the money they extracted at the start.[57]

It had once seemed a rosy future. An ever-expanding population of the elderly frail promised an endless income stream. Then came austerity and cuts in the fees local authorities were able to pay for places in care homes for those without private means, while new laws on minimum wages, applying to much of the care workforce, drove up costs. The business model began to fracture, being at breaking point even before COVID-19 arrived. The Conservative peer Ros Altmann described the sector as 'fragmented, financially fragile and without the capacity to cope in a crisis',[58] which was pretty much the view three years earlier when the report on Exercise Cygnus was produced. Now, as the pandemic has hit the sector, Britain's largest chain of care homes – HC-One – has noted in its accounts that the crisis may be so severe as to 'cast a doubt on its ability to continue as a going concern'.[59]

Yet the sector seems simply to have been cut adrift during the pandemic, apart, that is, from its unhappy role on the receiving end of the industrial transfer of patients out of hospital. The charge list is long. No strategic plan was produced for care home support until mid-April 2020. The supply of limited and inadequate PPE from central government stocks went mainly to health settings while care homes received little or none of what was available. Access to testing in care homes was inadequate for weeks. Hence, struggling with an underpaid and demoralised workforce – often propped up by agency workers who moved between homes and could not afford to be off sick – the conditions for the spread of infection were optimised, despite the hard work and best intentions of individual care homes and their staff. We know what this meant for deaths of care home residents, but it is less well-known that care workers, too, suffered one of the highest death rates from COVID-19, well above that of health care workers.[60] The only silver lining in all of this is that the whole miserable experiment in the privatisation of a public service – social care – will surely need radical revision. Public opinion will demand it even as mounting provider bankruptcies necessitate it.

A Dysfunctional State

Meanwhile the sloppy, ineffective governance that is a hallmark of democratic capture was on full display in the handling of the pandemic. Some of this was just a lackadaisical disinterest in or inability to grasp the minutiae of the government brief. But it was also about protecting their own – 'jobs for the boys', and of course these days the girls, too. In many ways this was simply making more visible the cosy relationships within the UK's predominantly public school educated elite, occupying as they do more than half the senior positions in the country from the cabinet to the civil service, journalism and the judiciary.[61] Many of those in this charmed circle – which is not by any means limited to one particular political party – may indeed be very talented. Kate Bingham, who led the Vaccine Taskforce, is arguably one of them. But equally one has to wonder how much talent and how many fresh perspectives we are missing from those not allowed in.

It is no surprise, then, that so many of the hastily let pandemic contracts went uncontested to close associates of ministers or MPs, indeed there were explicit processes created within government to establish a 'high-priority' lane for trusted contacts. Consultancy firms such as Boston Consultancy Group, PricewaterhouseCoopers and Deloitte, who already had close relationships to government, were another beneficiary of the largesse, although with executive day rates as high as £6,000 it was hardly concessionary 'mates' rates' on offer.[62] Value for money didn't seem to be much of a consideration in many of these contracts if we are to believe reports that a Spanish 'go-between' working for a Florida-based jewellery designer turned PPE contractor (no you couldn't make it up) was being paid £21 million of UK taxpayer's money for his role in this merry-go-round.[63]

Then there was the £347 million COVID-19 testing contract that went to Randox, sponsors of the Grand National, in October 2020, without other firms being asked to bid, and despite the warning flag raised after issues of contamination had affected their testing kits over the summer.[64] Randox is advised by the Tory MP Owen Paterson, who receives a fee of £100,000 a year for his services. Even Matt Hancock's former local publican, Alex Bourne, got in on the act, winning a £30 million contract to supply plastic vials for test kits despite having no prior experience of manufacturing highly regulated medical products.[65]

And how charming that Dido Harding, a Conservative peer, wife of a Conservative MP and chief executive of TalkTalk during its catastrophic data breach debacle, for which it received a record fine, should have been appointed without competition to lead the privatised 'NHS Test and Trace' body, responsible for nothing other than the sensitive task of gathering contact tracing data in the pandemic. With no background in public health to speak of and a senior team unable to make up that deficit, she presided over a monumental breakdown of the testing system at the most critical moment, in early September 2020, when children were returning to school.

Harding was apparently unable to predict the likely surge in demand for testing as classrooms filled up again, with the result that families with feverish children were being diverted by the system to appointments hundreds of miles away or, most likely, simply unable to get tested. That loss of control over the whereabouts of the virus at the end of the summer made a mockery of targeted

Image 11. Dido Harding outside Downing Street, 16 September 2020.
Source: NurPhoto / Getty Images

self-isolation, and was highly likely to have been instrumental in pushing the country into the necessity of much larger-scale and economically damaging blanket restrictions later on.

By late November 2020 the overall budget for NHS Test and Trace had risen to £22 billion, not far shy of a fifth of the entire annual NHS budget. Yet a National Audit Office investigation found it was still failing through the autumn in its core function, unable to meet testing targets or to identify and then reach enough of the close contacts of people who tested positive.[66] With a further £15 billion committed to it for 2021–22, and fees of up to £6,600 per day being dished out to 2,500 private consultants in March 2021 the Public Accounts Committee of cross-party MPs condemned what their chair, Meg Hillier, MP, called the 'unimaginable' cost of the programme (the NHS's current budget for staffing costs is just £56.1 billion) while finding 'no clear evidence' of its effects.[67] It had, the report noted, failed to prevent two further lockdowns, despite this being the rationale for the enormous sums of money thrown at it.

While other countries, notably Japan, were using sophisticated 'backward tracing' of contacts to identify the source of a cluster of infections – arguably a far more effective system of disease containment – the UK struggled throughout to get even basic onward contacts identified.[68] Compliance with self-isolation requests once contacts were located was in any case so low that it is arguable that the money spent on tracing people was barely worth the candle, without further thought being given to the incentives and support that people would need to isolate effectively, recognised as critical since the 1604 Plague Act.

Financial support is obviously a key issue, but the limited scheme eventually introduced six months into the pandemic to provide £500 to those self-isolating was available only to a restricted group of people and applications had a very high rejection rate.[69] So no one could begin a period of self-isolation after a positive test or contact with someone infected with any confidence that their lost income would be replaced. That probably explains why so many on low incomes just decided to carry on regardless. Research data collected during the many months of the pandemic showed that those experiencing financial hardship were significantly less likely to isolate after a positive COVID-19 test, with 'going back to work' the second most common reason for breaking self-isolation.[70]

In any case effective self-isolation is as much about people's living conditions – how easy it is to avoid the risk of spreading the virus to other household members – as it is about income. Plenty of other countries seemed to have been able to work that out. The New York 'Take Care' scheme, for instance, offered free hotel accommodation, food and even pet care for those needing support and space to self-isolate.[71] It showed an admirable display of joined-up thinking that was evidently beyond the capabilities of the UK government and its privatised contractors.

It might seem churlish to fuss about the panoply of other uncontested pandemic contracts, were it not for the fact that so many of them did real harm. A company called Edenred swerved competition to land £234 million from the Department for Education during the 2020 spring lockdown.[72] Their job was simple: to provide free school meal vouchers for children who were not attending school but would normally have a meal provided. But head teachers reported unending problems with accessing the vouchers via an online system that required hours of queuing, with codes being issued that didn't work or were rejected by supermarket systems, leading to widespread reports across the broadcast and print media of families not getting food relief for what in some cases was a matter of weeks.[73] One wonders what the accountability and penalties built into this non-competitive contract will have been?

And then there is the shabbiness of government itself, starting from the top down with a prime minister who complained at one point of the amount of 'sherpa time' that was needed to prepare for committee cross-examinations. This came during a grilling by the parliamentary Liaison Committee in which he admitted that he didn't know what 'No Recourse to Public Funds' meant when it was put to him that people with temporary immigration status were losing their homes because of it.[74]

This cavalier approach to policy detail fed U-turn after U-turn, one of the most spectacular coming from an education secretary who apparently did not understand that an exam algorithm he had already been warned was seriously flawed might downgrade pupils unfairly although, coincidently of course, private schools looked as if they might not be so badly affected.[75] Gavin Williamson himself escaped any ministerial markdown in the furore that followed. Then there was the incredible decision to tell people on a Sunday night in May who were not able to work from home that they should return to work on Monday, twelve hours later – no consultation, no thought that anybody might have to arrange childcare, and farcical levels of pre-warning to all the employers who would have to adapt their workplaces. It seemed the country was being governed by people who had never needed to think through the full implications of anything they were asked to do. Yet they were not prepared to cede any powers or responsibilities or even at times to consult with those who could.

No doubt one reason for the mistakes and botched decision making was the lack of the basic intelligence needed to inform policy. To collect information of course costs time, effort and money, which doesn't look like a good deal for a government committed to austerity and cuts. But the longer-term price paid for this 'cultivated ignorance' can be devastating.

For a start, when the pandemic hit, the government didn't have a sufficient grip on where its stock of PPE was and what condition it was in. Then, once the government realised there was an enormous backlog building up in the nation's courts as a result of the disruptions due to the pandemic and that it needed to go online with socially distanced proceedings, it discovered it didn't have data on how many trials were happening and how many defendants were in criminal court. More disturbing still, according to a report published in early 2021, the pandemic 'exposed a black hole in the UK's information on social care', something the government was already aware of, and which now meant that 'vital information that should have helped slow the spread of the virus [in care homes] was simply not available'.[76] This culture of winging it, of failing systematically to collect and analyse data and intelligence, symptomatic of the diminished state, not only has serious consequences for effective government. In a pandemic, such failings can be lethal.

Ministers and their advisers, as the Dominic Cummings lockdown escapade shows, took no responsibility for mistakes, however serious.[77] Yet in the first six months of the pandemic the head of the civil service, four other departmental chiefs and the head of the exam regulator were all removed from post, with one pursuing a claim for constructive dismissal. A scurrilous attempt was made to blame the care sector disaster on care homes themselves, alleging their misunderstanding of procedures, and Public Health England became the fall guy for the errors in health policy. It was abolished and incorporated into a new body – the National Institute for Health Protection – which took on only half its remit and was to be run by the aforementioned, ill-qualified Dido Harding.[78]

The Ministerial Code might say otherwise but ministerial accountability was nowhere to be seen in this period. Indeed, by November 2020, Boris Johnson in effect all but repudiated the validity of the Ministerial Code when he failed to sanction his home secretary, Priti Patel, for a breach of expected standards of ministerial conduct in her treatment of Home Office staff. It precipitated a further senior resignation from the official who had led the inquiry into the bullying allegations against her, one more public servant forced to fall on their sword while ministers appeared serenely unperturbed by any attacks of conscience.

Richard Horton, editor-in-chief of *The Lancet*, vividly described in the first weeks of the pandemic a political philosophy that had 'blunted the ambition and commitment of government to protect its people. The political objective was to diminish the size and role of the state. The result was to leave the country fatally weakened.'[79] He was talking in that instance about the years of austerity, but he might just as well have been summing up the whole forty-year period of the neoliberal project. The tragedy is that it did indeed leave the country fatally weakened, unfortunately literally so.

4 INEQUALITY SAPS RESILIENCE

Inequality and the Laissez-Faire State

We have seen what neoliberalism meant for our economy and public institutions in the years prior to COVID-19. What about individual lives and life experiences? Who was thriving and who not? How were opportunities for ordinary people affected and what happened to those who fell on hard times?

Reflecting what was happening in the wider economy, the world of work was soon transformed under the aegis of neoliberalism and its disinterment of the nineteenth-century 'free-market' philosophy, so that it was no longer providing the guarantee of secure work and rising incomes that people had come to expect. Thatcher's experiment with monetarism on taking office in 1979 had instead brought recession and steeply rising unemployment as the 'price' for reducing inflation, crippling labour's bargaining power in the process. A symbolic showdown with the miners after the bitter and protracted strike of 1984–85 cemented the transfer of power. Trade union rights became heavily circumscribed by new legislation, union membership plummeted and the share of output going to labour fell. By early 1984 there were well over 3 million unemployed and for nearly two decades there was a new norm of mass unemployment, which was never below 2 million in the period 1981–97.

Rising wealth and income inequality soon became the motif of the neoliberal project. Champagne corks had popped in 1979 when the top rate of tax for high earners was reduced from 83 per cent to 60 per cent and again less than ten years later when a further reduction to 40 per cent was handed out. Executive pay took off in the newly confident corporate world, with a vast gulf opening up between salaries for the 'fat cats', as they became known, and the pay of ordinary workers. In the early 1980s a chief executive of a top UK company was earning twenty times as much as the average worker. By the turn of the millennium it had risen to fifty times and by 2019 they were earning 120 times as much.[1] It stretches credibility that this could have reflected a six-fold increase in productivity.

Data from the Institute for Fiscal Studies give a very clear picture of how all of this played out.[2] As Figure 1

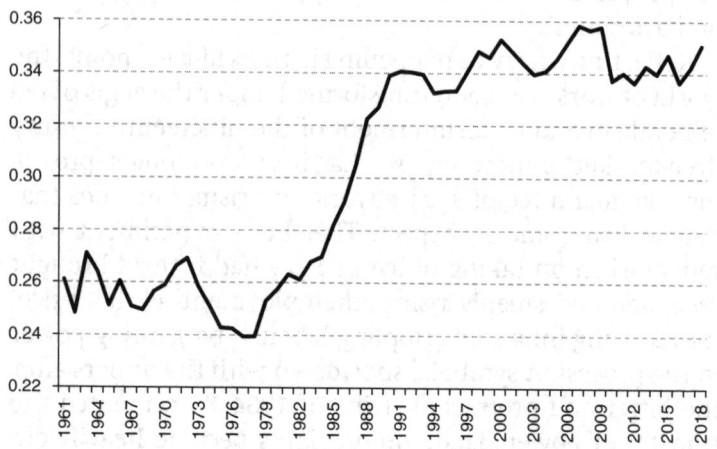

Figure 1. The Gini Coefficient of income inequality in Great Britain, 1961 to 2018–19.

Note: Incomes have been measured net of taxes and benefits but before housing costs have been deducted and have been equivalised using the modified OECD equivalence scale. Years refer to calendar years up to and including 1992 and to financial years from 1993–94 onwards. Figures relate to GB households.

Source: Bourquin, Joyce and Keiller (2020), Institute for Fiscal Studies: authors' calculations using the Family Expenditure Survey, 1961 to 1993, and the Family Resources Survey, 1994–95 to 2018–19.

shows, income inequality – as measured by the international standard known as the Gini Coefficient[3] – had been broadly stable or falling from 1961 to 1979, but then rose suddenly and rapidly from the moment Thatcher took office until more or less the day she left in 1990.[4] Despite some small variations up and down since then, it has stubbornly remained at this new higher level for the last three decades, making the UK one of the most unequal countries in Europe, although less unequal than the USA.[5]

This is a picture of income inequality *after* taxes have been deducted and benefits added on. Before these transfers, inequality is far higher and stands above that in nearly all comparable nations including the USA. So, the welfare state has a much bigger job to do in the UK than elsewhere if it is to make a real dent in inequality. As John Hills, the guru of welfare state analysis, writes, despite the welfare state's redistributive efforts, 'we still end up [after taxes and benefits] as one of the most unequal countries in the rich world because there is so much inequality [at the outset] in the income people receive from the market compared with elsewhere'.[6]

With rising income inequality, wealth inequalities grew, too. Our collective wealth pot stood at £14.6 trillion in 2018, seven times the size of our whole economy – something not seen in this country for over 100 years – and far greater than in the 1970s when it was only a multiple of three. But the gulf between the haves and have nots grew, too, so that in 2018 it was estimated that each household in the top 10 per cent ranked on wealth had £2.5 million more accumulated wealth than those in the bottom 10 per cent, be this property, pension pots, stocks and shares, works of art or just piles of cash.[7]

A view grew up (endorsed even by Labour cabinet minister Peter Mandelson in 1998) that we should be relaxed about people getting rich – that what was important was that we were freeing up the economy.[8] If entrepreneurs are incentivised to invest, innovate and generally do what they do to make the economy grow, while keeping them free from burdensome taxes and regulations that might get in the way, then everyone will be better-off. Sure, the rich will get richer but the rest will still be in a better position than they otherwise would have been.

This was the story of 'trickle down' – when those at the top are helped to prosper, for instance through lower taxes, the benefits permeate down to those below.[9] It was an idea caricatured by the great American economist John Kenneth Galbraith as 'horse-and-sparrow' economics: the less than elegant metaphor that 'if you feed the horse enough oats, some will pass through to the road for the sparrows'.[10] Today's politicians prefer the rather more uplifting metaphor that 'a rising tide will lift all boats'. Economic growth is the aim. How it is shared out and how much taken as a levy to pay for public services is not seen as a big deal because as the tide of growth rises everyone is raised up.

In practice this textbook picture was tenuous at best. The UK post-Thatcher had become a rentier economy – one where profit is gained from control of scarce resources – in which capital was being diverted as much to property and asset investment as to anything that would foster productive growth. In his book *The Corruption of Capitalism*, Guy Standing is scathing in his assessment: 'Rentier capitalism is fundamentally fraudulent. The neo-liberal rhetoric has extolled the virtues of free markets. Yet neo-liberals have constructed the most unfree market system imaginable.'[11]

Finance was booming but at the expense of resources that might have been better deployed elsewhere. Much of the time a heavily financialised economy was simply moving money around between its own institutions to little productive end, or as Ha-Joon Chang puts it in his best-selling guide to capitalism, aiding 'impatient' capital to 'slosh around the world at very short notice and in "irrational ways"'.[12]

All the while the burgeoning ranks of the super-rich would do disproportionate damage to the environment as they – a 'polluter elite' – indulged in their private jets and unsustainable spending habits.[13] Their conspicuous consumption would tempt others to emulate and live beyond their means, even if they had to borrow to do so. As Joseph Stiglitz has rightly said, 'trickle-down economics may be a chimera, but trickle-down behaviourism is real'.[14] The greater the level of inequality, the more competitively induced and environmentally damaging consumerism is encouraged, as people strive to keep up with the rest.[15]

Throughout all of this, business investment, whether in productivity enhancing technology or in better-trained workers, became increasingly conspicuous by its absence.[16] Following the financial crash of 2008, the UK economy saw a sustained and largely unexpected growth in employment that would have been good news had it not been accompanied by more than a decade of falling wage growth. Earnings after inflation had barely returned to their pre-crash level by the time that COVID-19 arrived, following the longest decline in real wages since the Napoleonic era.[17] Where exactly in all of this can we say that rising inequality had been justified by any compensating benefit? It certainly didn't seem to have helped the economy. Figure 12 (Chapter 11) shows quite how unimpressive growth had become in the decade prior to COVID-19.

Without sufficient trade union strength an informal workforce of low-paid gig economy workers – characterised by insecure contracts, often with no fixed guarantees of work, poor training and minimal rights – had grown up. A cheap alternative for employers to more risky capital investment in the aftermath of the financial crash and then the looming Brexit uncertainties, it is a development that surely helps to account for the UK's collapsing productivity growth – the much discussed 'productivity puzzle' of the last decade.

Yet there has been little attempt by a hands-off, business-friendly state to stop the abuse of zero hours contracts or the denial of sickness and holiday pay by employers who could use 'self-employment' and outsourcing as a screen to avoid taking responsibility for workers' welfare, lining their pockets in the process.[18] This has produced the ridiculous travesty of increasing in-work poverty and precarity within a casualised gig economy, and the dangerous consequences for a family if, for instance, somebody were to fall ill, as was so powerfully depicted in Ken Loach's 2019 film, *Sorry We Missed You*.

Loach was exposing the practices of a fictitious delivery company and their treatment of their drivers. His film was made not long after a tragic case in which Don Lane – a courier who had worked for the parcel company DPD for nineteen years – was fined £150 for taking time off for a medical appointment. Less than six months later, Lane, who had diabetes, and had already previously fallen into a diabetic coma while in his van, collapsed and died at the age of fifty-three while still working for DPD, telling his wife in the days prior to his death as he became increasingly sick, 'I really don't want to work, but I have to.'[19]

The presumed automatic trickle down of prosperity is perhaps looking like wishful thinking. A hands-off, laissez-faire state has certainly produced a more unequal society. But it is also one in which those at the bottom are increasingly excluded. As Carys Roberts, executive director of the Institute for Public Policy Research (IPPR) wrote in 2019:

> *Over the last 40 years, only 10 percent of national income growth went to the bottom half of the income distribution. The UK is Europe's most geographically unbalanced economy, with wide disparities in wealth and power between nations and regions, and once-thriving communities suffering economic decline.*[20]

In Britain's old industrial towns, many of which had never recovered from the 1980s recession and the poverty it brought, one in twelve working age people were by this point receiving incapacity benefits for poor health. Five of the ten local authorities with the highest rates of unemployment in the UK were coastal towns in decline, where low-paid seasonal work or sporadic gig economy jobs were often the only ones on offer.[21]

Nevertheless, there were still those who persisted in their belief that the problem lay with the poor themselves. Echoing Norman Tebbit's moralising at the Conservative Party Conference in October 1981, at a time when nearly 3 million people were unemployed, that the solution was to do as his father had done and get on your bike and look for work, the post-2010 government peddled the same old myth: that the unemployed had become detached from work, that perhaps benefits were too generous and incentives to find a job insufficient. No problem – they had a solution to hand.

'This Is Not an Easy Life Any More, Chum'

At the Conservative Party conference on 7 October 2002 Theresa May, then the party chairwoman, had stood up on stage and said, 'you know what some people call us – the "nasty party"'. After five years in opposition, it was an image, she said, that the party needed to ditch, to stop the 'glib moralising' and 'hypocritical finger-wagging'.

Perhaps Iain Duncan Smith didn't get the memo or maybe it's just that things are different when you get into power. In any event after his appointment as Secretary of State for Work and Pensions in 2010, he applied himself with gusto to the task of achieving Chancellor George Osborne's stated aim to cut billions off the welfare budget in a bid to shrink the state. None of the cuts were to fall on pensioners in case they fought back – it was the 'workshy' and the 'slackers' who were in his sights.

It was Duncan Smith's bright idea to simplify existing benefits for both the unemployed and the low-paid into a single household payment that would be known as Universal Credit. This was perfectly understandable if it was just a matter of tidying up a system that had got rather too unwieldy. But he didn't want to stick at just that. His mission was to reform the system so that it would 'make work pay'. Part of this was about making sure that people didn't have benefits such as housing or child support taken away too abruptly as they started back at work. The tapering away of support had to be gradual enough for people to see how much more they could get by working. The reforms came with a big increase in free or subsidised childcare for those taking on lower-paid jobs. But the stick wielded alongside all of this was much bigger than the carrot. Making work pay was also about making the experience of being out of work a thoroughly unpleasant one. Duncan Smith had an arsenal of measures to back up his taunt in 2012 that 'this is not an easy life any more, chum'.[22]

Anyone claiming benefits because they didn't have a job would be expected to provide exhaustive evidence to DWP officials of what they were doing to get work. It was a tightening of 'conditionality' that went hand in hand with a hardening of sanctions, mostly the threat of or actual withdrawal of benefits, which could be for something as trivial as missing an appointment because of a late-running bus. Single parents would from 2017 be required to be looking for work as soon as their youngest child turned three (it had been ten in 2009). For those on sickness and disability benefits, including those with mental health issues, conditionality was to mean work capability assessments carried out by private companies whose assessments were in far too many cases shown on appeal to be wrong.[23] Thousands of people have died after being declared fit to work in these assessments and having their benefits reduced or removed and scores of suicides have been linked to DWP's handling of benefit claims.[24] They include the very sad case of Philippa Day, a twenty-seven-year-old mother with a history of mental illness, who took her own life in August 2019 after her benefits were cut for months when she failed to return the correct form. The inquest into her death documented twenty-eight mistakes in how her claim was managed.[25]

Apart from making it harder for people to be on benefits, the other main way the welfare bill was to be cut was by paying everyone less. A good start was made by making everyone claiming Universal Credit wait six weeks before their first payment was made – a delay that was magnanimously reduced to five weeks in February 2018 after years of protest. With the DWP's new 'digital by default' application system, the delays could be even longer for those finding internet access a problem – if for instance they were too poor to own a computer or not sufficiently IT-literate. Cynically the government allowed – indeed encouraged – food banks to step in to provide support during these waiting periods, with the Trussell Trust alone giving out 1.3 million emergency food packages in 2017–18. This was exactly what those warning against the Conservatives' 'Big Society' had predicted – it was a smokescreen for reducing tax-funded state support and leaving the poor to charity.[26]

Keeping up pressure on the bottom line also meant benefits being cut or withdrawn. A 'benefit cap' was introduced to limit the total amount any one family could receive in benefits. Housing Benefit was cut for anyone deemed to have more bedrooms than they needed, whatever the reason and whether or not they were able to move (the so-called 'bedroom tax'), while the amount of help given with Council Tax payments was reduced.

Worst of all, though, was the now infamous 'two-child limit'. This draconian new rule meant that from April 2017 families would not get means-tested benefits for a third (or subsequent) child born after that date. It was a strictly British innovation quite at odds with how other European countries support families with children. Of course, as with any good bureaucracy, exceptions are allowed: for a disabled child, a second pregnancy producing a multiple birth or a 'proven' rape, provided there was no continuing contact with the perpetrator. The form to claim support for a child born as a result of non-consensual conception is easy to find on gov.uk – even helpfully titled NCC1. Perfect for all those women who have managed to get shot of their abuser, find a corroborating witness and all the while keep hold of a PC or smartphone.

Even for the happiest of families the two-child limit will restrict the help provided to any who claim Universal Credit, including during the pandemic, should they have gone over the acceptable reproduction level of two. As time has gone by, more and more families have been affected. The government's own figures show that by April 2020 almost 250,000 households were being denied benefits for a third or subsequent child. This has knock-on effects, of course, for all the children – over 900,000 in total – who are living in families with these reduced benefits.[27] This is a measure put in place by a cabinet full of male millionaires not distinguished for their own procreational continence. Duncan Smith himself has four children, no doubt blithely consuming all manner of public services short of benefits.

The icing on the cake though was the decision to stop increasing benefits at all. All working age benefits both for the unemployed and top-ups for those on low pay were frozen for four years from April 2016. That followed three preceding years in which they had been uprated by 1 per cent instead of by the full rate of inflation. Even the universally popular Child Benefit was hammered. Housing Benefit was subjected to the same treatment, pared back over time so that people would be forced to rent the very cheapest properties in their area. Frequently in damp, overcrowded accommodation or lacking access to basic amenities, they were too scared to challenge unhealthy living conditions for fear of eviction by landlords doing very nicely hoovering up benefits from the state.

It did the job. Osborne, Duncan Smith and their successors put in place a regime that succeeded in cutting in the region of £20 billion in real terms from the bill for non-pensioner social security, bringing spending on working age benefits down from 6.5 per cent to 4.4 per cent of GDP in just ten years.[28] Benefits for living costs and housing were worth 10 per cent less by 2020–21 for an average out-of-work household than they had been in 2011–12, cutting £1,600 off their income in real terms. For those with children – the ones most battered by the austerity cuts – benefits were worth 12 per cent less than in 2011–12. That's equivalent to a loss in income of £2,900 a year.[29] Indeed had Universal Credit not been increased by £20 a week when COVID-19 hit, the real-term cut in benefits would have been much higher – 15 per cent for the average out-of-work household and 16 per cent for those with children.

No surprise, then, when child poverty started to rise again. It had once again reached 31 per cent by 2019–20 – double the level it had been in the 1960s and 70s, before the policies of the Thatcher era saw it rocket upwards, as can be seen in Figure 2. But child poverty was expected to rise much further once the full effects of the two-child limit and the four-year benefit freeze had been reflected in the figures. At the time of the December 2019 General Election the Resolution Foundation – a leading think tank concerned with poverty and low pay – forecast that it could reach a record-equalling high of 34 per cent by 2023–24.[30] If that turns out to have been correct austerity would have undone all of the hard-won progress in tackling child poverty that had been made under New Labour after the ravages of the Thatcher years.

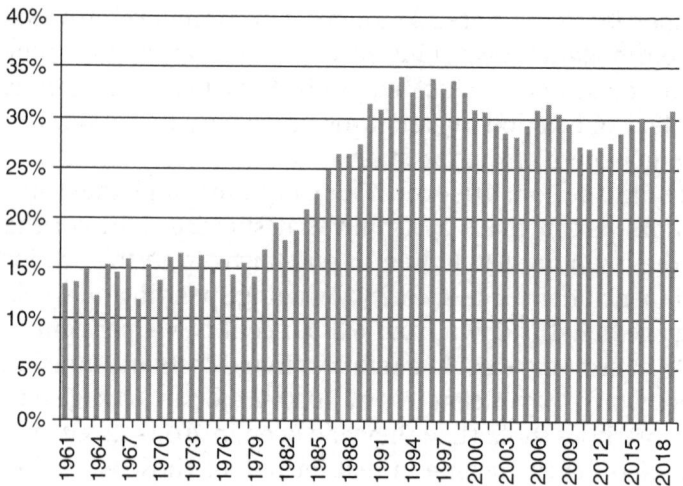

Figure 2. Percentage of children living in relative poverty (after housing costs), 1961 to 2019–20.
Note: Children living in households with less than 60 per cent of median household income after housing costs. Financial years after 1993. Great Britain only before 2002–3, UK thereafter.
Source: Institute for Fiscal Studies, www.ifs.org.uk/tools_and_resources/incomes_in_uk

Despite popular pronouncements about work being a route out of poverty, a large proportion of children living in poverty in fact have a parent in work, with poverty most acute for single parents and for families living in privately rented accommodation. It is estimated in both cases that more than half of children in these families live in relative poverty once their parents' housing costs are taken into account.[31] Meanwhile child poverty rates in Pakistani and Bangladeshi families are double the national average.[32]

The potential upward trajectory of child poverty, forecast in December 2019 by the Resolution Foundation, now critically depends on whether or not the £20 uplift to Universal Credit granted during the pandemic is maintained beyond September 2021. At least 6 million households, including those on low pay as well as those out of work, stand to lose £1,000 a year if the measure is reversed, pushing many families below the poverty line exactly as feared when the 2019 forecast was made.[33]

Compounding all of this, evidence was emerging in 2018–19 that poverty was deepening, with more families and children living on sums of money that were significantly below the official poverty level of 60 per cent of median income. A record 13 per cent of children in that year were to be found in families having to get by on less than 40 per cent of median income.[34] A study by the Joseph Rowntree Foundation published in December 2020 but relating to the year preceding COVID-19 similarly showed a 35 per cent rise in the space of two years in the number of households experiencing such extreme poverty that it amounted to destitution. The picture was even more stark for children, where the number of children experiencing destitution at some point during 2019 rose by 52 per cent, to more than half a million children. According to the Foundation's definition, these would be children in families who had extremely low or no income at all, or who were unable to afford essentials such as food, heating or clothing.[35]

The more we look at it the more it becomes clear that the political agenda in the UK in the years after 2010 was no longer just about tolerating inequality. It was about a conscious disregard for poverty, too. It was a calculated move by the government to cut many of the strings of the safety net that lay between decency and destitution, even extending to making people wait in penury to receive their benefits. According to an investigation by the Select Committee for Work and Pensions some women were resorting to 'survival sex' for money as the only way they had to feed their children during the Universal Credit waiting period.[36] Still others would fall into the hands of loan-sharks with their usurious interest rates. Many others were resorting to abortion – with data showing a sharp increase in the abortion rate after the introduction of the two-child limit and abortions rising most among those who already had two or more children.[37]

The UN special rapporteur on extreme poverty and human rights, Philip Alston, concluded in 2019 after his investigation into conditions in the UK,

> The bottom line is that much of the glue that has held British society together since the Second World War has been deliberately removed and replaced with a harsh and uncaring ethos … [that has] … continually put people further into poverty.[38]

On the specifics of the benefit reforms, he described the regime created to make work pay as akin to

> a digital … version of the 19th Century workhouse.

Image 12. A woman walks past a homeless tent in Bradford City Centre, 12 February 2021.
Source: Nathan Stirk / Getty Images

Are We Bothered?

There will always be those who say that, while of course we want to do something about poverty, we shouldn't worry unduly about inequality. We can't all be the same and those who work hard and use their talents for the good of us all deserve to be rewarded. People need something to motivate them, something to aim for, a driving aspiration for betterment, evocatively captured in the fantasy of the 'American Dream'.

In Western liberal democracies this is associated with the idea of 'meritocracy' and the potential for upward social mobility – getting to a better place than where you started – which it appears to promise. It's supposedly the prize that's there to encourage us all to strive. The problems come, though, when meritocracy is exposed as an illusion, when it starts to become clear that the competition, not just to get to the top, but to get ahead at all, was fixed from the start.[39]

This is how it works. The children of better-off parents go to better-resourced schools, have more money spent on them, have none of the stresses of cold, overcrowded homes and poor nourishment and so are more likely to thrive and succeed. This helping hand up the ladder is magnified among the wealth elites, for whom there is a long history of privileged access to the top through elite schooling and networking. It currently costs an average of £17,000 a year for each child educated in private schools (£40,000 at Eton). In return, by the time they have left, each pupil taught in these fee-paying schools has had the benefit of exactly three times as much funding and twice as many teachers as the remaining 93 per cent of the population in state schools.[40] All of this is subsidised by the taxpayer through the public schools' charitable status. As the historic commentary to a new wide-ranging study of inequality in the UK argues, 'the powerful role of these separatist institutions in perpetuating their privileges ... should be considered as one of the strongest and most pervasive influences on the reproduction of inequality'.[41]

What's more, in a very unequal society all parents, not just the rich, are aware of the high penalties of falling down the pecking order – the downward mobility that will happen if someone else's children succeed instead of theirs. In more equal societies, where the divergence in children's future life outcomes is less extreme, parents can be more relaxed. But in the UK parents know what is at stake. They have every incentive to move to the right areas for the best schools, pay for private education or extra tuition if they can afford to and organise internships, often unpaid, through their networks.[42] It's called 'opportunity hoarding', putting a glass floor underneath their offspring that they can't fall through. It's why social mobility has become a distant memory in the UK, why you are 80 per cent more likely to get a top job if your parents come from a professional background.[43] Fair access to opportunity is far harder to achieve when inequality makes the price of failure too high.

It's also far harder to achieve when investment in public services – health care, education, housing and early years support – is being cut back. These services are the real levellers in our society because they help those without other means to have a shot at overcoming the odds stacked against them. Modern welfare states were designed to do this by 'de-commodifying' these services – in other words taking them out of the market so that they are funded by taxation. That then means that it is citizenship, not class or ability to pay, that gives people access to them.

In economic terms, public services are sometimes described as a virtual income or even as a 'social wage', a benefit given out on top of other income. They help prevent inequality arising in the first place through the *pre*-distribution of resources, instead of being faced with the need for redistribution later. Everyone gains but the least well-off, of course, proportionately gain the most. Although it is not captured in measures of income and wealth inequality, government figures show that the universal benefits in kind of the NHS and of education were in 2017 worth 60.9 per cent extra on top of the disposable income of the poorest one-fifth of the population, but only 8 per cent to the richest one-fifth.[44] And there's the problem.

Generous public services provision is anathema to the small-staters. Any government cutting taxes and with big ideas about balancing the books will need to cut the amount spent on public services to compensate for the lower tax revenue. Actually, whether they need to or not, the neoliberal philosophy is to pare the state back. And – with a marked interruption during the New Labour years – that is precisely what has been done for the last forty years. It has consequences.

Let's take education. During the post-war years investment in education was expanded massively, more or less doubling as a proportion of GDP from 2.9 per cent in 1955–56 to peak at 5.6 per cent in 1975–76, with free secondary school education mandated up until the age of sixteen by the end of the period. But then came two decades of retreat in which the percentage of GDP devoted to education was cut back drastically, as can be seen in Figure 3.

By the time New Labour came to office it had fallen by well over a quarter and was back down to 4 per cent of GDP, the same as the early 1960s. Teachers in state schools had been cut by 50,000 – one in ten of the workforce – with the result that by the late 1990s every private school had twice as many teachers per pupil as state schools.[45]

While New Labour reversed the cuts, investing at all levels from the crucial early years, through schools, further education and higher education, this was not sustained after 2010. Austerity slashed education spending again right back down to where the Conservatives had last left

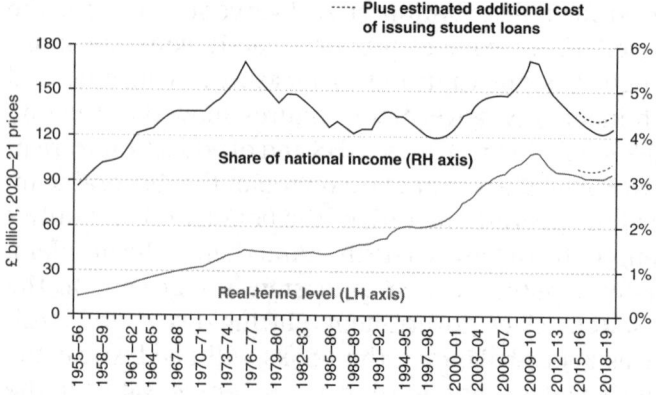

Figure 3. Trends in UK education spending, 1955–56 to 2019–20.
Source: Britton et al. (2020), Institute for Fiscal Studies

off, this time bringing unprecedented cuts in real-terms expenditure, too. That this happened at a time when far more young people were staying on in education to the age of eighteen and when nearly half of each year cohort progressed on to university is quite some feat. As an advanced, knowledge-based economy our education needs were soaring but we were squeezing the last drops out of the hapless institutions trying to meet them.

The cuts fell particularly harshly on sixteen- to eighteen-year-olds in FE colleges and state school sixth forms where, adjusting for inflation, spending per student fell by 12 per cent and 23 per cent respectively between 2009–10 and 2019–20.[46] Students from less well-off backgrounds also lost the Educational Maintenance Allowance introduced by New Labour that had helped support them through post-sixteen education. Less extreme but still significant is the 9 per cent fall in real-terms spending per student in primary and secondary schools over those ten years, which left spending per pupil in England at a level of £6,100 (far behind the £7,300 spent per pupil in Scotland).[47] Cuts on this scale will inevitably come home to roost in poorer economic performance and increased inequality in the future.

Overall public spending per person has been falling year on year since 2010 after allowing for inflation, meaning that the welfare state is retreating ever further from its social investment function.[48] Sure Start Children's Centres, which had been established right across the country under New Labour as part of their 'early intervention' programme, were one of the first casualties of austerity. Yet we know that their baby clinics and tailored health advice would have helped improve the health and well-being of poorer children.[49] We know, too, that the structured support they provided was designed to help narrow the gaps with their better-off peers as they prepared to start school. Parents, too, were given help with claiming benefits and accessing opportunities to return to work if they were ready, or support with parenting and money management if they needed it. It was all part of New Labour's Every Child Matters agenda designed to boost the life chances of those who started off with the least in life. The knock-on effects of cutting services like this will feed through into reduced social mobility and make social justice and the much trumpeted 'levelling up' look like rather empty catchphrases dreamed up by an advertising company, which is probably what they were. As has been said by others, 'a rising tide can't lift all boats if some can't even get launched'.[50]

While austerity took money away from nearly every government department, local authorities were particularly hard hit, sustaining crushing losses from cuts to local government grants, with some ending up close to insolvency. Spending on care services, including for the frail or disabled, was severely affected, to the detriment not just of those whose care needs could not be met, but also the hard-pressed families who had to take up the slack. The pressures, though, have fallen unevenly. In the most deprived areas adult social care spending per person fell by 16 per cent but in the least deprived areas it fell by only 3 per cent as can be seen in Figure 4.[51]

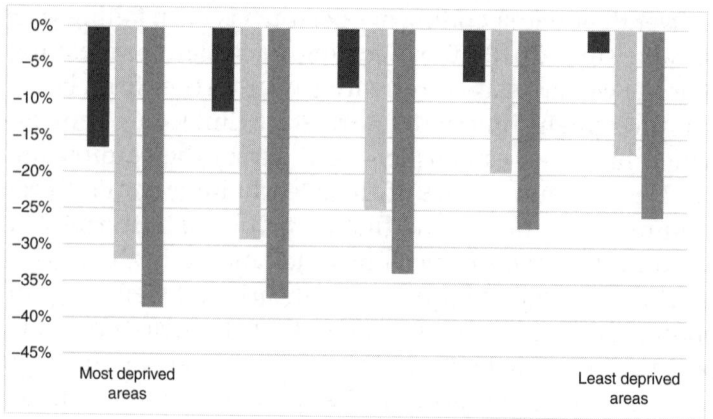

Adult Social Care spending per person
Total Local Authority service spending per person
Other service spending per person

Figure 4. Average percentage change in council service spending per person by local area deprivation, 2009–10 to 2017–18.
Source: Phillips and Simpson (2018), Institute for Fiscal Studies

Local authority spending on services other than adult social care has been cut even more severely. Again, the most deprived areas fared worse, with spending falling by 38 per cent per person over the years of austerity. Even in the least deprived areas it fell by more than a quarter.

This somehow seems the wrong way round. Local services that had been working well in reducing inequalities – delivering early years and youth provision as well as core public health interventions targeting obesity and smoking and providing mental health and addiction services – were all hit by Osborne's swingeing austerity. It was a short-sighted move that was storing up trouble for the future as social problems and health inequalities were left to magnify. Almost inevitably the longer-term costs will outweigh any short-term gain.

With so much of social provision cut across so many areas of people's lives inequality by 2020 was about far more than just gaps in income and wealth. It was seeping ever deeper into life chances and life outcomes. For thirty years between 1980 and 2010 life expectancy at birth in the UK had been rising steadily, as indeed it had for the whole of the twentieth century. Every five years females would on average gain another year of life expectancy and males were notching up an extra year every four years. But the pace of improvement decelerated abruptly in the years after 2011. It was a reversal that left us lagging behind nearly all other high-income countries, with the notable exception of the USA.

There was a penalty to being born poor, too. Boys born between 2017 and 2019 could expect to live more than ten years longer if they were born in Westminster than if they were born in Blackpool, and girls could expect to live nearly eight years more. Then, with this life expectancy gap based on poverty already starting to widen, new data emerged that showed that life expectancy at birth had actually started to go backwards for girls who were unfortunate enough to live in the most deprived 10 per cent of communities.

As the eminent public health expert Michael Marmot wrote in February 2020 summing up these findings in his review of health equity, ten years on from the first 'Marmot' report,

> health is closely linked to the conditions in which people are born, grow, live, work and age and [to] inequities in power, money and resources – [these are] the social determinants of health … . Austerity will cast a long shadow over the lives of children born and growing up under its effects.[52]

It's the Economy, Stupid

In 2019 the Nobel Prize winning economist Angus Deaton was asked by the UK Institute for Fiscal Studies to lead a review of inequality and how it should be understood in the twenty-first century. The first cut of the evidence, published by the IFS that year, concluded that '[i]nequality cannot be reduced to any one dimension: it is the culmination of myriad forms of privilege and disadvantage, many of which re-inforce each other'.[53]

This matters on one level because it makes us feel uneasy about the injustices done to those disadvantaged unfairly. But it turns out that inequality is bad for the economy, too, not least because the better-off save a higher proportion of their income than those on lower incomes. In a more unequal society there is just less money being spent and therefore less economic demand to drive growth.

Researchers at the International Monetary Fund have looked in detail at some of the wider economic effects of inequality, finding that reducing inequality in fact benefits growth.[54] Their analysis of cross-country data on growth, inequality and redistribution over a five-year period showed that 'lower ... inequality is robustly correlated with faster and more durable growth' and that efforts to remedy inequality through redistribution (by taxing the better-off) did not harm growth except in extreme cases. This, they say, confirms their earlier findings showing a 'multi-decade cross-country relationship between inequality and the fragility of economic growth'. The explanation they offer is that inequality can 'undermine progress in health and education, cause investment-reducing ... instability, and undercut the social consensus required to adjust [to] shocks, and thus ... tend[s] to reduce the pace and durability of growth'. The economist Piketty has also suggested that inequality can create a reactive nationalism that is further damaging to the social fabric.[55]

Discussing these findings at the time in the *Financial Times*, the leading economic commentator Martin Wolf noted that, in Europe, the highly redistributive Scandinavian economies have outperformed their less redistributive peers and that the far more equal East Asian countries, especially Japan and South Korea, vastly outperformed the far less equal countries of Latin America after the Second World War. Lower inequality, Wolf argues, increases 'the ability of the entire population to participate, on more equal terms', although only so long as 'politics is not unduly beholden to wealth'.[56]

By contrast, work by social epidemiologists Richard Wilkinson and Kate Pickett has shown that deprivation and the acute awareness of lower social status that comes from living in a highly unequal society has the opposite effect. The stigma of low status and poor social relationships, including the experience of racism and other forms of prejudice, affects both physical and mental health and may promote addictive behaviour, reduce educational performance, damage social cohesion and be linked to increases in violence (including self-harm) and imprisonment.[57] These problems of prejudice and status are heightened by larger income differences, and all of their consequences make our society and economy poorer.[58]

Other research shows that where inequality is associated with high levels of poverty it can lead to children growing up in chaotic and insecure environments due to the pressures their parents are under. Many parents under stress behave – often without knowing it – in ways that are harmful for their child's development, producing disoriented child–parent attachments that can have deeply damaging intergenerational consequences.[59] Children with disorganised attachment are likely to be less able to learn effectively or behave 'normally' in schools, degrading their own future capacities to acquire skills, to remain healthy and socially connected and to integrate into their society, all part of the cycle of transmitted deprivation and social exclusion.[60]

If social instability and a loss of consensus is, as the IMF research suggests, one of the consequences of high and persistent inequality, this should be ringing alarm bells in the

UK in the aftermath not just of a divisive Brexit vote that triggered two subsequent general elections in the space of three years, but now the worst health and economic shock for generations. Low trust and poor social cohesion arguably make it much harder for the government to take the population with it when it calls for continuing and potentially long-term sacrifices to manage and then recover from COVID-19. Securing the comprehensive vaccination take-up that the government is banking on is also a bigger challenge where low levels of trust and widespread disengagement have become engrained.

The 'Burning Injustices'

The stepping down of the Cameron–Osborne political partnership after the unexpected 'Leave' vote in the 2016 Brexit referendum marked somewhat of a watershed in attitudes – at least publicly – as politicians began to digest its implications. The new prime minister, Theresa May, promised that there would be action to tackle what she termed the 'burning injustices' afflicting those now called the 'left behind'. She cited lack of access to university for white working-class boys, privileged access to the professions by those from private schools, the life expectancy gap, the gender pay gap, the exclusion of the young from home ownership, insufficient mental health support and the harsher treatment of people of colour, especially by the criminal justice system.

It was a reasonable diagnosis of the problems of contemporary Britain. But these were long-term problems stemming in no small measure from the policies her party had so vigorously espoused. Turning that juggernaut around would be no easy matter. There was no mention of the poverty experienced by those 'left behind' due to the continuing cuts in benefits, or to the rise in 'deaths from despair' – from suicide, drug and alcohol overdose – that had started to push up mortality rates in the middle-aged since 2010,[61] nor of its possible link to any of her burning injustices.

After a while talk of burning injustices gave way to the more sanitised political lexicon of 'levelling up'. It was an idea taken up with enthusiasm in 2019 by Boris Johnson's administration after the Conservatives had broken through the 'Red Wall' of traditional Labour support in the Midlands and the North in that year's election. Hence levelling up the regions, tackling the inequalities and infrastructure deficiencies of left behind places, as much as helping left behind people, was a key motif of his early months in government.

It was an ambitious task. The UK's Industrial Strategy Council, chaired by the Bank of England's chief economist Andy Haldane, published a report in early 2020 that showed the scale of the challenge. Their research showed the UK to be one of the most regionally unequal countries in Europe, its productivity gap worse than every other country apart from Romania and Poland. Furthermore, according to the report, regional disparities in the UK had risen to their highest level in more than a century – regional differences in average worker income were about as large in 2019 as they were in 1901.[62]

Conditions in some of the left behind places were miserable indeed, with many recording shocking increases in child poverty during the years of austerity as static incomes combined with rising housing costs to push households to the brink. In Middlesbrough 41 per cent of children were estimated to be living in relative poverty in 2018, an increase of 12.5 percentage points in four years. Birmingham, Manchester and Oldham also had child poverty rates over 40 per cent by 2018, and Newcastle was not far behind, having also seen one of the fastest rises – more than ten percentage points in four years.[63]

In the event the levelling up measures announced in Johnson's March 2020 budget were simply swept away by events. The UK met the pandemic head on with both its public services and many of its citizens lacking the resilience to cope with its impact. As the lockdown began and deaths began to soar, the broadcaster Emily Maitlis was quick to debunk the idea that at least in this regard everyone was on an equal footing. Her plain speaking on live television – 'They tell us coronavirus is a great leveller. It's not. It's much, much harder if you're poor' – went viral.[64] Let's take a closer look at why this would be the case.

For a start the many years of stagnating real wages that followed the financial crisis had left many people in a very precarious position and unable to save for the proverbial rainy day. Indeed, many had run up debts that were taking a chunk out of their income each month.[65] Not surprising, then, that one in eight people surveyed for the Financial Conduct Authority's 'Financial Lives' study in 2017 had no savings at all, a figure that rose to one in six of those living in the North East and North West.[66] Around a third of low-income households also said in the lead-up to COVID-19 that they would not be able to manage to get by even for a month if they lost their main source of household income.[67] Of course, these were the very households – often in casualised jobs in retail and hospitality – most vulnerable to loss of income or redundancy.

The fragility of their position became clear very quickly as reports of families going without food and an unprecedented call on food banks for emergency supplies emerged within days of lockdown. A YouGov poll carried out for the Food Foundation three weeks into the first lockdown estimated that around 1.5 million people had not eaten for a whole day because they had no money or access to food. According to the survey estimates, more than a million people reported losing all their income because of the pandemic, with over a third thinking they would not be entitled to government help.[68] Communities, schools, families and neighbours stepped in to provide emergency food, and food bank charities worked round the clock to meet need. But this was not just a short-term response. By September 2020, the Trussell Trust, the leading food bank charity, said that it expected demand to surge in the winter as unemployment rose, with families with children hardest hit. At that point they were anticipating giving out six parcels every minute between October and December – not far short of a million in total – unless something changed.[69]

Poverty hits in other ways, too. Susceptibility to COVID-19, including the risk of dying, is known to be associated with a range of underlying health conditions. These include diabetes, coronary heart disease, high blood pressure, chronic bronchitis, asthma, cancer or malignancy and obesity. Although this is true the world over, more unequal countries, such as the UK and the USA, are particularly vulnerable to the impact of these comorbidities, given their link to ethnicity, low income and deprivation and constrained living conditions.

The poorest third of the UK population has a 50 per cent higher chance of having an illness that puts them at medical risk than those in the top 20 per cent.[70] Such high levels of underlying poor health in the UK, arising from our higher levels of inequality, undoubtedly reduced our resilience in the face of COVID-19. It was made worse by the fact that many of those most affected, including people of colour, were either key workers or in jobs most exposed to infection, as Michael Marmot's COVID-19 review in December 2020 – Build Back Fairer – so clearly shows.[71] It was a double jeopardy for them.

Moreover, front-line workers, vulnerable themselves but also liable to transmit infections to others, could be severely financially compromised if they became ill or were expected to self-isolate after a positive test or contact with an infected person. Some might qualify for statutory sick pay if they took time off, but this now stood at

£95.85 a week. No one could possibly argue that this was enough to cover reasonable living costs – for many people it would not even cover their rent. In any case, in this largely non-unionised world, many had no access at all to sick pay either because they were in casualised work in the gig economy or because their pay was too low to meet the threshold to qualify. Inevitably this led to many people being scared to even get tested, 'because they knew they could not afford to isolate'.[72]

For those who could claim statutory cover for sickness, or who were covered by a more extensive workplace scheme, it was employers – with some relief for smaller businesses – who had to pay out from already shrinking incomes.[73] Unfortunately, with employers under the cosh and many workers facing sub-subsistence levels of sickness pay, both sides – unless literally bed-bound – have a very big incentive to just insist that they can carry on working, whether ill or not. Equally, as the Test and Trace app began to function and 'ping' to alert people to self-isolate as a result of a detected contact with someone testing positive, reports emerged of people simply switching off the app, often at the behest of employers.[74] That's not a great idea in a pandemic.

Nor are overcrowded and poor housing conditions. We know from the historic study of cholera, typhoid and TB transmission that poor-quality, cramped housing and overcrowded neighbourhoods are vectors for the rapid spread of disease and present a particular nightmare for epidemic control. Yet this seems to have eluded a distant Whitehall machine pumping out directives on self-isolation without considering how this could be done safely. If you are in a house not suited to living separately, maybe including older or medically vulnerable people, then you are just going to magnify disease risk if you lock yourself in with them when you are sick or think you might be. It's surely blindingly obvious, as professor of global public health

Devi Sridhar wrote, when the second wave of COVID-19 took off, that 'given that we know the virus spreads easily through households, those who test positive should have the offer to isolate in external facilities such as hotels'.[75]

We did this when people were first airlifted out of Wuhan to the UK, placing them in emergency hostels for a full two weeks, and other countries have kept these sorts of arrangements in place permanently. A policy to enact this would be exactly comparable to the practice legislated for over 120 years ago in the UK through the Notification of Diseases Act, to empower local authorities to fund the removal of sick patients from crowded households to isolation hospitals.[76] A properly mobilised local support network to oversee testing, tracing and isolation throughout the pandemic could have identified vulnerable households to ensure they could be protected in exactly this way when someone tested positive. A distant call centre operator quite clearly could not. No wonder there were reports emerging over the summer of 2020 that COVID-19 had become endemic in many deprived urban communities where there were large intergenerational households with significant social mixing between families and concentrations of workers in high social contact jobs.[77]

5 THE PANDEMIC ONSLAUGHT

There are individual tragedies in every single one of the more than a hundred thousand deaths in the UK from COVID-19 itself and the as yet unknown number of deaths from all the knock-on effects of the pandemic in reducing access to normal medical treatment and diagnosis. Mary Agyeiwaa Agyapong, a nurse who worked at the Luton and Dunstable University Hospital, was thirty-five weeks pregnant when she tested positive for COVID-19 in April 2020, two weeks after her father had died from the disease. On admission to hospital her baby daughter was delivered safely by emergency C-Section, but Mary herself died shortly afterwards. Tens of thousands more such stories of suffering would follow in future waves of the pandemic, leaving families devastated as the death toll continued to rise.

But alongside these individual tragedies there is also a collective tragedy in our peculiar vulnerability to such high levels of fatality. This was not inevitable. It came on the back of decades of rising inequality and poverty, the result of the policies favoured by neoliberal ideology.

Those Who Lived and Those Who Died

Figure 5 shows with great clarity just how much higher COVID-19 death rates were in areas of high deprivation – more than twice as high as in the least deprived areas. Deaths from any cause creep up across the spectrum of deprivation as Figure 5 also shows, but it is a steady gradient, not the stark jump that was seen with COVID-19 deaths.

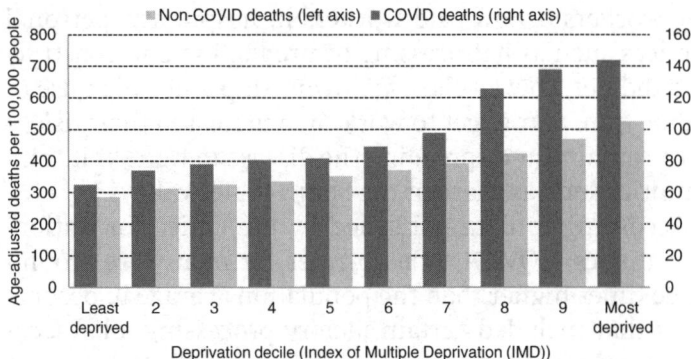

Figure 5. Deaths by local area deprivation, 1 March to 31 July 2020.
Note: Age-adjusted deaths per 100,000 people using different scales on left axis (non-Covid) and right axis (Covid).
Source: Johnson, Joyce and Platt (2021), Institute for Fiscal Studies

No surprise, then, when Public Health England's report *Disparities in the Risks and Outcomes from COVID-19* concluded with some understatement, that 'the impact of COVID-19 has replicated existing health inequalities and, in some cases, has increased them'.[1]

This deadly outcome for deprived communities in essence boils down, firstly, to a greater likelihood of contracting COVID-19 and then, secondly, to a greater vulnerability to its effects, once contracted. People in lower-paid jobs are much less likely to be able to work from home and more likely to use public transport to get to work, both of which expose them to greater risk. Rhondda Cynon Taf in Wales, an extremely deprived former industrial area, suffered the UK's highest COVID-19 death rate in the first ten months of the pandemic. Neighbouring Merthyr Tydfil had the second highest. More than three in five people in Rhondda work in jobs that cannot be done from home. So, while professional and executive occupations had the added protection of homeworking during the pandemic, key workers or low-paid workers in hospitality, personal services such as hairdressing or production and construction did not. Low levels of car ownership and a high use of public transport to get to work then increased their risk of both catching and spreading the disease in tight-knit communities such as those of the South Wales valleys.[2]

According to data published by the Office for National Statistics, COVID-19 death rates for men were around three times higher than the population average in occupations that included certain factory processing jobs, security guards, care workers, taxi drivers, chefs and nursing auxiliaries. Although death rates for women were lower overall, key worker occupations such as care workers, social workers and nurses as well as public facing officials, retail workers and some factory processing roles had much higher than average death rates.[3] This elevated chance of dying was significantly above what would occur in these occupations in normal years.[4]

A greater chance of being exposed to COVID-19 in certain occupations is further compounded by a greater vulnerability to serious illness for those with underlying health conditions – such as cardio-vascular disease, obesity and diabetes – that interact with the virus. This affects not just those contracting the disease, but also family members who may share these same vulnerabilities. It is particularly problematic in large or multi-generational households or highly connected communities where disease transmission is likely to be high and older people may be at risk. These co-morbidities are precisely the diseases that the 2020 Marmot report had shown were much more prevalent among people from disadvantaged backgrounds and those living in deprived areas, as well as among people of colour, contributing to their higher death rates.[5]

Disproportionate deaths among people of colour were one of the early alarm bells of the pandemic and will continue, along with care home deaths, to be the subject of future scrutiny. Men of black African background had a death rate 2.7 times that of men of white ethnic background; women of black Caribbean background had a death rate 2.0 times that of women of white ethnic background and all non-white ethnic groups other than Chinese had a higher death rate than the white ethnic population for both males and females.[6]

A report by Independent SAGE on disparities in the impact of COVID-19 considered the many factors driving the higher death rate among people of colour, concluding that 'structural racism is particularly likely to impact [their] infection and mortality rates through systematic social and economic inequalities that drive health status'. There is plenty of evidence that documents the lower incomes and higher poverty levels experienced by people of colour in the UK,[7] and the risk that this will now be exacerbated by their greater exposure to job losses in the pandemic.[8] Independent SAGE's argument is that it is underlying structural discrimination that sets the stage for the jobs people get, the living conditions they experience and the many other ways in which they are exposed to higher levels of infection.[9]

However, they do not stop there. They go on to discuss the ways in which direct racism may also have had an impact on outcomes from COVID-19, arguing that 'racism renders people precarious and those in precarious positions are less able to challenge conditions (particularly at work) which place them at risk'. Certainly, people of colour within the NHS were, as they report, experiencing far higher COVID-19 deaths rates than those from a white background at all levels from nursing and support staff right through to doctors and dentists.[10]

Clearly there will be many compounding factors in this, but it is alarming to note that Independent SAGE reports survey evidence from the Royal College of Nursing that nurses from a non-white ethnic group were much less likely than white nurses to say they had received eye and face protection equipment and more likely to say that they had been asked to reuse single-use equipment. Independent SAGE places this in the context of Public Health England's own view that racism and stigma may well have made people of colour working in the NHS more vulnerable to succumbing to COVID-19.[11]

It is an uncomfortable indictment of the inequalities and prejudices engrained in our society, all too apparent in the scandalous treatment of the Windrush generation over the preceding years and the 'hostile environment' imposed by Theresa May's Home Office on those who had been invited to the UK to rebuild our post-war society, including the NHS itself.[12]

Perhaps no surprise then that by the summer of 2020, as the publicity surrounding the mounting toll of deaths of black Americans at the hands of the police in the USA

Image 13. NHS nurses protest outside the entrance to Downing Street, 3 June 2020.
Source: Wiktor Szymanowicz / Barcroft Media / Getty Images

was compounded by the realisation of COVID-19's impact on people of colour, that Black Lives Matter caught fire as a protest movement around Britain and professional footballers, too, began to 'take the knee'. These twin tragedies became caught up in the urgent issue of structural racism in the UK as in the USA. The most spectacular expression of this rising emotion was seen in Bristol on 7th June when the statue of Edward Colston, a prominent eighteenth-century philanthropist heavily involved in the slave trade, was dramatically torn down by protestors and thrown into the harbour.[13] In the febrile atmosphere of the pandemic, race and racism were moving firmly centre stage.

The Tattered Safety Net

We have seen that we approached the pandemic with benefit levels that had been slowly and steadily cut back over many years. The Resolution Foundation has calculated that the basic benefit that could be claimed under Universal Credit by someone made unemployed was at its lowest real-terms level for nearly thirty years when the pandemic struck. As a proportion of average earnings it was at an all-time low, well below the level set when unemployment benefit was first introduced in 1948.[14]

This is what it meant in hard cash. On 19 March 2020 a single adult over twenty-five claiming basic Universal Credit could expect to get £73.10 a week, rising to £74.70 in April, thanks to the first increase for four years. This was at a time when someone with earnings in the middle of the pay distribution was getting £586 a week if working full-time and a low-paid worker on the national minimum (living) wage and working a 38-hour week would be paid £312.[15]

Miraculously, on 20th March, as lockdown day approached, the chancellor decided that this was all far too stingy and announced that Universal Credit would be increased by £20 a week. Next it was decided that restrictions on Housing Benefit would be relaxed – with ministers evidently now thinking it would be good if people could at least afford to pay rent on the cheapest 30 per cent of properties in their area, which until then had been deemed too generous. All those years of carefully crafted benefit cuts were simply being thrown to the wind.

Why? Let's not beat about the bush. The government was embarrassed because it was about to be caught out. Ordinary people, potentially millions of them, indeed potentially millions who had voted them into power, were going to find out what the crusade against the 'something for nothing' society really meant for those caught on the sharp end of misfortune or disadvantage. Ministers knew only too well the political risks they faced from the inevitable economic fallout of the shutdown they were now reluctantly imposing.

The welfare safety net in the UK provides for a flat-rate payment to the unemployed, meaning that no account is taken of previous earnings when people lose their jobs. This hasn't always been the case. Between 1966 and 1982 there was an earnings-related supplement to unemployment benefit so that people had a cushion that was closer to their previous income while they tried to get back on their feet. These days, Universal Credit, with its very low flat-rate payment, is topped up with extra allowances for anyone with dependents to support, subject to meeting the qualifying means-test and, of course, the two-child limit. Similar conditions are put on entitlement to Housing Benefit, both the means-test and also stipulations about the maximum rent and the number of bedrooms allowed.

Many of our European neighbours, by contrast, have systems of unemployment insurance that *do* directly link to previous earnings. Germany pays 60 per cent, Switzerland 70 per cent and Denmark 90 per cent of previous earnings up to a capped threshold, and these rates increase for those with children to 67 per cent in Germany and 80 per cent in Switzerland.[16] For the first time in decades, the UK furlough scheme introduced at the start of lockdown mimicked this continental approach – paying people 80 per cent of their earnings (up to £2,500 a month) if they were unable to work due to lockdown. The government's immediate concern was to protect viable businesses but it was also protecting workers from meeting a sudden cliff-edge of financial loss in a situation it was hoped would be temporary. In the worst eventuality, for those whose jobs did not survive, it had bought them time to prepare for what was to come when they encountered the downward plunge into what is our actual safety net.

As the economy went into lockdown in the spring of 2020, around 9 million employees were furloughed, with the government picking up 80 per cent of the wage bill. The Resolution Foundation has looked at each of the different forms of government support provided during the long months of lockdown to see what they actually meant for a typical worker on median pay. On the furlough scheme, they calculated that this hypothetical individual would have lost just 10 per cent of their income, after adjusting for tax. The hit to take-home pay would have been rather more – 15 per cent – on the Job Support Scheme that it was planned would replace furlough.

But if this same individual moved out of work and on to Universal Credit they had a much bigger shock in store. Even after payments to support their families were added in they would be on course to lose more than 40 per cent of their previous disposable income.[17] In a sense they were lucky. Had Universal Credit not been increased by £20 a week at the time of lockdown, they would have lost even more. Nevertheless, this was now a sword of Damocles hanging over everyone because the chancellor had failed to guarantee that the March 2020 benefit increase – pencilled in for twelve months – would be anything other than temporary.

On any analysis, then, what we had in 2020 was a safety net that for the vast majority of people would not come anywhere near to meeting their previous commitments if they were to find themselves unexpectedly without work. Most people in this position have limited scope to cut back spending since their income is largely spent on essential purchases and bills – only those on higher incomes are likely to have the leeway to forgo luxuries quickly if they need to. The chancellor appeared to be explicitly recognising this when he announced the furlough extension up to December 2020, in order, he said, to support people 'to continue to provide for their families'.[18] That sounds very much like an admission that the alternative of claiming benefits could not guarantee to do that – that our welfare system was indeed woefully inadequate as an insurance against hard times.

By the winter of 2020 hundreds of thousands of workers in the hospitality, retail, recreation and other vulnerable sectors found themselves made redundant and peremptorily ejected into the safety net, as businesses finally threw in the towel or cut everything back to the bone to survive. Redundancy rates during the first eight months of the pandemic rose faster than in the equivalent period after the financial crash and by December 2020 the number of employees on payroll had fallen by 819,000 since February.[19]

Meanwhile, 4.5 million new claims for Universal Credit were made between 13 March 2020 and 14 January 2021, including 1.1 million claims made in the initial two weeks after 13 March. Universal Credit is paid to help with living costs for those who are either working but on low income or out of work. What this reveals is that while the official unemployment figures did not rise by as much as might have been expected during the pandemic, the numbers claiming benefits skyrocketed. Not all would have had pressing family commitments. Many of those claiming Universal Credit may well have been young people living with their parents or other family members – just part of the COVID generation of young unemployed. Nevertheless, the fact remains that by early January 2021 there were 6 million people receiving Universal Credit – one in seven of the working age population who were either unemployed or on such low incomes that they could not adequately support their families without benefits.[20]

Although claims for Universal Credit were in the main dealt with promptly despite the huge pressures on the system, all new claimants were still made to wait for five weeks before anything was paid to them, during which time any emergency payments they requested would simply become a debt to be paid back later. Indeed, food banks were saying by the end of 2020 that benefit deductions to pay back these debts were frequently cited by those going hungry as the reason they were unable to afford basic food.

As time went on more people in executive and professional jobs were likely to begin to join the ranks of the unemployed, shining a light on some of the other problems with the benefit system that had until then not received sufficient attention. Housing Benefit would only cover the costs of the lowest 30 per cent of rented homes. Anyone with savings above £6,000 – which might be money in an ISA to buy a house, or perhaps something put aside for a postponed family wedding – would find it taken into account in calculating their benefits. Having a partner in work could also be a reason to be denied benefits. Some would find that the most they would qualify for in these circumstances would be the basic Job Seeker's Allowance, with no access to means-tested top-ups. For some reason this particular benefit had been left at its existing level of £74.70 a week and can in any case only be claimed for a maximum of six months.

Many families facing these barriers would find themselves in severe difficulties if they had large commitments such as a mortgage that they could not easily reduce. Even if they did qualify for Universal Credit, its limited support with mortgage payments would only be forthcoming after nine months of being unemployed. That's a little tricky when you consider that the maximum mortgage 'holiday' that the banks had originally been told they had to provide was set at three months with a later concession to extend it to six months.[21]

The consequences, unless further action is taken to protect those from all the many walks of life who have suffered a drastic drop in income as a result of the pandemic, will be as varied as are people's individual circumstances. But they are extremely likely to include rising debt, homelessness, repossessions, evictions, food and fuel poverty as people struggle to feed themselves or heat their homes; and yet more families and children fall into deepening poverty, with even Christmas already an unaffordable stress for many by the end of 2020. And it will without doubt play out in mental health crises, increased suicides, deaths from destitution, domestic violence, family breakdown and children permanently traumatised by their parents' anguished lives. Society will be picking up the costs for decades to come.

The COVID Generation

Whether the economy 'bounces back' relatively quickly or remains in the doldrums, the national and local lockdowns that were imposed to deal with COVID-19 will leave a generation of young adults who were just starting out in life scarred by the experience, in the same way that the massive recession of the early 1980s affected the life chances of those swept aside in its wake.

Young workers were of course much more likely than others to lose their jobs as a result of the pandemic, as socially facing work in bars, restaurants and similarly exposed sectors was lost. Those who were coming out of schools and universities in 2020 and looking to enter the world of work would find their hard-won qualifications of little help as recruitment plummeted, leaving them with few options beyond a dispiriting first experience of unemployment, most likely spent at home with their parents. With this start to adult life Generation Z will be hard-pushed to avoid falling behind even the less-than-inspiring trajectory of Millennials before them, similarly locked out of home ownership and security and progression in work. No wonder, then, that mental health problems were soon magnifying in young adults.[22]

Yet the real problems are probably still in the pipeline. Children missed almost six months of in-school teaching during the first lockdown unless they had parents who were key workers or were deemed vulnerable in some way. A further two months were lost in the early 2021 lockdown. Unfortunately, the evidence is that this is likely to accentuate already entrenched educational inequalities, with some educationalists believing that many children will never catch up on what they have missed.

Some children will have had good access to broadband and high-quality laptops or similar, as well as space to work in and support from their schools and parents for keeping up their learning. Others will have had little such support. Plenty of poorer children were in households without adequate IT, potentially sharing one phone between several siblings to try to get homeworking assignments done. Many will not even have got as far as that if distressed circumstances and distracted parents left them disengaged from schoolwork and potentially lacking adequate food or exercise, or in extreme cases exposed to the violence and abuse that increased in the confined conditions of the lockdowns.

Figure 6 gives an indication of the impact of family background and resources on learning in the early weeks of the spring 2020 lockdown. Children in better-off families were spending more time on just about every educational activity than those in poorer families and were also accessing higher-quality support from schools such as online classes and, for the better-off, private tutors.[23]

Before the pandemic we were already in the position where education spending had been falling in deprived areas[24] but not in more prosperous areas and significant gaps in attainment were correlated with socio-economic background.[25] It was already the case that children were three times more likely to go to university if their parents were in the top fifth of the social distribution than those in the bottom fifth and nearly seven times as likely to go to one of the top universities.[26] Those gaps will now widen. Long after COVID-19 has receded we will still be counting the costs of the inequality and lack of opportunity that had been allowed to take root over many decades, only to be further amplified under the stress of the pandemic.

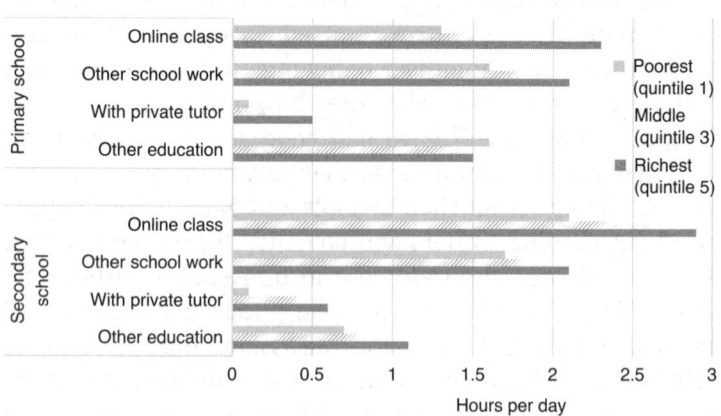

Figure 6. Children's daily learning time: gaps in educational activity. Source: Andrew et al. (2020b), Institute for Fiscal Studies

Where's Next?

By autumn 2020 new and deeply worrying regional disparities in COVID-19 susceptibility were emerging. Leicester in the East Midlands had been the first area to be placed under new restrictions to contain rising infections.[27] Rates of infection and hospitalisation then started to escalate in parts of the North East, North West, Yorkshire and Midlands including large areas around Newcastle, Liverpool, Manchester, Sheffield and Birmingham.[28] Restrictions on opening hours for bars and restaurants that had been imposed nationally were followed by compulsory full closures of hospitality venues, leisure centres and gyms in selected localities beginning with the Liverpool City region. This was part of a 'three-tier' response short of full lockdown that was to impact heavily on the North of England.[29] Scotland and Northern Ireland brought in similar partial lockdowns, while Wales moved to a full seventeen-day 'firebreak' lockdown to begin as schools broke up for the October half-term.[30]

A scheme that replaced two-thirds of wages (up to an upper cap) for businesses forced to close by these new tiered restrictions was announced – giving an extra six months' support after the planned ending of furlough but on less generous terms.[31] Manchester's mayor, Andy Burnham, challenged Whitehall's approach and the local funding offered, concerned about the economic devastation that new restrictions would bring to businesses that had still to recover from the earlier national lockdown and especially the ability of workers on the minimum wage to subsist on two-thirds pay.

A bitter and highly public row ensued with Burnham accusing the government of scaling back support for those in tier-three lockdown in the North, 'grinding people down … to accept the least they can get away with'[32] and 'playing poker with places and people's lives through a pandemic'.[33]

Image 14. Greater Manchester mayor Andy Burnham speaks to the media on 20 October 2020 after the failure to agree a financial package to help those whose jobs were threatened by a tier-three lockdown. Source: Christopher Furlong / Getty Images

Whitehall's case was not helped when it suddenly found money to support a return to the more generous furlough scheme when the rest of England was hastily put in full lockdown in early November. It inevitably led to accusations that lives in the North were deemed to be worth less than those in the South.[34]

There is no doubt that during this period both the health and economic impacts of COVID-19 were hitting people hard in the Midlands and the North with every likelihood that this would deepen already engrained inequalities of place. With many people's livelihoods already on the edge, analysts calculated that if on top of everything else the temporary increase in Universal Credit was reversed in April 2021 it would be the 'Red Wall' seats in the North and the Midlands that would bear the brunt, with one in three working age households in these constituencies likely to suffer a drop in income as a result.[35] Many of these are the communities who voted 'Leave' in the 2016 Brexit referendum, for a whole host of reasons, of course, but at least in part because they were aggrieved by a sense that their needs had been ignored by the prevailing London establishment.

The process of leaving the EU is already creating tensions that are endangering the continuation of the Union, especially the position of Scotland and Northern Ireland within the United Kingdom.[36] Further instability and loss of national cohesion are now a very real risk, particularly if parts of the country, including the former industrial regions in the North, perceive that they have suffered disproportionately not just from COVID-19 but also from an ill thought through and damaging Brexit to which they were simultaneously being subjected.

Looking to the Future

The extensive damage inflicted by COVID-19 has seen a grievous worsening of the harms wrought upon the more vulnerable sections of the population for decades. For its instigators, the idea of austerity legitimated deep cuts to welfare benefits and publicly funded services, which had served the working classes so well in the post-war decades but which, according to the neoliberal ideology, were a wasteful tax burden on the market economy.

The obsession with putting the interests of business first was stubbornly pursued into the pandemic itself with disastrous consequences. The government blundered repeatedly by prioritising keeping the economy open for too long when it should have locked down earlier and by insisting on employing private companies to do public health work they had no expertise or capacity to deliver effectively. There were many opportunities over the course of 2020 and beyond to move forward to establish a new, more responsible relationship with business, although precious few were taken.

The experience of COVID-19 should now be a catalyst for change, a re-examining of power relationships and a recasting of our public sphere after the shock that has hit right across the economy and society. Part III of this book will lay out the choices we face and the huge challenges that remain in achieving the aspiration that it seems everyone is agreed on: to 'build back better'.

PART III
HOW COVID-19 CHALLENGES US TO CHANGE

6 'TOO BIG TO FAIL?' WE NEED A PAYBACK THIS TIME

Power relationships change when the state steps in to manage a deteriorating economic crisis. Governments have a unique lever in this situation to negotiate something in return for being the backer of last resort. The bank bailouts in 2008 were a missed opportunity to secure this sort of payback. The unprecedented injection of support under the furlough and business loan guarantees during the COVID-19 lockdowns offered a new chance for governments to add some conditionality, to re-engineer a move towards a more ethical capitalism.

Lessons from the 2007–8 Financial Crash

Of course, nothing is actually too big to fail. It's just that some things are so big that it's dangerous if they do fail. Take banking, for instance. In September 2008, as the financial crisis was gathering pace, the US government decided to let Lehman Brothers collapse rather than come to its aid with a rescue package.

When this threatened to unleash a domino effect of further bank failures around the world there was a panicked reversal. Economists began to mutter about the 1929 crash and the mistakes made then in letting banks go to the wall. Politicians agreed and suddenly funds running into billions were being poured into saving the banks, the UK no exception. The argument was that while individual banks may have loaded themselves with toxic debt without sufficient cover against default, banking as a whole was too crucial, it had to be bailed out. The alternative, too

Image 15. Worker leaving Lehman Brothers' European headquarters, Canary Wharf, 15 September 2008.
Source: BEN STANSALL / AFP / Getty Images

bad to contemplate, was systemic – whole economy – failures because ultimately banking is what oils the wheels of everything we do.

Not everyone was happy with this. Mervyn King, the governor of the Bank of England, called it the 'biggest moral hazard in history' and he was probably right.[1] To paraphrase the argument, moral hazard is the temptation to push boundaries when you know someone else is on the hook if things go wrong. If I know that whenever I spend too much on my credit card there is a rich relative who always obligingly pays it off, maybe it's only going to encourage me to spend even more recklessly. 'Too big to fail' is exactly the same. Once business leaders believe the government will step in to support them no matter what happens, why wouldn't they take a few more risks? Either their gamble will pay off or they'll be bailed out – a one-way bet.

Arguably, though, governments can deal with this by asking for some sort of payback for acting as backer of last resort. When faced with the prospect of mass business failures they may throw public money at the problem, but they have to come in hard behind with a crucial question that deals with the moral hazard. Specifically, that question should be: what will the public get in return? Or, in the case of a bank-induced crisis, what will you do to stop this happening again? That debate needs to happen swiftly, while the government still has the upper hand. After the financial crisis there was a bit of this. In the UK, where finance had become so dominant in the economy, some banks were taken into public ownership, giving taxpayers the prospect of some future financial return. Regulators were shaken up, reorganised and told in no uncertain terms to keep their eye on behaviour that was putting the whole banking system at risk. Banks were made to keep much more capital in reserve so that if their money started flying out again in bad debts, they still had something left in the till.

This was of course shutting the stable door after the horse had bolted. But there will be many more horses trying to bolt in the future – financial crises tend to come around more often than pandemics. That's the reason why banks were also made to separate everyday branch banking – the place where customers and firms do their business – from their risky investment banking. That important change finally came in 2019. It means that in the next financial crisis we can just decide to let the risky stuff banks do take the hit without jeopardising the bread-and-butter banking functions that the economy depends on. And the banks now know this.

The trouble is this wasn't really enough. The public purse had picked up an eye-watering bill. The banks had been given a cash injection of £133 billion but it was the long-term damage done by the financial crash that was the real problem.[2] When it was all added up the crisis and its aftermath of plummeting growth, falling incomes and disappearing tax had bumped up the national debt by about £1 trillion – over half the value of the entire economy, and far in excess of the COVID-19 debt hit that was to come.[3] Yet incredibly no one seemed to have a plan for holding the financial sector to account for this.

The bailout had gone way beyond saving flagship banks from collapsing. So severe was the potential damage to the economy as the financial sector buckled that interest rates were cut rapidly from 5 per cent in September 2008 to 0.5 per cent by March 2009 in a bid to keep money flowing in the economy. Just to put this in context: 0.5 per cent interest was the lowest rate ever set in the more than 300-year history of the Bank of England by some considerable margin (although, as with so much else, COVID-19 was to smash that record, too). Prior to 2009 the lowest that interest rates had ever been down to was 2 per cent, which was the rate in force for almost all of the long period of depression and war from 1932 to 1951. But in 2009 even this extreme move to cut rates to 0.5 per cent proved insufficient. At this point a new phrase – quantitative easing – came into the language as the Bank was forced to pump in even more money behind slashed interest rates, of which more later.

The best news to come out of this is that we didn't experience a global depression on the scale of the 1930s, which is what many people feared. Though he has barely received the recognition he deserves for it, this was down in no small part to the quick work of the UK prime minister at the time, Gordon Brown, in galvanising fellow world leaders to keep spending as central banks kept money flowing. The less good news is that the economy did nevertheless contract. The UK along with many others saw the biggest fall in output in generations (see Figure 12, Chapter 11). Gordon Brown and his chancellor, Alistair Darling, worked hard to get things going again, understanding the urgency of kickstarting growth. They cut VAT, announcing that this would be temporary – a ploy to get people to go out quickly and spend on big ticket items. Next up was the car scrappage scheme – again putting money in people's hands to upgrade their cars and keep assembly lines rolling. A couple of years after the financial storm had struck, things did indeed look more hopeful when welcome green shoots of recovery began to push through.

Then the election in 2010 returned a coalition government with the Conservatives as the senior partner. With David Cameron as prime minister and George Osborne as chancellor, they changed economic tack in a big way. The mounting debt from the devastation of the financial crisis was now viewed as a millstone around the country's neck. They declared it should be paid off quickly, which they decided would be done through cuts in public spending and no increases in pay for anyone on the public payroll (or indeed, as it turned out, for just about anyone else). When the Conservatives were returned again in 2015, this time as a majority government, they went in hard on the welfare budget, promising swingeing cuts to address 'the damaging culture of welfare dependency'. The toll was high – according to the Institute for Fiscal Studies, outside of health, the amount spent per person on public services in the UK fell in real terms by 25 per cent over the decade 2009–20.[4]

What seems to have largely escaped public notice is that while all these cuts were happening, the rich were being made better off by the very same politicians who were bearing down on the poor. Corporation tax on business profits was 28 per cent in 2008, around the OECD average. By 2020 it had been cut to 19 per cent, which was now the lowest of the main G20 countries by a considerable margin and lower even than the USA.[5] The new top rate of income tax of 50 per cent that had been introduced in 2010 for those earning more than £150,000 was also cut – going down to 45 per cent in 2013. This evidently wasn't enough, though, to satisfy the demand for ever-higher rewards since executive pay and bonuses continued to soar.

But arguably the biggest piece of luck for the wealthy was the – possibly unintended – consequence of quantitative easing (QE), the tool used by central banks to stimulate the economy during the financial crisis with newly created electronic money. The era of QE began in 2009, with the Bank of England using its new money to buy government bonds from banks. The idea was that this would transfer over cash from the Bank of England which the banks would then lend to hard-pressed businesses. Sitting side by side with ultra-low interest rates, it was a stimulus that was meant to be strictly temporary.

The effect of the Bank of England's buying spree was to push up the price of government bonds, reducing their effective interest rate, thereby depressing economy-wide borrowing costs. Despite the stated intention that this would be a temporary stimulus there was no subsequent tightening of policy under three successive Conservative chancellors, so that interest rates simply flatlined for the best part of a decade. With abundant cheap money sloshing around it was an invitation to investors to jump on board and hoover up whatever assets – housing, shares or similar – they could. This they did, feeding a speculative frenzy of rising prices as buyers thought the only direction was up. Those who had acted quickly or who owned assets already were laughing all the way … to the bank.

The burgeoning of wealth in the years after the financial crash as this all unfolded was indeed staggering. Between 2013 and 2018 the *increase* in the value of housing wealth for those lucky enough to own bricks and mortar was a cool £842 billion in London and the South East alone.[6] That is more than a whole year's worth of public spending in those austerity years. Remember this was a return for doing absolutely nothing! Much of this housing was unencumbered by mortgages, being in the hands of the over fifties. Many, eager to benefit from ever-rising prices and buoyant rents, had then used an inheritance, buy-to-let mortgage or pension pot to acquire additional property. With the young unable to get a toehold on the property ladder, the reach of those who already owned property was such that more than 10 per cent of the adult population owned two or more houses.[7]

Similar forces were at work in the market for financial assets. From its 2009 low of 3,512 the FTSE 100 index of UK stock market value more than doubled to stand at 7,675 in January 2020 in what has been dubbed the longest bull run in history. Not only had we let bankers escape scot-free from clearing up the mess of the financial crash. We'd also allowed the wealthy to sit back while the population endured a decade of austerity and cuts, only to wake up each day a little bit richer as their mansions and asset portfolios delivered the proverbial golden egg.

What Does All This Have to Do with the 2020 Pandemic?

The consequences of our actions in responding to COVID-19 will be with us for decades to come both in terms of economic scarring and in sheer human cost. So, this time it's really vital that we get this right. We must work out how we devise a fair payback for everyone from the public money put into shoring up and then rebooting the economy.

That includes making sure that the already well-off do not, yet again, gain at the expense of everyone else.

In late March 2020, once the decision had been made that there was to be a full-scale lockdown to contain the escalating pandemic, with much of the economy simply halted or moved overnight from offices into workers' homes, the government had no option but to step in and step in big. Just as with the financial crash a little more than a decade earlier we were back to the government as backer of last resort.

But two things (at least) were different this time. The first is that it was the government itself that had, of necessity, mandated the shutdown. This was not a run-of-the-mill crisis caused by the workings of the economy or any particular players in it. It was an emergency public health response and it was worldwide. As Kristalina Georgieva, managing director of the IMF, said in early April 2020, 'this is a crisis like no other … [n]ever in the history of the IMF [have we] witnessed the world economy coming to a standstill'.[8] The second, of course, was that it touched absolutely every business serving the many parts of our national life that were summarily put on ice. From cars to clothing, culture, cafés and coiffure, businesses – whether large, small, innovative, traditional, dazzlingly profitable or barely surviving – were stopped in their tracks as the economy contracted by 25 per cent in a few short weeks. Unprecedented in scale and severity, it needed an unprecedented response. It was not just one vital enterprise, or one key sector of the economy that was too big to fail – this was an emergency facing the whole economy and all the millions of people working in it.

On 20th March Chancellor Rishi Sunak announced with admirable speed the first details of the government's support package. The Coronavirus Job Retention Scheme would pay 80 per cent of wages (up to a monthly limit of £2,500) for staff unable to work as a result of lockdown –

henceforth known as 'furloughing'. Subject to certain eligibility conditions, the self-employed were able to claim temporary cash grants while businesses in retail, hospitality and leisure had their business rates waived, with some also getting a one-off grant, a provision that was to be repeated in the 2021 budget. Businesses across the board could apply for one of a selection of Coronavirus Business Interruption Loan Schemes – including a small business bounce back scheme – which would give a lifeline cash injection to those whose revenues had dried up. The government undertook to underwrite the bulk of these loans, which it expected the banks to provide, thereby minimising their risk in the event of future defaults.

The hope was that by cocooning businesses and jobs in this way during what was in effect a period of economic hibernation, the long-term damage of lockdown would be lessened. By late June 2020 it was estimated that 1.1 million employers had furloughed 9.2 million workers – covering roughly a third of all jobs![9] There were still gaps that people could and did fall through, especially the self-employed, and some – no doubt justified – complaints that banks were dragging their feet on loans. Nevertheless, the government had effectively stepped in to socialise a large part of the costs of the economic shutdown for the very simple reason that it needed there to be an economy still standing at the end of the crisis.

A First Look at the Winners and Losers

Taking the Treasury first, the cost of the original furlough scheme was roughly £10 billion a month (less after the first four months when the payments became less generous). Grants to the self-employed added more than £2 billion per month in the first tranche at least, and billions more were at risk in guaranteed business loans.[10] The plan was that from 1st November the furlough scheme would end and be replaced by the Job Support Scheme, which had a far less generous, and therefore less costly, level of wage replacement. The new scheme attracted considerable criticism, however, as it appeared poorly designed to meet its stated objective of helping employers keep workers on at least part-time and hence – many business groups argued – was insufficient to avert large-scale redundancies.[11] In the event the furlough scheme was reprieved at the eleventh hour, when a second full lockdown implemented in November – followed by a third from early January 2021 – put it firmly back on the table for weary businesses now facing the loss of much of their winter trade. For many workers, though, this was too late as employers had already made decisions on redundancies, which soared to record levels over the autumn of 2020.[12]

Figures released at the time of the March 2021 budget estimated the cost to the public purse of supporting workers' incomes as the economy was put into repeated lockdowns at £80 billion in the 2020–21 financial year, with more to follow in the coming months.[13] That was for furlough and self-employment support. It was just one part of the extra £300 billion that the government expected to borrow that year as it poured money into welfare payments, emergency funding for public services, especially the NHS, while also having to contend with having much less money coming in from taxes as output collapsed.

Let's take a look at the beneficiaries of all the money that was flowing through these government support schemes during lockdown and beyond. When you get into the detail you can see that they worked by propping up the *income* of furloughed workers and the self-employed. What people didn't get was any help with *outgoings* even if another family member had lost their job. If as a result they got into difficulty with their regular payments, as many did quite quickly, the official advice was to seek a mortgage 'holiday' from their bank or rent deferral from their landlord.

This apparent nod towards clemency was backed up with legislation temporarily banning evictions and a mandated halt on mortgage repossessions. But the fact remains that the missed payments were not forgiven – interrupted mortgage payments would need to be repaid sooner or later, as would rent – unless an accommodating landlord chose to waive it. A report by the debt charity StepChange in early June 2020 found that 4.6 million households were at risk of building up crippling levels of debt as missed payments on Council Tax, utilities and credit card payments compounded housing cost arrears.[14] Similarly, while banks would do very nicely from the interest on loans underwritten by the government, struggling businesses knew that in a fragile post-lockdown economy they would still have to pay back the money they had borrowed to get through the pandemic unless they were actually bankrupt.

The Institute for Public Policy Research (IPPR) has looked in more detail at this asymmetry of power and calculated that as much as 45 per cent of the money from the Job Retention Scheme was probably being paid directly to landlords, mortgage lenders and banks.[15] They conclude that 'in the absence of measures to freeze outgoings such as rent and debt repayments, the Job Retention Scheme and other household income measures … [were] in part an indirect way of protecting income streams for asset owners'. With many ordinary households and businesses likely to end up racking up debt as they tried to keep going, IPPR conclude that 'most of the … crisis response measures amount to pumping more money through a highly unequal economic system' such that it is 'perhaps inevitable that most … will … end up in the hands of the rich and powerful who already benefit most handsomely from our economic settlement'.[16] Landlords and banks were, they argue, getting an implicit government bailout without incurring losses themselves.

It doesn't stop there. The former trader Gary Stevenson has eloquently described the merry-go-round of cheap money and asset prices rises to be expected as the government moved to prop up the economy – a repeat in effect of what happened in the aftermath of the financial crisis, although with an extra twist. The richest segment of the population had been saving money during the lockdowns. Likely to be high earners able to work from home on full pay, they were stuck indoors bereft of the restaurant meals, theatre trips and overseas holidays that normally took care of their surplus income. Many will have joined the investor class to make a killing stocking up on assets before prices rose again. The crisis set in train by COVID-19 could start looking like Groundhog Day if this sees wealth inequalities deepen yet further.[17]

Certainly, wealth concentrations were growing from very early on. A report by UBS and PwC published in October 2020 charts the rise in the fortunes of the world's billionaires during the first months of the pandemic as stock prices responded to government stimulus packages and, for companies such as Amazon, the extremely favourable trading conditions of the pandemic itself. From the beginning of April to the end of July 2020 the collective fortune of this billionaire club rose by more than a quarter to a record $10.2 trillion, surpassing the previous peak of $8.9 trillion reached at the end of 2017, and almost certainly set to rise significantly further.[18] Some of this largesse would no doubt find its way into worthwhile philanthropic causes. Nevertheless, it does perhaps merit some further debate when you consider that this billionaire wealth pot – in the hands of just a couple of thousand people – is practically half the size of the USA's economy and twice that of Japan's!

Meanwhile behind the scenes during the summer lockdown and its aftermath some of the UK's biggest businesses, finding their fortunes going in the opposite direction, began petitioning the government for support, no doubt bringing in the 'too big to fail' argument in one guise or another. Some, particularly the big airlines whose revenue had all but disappeared, were haemorrhaging money.[19] The Covid Corporate Financing Facility was created using new money from the Bank of England to bolster large firms' cash reserves via bespoke debt facilities. These were made available at pretty attractive rates, certainly better than the commercial loans smaller businesses had to take. As Edward Luce wrote in the *Financial Times* at the time, big companies were 'drink[ing] deep from the hose of central bank liquidity, while their smaller counterparts fight over the trickles to survive'.[20]

By early June 2020 it was revealed that fifty-three big corporations had borrowed a total of £16.2 billion, although provision had been made available for nearly four times that amount. They included easyJet, Ryanair, British Airways, Burberry, John Lewis, Marks and Spencer and overseas companies Bayer, Chanel, Nissan and the car finance arms of Toyota and Mitsubishi.[21]

Around the same time the government announced a new programme – Project Birch – to rescue firms whose failure would 'disproportionately harm the economy'. Fortunately, railways had already been dealt with at the start of lockdown when franchise arrangements were summarily ended and the rail network was effectively brought back into public control. It was as if the arguments of recent decades over rail re-nationalisation had never happened. For other critical businesses operating in the commercial sector Project Birch would combine loans with possible equity stakes to bail out those still considered viable who had exhausted all other options. Names in the frame over the summer included Jaguar Landrover, Virgin Atlantic and Tata Steel, although by the autumn Celsa Steel UK had been the only one to actually receive funding, to the tune of £30 million.

All of these were no doubt sensible short-term measures to protect the hundreds of thousands of jobs and livelihoods at risk. Any big economic contraction carries the extra risk that businesses that go bust remove capacity and skills from the economy that cannot be quickly regained, making it harder to bounce back when things improve. Targeted interventions to avoid that happening clearly make eminent economic sense.

Nevertheless, the public was sceptical from the start about what some of the better-known companies were up to, with some facing a public backlash as they lined up for funding. Newspapers called out the personal wealth of well-known figures such as Victoria Beckham, questioning her plan (later withdrawn) to use the furlough scheme and scrutinising how she was treating her staff during lockdown.[22] Richard Branson's use of offshore facilities to shield his private fortune, although not his businesses, from UK tax was the subject of much criticism when he sought to throw himself on the goodwill of those who had paid their dues.[23] In the discussion of who should and who should not be in the frame for support, it was not lost on people that countries such as France, Poland and Denmark were denying government funding to businesses registered in tax havens. The message in those countries was crystal clear – if you don't contribute to our tax base, don't come asking to be bailed out with our taxes when you get into trouble.

Particular criticism was levelled at businesses who were willing to take government support that many thought they didn't need. This came to a head when some continued with routine pay-outs to shareholders and top executives. Tesco – a business that was clearly a beneficiary not a victim of lockdown – was taken to task for disbursing £635 million in dividends straight after being excused business rates of more than half a million pounds, money it eventually paid back nearly eight months later.[24] EasyJet attracted some opprobrium when it sought bailout funds to the tune of £600 million having only recently paid a massive dividend to its shareholders.[25] A public row broke out, too, over Premier League football clubs who wanted to use the furlough scheme to subsidise low-paid workers but appeared unwilling to cut back exorbitant player and manager remuneration before seeking external support.[26]

The business and political elite was, it seems, walking somewhat of a tightrope of public opinion. People had known from pretty early on that deaths from COVID-19 were higher in lower-income groups and among people of colour and that job losses were hitting the lowest-paid hardest. When the prime minister continued to insist – until his own backbenchers stopped him – that the country couldn't afford to treat immigrant health workers for free in the very hospitals where they were putting their own lives at risk, people began asking in earnest, 'how are we all in this together?'[27]

They may well ask.

In the years leading up to the pandemic we now know from independent research that the UK's biggest companies paid out almost half a trillion pounds in dividends and share buybacks, not to mention eye-watering senior executive salaries. Many did so despite it leaving them weaker and potentially exposed in the event of a crisis. Over the eight-year period that the researchers looked at, the UK's 100 largest non-financial companies had simply handed over a staggering two-thirds of their net profits to shareholders rather than investing them or retaining them for a rainy day.[28]

One high-profile and shocking example is Arcadia, which went into administration in December 2020 with 13,000 jobs on the line and a £350 million hole in its pension scheme.[29] A few years earlier Tina Green, wife of Arcadia's owner Philip Green, was paid an untaxed dividend of £1.2 billion from the business. Industry sources are in no doubt that stripping funds out in this way deprived the business of vital investment in its retail brands (which include Top Shop, Burton and Dorothy Perkins) particularly in the essential task of preparing to take on the online market to secure long-term survival. The retail empire's eventual collapse during the pandemic was no surprise to anyone after such unprincipled value extraction. Tina Green's dividend payment in 2005 was the biggest in British corporate history; fifteen years later Arcadia Group was branded '"worthless" due to huge debts'.[30] Tragically, Arcadia took the department store Debenhams down with it, due to the multiple 'concessions' it held in their already struggling stores, putting a further 12,000 jobs at risk.

Just as the banks' poor financial cover and excessive risk-taking had been implicated in the 2008 financial crash, then, it seems that the inexorable drive for shareholder gain and profit extraction had continued right across the economy in its aftermath, leaving many businesses much more vulnerable than they should have been when the new crisis hit. It was as if nobody had learned anything from 2008; or perhaps more accurately, as Mervyn King had foretold with his comment about moral hazard, they had learned that they did not have to change their behaviour one jot. Perhaps moral hazard had played another role, too. With memories of the 2008 bailout still fresh, businesses and their well-heeled executives were quick to come forward to seek taxpayer support in the pandemic. This time, one would have thought, it must surely come with strings attached.

Securing the Pandemic Payback: How Are Things Looking This Time?

As luck would have it, an unlikely alliance between a hedge fund manager and an American academic, whose jointly penned book *Angrynomics* was already at the printing press, gives us a perfect springboard for thinking about the economics of the pandemic.[31] Rapidly adapting their insights, Eric Lonergan and Mark Blyth rushed out a paper in March 2020 contending that 'the current crisis is a huge opportunity to transform and improve the structure of our capitalism'.[32]

The original idea that the pair were promoting in their book was that with interest rates below inflation (i.e. negative in real terms) it was a no-brainer that governments should get in on the act. After all lenders were in effect paying people to borrow from them. Why would governments not do what fund managers were already doing – namely use this cheap money to invest in assets? The only difference being that, if the government did it, the assets would exist for everyone's benefit. And why would they not do this in every economic downturn if the opportunity was presented to acquire assets cheaply?

In the midst of the pandemic Lonergan and Blyth saw a new opportunity. With businesses such as the airlines looking for big money injections and in no position to bargain, the government could get on the front foot and insist on purchasing a substantial equity stake in return for cash support. Shareholders would be taking a hit, but wasn't everyone supposed to be in this together? If priced correctly – and the pair had very clear views that the government must drive a hard bargain – it would create significant value for the state, meaning for us, the ordinary tax-paying citizens. After all, outside a pandemic, most of these businesses were fundamentally very strong.

In other words, rather than passive interventions pouring money into businesses that would get repaid later with little to show for it, they argued for a much more assertive stance. Here was a unique chance to secure part ownership of large corporations at favourable prices – surely any sane government would seize it. They even offered a detailed blueprint for how it should be done. For Lonergan and Blyth it was a win, win, win:

By issuing debt when interest rates are so low and, in effect, buying assets at very cheap prices, in the medium term the state will simultaneously ensure businesses survive, workers keep their jobs and the state emerges an owner of significant assets.[33]

For it to work in the wider public interest, the government, they argued, should move the assets into a publicly owned wealth fund and certainly not sell them off precipitously as was done after the financial crisis. As they grew in value, they could then be used by the public for whatever collective purpose they prioritised – education, health or social care or a capital payment to young adults to support them with housing, education or similar. It has long been argued that wealth funds of this sort, created for the public interest, produce greater equality of wealth ownership, and are therefore a counterweight to the tendency towards ever-greater concentrations of private wealth ownership.

There would also be scope, having acquired an equity stake, to influence how corporations are run and who makes the decisions, using this newly gained muscle to put the case for the long-term interest of the business and its employees over short-term quick fix pay-outs to shareholders. These were ambitious, even audacious, ideas. If pursued successfully they would fulfil the authors' aspiration that we should be able to look back at this period and say that society was both 'compensated for the support it … provided and share[d] in the gains from recovery'.[34]

While their masterplan remains on the printed page for the time being, Lonergan and Blyth had painted a bigger picture, conveying an urgency to shake up the relationship between state, citizens and business. It was a vision that chimed with others now pushing for the government to use its new authority to get something back from those businesses who had taken a handout – and goodness knows there were a lot of them out there. Environmental goals, ethical goals, better corporate behaviour, better treatment of workers – all were now potentially in the policy melting pot.

Commentators, opposition politicians and lobby groups came forward with ideas but there was little sign of the UK government taking the initiative to secure concessions on any front. Airlines, large oil companies, car manufacturers and others with a large carbon footprint were all, it seems, accessing the government's Covid Corporate Financing Facility without any questions being asked. Greenpeace was blunt in its criticism, focusing on airlines who, they argued, had 'been given billions in cheap and easy loans to keep them polluting without any commitments to reduce their emissions or even keep their workers on the payroll'.[35]

Across Europe, by contrast, many of the pandemic rescue packages had built in social and environmental conditions from the start. Job retention payments in Denmark, for instance, were conditional on avoiding redundancies. Not only was this condition not applied in the UK, but there was also no clear expectation set out that businesses which could afford to pay furloughed staff should do so before seeking any public money. Even measures to restrict dividend payments and share buybacks while in receipt of government support took weeks to be agreed in the UK.[36]

Airline bailouts in Europe, meanwhile, were being crafted to include new environmentally friendly targets. Austrian Airlines' €600 million rescue package put together by the Austrian federal government and Lufthansa was trumpeted as coming with 'binding commitments … to strict ecological requirements'. There were to be rapid improvements in jet engine efficiency, targets for reductions in CO_2 emissions and short-haul passengers diverted from flights to viable train services.[37] Very similar conditions were placed on an Air France bailout, including the stricture that they were not to compete with the national rail network's fastest TGV routes.[38]

The lacklustre performance of the UK government in thinking through how to secure a pandemic payback also gave banks a latitude that they should not have had at such a critical time. At the start of the lockdown several of the banks had tried to take collateral from businesses applying for loans despite having a government loan guarantee.[39] One can only assume they would have called in both in the event of default. The banks retreated on this under protest but dragged their feet anyway on lending until the government was forced to step in to increase guarantees to 100 per cent on smaller loans.

Evidently banks were not actually short of cash as they had every intention of continuing with dividend payments until the Bank of England decided to take a stand. As IPPR put it, the Bank of England had to 'force the big five banks to cancel their dividends, in the teeth of fierce resistance, at the same time as they seemed unable to fulfil their core public function of financing the real economy'.[40]

The Swiss government was one of many who, like the UK, made provisions to guarantee bank loans to businesses during the economic shutdown.[41] However, the Swiss had additionally placed an upper limit of 0.5 per cent on the interest that banks could charge for these loans. The UK government had at least had the good sense to offer to pay the first year's interest for businesses getting a credit line, although in the case of bounce back loans this meant pouring an estimated £1 billion into the banks' coffers for loans that were 100 per cent backed by the state.[42] After that, though, its only stipulation on what banks could charge was a 2.5 per cent interest rate cap on bounce back loans up to £50,000. For those requiring loans above £50,000, which were provided via the Coronavirus Business Interruption Schemes with their slightly lower 80 per cent guarantee, there were no limits set on interest rates.

Reports soon emerged that the average interest rate being charged was over 5 per cent, at a time when the Bank of England base rate was 0.1 per cent.[43] With hindsight this will surely look like a double whammy for the government. It was putting its own money at risk on behalf of the banks but allowing them the leeway to charge rates of interest that could mean that the very businesses it wanted to protect would struggle to survive.

There is a greater structural risk here, too. If a large number of smaller firms are overburdened with debt and in the carnage of the pandemic lockdowns either fail or get swallowed up by larger predators, market power will become even more concentrated. This benefits no one other than those who can take advantage of the loss of competition to bolster profits. One might think that there could be a public solution to this. For instance, perhaps a state company could be formed to purchase viable small or medium enterprises in distress, providing a respite that might avoid mass bankruptcies and a rush of hostile takeovers. Let's watch this space.

To conclude, the verdict on the UK's success in gaining a payback for the public in return for the money poured into the economy during the pandemic was, as with the rest of its handling of the crisis, somewhat underwhelming. Much was made in the spring 2021 budget of the announcement that corporation tax was to be raised in 2023 from 19 per cent of profits to 25 per cent. Small businesses were exempt from the increase, which was to apply to larger and more profitable companies only. Inevitably the rise was presented as businesses paying their dues for the pandemic support they had received, and it was certainly a very bold reversal of the Conservatives' own business tax policy. But in practice it was a measure that still left corporation tax below its level in 2008, when it was at 28 per cent. Even at the new rate of 25 per cent it remained below that of all other G7 economies, many of whom were in any case likely to raise their rates soon. It was a fiscal measure that smacked of expediency, could easily be reversed in the future and, crucially, did nothing to change any fundamentals.

While other European countries had spent the pandemic carefully designing ways to lessen the long-term risk to jobs and small businesses and locking bigger players into new behaviours and commitments, no equivalent strategy can be discerned in the UK response to the pandemic. If, as Lonergan and Blyth argued, the crisis was indeed an opportunity to transform and improve the structure of our capitalism, the UK government, deeply invested as it was in the status quo, took precious few steps during lockdown or afterwards to avail itself of that opportunity. Still as committed as strongly as ever to the ideology of hands-off laissez-faire economic management, this apparently left it blinkered to the possibility of engineering something better for everyone.

Is the Old Order Beginning to Crack?

So, what needs to happen next? After the immediate crisis has passed how should we respond to the fault lines it has exposed? It will be a moot point whether, after all that has happened, we can just return to 'business as usual'. As the Common Wealth think tank writes,

> *All crises buckle and reshape the order of things; in what direction and in whose interests depends on politics and the balance of power within society.*[44]

There are so many ways in which a reshaping might take place. A (real) Green New Deal of the scale needed – echoing Roosevelt's New Deal in 1930s USA – would provide an opportunity for jobs-led growth geared to green technology and away from fossil fuel dependency. Young people and other workers displaced by the pandemic job losses could be trained to retrofit homes with new green boilers, to manufacture batteries for electric cars and build the new charging infrastructure, or to get involved in the many initiatives needed to bolster flood defences.

Businesses themselves seemed to be up for this. While the economy was still in lockdown in the summer of 2020 almost 200 chief executives sent a letter to Boris Johnson calling for 'a clean, just recovery' and asking for government interventions to be 'aligned with the UK's legislated target of net zero emissions by 2050 at the latest'. Signatories included Aviva, HSBC, Lloyds, BP's UK business, National Grid and Heathrow airport.

These heavyweights wanted stimulus packages that would require anyone getting government money to align their business strategies to national climate goals; tax incentives for investment in low-carbon technologies; targeted public investment to the same end; and a focus on supporting parts of the economy most likely to stimulate jobs and lower emissions.[45] Perhaps they understood that it was shareholders and asset managers who would be stopping their corporations from acting responsibly to mitigate climate change.[46] Perhaps they wanted a more directive government stance that would counter that – but only if everyone had to comply.

Which of course brings us on to politics and the balance of power within society. Surely it would take an almighty reversal out of neoliberal ideology to cut through the tangled web of financialised power sustaining the current order. Yet on 3 April 2020 the *Financial Times* – the world's leading business newspaper – put out an editorial advocating something that looked remarkably like it:

Radical reforms – reversing the prevailing policy direction of the last four decades – will need to be put on the table. Governments will have to accept a more active role in the economy. They must see public services as investments rather than liabilities and look for ways to make labour markets less insecure. Redistribution

*will again be on the agenda; the privileges of the elderly and
wealthy in question. Policies until recently considered eccentric,
such as basic income and wealth taxes, will have to be in the
mix.*[47]

Quite some statement to be coming from the financial services' house journal. It would seem unlikely, though, that
the reversal of policy direction called for by the *FT* could
happen without radical change in how corporations are
governed and a big shift in thinking about who they are
set up to serve. Shareholder capitalism and the wholesale
channelling of corporate profit into dividends and share
buybacks are a pretty hard nut to crack you would have
thought. Maybe though their number was already up. In
late 2019, before COVID-19 was even a thing, the World
Economic Forum published its grandly titled, 'Davos Manifesto 2020: The Universal Purpose of a Company in the
Fourth Industrial Revolution', which appeared to be doing
just that.

Following on from a pronouncement earlier in the year
by the US Business Roundtable, the Davos Manifesto told
the world that the purpose of the company was now 'to engage all its stakeholders in shared and sustained value creation'. Furthermore, it proclaimed that 'a company serves
not only its shareholders, but all its stakeholders – employees, customers, suppliers, local communities and society
at large'. They must, it was now declared, work together
'through a shared commitment to policies and decisions
that strengthen the long-term prosperity of a company'.

These were words that harked back to an earlier, almost
forgotten, era of corporate responsibility. Klaus Schwab,
the World Economic Forum's founder and executive
chairman, presented the manifesto and its promotion of
'stakeholder capitalism' to replace 'shareholder capitalism' as the culmination of a vision he had first sought
to implement half a century ago. Stakeholder capitalism

Image 16. Klaus Schwab (right) with staff at the World Economic Forum, Switzerland, 20 January 2020.
Source: FABRICE COFFRINI / AFP / Getty Images

provides, he said, a model that 'positions private corporations as trustees of society', who 'should pay their fair share of taxes, show zero tolerance for corruption, uphold human rights throughout their global supply chains, and advocate for a competitive level playing field'.[48]

These words now need to be backed up with action. Corporations must have their feet held to the fire in the push to reinstate value creation above value extraction. Even so, exhortation might not be enough to move hypothetical aspirations on from worthy statements to concrete outcomes. In that vein, the authors of *Commoning the Company* proposed an amendment to the UK's Companies Act 2006 that would use the law to actualise change, obviously only in the UK, but no doubt it could be generalised. They argued, along the same lines as the 2020 Davos Manifesto, that this should be done by making the primary duty of directors – backed up in law – the promotion of the long-term success of the company, not the maximisation of short-term shareholder interest.[49]

Indeed it is salutary to reflect in all of this on the fact that the corporation, as a legal entity to conduct business activities, has an ancient and continuous history found in many cultures and that a public and social purpose was always essential to its legal privileges.[50] The idea that a corporation should be an impersonal machine for profit-max-imisation, with no balancing duty to the public sphere, is in fact a new and dangerous cuckoo in the nest.

Cracks in the neoliberal order were, then, already open-ing up when the pandemic hit. As the crisis unfolded more insistent voices could be heard through these cracks call-ing for a new ethics of business behaviour. Could we real-ly return to the situation where risible levels of sick pay made taking time off work unaffordable, where workers could have a contract for work with no actual hours, where people were only told which days they were working at such short notice that they could not plan their lives, their holidays or even their childcare?

An interesting early feature of lockdown in the UK was the increase in contacts made with trade unions. Many people were evidently fearful of returning to work without reassurances that there would be adequate social distan-cing and other safety measures in their workplace. Many also understood that their jobs hung by a thread and would have wanted to understand their rights. Perhaps the new world of COVID-19 had opened a door that many workers didn't even know it was possible to walk through.

Certainly, the issue of worker representation is likely to be rising up the agenda in the jostling for a post-pandemic settlement, both representation in the workplace but also on the executive bodies of the major corporations. So, too, is full and fair payment of tax and, whisper it quietly, the under-taxation of wealth. Perhaps, too, pay inequality and the astonishing gap between the highest-paid executives and their average worker will surface in the discussions to be had. In the light of the Black Lives Matter movement pay gaps experienced by people of colour may even take their rightful place in the debate alongside gender pay gaps, and that is not to mention LGBTQ+ discrimination.

We may not have seen a pandemic payback yet from those who hold the power in our economic system, but the pressures are building.

7 NO TIME FOR AUSTERITY NOW

So We Found the Magic Money Tree

With COVID-19 circulating freely in those dangerous days in March 2020 the world's stock markets looked to be teetering on the edge of meltdown. That tends to make governments move quickly and the UK was no exception. Confidence is everything in a situation like this and not just for businesses and investors. Everyone's world was being turned upside down and everyone needed to be told it was going to be OK. That's when we found the magic money tree – the fantasy pot of money so derided by Theresa May and her entourage a few short years earlier to discredit her supposedly open-walleted opponents in the 2017 General Election campaign.

People were told what they wanted to hear – the government would be providing 'whatever it takes'. No stone would be left unturned. Businesses and jobs would be supported. Whatever the NHS needed, it would have. There were no fiscal rules or constraints, no budget limits. The government's credit was good and it would find the money.

In the space of a few short months the government's anticipated budget deficit (the gap between what the government spends each year and what it receives) shot up to £355 billion, 17 per cent of GDP, as the government put its money where its mouth was and poured cash into saving the economy.[1] That was several multiples higher than the £55 billion previously pencilled in for 2020–21, a figure out of date practically the moment it was uttered by the chancellor as he delivered his first budget on 11 March 2020 to a parliament still trying desperately to pretend things were normal even as the virus was almost certainly spreading in that very building.

All that extra outlay gets moved on from the annual accounts and added to the national debt. The best guess in March 2021 by those who did the sums was that the stock of public debt could now rise to 100 per cent or more of annual GDP in 2020–21 as a result of the pandemic response.[2] This would be the highest it had been since the 1960s, although, to be fair, the fallout from the financial crash had broken that record, too. Debt has been at least 80 per cent of GDP since 2014.[3]

It's worth just pausing for thought here for a moment. If we could find these seemingly mind-boggling sums of money in 2020 why didn't we find them a bit sooner? Was the era of austerity that started in 2010 and notched up a gear in 2015 actually not necessary? Were we conned into acquiescing in a decade of mounting inequality and poverty that could have been avoided?

There are economists who had been saying for years that austerity was a small-state ideology, a belt-tightening myth that actually did more harm than good.[4] Every economist knows that cutting back is not what you do when the economy is struggling because it makes things worse. You need to be putting demand into a stressed economy, not taking it out.

In any event, all of that paring back to the bone went out of the window in early 2020: rail nationalisation, state loan guarantees, furloughing and all the other measures pulled out of the hat as we entered lockdown. Small-state neoliberalism overturned at a stroke. In a moment of supreme irony we saw the penny-pinching Conservative establishment morph overnight under the weight of the pandemic into the most expansionist, statist operation for over a generation. It was positively Keynesian, almost,

"Any time you need more, the money tree is here."

Image 17. Finding the magic money tree.
Source: www.cartoonstock.com/cartoonview.asp?catref=aton4795

well … socialist. Certainly way beyond the measures in Mr Corbyn's 'magic money tree' election budget. As Chancellor Rishi Sunak himself said in March 2020 as he announced the momentous volte-face, 'this is not a time for ideology and orthodoxy'.[5]

When Austerity Was in Vogue

Boris Johnson has apparently never liked the 'A' word.[6] To give him his due, he had already announced a considerable spending rebound in the 'levelling up' budget just prior to the pandemic – the reward to the ex-Labour voters who had turned the 'Red Wall' blue in the winter election and whose votes he knew were 'on loan'. In Johnson's playbook, austerity was the policy of his predecessors, and especially his predecessor but one, David Cameron and his chancellor George Osborne.

Osborne had been the one who had first turned the screws on departmental spending, who had cut local authority budgets so hard that some were barely able to fulfil their statutory duties and who had sought to get the public onside with the Conservative's war on the 'benefit scroungers'. His justification was that we had to tackle our national debt because it had reached a level that was unsustainable. He told a good story on that, on how we risked a downgrading of our credit rating so that we had no option but to pay the debt down.

Osborne deflected attention away from the reason the economy was in such a mess in the first place by seeking to blame the previous Labour government for profligate spending – a perennial if rather lazy mantra from Conservative politicians. The shallowness of the argument does not survive even the most perfunctory of analysis. Most of the developed world was in crisis in the years after 2008 and it would be a brave economist indeed who could suggest that that could all be down to one government's alleged domestic overspend. Of course, no one in the party wanted to mention the Labour government's other more plausible role in the financial crash – their lax regulation of the financial sector – for fear of drawing attention to the Conservatives' own rather more culpable record on that score.

The confected story about who and what was to blame – Labour government spending, the dependency culture, the fear of losing the international line of credit – enabled the government to press ahead with the swingeing cuts that their anti-state ideology demanded. It was a superb smokescreen for tax-cutting bungs to the better-off. Everything was perfectly justified by the need to get government out of people's lives so that the hard-working entrepreneurs could get on with making things better.

If it had to be backed up with a little bit of myth making then the Conservatives were not averse to that, in fact they positively promoted it. The ancient story that welfare makes people lazy and encourages scroungers – a twenty-first-century version of shaming the poor[7] – is a ridiculously easy one to peddle: when money is tight, something has to be cut. This appeals at a basic level to everyone's sense of household economics. If support to the poor is seen as a luxury that has perhaps got a little too generous, then at a time when everyone is feeling the pinch, it is, politically at least, a low-hanging fruit to pluck.

But the narrative that the welfare state can be cut with impunity is revealed time and time again to be one of false economy. The 2010–20 era of austerity brought with it the rise of the food banks and the desperation of the five-week waiting period for benefits. It saw rising poverty, especially child poverty, as targets for reducing the welfare budget started to bite. But we know that children living in poverty don't thrive and we know they don't learn if they are too hungry to concentrate. Why would we want to hold back our precious future workers and citizens in this way?

With almost a cruel irony, the cuts demanded by austerity in practice made it *more* difficult for the government to pay down the debt burden that was the whole point of the exercise in the first place. Osborne's ill-advised policy choked off the more favourable growth path that had in fact started in 2009, cutting government tax receipts with it.[8] No wonder debt continued to rise during his chancellorship – it stood at 64 per cent of GDP in 2010 but was over 80 per cent by the time of his departure for pastures new in 2016.[9]

The post-2010 regime of austerity was miserable all round. It lowered GDP in relation to its expected trajectory in every subsequent year. The New Economics Foundation has estimated that in 2018–19 the UK's economy was around £100 billion – nearly 5 per cent – smaller in than it would have been without the spending cuts of austerity.[10] The International Monetary Fund (IMF) corroborated this, its chief economist admitting as early as 2013 that they were wrong about austerity, grossly underestimating the damage it would do to European economies.[11]

As if that were not enough, the decade of austerity also saw earnings after inflation falling year after year and gave us a new economic conundrum – the so-called 'productivity puzzle'. After the 2008 financial crash the annual increase in productivity – the amount each worker produces – slumped to just 0.3 per cent, lagging well behind our competitors, and lower than any previous period in our modern history.[12] It was so extraordinarily bad that in December 2019 the Royal Statistical Society hailed this dire productivity performance as the 'UK statistic of the decade'.[13]

Prior to this productivity had been increasing at 2 per cent for years, keeping pay rising in real terms, too, as workers took a share of the gains.[14] Once productivity took a nosedive for all those years and pay rises started to drop below inflation, workers with less money paid less in tax and claimed more in top-up benefits. It was a self-defeating cycle that further weakened the public finances.

Would we have put ourselves through all that pain if we had known what we know now? Would we not have taken a different path if we had known what the net effect of austerity would be? Yes, the wealthy benefited, but the poor were driven to the edge, the middling workers were squeezed and all we managed to do was to weaken our economy without actually making any kind of dent in the national debt.

Worse still is that George Osborne's austerity message was actually based on an outright falsehood. It was

founded on the work of two academics – Reinhart and Rogoff – who Osborne had eagerly drawn on to formulate and
justify this policy.[15] Unfortunately, it turned out that their
key paper contained a series of spreadsheet errors. This
now infamous 'Excelgate' incident had suggested that government debt in excess of 90 per cent of GDP would prove
unsustainable, hence requiring the belt-tightening that
the government had embarked on with such alacrity.[16]

Although the spreadsheet errors – a combination of
mathematical mistakes and data omissions – that produced this conclusion were exposed by academics in 2013,
ideology and the narrative of austerity nevertheless prevailed.[17] Osborne's 'nonsense on stilts' policy continued
under consecutive Conservative chancellors for seven
more years even though the government knew that the
suffering imposed, as so powerfully evoked in Ken Loach's
searing 2016 film on the personal toll of austerity, *I, Daniel
Blake*, wasn't necessary even on its own terms. Our debt
level was not in fact at risk of becoming unsustainable,
which is pretty fortunate when you consider that austerity
had had zero success in bringing it down.

Let's Just Put It on the Tab

Which brings us on to our current situation. With the financial crisis having already pushed up the national debt
from 34 per cent in 2008 to 80 per cent of GDP by 2014,
where it had stayed for the next five years, it will now rise
to above 100 per cent of GDP as we pay the bills for our
COVID-19 response. How big is that really?

History is always useful in providing proper perspective
and we have the benefit of another pandemic publication,
this time from economic historian Duncan Needham, to
guide us here.[18] What Needham's key chart – Figure 7 –
tells us is that a debt level of around 100 per cent of GDP

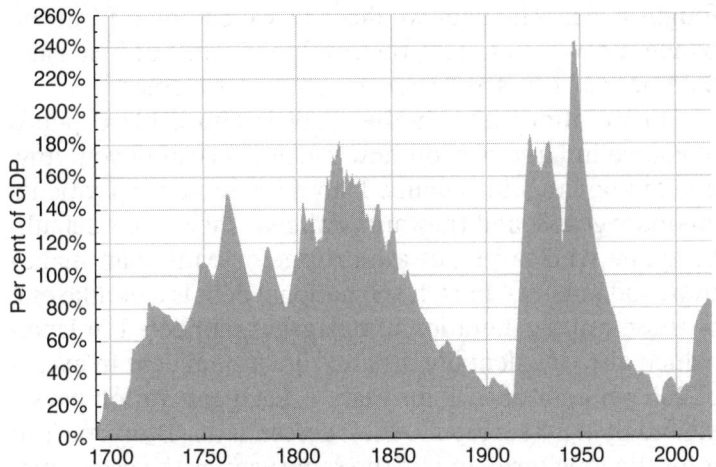

Figure 7. National debt as a percentage of GDP, 1693–2019.
Note: Financial year data for the UK.
Source: Needham (2020) and data from www.ukpublicspending.co.uk

is, in his words, 'in line with the average since the Glorious Revolution [of 1688–89] but considerably below the post-Napoleonic and Second World War peaks'.

Wars, it seems, are drivers of debt. Faced with an extreme national threat, tolerance by the governing elite for higher spending is suddenly transformed. Each peak in the chart shows the costs of funding a war – the Seven Years' War and American War of Independence in the eighteenth century, the Napoleonic Wars in the nineteenth century and then the two twentieth-century world wars. After the second of these, debt peaked at an alarming-looking 243 per cent of GDP.

So, the prospect of debt rising to a peak in 2023–24 of almost 110 per cent of GDP, as was forecast in early 2021,[19] is, well, average really, when you take the long view – it's been higher in 112 of the last 300 years. What is more unusual is seeing debt at such a high level without having fought a war. The debt we faced as we emerged from the pandemic was, uniquely, the combined effect of first a global financial crisis and then a global health crisis.

Can we afford it? Whether debt is affordable depends of course in large part on how much it's costing you. Anyone can be sanguine about a loan if the monthly payments are manageable and they are confident they won't default. Everyone who takes out a mortgage or bank loan makes those judgements. In fact, the national debt is a bit like one of those multi-generational mortgages pioneered in Japan (which also, incidentally, has had a national debt in excess of 200 per cent of GDP for years[20]). Each generation pays a bit and then passes it on to their descendants. Everyone is in it for the long term. In just the same way, as the economist Martin Slater has argued, the national debt is 'permanent by design, not simply through fecklessness'.[21] It is a planned long-term commitment that has to be serviced by each generation according to the actions of their predecessors.

After the Nine Years' War in 1697 this didn't look like such a good prospect. Just paying interest on the national debt was consuming nearly a third of national revenue, as can be seen in Figure 8. A few years later, in 1714, the War of the Spanish Succession had forced the government into an even worse position in which over 50 per cent of its annual revenue was absorbed by interest payments. This dire situation was reached again during the Seven Years' War in the mid-eighteenth century and repeated a few decades later in the Napoleonic Wars that ended with the Battle of Waterloo in 1815. As Needham shows, the stresses created at these pressure points led the incumbent governments to dream up all sorts of ingenious new methods for re-financing the debt to dampen down these massive interest payments – starting with the founding of the Bank of England itself in 1694.[22]

Over time they got this working pretty well. Hence we can see in Figure 8 that although the two world wars saw

Figure 8. Debt interest payments as percentage of total annual revenue 1680–2020 (and forecast 2021–25).
Note: Financial year basis (breaks in the length of the financial year in 1751, 1800 and 1855).
Source: Emmerson and Stockton (2020), Institute for Fiscal Studies

the highest ever levels of national debt in relation to the size of the economy, the debt was more easily serviced than it had been after earlier wars, taking up quite considerably less of annual revenue. Figure 8 looks suddenly rather encouraging when we consider the historic position.

Debt interest as a share of government revenue had actually reached a 320-year low by 2020. It only takes about 5 per cent of government revenue to service our debt these days and even when debt rose so much after the financial crisis the increased interest payments were no big deal.

Of course, when you think about it, that makes sense – the key feature of the financial crisis was the massive and historic fall in interest rates that was never significantly reversed. No surprise then that the costs of paying the interest on our debt were held in check.

But the most astonishing news is this: when the government cut UK interest rates to 0.1 per cent – a further historic low – on 19 March 2020 to cushion the pandemic impact, it again had a knock-on effect on the cost of servicing the national debt. The Institute for Fiscal Studies was able to say at the beginning of July that year that, although debt *levels* had been pushed up by the cost of lockdown to a point not seen for over sixty years, debt interest *payments* in 2020–21 would almost certainly be *less* than the amount we had been scheduled to spend even if COVID-19 had never happened![23] That's how much difference cutting interest rates made – more than enough to completely neutralise any increased interest payments arising from COVID-19.

Three cheers all round then! There's no need to stress – at least for the moment – about whether we can afford the extra costs of the pandemic response: we can. No need, either, to even be talking about austerity cuts to 'pay for the crisis' – it isn't costing us anything extra. The economic threat from COVID-19 in the short term isn't from higher levels of debt. It is the very real risk of not getting the economic revival after lockdown that is needed to sustain businesses and jobs.

Don't just take our word for it. Let's look at what the economics profession has been saying. In fact, leading economists reached a rapid consensus at the start of the crisis that the costs of the response to COVID-19 should be added to the national debt. Writing in the *New Statesman* on 4th May, Nobel Prize winning economist Professor Christopher Pissarides put it as succinctly as any when he said, 'the level of debt will probably not exceed 100 per cent of GDP, a manageable level in an era of near-zero interest rates'. Eminent academic Professor Jonathan Portes agreed, saying 'we could finance [the increased debt] for £2bn a year; trivial in macroeconomic terms'.[24] Debt did in the event rise above 100 per cent of GDP – it has been predicted to peak in 2023–24 at just under 110 per cent – but the fundamental point about the low cost of servicing the payments while interest rates were so low remained intact, as we shall see.

There were, predictably, some politicians who suggested that a return to the spending cuts of austerity would be needed at some point to defray the costs of the crisis – George Osborne, sounding somewhat like a broken record, warned of the need for a future 'period of retrenchment'.[25] But no one realistically thought that would be acceptable after everything that the population had been through. Torsten Bell, chief executive of the Resolution Foundation, joined others in cautioning that a repeat of austerity 'makes no sense economically or politically'.[26] Osborne's former colleague David Davis didn't mince his words in getting across the same message, proclaiming that 'austerity would launch the economy into so many brick walls it would be hard to list them all. It's a bonkers idea.'[27]

There was no need either, according to the economists, for the UK government to worry about how in practice it would get its hands on the money needed to support the package of COVID-19 measures. Having established that the government could relax for a while about the future interest payments, this is equivalent in household terms to the question, 'Ah yes, but can I find anyone who will give me a mortgage?' It's one of the many false concerns that economic historian Adam Tooze would remind us of, contradicting the previous decade's fear-mongering about the taps being turned off on government borrowing. As Tooze says, 'we are not in the position of a subordinate debtor nation. ... Advanced economies borrow in their own currencies and overwhelmingly from their own citizens ... we merely owe government debts to ourselves.'[28] And if borrowing in our own currency were ever to become a problem, there are plenty of historical precedents for the government using its influence to get banks and insurance companies to take on the extra debt.

If we are reconciled to putting the bill for the pandemic lockdowns on the national debt, we should nevertheless also be alert to the possibility that there could be another shock hitting us at any time. It is to be hoped that we have put in more robust protections now against future costly financial crises, although this remains an area for vigilance. But we could still in the future have further serious or protracted COVID-19 outbreaks, if we don't succeed in bringing things properly under control, or indeed we could face a new pandemic-causing pathogen. We could – heaven forbid – be drawn into a costly war or face a climate-related economic emergency. We would do well, therefore, to think about how we build a buffer against further unpredictable shocks impacting the public finances.

Going back to the historical evidence, one reason why debt reached its pinnacle of 243 per cent of GDP after the Second World War was that it hadn't really had long enough to recover from the First World War and the economic wasteland of the 1930s depression before war hit again. That wasn't a good place to be in. Taking that long view of course also gives us the clue to how debt gets 'paid off'. In practice it mostly gets eroded over time by a natural process of growth. As GDP rises, historic debt is an ever-smaller proportion of the total. It's pretty simple and it's the key to getting debt down again if we want to secure that all-important buffer for the future.

To reinforce this point, take a look again at Needham's chart (see Figure 7). Each time you see debt spike upwards, the drop back down is almost as steep. Some of this reflects government action to offset the costs of a crisis. Income tax was famously first introduced as a temporary measure during the French Revolutionary Wars. Mostly, though, as Needham points out, the debt pile has been lessened by a combination of rapid economic growth, as happened in the nineteenth century, and – even better for debtors – rapid economic growth combined with inflation, as happened after the Second World War.[29]

In 2020 we were in a different inflation regime, with an independent Bank of England operating to a target to keep inflation at around 2 per cent. While that remains, the likelihood of inflation providing a direct route to devalue debt is limited. It also makes little sense, as discussed, to stress about using government revenues to pay off actual debt, rather than simply servicing the interest on that debt, if interest rates stay at current lows. That being the case, it is growth – of the green and sustainable variety of course – that should be the mechanism for us to get over the top of the debt mountain and start the descent back down the other side.[30] As this happens a fixed level of debt will automatically become a smaller slice of a bigger pie.

As Needham concludes in a dismissive review of Reinhart and Rogoff's erroneous 'finding' that the economy could not deal with debt levels over 90 per cent, 'While we should of course worry about rising debt … the British experience shows that it is possible to grow out from under much higher debt levels' than 90 per cent.[31] If only Osborne had known his history.

Storm Clouds Ahead?

A fair amount hinges in all of this on the fortuitous affordability of debt interest payments. We have to remain mindful, therefore, of the ongoing dynamics of all this extra debt. It might not always be quite so easy to keep up interest payments if interest rates were to rise, for instance. But actually we can get clever about that, too, again learning the lessons of history. Just as people applying for a mortgage might decide on fixing the interest rate when that looks favourable for them, it's possible to do something similar with the national debt, sometimes for decades it seems.

We did it in 1946 and now, two generations on, Warwick Lightfoot, a former special adviser to no fewer than three Conservative chancellors, was gunning for the UK to do it again, saying he had changed his mind on debt because 'the caravan has moved on'. In a paper for the right-leaning think tank the Policy Exchange, he urged the UK to 'lock in the present historically very low rates of interest ... by ... issuing much longer dated fifty- and hundred-year maturity gilts in the manner that other countries ... have done'.[32] Duncan Needham and leading economist Charles Goodhart were up for it, too.[33] Sounds like a smart idea – if you have to borrow money, taking out a long-range mort-gage at an interest rate of almost zero (below zero after inflation) is a pretty good way to do it. Indeed, as Needham reminds us, that is precisely what Britain has done for most of its modern history.

Although debt may be parked as a worry if the right action is taken, our capacity to afford current day-to-day spending on the nation's many needs depends on what happens to the economy and especially how soon it gets back on track after the unprecedented contraction of lock-down. The government's coffers need tax revenues to start coming back in to help finance all the many calls on spend-ing; and an economic bounce back would also reduce the calls on the social security budget.

The question that people began to ask, then, starting in the long summer of 2020 was if, and critically when, an economic recovery might happen. Ever good for a metaphor, Boris Johnson was candid in June 2020 as the economy started to open up in predicting that the health crisis of the spring would soon seem like a flash of light-ning heralding the thunderclap of the economic fallout to follow.[34] This may have been part of his strategy to turn the conversation away from the government's performance in the health sector towards the issue of rebooting the econ-omy. Nevertheless, politics aside, the near-term trajectory of growth was indeed a serious issue.

While nobody knew what was to follow, economists amused themselves by speculating about which letter of the alphabet might best describe the economy's future course. There were those, like the Bank of England's chief economist, who thought we should be anticipating a V-shaped economic recovery.[35] The first part of the V represents the economy plunging down, contracting by a quarter during the summer shutdown – that much everyone knew did happen. The other side of the V was the optimistic idea that it bounces back pretty quickly to somewhere close to where it was before. Another possibility was that we might see something more U-shaped – a rebound but with a bit of a trough at the bottom first. A more complicated variant was the W-shaped path, where the economy does the V down and up, but then gets hit by a second crisis and goes through it all again. What everyone feared was the L-shaped scenario – a downward dip that we got stuck in because we'd lost too many jobs and businesses and consumers themselves had lost too much confidence for us to have the oomph to bounce back.

Only hindsight would show which one of these scenarios was closest to the truth. But the trick at the time was to strain every sinew to make the V-shaped outcome the most likely, with any additional spending outlay to help make this happen more than justified. Think tanks churned out ideas like there was no tomorrow. Some joined with the Labour Party to argue for a more targeted job protection scheme to replace furlough specifically to preserve those jobs that were still salvageable in the hard-pressed hospitality, retail, leisure and arts sectors. Some suggested pumping money into job creation schemes with social aims such as rebuilding the social care workforce. Another idea was to stimulate spending by cutting VAT or by giving everyone a voucher to spend cash where it was thought to be needed most.[36] The 'Eat Out to Help Out' scheme was the chancellor's eventual choice for this purpose, serving up a hearty £840 million of cash subsidy to the nation's diners in the four weeks it was in operation over the summer of 2020.[37]

Image 18. The 'Eat Out to Help Out' subsidy, August 2020.
Source: OLI SCARFF / AFP / Getty Images

But as 2020 progressed, bringing new autumn and winter lockdowns to contain infection levels that were again threatening to overwhelm the NHS, the outlook for the UK economy was far from rosy. A brief period of recovery over the summer had been brought to a halt as much of the economy was closed down once again. By the end of 2020 the economy had recorded its biggest contraction since the Great Frost of 1709, ending up close to 10 per cent smaller by the end of the year than it had been at the start. Still waiting for the V-shaped bounce back then. Worse still, the fall in output in the UK had been bigger than in any other G7 economy, exceeding by some considerable margin the USA's 3.5 per cent, Japan's 4.8 per cent, Germany's 5 per cent, Canada's 5.4 per cent, France's 8.2 and Italy's 8.9 per cent, a fact that had not gone unnoticed by our friends overseas.[38]

The international ratings agency Moody's had already put out a statement in mid-October 2020 in which they lowered the UK's credit rating, citing growth that 'has been meaningfully weaker than expected and is likely to remain so in the future', and cautioning that the 'negative … dynamics would be exacerbated by the decision to leave the EU … and the UK's subsequent inability to reach a trade deal [that] replicates the benefits of EU membership'. All these challenges were compounded by what they described as a 'weakening in the UK's institutions and governance'.[39]

The IMF, which was also monitoring the UK economy, stepped in as a critical friend urging the UK to stay focused on its response to the crisis, and deliver an additional 'fiscal push' (i.e. greater spending) to bolster the economy and invigorate a recovery. The IMF had argued earlier, with more than a hint of old-style Keynesianism that every £1 invested by governments at this stage would produce £2.7 of additional economic activity as jobs and investment were supported, a growth 'multiplier' that would pay back the investment in spades. Their managing director, Kristalina Georgieva, now called on the UK to take this 'opportunity to "build forward" and address the UK's climate targets, reduce regional inequality, and help those who do end up losing their livelihoods'.[40]

The message coming across was loud and clear. The biggest risk the UK was facing was not the sustainability of debt, but the state of the economy. The IMF's warning was unequivocal: prematurely withdrawing fiscal support in this situation was the worst thing to do. Remember, you don't cut spending in a recession because it just makes everything worse. And, as history shows, you pay off debt by growing your economy. The alternative downside risk of economic stagnation, which would make debt a bigger drag on GDP, was to be avoided at all costs.

The urgency of the position was all too clear by the time it came to the March 2021 budget. January 2021 had seen the imposition of a third full national lockdown with a pretty uncertain roadmap out of it, contingent in large part on the success of the vaccination programme. Sunak's plan, announced in the budget on 3rd March, was to continue borrowing to the tune of 10 per cent of GDP in the coming year in a bid to sustain the economic rescue, announcing a flotilla of schemes from low-tax freeports to a super deduction of tax to support immediate business investment.[41]

With the looming threat of business failures and redundancies to come and the now evident disruptions of Brexit, Rishi Sunak also had little option in the spring of 2021 but to announce a further extension of the furlough scheme, leaving it in place to the end of September, while also extending and widening the eligibility for self-employment support. Sunak knew, too, that it would not remotely make economic sense to add to the grief by reversing the £20 benefit uplift, a move that would take £6 billion of spending power out of the economy. That was reprieved in the March 2021 budget as well for a further six months. Sunak's spending plans would of course feed through into higher debt, which, as he said, would be for many governments over many decades to pay back.

To what extent these measures would work in allowing space for the economy and livelihoods to recover, rather than simply kicking the problem down the road, remained to be seen. The risk was that family incomes would plunge in the autumn of 2021 as a wave of post-pandemic redundancies materialised after the ending of furlough and just at the moment when the £20 Universal Credit uprating would finally be removed. A K-shaped recovery was therefore looking like a distinct possibility – a widening of inequality in which those already able to access better-paid jobs in secure sectors of the economy benefited from the hoped-for bounce back – the upward leg of the K – while those whose position was most precarious as we went into the pandemic were once again left out in the cold.

8 WHO HAS THE DEEPEST POCKETS?

A Better Future and a Proactive State

COVID-19 was an emergency that had to be dealt with quickly and decisively – the spending as necessary as in a war. The extraordinary outlay on the pandemic support packages was a one-off shock that has to be absorbed, just as historic war spending has been, and that happens by adding it to our national debt, not by any futile attempt to 'pay it back'. Nevertheless, we can't countenance a future in which every year we add another great big blob of debt to our national tally. Fair enough in an emergency, and for a short period afterwards – everyone gets that. But after that there needs to be a bit more of a mature discussion about taking responsibility and fairly apportioning the necessary fiscal balancing-up that will have to come next.

In his virtual speech on 5th October to the 2020 Conservative Party conference Rishi Sunak had promised, somewhat optimistically, that 'this Conservative government will always balance the books', which he considered to be not just a fiscal rule but a 'sacred' duty.[1] It was clearly a premature commitment given where we were then, and most likely intended mainly to calm nerves. But some sort of fiscal rules – to set government spending in relation to the money coming in – do at some point need to come back on the radar. It's important – as the IMF had telegraphed in no uncertain terms – that this doesn't happen before we are confident that the economy is back in good shape again, but equally it can't be avoided forever.

It was a point Sunak had again signalled he would stick to as he presented his forecasts in his March 2021 budget, arguing that in normal times the state should not borrow to finance day-to-day public spending.

In 2020–21 our public sector deficit – the amount by which the government had overspent – was without contest the highest peacetime deficit on record. Each year this public sector deficit (the annual overspend) just gets added to the national debt. So our debt is basically the total of all the annual overspends accumulated in the past. The trouble was that the economic aftershocks of the pandemic would mean that for several more years spending would of necessity be well above the money the government had coming in on existing plans, so each year we would be facing another high deficit. If furlough and the schemes to support the self-employed and struggling businesses had been the rescue plan, the next requirement would be for an economic recovery plan, which would not be cheap. It doesn't take an Einstein to work out that one way to prevent a recurring deficit, if you are not going to be cutting spending, is to try and increase the amount you have coming in via taxes to support it.

The March 2021 budget tried to square this circle. Rishi Sunak used his budget speech to announce significant tax rises, which would be phased in when things had stabilised. Corporation tax (a tax on business profits) would rise from 19 to 25 per cent. Alongside this, personal tax allowances were to be held constant, instead of rising with inflation, using a process known as 'fiscal drag' to bring more people into the tax net, including dragging more into the higher-rate tax bands.

But Sunak's budget also ploughed ahead with plans to cut public spending relative to pre-pandemic plans (and in fact accelerated the cuts) in all the 'non-protected' departments, which included local government, despite many authorities being already on their knees. He also appeared to have made no provision to enhance spending in 'protected' areas such as health and education after 2021–22, despite the very obvious need for such spending, a glaring omission that led commentators to question the credibility of his forecasts for bringing the public finances back under control. Within twenty-four hours of the budget speech, the Institute for Fiscal Studies' director, Paul Johnson, had given a public briefing in which he suggested that Sunak's planned tightening of spending would, in his opinion, unravel pretty quickly, saying he would offer odds of 10 to 1 against it actually happening.[2] If Johnson turns out to be right on the spending outlook, then clearly Sunak's push for fiscal balance can only imply a rethink on taxation. The Institute for Fiscal Studies pointed this out, too, as did the Office for Budget Responsibility in its published assessment of the risks in the budget spending forecasts.[3]

Whichever way you look at it, spending pressures were going to be coming in thick and fast from all directions. The shopping list of demands in the post-pandemic world was long, starting with the multi-billion cost of maintaining a mass population vaccination programme, very possibly a continuing and hopefully better test and trace function and certainly an adequate PPE supply. And that was before making allowance in the health budget to deal with the vast backlog of diagnostic work, operations and routine treatment that had built up and now needed urgent action, as well as the long-term health needs arising from the phenomenon of long COVID.

Then there would be pressures to get to grips with the inequalities that had only intensified during the pandemic. At the very least there would be calls for a more tangible recognition – beyond the weekly clapping of the lockdown – of the immense sacrifice of health and care workers, who had forfeited such a lot and been exposed to so much danger. Just as pressing would be the retraining and support

needed for those especially young people, who were
without work, not to mention funds for the educational
catch-up that was going to be required, especially for more
disadvantaged pupils. A deepening poverty crisis in the autumn of 2021 when the economic support schemes were
due to end, including an almost certain rise in demand for
supported housing as people lost their homes, and, one
presumes, urgent action to tackle food poverty, would
only pile on further pressures.

Politicians also know that sooner or later (preferably the
former) we would need to face up to the climate emergency
and start getting properly serious about spending on that.
Add in the still-unresolved issue of how to pay for the costs
of an ageing population and their inexorably rising need
for health, social care and pension support and an inevitable logic was emerging. If we need to *spend* more money,
indeed if we want to spend more money, then we'd need
to *have* more money, and rather a lot of it by the looks of
it.[4] The days of the low-tax, low-spend state were looking
well and truly numbered.

Surveys testing the public mood confirmed it. An appetite not for cuts but for raising public spending, even if it
meant tax rises to fund them, had been coming through
loud and clear for some time.[5] It may have escaped the notice of the party in power, but the drivers for a bigger, more
proactive state that had come to the fore in the emergency
of the pandemic were not going to be so easily put back
into the bottle now that the genie was out.

If an enlarged public sphere was where we were now
heading, a key question remained over how we would
choose to pay for it all after the dust had settled on the
immediate crisis and spending needed to be supported by
money coming in. Were we just going to say that everyone's taxes would be going up? That the younger generation, whom we had already confined indoors when they

should have been socialising, building relationships and progressing their education and careers, would be asked to pay more? Or that ordinary workers who had scraped along through lockdown would be hit with tax rises or sustained pay freezes, as appeared to be part of the plan? Or somehow contort to blame the old (those who had survived) and ask them to pay?[6] Or was there a fairer, and indeed, a more obvious, alternative?

Will We Find the Pot of Gold?

Many of the extremely wealthy appeared resigned to what might be coming their way. As early as April 2020, Deloitte's regular survey of chief financial officers had asked them how they thought policy would change in response to the pandemic and its fallout. They were hard-pushed to find any who, even at that early point, were not expecting rises in corporation or household taxation.[7] In the same month, the columnist Merryn Somerset Webb published an article in the *Financial Times* titled 'The Pandemic and the Radical Change in Wealth Distribution to Come'. She drew on history to argue, with evident unease, that '[t]axes are bound to go up on those with unearned income'.[8]

It seems the wealthy had started to realise that this was what the population now wanted. A YouGov poll in May 2020 was pretty unequivocal – 61 per cent of those questioned thought that there should be a wealth tax on those with more than £750,000 in assets excluding pensions and main homes.[9] It fits with the wider view from survey evidence that shows pretty clearly that people now viewed wealth gaps as too wide. In a pan-European survey, 20 per cent of British respondents thought differences in wealth were fair, but 59 per cent thought they were too high – see Figure 9 – a view repeated across most of the other European countries included.[10]

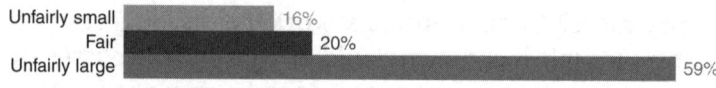

In your opinion, are differences in wealth in Britain unfairly small, fair, or unfairly large?

Unfairly small   16%
Fair   20%
Unfairly large   59%

Figure 9. Attitudes to differences in wealth.
Note: European Social Survey wave 9 (2018/19), adults in Britain.
Source: Curtice, Hudson and Montagu (2020)

Only a few diehards – funnily enough, mostly from the ranks of the super-wealthy – still seemed to think these issues could be put on the backburner. Of course, the government had been pretty distracted in mid-2020 with all the work managing the pandemic. It couldn't really have been expected to set up some kind of policy commission to pore over the issues involved in taxing the wealthy even if it had wanted to.[11] But the appetite for an almighty debate to decide who would be asked to put their hands deepest into their pockets appeared to be getting stronger. It was going to happen anyway, whatever the government did.

The Institute for Fiscal Studies helpfully stepped in to start the ball rolling. Even better, they got hold of Gus O'Donnell, former Treasury permanent secretary and cabinet secretary to three prime ministers, for an event in July 2020 to launch the work of a new Wealth Tax Commission, bringing together academics, policy makers and tax practitioners to look in detail at the case for a wealth tax and the practicalities of implementing one.[12]

O'Donnell spoke eloquently at the project launch of the 'burning platform' of debt and deficits, of the flip from spending reductions to tax rises as the public's remedy of choice and of the fairness of wealth taxes for a government committed to levelling up. Ever one to read the political runes, he knew that timing was all – a Conservative government with a large majority could seize the moment in a way that a Labour government could not when it came to tapping the wealthy for more.[13]

There are many ways to tax wealth. The Wealth Tax Commission was all about a tax on the ownership of wealth – houses, possibly the value of pension pots, land, works of art, cash holdings and so on. Despite lots of plus sides, the key blot on the copybook of a wealth tax is that it has failed so often before. Lloyd George's People's Budget of 1909 had included a land value tax that would apply to unearned increases in land value when land changed hands as well as levying tax on any increase in the value to land that resulted from public expenditure, for instance a new railway station. Although this was passed into law in 1910 it was repealed in 1920 on the grounds that it was too difficult to administer.[14] The Labour chancellor Denis Healey was similarly unable to find a way of implementing the wealth tax proposals in both of Labour's 1974 election manifestos that would produce enough revenue to justify the administrative and political cost. Switzerland, Spain and Norway are now the only major European countries that still retain a comprehensive annual wealth tax, with rates kept acceptably low.

The naysayers in any discussion of a wealth tax will no doubt point to the elderly pensioner living with just their memories in a large house they can barely afford as it is. They will argue for reliefs and exceptions that whittle away at whatever is agreed. There are ways round that. One would be to focus on reforming the way that wealth is passed between generations, reducing how much can be transferred tax free and perhaps making it an income tax on those who receive it, rather than an inheritance tax on an estate. There are plenty of smart proposals around for how to do this.[15]

Another way to approach it would be to have a one-off wealth tax – an emergency passing around of the hat, not a repeated raid. It could miss out the ordinary saver or homeowner and just be passed to the really big wealth holders, perhaps with an appeal to their public-spiritedness. And if they really couldn't afford it right now they could pop in an IOU and pay when they sold something or just leave it until after their death.

This, too, is an idea that has a long pedigree. The renowned British economist A.C. Pigou called during the First World War for a huge one-time levy – he proposed 25 per cent – on wealth holdings, arguing that 'considerations of fairness directly demand it', and pointing to the sacrifices that war had required of others.[16] But it was an ask that was never to be implemented.

The fact remains though that, according to those who make it their business to analyse this stuff, the taxation of wealth has not caught up with rising wealth accumulation.[17] With overall taxation standing at roughly a third of GDP, our vastly increased levels of private wealth still contribute only around a tenth of that revenue. Stretching right back to the 1960s and 70s wealth taxation has stayed stable at around 3 per cent of GDP.

But the stock of wealth has rocketed, more than doubling over that time, when expressed as a percentage of GDP, as in Figure 10, from three times to seven times its value. Nearly half of all this increased wealth (45 per cent) is in the hands of the richest 10 per cent of households. Yet nothing has been done to capture that enormous gain. Why should the yield from wealth tax remain at 3 per cent of GDP, when it would clearly be more proportionate and in line with its own massive increase if it now raised about 7 per cent? That lost opportunity appears in Figure 10 as the ever-widening crocodile mouth.

The rich, then, are getting richer *and* it seems clinging on to their ever-rising piles of wealth. Those who are investing their wealth productively in new business enterprises or similar will be taxed on the income they make from that capital investment. Those with 'idle' capital, not making a contribution to the economy, are by contrast taxed far less. This is another distortion that we could now start to address because it would actually be good for the economy – giving greater incentives to those who put their capital to productive use. In that sense it has been argued that a wealth tax 'acts as capitalism's handmaiden by rewarding good entrepreneurs and punishing bad ones'.[18]

Maybe in these extraordinary times we will work out how to take a slice of the wealth mountains that have been building for decades in a way that is genuinely workable. If Switzerland and others can do it on an ongoing basis by keeping realistic the amount of tax asked for, maybe the time has come for us to try, too. Or we could learn from the one-off wealth taxes that have worked at times of crisis in other countries, including in France, Germany and Japan after the Second World War and in Ireland after the 2008 financial crisis.[19] A one-off wealth tax also has the added benefit that it is particularly efficient as a tax because it doesn't lead to people changing their behaviour in the way

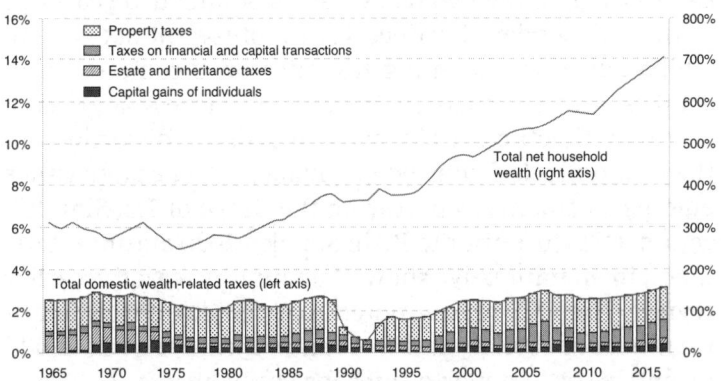

Figure 10. Total household wealth and amount of wealth taxed, each as a percentage of Gross Domestic Product in Great Britain, 1965–2017. Source: Bangham and Leslie (2019), Resolution Foundation

that permanent taxes do, providing it is kept secret until the point at which it is announced.

Clearly there are many who agree that introducing a wealth tax is now an appropriate move. A new insight into the public mood came from the think tank Demos, who published a report on the public's attitudes towards tax rises in September 2020 – fully informed by the devastation of the first wave of the pandemic. They found that 63 per cent of those questioned (in a representative sample of 2,000 UK adults) supported a one-off 10 per cent tax on wealth holdings over £2 million, excluding main homes and pension funds. Only 11 per cent opposed the idea.[20]

And, of course, besides a direct tax on wealth there are also what the tax guru Richard Murphy and many others see as more accessible low-hanging fruits. There is no reason, for instance, why the taxation of capital gains – the *returns* to wealth that come from asset appreciation – should not immediately be put on a par with the taxation of earned income. For that to happen, Capital Gains Tax would need to be raised so that it is equalised with income tax and the current offsetting allowances reduced or removed. A radical overhaul of the two taxes was recommended years ago in the independent Mirrlees Review of the UK tax system, which advocated 'aligning tax rates on income from all sources', not so much on grounds of fairness as of actual economic efficiency, because it reduces distortions in the economic decisions people make.[21] These same issues emerged again in a report from the Office of Tax Simplification (OTS) just prior to Rishi Sunak's 2020 autumn statement, in an impressive show of unanimity with the earlier review. The OTS review noted that the current different treatment of capital gains is 'counter-intuitive, creates odd incentives or … opportunities for tax avoidance'.[22]

Demos specifically examined this question, too.[23] They found that 46 per cent of people in their study supported the idea of equalising the tax on income from capital gains with income from work, exceeding by some margin the 18 per cent who opposed it. The OTS report concludes that 'more closely aligning capital gains tax rates with income tax rates has the potential to raise a substantial amount of tax for the Exchequer'.[24] The Institute for Public Policy Research had a go at estimating this, finding that taxing capital gains at the same rate as income and abolishing the annual exempt allowance would raise in the region of £10 to £20 billion a year, after allowing for people adapting their behaviour.[25] This is a pretty remarkable amount of extra revenue and it increases the efficiency of the economy to boot. What's not to like?

Now that we have started to bite the bullet on business taxation, raising corporation tax to nearer the OECD norm, why not also levy a one-off windfall tax on businesses whose profits have been supercharged during the pandemic? After all we did something similar in the 1980s when we taxed the oil companies' windfall profits. Those who found themselves in the right place at the right time were able to make a fortune on the back of the huge changes people made to their lives during the lockdowns. Amazon is one, benefiting from the mass switch to home delivery, and of course Zoom and other online meeting and e-learning platforms also made phenomenal profits, along with delivery companies, cycle and e-scooter businesses, toys, video games and streaming services to name but a few. Banks, too, were making money without risk from government-supported loans, arguably, therefore, another potential candidate for an ad hoc tax.

What about the elephant in the room? Council Tax was introduced in 1993, replacing domestic rates, a tax that was directly proportional to a property's market rental value. Council Tax, by contrast, is levied in broad bands based on a property's capital value, and has become increasingly regressive over the years. It is based on valuations of properties from 1991 that have never been updated, benefiting those whose property values have risen the most. This creates some quite absurd anomalies. Apparently a £150,000 home in Middlesbrough has a higher Council Tax bill than a £2.5 million mansion in Westminster![26]

On top of this, landlords not living in their house can simply pass the tax on to their tenants, although many – students for instance – don't have to pay it at all. If there is any justice in the post-COVID world, this anomalous mishmash will be at the front of the queue for reform when the politicians and committees start to get their teeth into all of this. We can't afford to continue losing out from such a botched and regressive attempt at a property tax.

The Institute for Fiscal Studies published an analysis in March 2020 showing how Council Tax reform could actually support the levelling up agenda, if more money was raised overall via a revaluation and was then channelled into less well-off areas. If properties are revalued and then taxed at a fixed percentage rate local authorities in areas with high-value properties would raise much more money and could be given less central government funding. The money saved could instead be allocated to areas whose tax base had been reduced by the revaluation. This redistribution in effect from the wealthier South to the North and Midlands would significantly benefit households and authorities in those regions and at the same time help in reducing regional inequality.[27]

It can hardly be claimed that the wealthy are hard done by in our current system. Little more than 1 per cent of wealth has been taken each year in tax since 1990, roughly half of the percentage taken during the 1970s and first half of the 1980s.[28] And wealth is the gift that keeps on giving (but only to those who have it). We've already seen how the better-off had been building up savings while confined indoors by COVID-19, how furlough protected landlords' income, and how those who are already wealthy are likely to benefit from further asset appreciation in the years ahead, with some having already banked big gains during the pandemic. That will be piled on top of the earlier increases in wealth concentrations that were allowed to build unchecked in the era of neoliberalism. There is indeed a rich seam to mine here.

That there is a case for a focus on wealth in the wake of the pandemic is hard to deny. Torsten Bell, chief executive of the Resolution Foundation, set out the argument with admirable clarity,

Wealth has grown much faster than income in recent decades. But wealth taxes have not risen at all and are riddled with problems. That is not a situation a post-virus Britain can afford.[29]

There is a moral issue here, too, sitting alongside any economic case. The rich have benefited from the crisis far more than anyone else, and, just as they did a decade ago, have the capacity to contribute to resolving it. If we can't find a way to make this happen now, the risk is that we will end up unable to respond to the very real economic and social challenges we are going to be facing in the coming years.

Today's politicians would do well to consider the example of Robert Peel in 1846. Although as leader of the Conservative Party he was there to represent those with wealth, it was Peel who led the movement to repeal the protectionist Corn Laws of 1815, which were simply lining the pockets of wealthy landowners. In the crisis caused by the potato blight, which was threatening the Irish population with starvation, Peel needed to take action, choosing to abandon a policy that had served the most wealthy in society for decades.[30]

What will it take to deliver an equivalent response today? COVID-19 has magnified inequalities, and the sense of resentment will build like a pressure cooker. The need to pick up the tatters of our minimalist state and welfare system will have to be addressed sooner or later. We saw the young footballer Marcus Rashford appeal directly to Boris Johnson to protect free school meals through the summer of 2020, passionately championing children whose well-being was hanging by a thread, as his own had been a few short years earlier.[31] Successful then and awarded an MBE shortly afterwards, he was unable to break through the Conservatives' resistance a second time when it came to free school meals during the autumn half-term. Despite amassing over 1 million signatures on his petition to parliament to keep children adequately fed, it was left to local businesses and cash-strapped local authorities to step in to fill the gap on that occasion.

When northern cities went into partial local lockdowns in October 2020 Louise Casey, an adviser over twenty years to governments of left and right, warned of poverty and destitution in the months ahead and her fear of a return 'to the days where people can't put shoes on their children's feet'.[32] As the rest of the country followed into a full lockdown in November that, after the brief December unlock, was to continue for months, with all the additional hardship this would bring, one key question still remained to be answered: what will the richest in society do to respond?

When the Wealth Tax Commission reported in December 2020, they looked at possible options for a one-off tax on wealth that would include property and pensions. They concluded that a 1 per cent levy on all wealth and assets over £500,000 (£1 million for a couple owning their assets jointly) and levied each year for five years would raise £260 billion, the same amount of money as a 6p rise in VAT or an increase in the basic rate of tax of 9p over the same time period.[33] They also, incidentally, found that the administrative costs of raising a wealth tax that had so exercised both Denis Healey and Lloyd George in the past were no longer an issue – now amounting to no more, as a percentage of the tax raised, than the cost of PAYE administration.[34]

As Arun Advani, one of the academics who worked on the Wealth Tax Commission, said when the report was published,

We're often told that the only way to raise serious tax revenue is from income tax, national insurance contributions, or VAT. That simply isn't the case, so it is a political choice where to get the money from, if and when there are tax rises.[35]

9 RETHINKING WELFARE

Is It Time for a No-Strings Attached Universal Basic Income?

The short answer is no. As emotions ran high in the dark days of the COVID-19 pandemic the idea of a Universal Basic Income (UBI) – a regular sum of money paid to all citizens with no questions asked and nothing expected in return – resurfaced with renewed vigour. It is easy to see why this might be seen as a solution to the economic hardship that people were anticipating.

First of all, the current welfare safety net was so flimsy and full of holes that anything that promised a more substantial backstop against poverty and loss of entitlement was bound to be appealing. Secondly, fears had been swirling around for some time that artificial intelligence (AI) would soon displace workers with automated alternatives. The so-called 'fourth industrial revolution' would, it was believed, put even skilled jobs such as medical diagnostics or financial advice in the firing line alongside the more routinised work that is always vulnerable to machine replacement. Thirdly, and now to the fore, it was feared that a prolonged period of social distancing could force large-scale restructuring and potentially permanent job losses in the most exposed parts of what has become known as the 'social' economy – high street retail, pubs, restaurants, leisure and the arts.

With pandemic losses and technological advances combining with calls to rein back our addiction to growth in the name of environmental sustainability, many see a 'post-work' world hovering on the horizon. It is a vista in which unpaid work in the home or community – caring or volunteering – and perhaps some part-time employment could become the norm for many if secured by an underpinning citizen's income. With increased time for leisure, new creativity and enhanced life choices might then replace stigmatised unemployment. Somewhere in the back of one's mind one thinks of aristocrats, such as the poet Lord Byron, cushioned by inherited wealth while they produced the great works of early nineteenth-century literature. Or bands like UB40 – who appropriated both the name of the benefit claim form and titled their first hit album *Signing Off* – rising to fame in the 1970s after an apprenticeship on the dole, conveniently free from any risk of being offered a job. A guaranteed income works in a myriad of ways for a myriad of people.

If UBI is, at least in the popular imagination, an idea whose time has come, it is not a new idea by any means. Milton Friedman – the right-wing libertarian behind Margaret Thatcher's monetarist experiment in the 1980s that pushed unemployment up over 3 million – had proposed something similar in the 1950s with his idea of a 'negative' income tax. Indeed, governments around the world of any and all political persuasions have been investigating UBI in one form or another for decades. That of course raises one or two alarm bells, since no country has actually gone on to introduce a fully comprehensive UBI. Is it at the end of the day unworkably utopian? So costly it could never be delivered? Too corrosive of the work ethic – a 'Shirker's Charter' in the words of Margaret Thatcher? Perhaps it is some or all of these. But before we get into that there is a more fundamental objection.

This is simply that Universal Basic Income doesn't change anything about who owns and who controls the power in our economy. As the economist Christina Berry wrote in the *IPPR Progressive Review* in June 2020, '[it] is still a form of redistribution, albeit on a grand scale … . It does not alter … . the true operating system of our economy.'[1] In other words a UBI that simply sits within a liberalised market system with all its distrust of regulation, including regulation of wages and working conditions, and its baked-in inequalities of wealth and power, may not actually provide the solution to poverty that people are seeking.[2]

This matters because in the hands of a right-wing administration UBI payments could be downgraded in exactly the way that benefits have been eroded under Universal Credit. Even a relatively generous UBI can lull people into thinking that they have done what needs to be done to ameliorate the big issues of poverty and insecurity, not recognising that it has only put a sticking plaster over them, without addressing their root causes. If on top of this the cost of delivering a Universal Basic Income means that money is diverted from vital public services – which some of UBI's supporters do indeed advocate – then it will weaken, not strengthen, the core of our welfare state. And that does most disservice to those who start off with the least, paradoxically running the risk of subverting the true spirit of 'universal' provision.

There is in any case a catch-22 that almost certainly scuppers a fully formed Universal Basic Income. Even its strongest proponents are aware that a UBI set at an amount that was enough to live off would be unaffordable – it would simply cost the state too much. But by the same token setting UBI at a level that was affordable to the state would be incapable of providing people with an adequate income to meet their living costs.

The difficulty is that the strength of a Universal Basic Income – that it is available without means-test or conditions – is also its Achilles Heel. Everyone – prince or pauper – gets it and they could win the lottery or marry a billionaire and still carry on getting it. That's an expensive commitment to universalism. The International Labour Organization (ILO) has estimated that, in the UK and most other high-income countries, a full UBI available to all without conditions and sufficient to live off would cost around 30 per cent of GDP each year.[3] This would be on top of all the other calls on public spending – the costs of continually maintaining and upgrading the nation's physical infrastructure, providing education, health and social care and so on.

There are, of course, ways of defraying the costs, and there is a small industry of modellers working away to illustrate how this might be done.[4] Some of the detailed options that have surfaced recently would abolish or significantly reduce the income tax allowance (£12,500 in 2020–21) and use this money to create a universal payment for all, adding in a basic income allowance for children, too. The authors of these models calculate that a Universal Basic Income of between £60 and £65 a week per adult and £40 per child could be partly paid for via the recirculated tax allowance and savings made on Child Benefit.

But their calculations also require higher rates of both basic and top rate tax and an increase in National Insurance contributions for higher earners to achieve even that relatively small income transfer.[5] These researchers celebrate the independence this small UBI payment would give to many who currently get no benefits at all – large numbers of (mainly female) carers for instance – and calculate that it would lead to a significant reduction in extreme poverty compared to the current situation. But they also acknowledge that a payment of a little over £3,000 a year would have to have other means-tested benefits including disability and family support grafted onto it in any realistic scenario. That being the case, one has to question whether it is really the best way of delivering resources within our welfare state. Would it not be better to focus on overhauling and better directing the support that we provide for those most in need?

'Dignity and Security'

In the middle of the COVID-19 pandemic a House of Lords committee put out a report with the self-explanatory title, 'Universal Credit Isn't Working'.[6] It was not Universal Credit per se that they had a problem with – if its attempt to integrate benefits into a streamlined system had done just that it might even have improved things. What their Lordships were concerned about was what they saw as unprecedented numbers of people forced to rely on food banks to feed their families and equally worrying numbers not able to afford their rent. As we know this stems from a toxic combination of inadequate payments and deliberate administrative delays, both of which were built into the operation of Universal Credit from the outset. They singled out the five-week wait for benefits as particularly harmful for the way that it 'entrenches debt, increases extreme poverty and harms vulnerable groups disproportionately'.[7] The report called for root and branch changes to make Universal Credit 'fit for purpose' as a dependable safety net, giving those seeking support the 'dignity and security' they deserve.

This appeal for a more compassionate approach to our fellow citizens might make us reflect for a moment on the meaning of the word 'welfare'. A contemporary dictionary definition states that welfare is simply 'help given ... to people who need it'.[8] Because that help is now often provided through state financial assistance, those receiving it are frequently described as being 'on welfare' or 'getting a handout', phrases bandied about not always in the most complimentary of tones.

But this seems to miss something rather more fundamental. If we say we are concerned about a person's welfare, we are generally seeking reassurance about their well-being, their health, comfort and happiness. Indeed, the origin of the word 'welfare' is believed to be the Old English phrase 'wel faren' – to fare well, get along successfully or prosper.

So rather than its current somewhat corrupted meaning as a handout, perhaps we should reclaim the idea of welfare – support given to others – as something that is there to help people to thrive and prosper.

If we can agree on the meaning of welfare, then we should be able to agree on the purpose of the safety net payments that welfare states provide. As Elizabeth I originally set out over four centuries ago in her far-sighted Poor Laws, a nurturing and protective state must provide its citizens with an entitlement to protection or 'relief' from specific vulnerabilities or circumstances, to which we are all potentially subject, and which might lead to destitution and insecurity. The core of this entitlement was to make sure people's most basic needs for food and shelter were met, without which well-being would suffer. Astonishing, then, that these are the very two things that the House of Lords' investigation found that the UK, the sixth richest country in the world, is not currently able to secure for some of its most vulnerable citizens, 420 years after having pioneered such a system – the first in world history.

How could we have got into this position? Clearly, a narrative of austerity framed as a battle against 'benefit scroungers' has enabled politicians with a particular agenda to press ahead with welfare reforms that would not be out of place in Dickensian Britain with its stigmatising workhouses. By late 2020 some politicians at least had stopped trying to pretend that they had any higher motivations in doing this. On 27th October, in an interview on BBC Radio 4 Stephen Crabb – and note this is the man who in 2016 succeeded Iain Duncan Smith as Secretary of State for Work and Pensions – made this quite breathtaking admission:

> one of the things that's been driving the increase in child poverty and this issue of food poverty is the fact that working age benefits in the United Kingdom have become too squeezed. There was a deliberate policy choice that was taken five years ago to do

that and the truth is that … surviving for any length of time just on Universal Credit is very, very difficult for a family and that's been one of the factors driving poverty rates in the country.[9]

Why are there no safeguards beyond the ballot box to stop this happening? Why is there no collective agreement on what a fit-for-purpose safety net would look like?

In 2019 when IPPR took a forensic look at the design of the UK's social security system they concluded that 'the calculation of benefit levels has always been based on historical precedent rather than any independent assessment of what is needed to afford the basic goods and services to get by'.[10] The economist Stewart Lansley agreed, writing in 2020 that 'Britain has never come close to creating a robust income floor' so that the current benefit system 'fails the key test of a robust defence against poverty'. Most benefit levels are, as he points out, below those in other comparable nations and in some cases lower as a ratio of typical earnings than in the 1970s and earlier.[11]

While the benefit freezes of austerity have undoubtedly accentuated the problem, arguably they couldn't have happened if we'd had some sort of locked-in guarantee of what a 'national minimum of civilised life' would consist of. This was the touchstone called for as long ago as 1909 by the social reformer Beatrice Webb.[12] Social commentators can and do work out how many people are living in absolute poverty or material deprivation (not being able to afford to heat their homes for instance) to show what a lack of that minimum guarantee looks like – it's not nice. But there is nothing that forces politicians to act on that and nothing that forces those graduating from comfortable middle-class upbringings to leafy southern constituencies to even confront it.[13]

In fact, on taking office in 2015 one of the Conservatives' first acts, now unrestrained by the Liberal Democrats in the 2010 coalition, was to repeal the closest thing we had at that time to an anti-poverty guarantee. New Labour's 2010 Child Poverty Act had set statutory targets for the reduction of both absolute and relative child poverty, requiring future governments to make sure policies were put in place to achieve this. Labour's original aspiration had been to eliminate child poverty within a generation. The Act included duties on local authorities to publish child poverty strategies and action plans for their locality. This was not only about benefits and income transfers. It was a holistic approach to poverty reduction that tackled issues from low skills and lack of work to school attendance and teenage parenthood.

While preparing to remove the Act from the statute books in 2016 the Conservatives had also planned to stop publishing official data that would enable trends in child poverty to be tracked. They backed down on this after vocal protests by campaign groups, charities and academics.[14] But they proceeded in any case to pursue policies that were bound to increase child poverty, having now successfully freed themselves from the constraints of the statutory targets.

Fast-forward to the autumn of 2020 and we find ourselves in the position where it fell to the president of the Royal College of Paediatrics and Child Health, Russell Viner, speaking on behalf of his profession, to spell out exactly how poverty was now affecting children, when he said that

We care for children who don't have enough to eat. We see far too many of them. It is heartbreaking that it has become a normal part of our jobs and hunger is all too common for millions of families in the UK.[15]

He and his colleagues were appealing to the government to support Marcus Rashford's campaign to extend free school meals into the October half-term to help families struggling to keep their heads above water. Many of the children that paediatricians were seeing going hungry will be those whose parents, either unemployed or in low-paid jobs, could not claim means-tested benefits for them because they had fallen foul of the two-child limit. As stated previously, by July 2020 almost a million children were living in families who were having benefit payments restricted because their families were deemed to be too big.[16] Why that should be taken out on the children is unclear.

If further evidence of the cruelty of the benefits system were needed, the British Pregnancy Advisory Service reported in December 2020 that over half of the women it surveyed who had an abortion during the pandemic and who were aware that they were facing the two-child limit cited it as an important factor in their decision. One mother said, 'If there was no two-child limit, I would

Image 19. Mural of footballer Marcus Rashford, MBE, with pizza boxes celebrating his campaign on child hunger.
Source: Nathan Stirk / Getty Images

have kept the baby, but I couldn't afford to feed and clothe it ... I've really struggled to come to terms with my decision.'[17]

It is surely a mark of the ethical bankruptcy of the Johnson government that the nation's moral compass had fallen into the hands of the young England footballer. As much as we applaud and admire Rashford's work and commitment, it should never come to celebrities corralling the government into feeding hungry children in a pandemic. Yet in an astonishing and completely disingenuous response to calls from all quarters backing Rashford's plea to keep free school meals going over the October 2020 half-term break, government ministers and many of their MPs repeatedly argued that the hike in Universal Credit earlier in the year had already improved the 'generosity' of benefits.

As we have already spelt out, the increase in Universal Credit in April 2020 added around £1,000 a year to benefits. The value of benefits removed from the average out-of-work family with children since 2011 is £2,900. Without the increase in Universal Credit they would have lost even more.[18] The government's position was smoke and mirrors. Of course, it helps if you give people back part of what you took away from them. But you can't relieve them from the actual poverty that you have put them in year after year unless you restore everything you removed.

The fact that anyone in government could even pretend that the level of Universal Credit was something to be celebrated arguably could only happen because there was no agreed standard for what a decent safety net should look like or how it should be provided. And it is that lack of any kind of anchor that enabled the government to seesaw once again into providing free meals for children in the Christmas holidays when things got too hot for them politically and Rashford stepped in once more to breach their defence.

That was of course another political sticking plaster, a reactive U-turn by a government who would have known that two weeks of food relief was not going to cut through to the real problem. When Scrooge in Dickens' *A Christmas Carol* gives his clerk Bob Cratchit a turkey to feed his family at Christmas, he doesn't stop there. He realises that he must also give him the pay rise that he had been so meanly withholding, without which, as the 'Ghost of Christmas Yet to Come' reveals, the clerk's disabled child, Tiny Tim, is sure to die. Published in 1843, Dickens' novel was a morality tale of its time, one we revisit each Christmas on our TV screens, and more poignant than ever in the year of COVID-19 to see the sickly Tiny Tim restored to health by Scrooge's new-found generosity.

What of today's Tiny Tims? The accelerating problem of child poverty, particularly for families with three or more children, was, by late 2020, leading some commentators to call for an emergency uprating of Child Benefit – the only remaining benefit not limited to two children. Gordon Brown, architect of New Labour's child poverty strategy, called for urgent financial measures to support those with children, including an immediate increase in Child Benefit, in a speech to an anti-poverty event organised by the Child Poverty Action Group in December 2020, in which he said, 'poverty now wears a very young face'.[19] This would have been a rapid and effective way of supporting families facing acute deprivation during the pandemic. Raising Child Benefit would target money at children far more directly than the £20 a week uprating of Universal Credit, applied per household. As a universal benefit, it would also support families facing severe difficulties who were not able to claim Universal Credit.

If we want to get serious, though, about making our safety net fit for purpose on a permanent basis we need to go further. First of all we need to take a step back and agree on what core goods and services are needed for people to live decently and to be able to participate in our contemporary society. We must then permanently commit to setting benefits at a level that will enable families to be able to afford them. Just as importantly there must be a legal guarantee for how benefits are to be increased each year to avoid a future government imposing benefit freezes as was done during austerity. None of this is difficult. It just requires the political will to do it.

To see what is possible, let's start with a good news story – pensioners. The Pensions Act 2007 set out a requirement for the state pension to be uprated each year at least in line with earnings. In fact the 'triple lock', announced by the Coalition government in 2010 and still in place in 2020, gives an even stronger guarantee, providing for pensions to rise in line with prices, earnings or 2.5 per cent, *whichever is the highest*. When the September 2020 inflation figure of 0.5 per cent was announced it was confirmed that state pensions would therefore increase by 2.5 per cent the following April as neither earnings (which fell during lockdown) nor prices were rising at anything close to that level. This is in complete contrast, then, to the convention, in any case now ignored for years, that all other benefits are just pegged to inflation.

Pensioners' special status doesn't stop there. They are also entitled to a guaranteed minimum level of income. Since 2003 this has been included in a payment called Guarantee Credit which is claimed via Pension Credit. The minimum guaranteed income for pensioners stood at £173.75 per week in 2020 for a single person and, like the state pension, it is required in law to go up each year by at least the same amount as earnings. Anyone who does not have a full state pension or sufficient other income can claim to have their income topped up accordingly.

Contrast this with the basic Universal Credit payment, still only £94.70 after the emergency uprating in April 2020. A single person aged sixty-five claiming basic benefits will find themselves getting £94.70 a week up until their sixty-sixth birthday at which point they suddenly become entitled to have their weekly income topped up to £173.75 through the Guarantee Credit payment. It's a nice birthday present – for once a vertical ascent instead of a cliff-edge fall. It explains why the WASPI women (Women Against State Pension Inequality) were so desperate for support during the extra years in their sixties when they were suddenly ineligible for retirement benefits after their pension age was raised on an accelerated timetable. With many unable to get suitable work due to age, illness, disability or caring responsibilities, falling back on working age benefits risked pushing them into poverty.

For those over pension age, though, all these new protections have at least coincided with a much welcomed reduction in pensioner poverty. While 26 per cent of pensioners were defined as below the poverty line at the start of the century this had fallen to 16 per cent by 2019, with much of the impact seen at the point at which Pension Credit was introduced.[20] The triple lock on pensions is likely to come under increasing pressure over the next few years as the older population rises to record levels, and cost savings are sought. That's if it even survives the pandemic. As and when this happens, it will become all the more important to ensure that the least well-off pensioners still have the security of the Guarantee Credit to fall back on.

It's worth noting that it's not just pensioners who have seen legal guarantees protecting their income put in place. Workers also have them in the form of the minimum wage, brought in as one of New Labour's first acts on taking office. The Low Pay Commission, established in statute by the National Minimum Wage Act 1998, advises on the level at which it should be set each year, after experts have weighed up the arguments of both workers and employers. The Commission's conclusions attract considerable political and media attention and once the new minimum wage is announced workers must then have their earnings uprated accordingly.

Why shouldn't we protect others in this way? The Institute for Public Policy Research has proposed that a 'Minimum Income Commission' should be created to advise the government on the calculation and uprating of benefits, just as the Low Pay Commission advises on wages.[21] That would be a good start. We could throw in the idea that there should be legislation to *require* that Universal Credit payments, after being initially reset at an acceptable level, are uprated according to an agreed annual benchmark, mirroring the guarantees we give to pensioners. In the aftermath of the pandemic there is also an even stronger argument for re-establishing targets on poverty along the lines of those in New Labour's 2010 Child Poverty Act.

Each year in Britain there is an official survey of 'social attitudes', seeking views on issues as diverse as gender relations, sexuality, race and immigration, the behaviour of businesses and, always without fail, whether people think welfare benefits are too generous or not generous enough. For the first time in more than two decades more people in 2019 agreed with the statement that benefits are 'too low and cause hardship' than those who thought they were 'too high and discourage work'.[22] That's a good springboard for doing something about it. And if that was what people thought *before* COVID-19, heaven knows what the 2020 survey, taken after all the months of lockdown, will have had to say on the matter.

Surely, though, we can devise a rather more sophisticated method than an annual opinion poll to act as a catalyst for change. What we urgently need now is a national conversation about how we redesign our safety net so that we can guarantee the dignity and security – the welfare – of our fellow citizens, including our nation's children, in good times and bad. We've seen now what the bad times really look like. Let's get serious about doing something about it.

Universal Services

A modern welfare state needs to be about much more than its safety net, important though that is. On top of ensuring people do not fall into poverty or destitution, it must also provide empowering positive freedoms – the freedoms to participate and prosper and to make one's own life better. This requires us, as the renowned economist Amartya Sen has argued, to nurture what he calls people's 'capabilities'.[23] We must support people to thrive as healthy and empowered citizens able to make genuinely free choices, informed about the options and consequences and with equitable access to the opportunities and alternatives that their society affords.

Back in 1942 when William Beveridge produced his famous report laying the foundations for the UK's post-war welfare state, he famously evoked 'five giants' that must first be overcome if the working classes were to prosper. These colossal barriers were, in his words, want (poverty), disease, ignorance (lack of education), squalor (poor housing) and idleness (lack of work).[24]

Image 20. William Beveridge's five Giants: Want, Ignorance, Disease, Squalor and Idleness.
Source: Fabians.org.uk

Beveridge's approach was both a diagnosis of and a remedy for the ills afflicting his society. The great post-war initiatives to establish the National Health Service, give free secondary education to all, provide affordable and decent homes and take action to secure labour rights and full employment (at least for men) all sought to overcome these scourges of deprivation and disempowerment.

Although it faced a mammoth task and it was certainly the case that engrained poverty remained a persistent challenge, the scope of the welfare state's vision had embraced the capabilities that Sen was later to champion. Overcoming the obstacles to this was not only a matter of social justice. The post-war investment in a healthier, better-educated, properly housed population would also go on to power a high-performing economy. Investing in our people was every bit as important as investing in our physical capital.

Public services investment today still forms the mainstay of welfare state spending in all advanced economies, far exceeding amounts spent on safety net – 'Robin Hood' – transfers between people.[25] Where good-quality services are made available universally so that everyone, rich or poor, is able to benefit, public buy-in to keeping them well-funded is likely to be high. If, however, the quality of public services is degraded by budget cuts or access is made more limited or only partially funded, as is the case with health care in the USA, then divisions start to emerge. Those who can afford to will move back to paying for services privately, often taking out insurance to do so. Employers may also contribute as part of a package to retain workers, actively encouraged in this of course by cost-cutting governments. Those who can't afford to, or who are not willing to go into the private market, will find service levels most likely further eroded and, in the case of health, some will be forced to endure pain and illness as they wait for access to treatment.

Austerity has, as we have shown, severely impacted public service provision in the UK, in effect devaluing our 'social wage' – the value of the services we receive as of right on top of our earned income. We are no longer investing effectively in our population's welfare. Instead entitlements and public service spending have been cut back, despite our growing and ageing population, so that we have become a 'consolidation state', that is, a state focused on reducing fiscal deficits, instead of an 'investment state' in which higher taxes fund generous social spending.[26]

Without the counterbalancing force of well-funded, valued public services, we have reached the point where years of state retreat have produced widening inequalities in both income and life chances, now further magnified by COVID-19. It is an inequality that also risks undermining social solidarity further because where there is less interaction between different sections of society, this can have the fiscal effect that the wealthier are less willing to fund public services they don't use for people they don't know.[27]

Even before the pandemic the New Economics Foundation (NEF) had flagged up the 'challenge of resuscitating and re-inventing the frayed post-war social contract', necessary in their view after the years of 'asset-stripping, finance crisis and austerity'.[28] They argued that this would now mean 'expanding and deepening' universal services. They proposed, along with others, that a set of Universal Basic Services (UBS) should become the bedrock of a revived welfare state. These would need to address the deficits in current provision in education and health, including mental health. But, it was argued, they would also need to be expanded to include transport services, housing, free childcare, universal internet access and sufficient food for all.[29] For this to be genuinely levelling, support from these broadened-out universal services should also meet the criterion of proportionate universalism – that those who start with the least get compensatingly more and better support.[30]

All of this resonates even more in the era of COVID-19. Urgent and highly visible, it was food security, especially for children, that became a political flashpoint repeatedly during the summer and autumn of 2020. So extreme was the problem that in November 2020 the Trussell Trust called for people to join the campaign for a Hunger Free Future. That was after it had published data showing that the Trust had been providing 2,600 food parcels for children every single day during the first six months of the pandemic, a figure it said was certain to have been just the tip of the iceberg of food aid provided.[31]

Digital exclusion, too, came to the fore as a critical dividing line during the pandemic. In December 2019, the Labour Party's General Election Manifesto had offered free broadband to every household as well as a guarantee that remote or rural parts of the country would finally all be connected up. Proposing, in effect, to make free access to digital information a full universal service commitment, they were met with incredulity and derision.

In the pandemic, however, it became all too clear what it meant to be excluded by technology. As libraries shut their doors so that free computers were no longer available to those without laptops or smartphones, a 'digital by default' benefit system piled further injustice on the poor. But once again it was children who revealed the full implications of the digital divide as schools were emptied of all but a minority of pupils over the long spring lockdown.

A study of children learning at home during this period showed that around one in seven primary school children in the poorest third of families had no access to a computer or tablet, two and a half times more than in the richest third of families. Among secondary school children, nearly one in five in the poorest third of families were only able to use a phone or had no device at all for schoolwork. For the richest third only one in ten faced this barrier.[32] This will inevitably have contributed to widening educational inequality in the extreme circumstances of that first COVID-19 lockdown, where home learning was the default for most children, and lessons and homework had to be accessed online.

It will no doubt have been ameliorated by government efforts and work by charities to supply children with devices for home learning as the pandemic lockdowns continued in the autumn. But it doesn't take much imagination to see that digital exclusion must already have been amplifying existing inequalities even before lockdown, as poorer children were less able to make use of the internet's vast learning resources. All that COVID-19 did, as in so many other areas of our lives, was to make it much clearer how structural disadvantage had been working in the many years prior to the pandemic.

Who Cares?

The post-war welfare state was of its era. It was predicated on a model of the family headed by a 'male breadwinner', whose employment needs took priority. A basic family allowance was paid to mothers for second and subsequent children from 1946 to help with the subsistence costs of raising children. But the actual care of children or other family members was a service that it was simply assumed would be provided by women for free – the flip side of the male breadwinner assumption – so that the welfare state had no need to intervene to provide support. This blindness to the value and contribution of what sociologists call female 'reproductive labour', including caring and unpaid work in the home in general, also has a long pedigree in the economics profession. 'Who cooked Adam Smith's dinner?' is a challenge posed by contemporary feminist economists to shine a light on this omission.[33]

The history of how GDP – our core measure of national output – was first developed as an economic indicator in the middle part of the twentieth century shows quite how comprehensively women's unpaid work in all its many manifestations was excluded – by deliberate design – from being counted as part of national output, despite the strong objections raised at the time.[34] As has been observed by many economists, this carries the corollary that if a man marries his housekeeper (changing her status from paid employee to unpaid wife) he is single-handedly reducing GDP, which is pretty problematic when you think about it.

Full employment policies in the post-war era were, unsurprisingly then, focused on jobs for men – the breadwinners. Employers remained wary of the 'risk' of employing and training women of childbearing age, and until the 1970s women were frequently sacked if they became pregnant.[35] Prior to 1977 married women could and usually did opt out of paying full National Insurance contributions in the UK, putting at risk their entitlement to benefits and a future pension. The view that a woman's place was in the home and that married women with families to look after were less effective workers remained widespread among employers. Some persisted with a 'marriage bar' to block the employment of married women even until the 1960s (Barclays Bank) and 1970s (Foreign Office).[36]

All of this began to change with the Sex Discrimination and Equal Pay legislation of the 1970s, reflecting changing social attitudes as well as the sacrifices of women such as the Dagenham machinists who fought their employer to eventually win the case for equal pay.[37] We no longer have a male breadwinner society, if indeed we ever did.[38] Women go to work. They stay in school, get qualifications and perform crucial roles in our economy. They may get married, and many may get divorced. Those who head single parent families are pushed back into work by our benefit system at the earliest opportunity.

While the 1970s saw the introduction of rights to maternity pay and maternity leave, the welfare state's treatment of care remains behind the curve. Only one of the main political parties in the 2019 General Election – the Liberal Democrats – was offering to introduce free childcare for all children from the age of six months. It also happened to be the only one led by a woman and working mother. The fact is that women who wish to work outside the home continue to be held back by childcare responsibilities and now by growing pressures to care for ageing parents.

And while gender roles are undoubtedly changing, especially as a result of the upheavals of COVID-19, it is interesting that a study in the UK of time spent on work and childcare during the spring 2020 lockdown shows that women were still doing far more of the childcare in two-earner heterosexual couples than men and were also putting their jobs under greater pressure. Mothers who were in paid work reported that nearly half of their working hours were simultaneously spent taking care of

Image 21. Mother combining work and childcare during the coronavirus pandemic.
Source: Sergii Sobolebskyi / Shutterstock

children. Fathers also experienced childcare pressures as they became more involved, although only a quarter of their working hours were also spent looking after children. This contrasts with regular weekdays in 2014–15 when only around 10 per cent of both mothers' and fathers' working time was simultaneously spent on childcare.[39]

The gender pay gap, which saw women in the UK earning nearly a sixth less per hour than men in 2020, is reducing, although painfully slowly. Women are still more often in lower-paying jobs than men – frequently those focused on nurturing and caring. And while educational gaps between the genders have closed, men are still more likely than women to have taken science and technology qualifications, which generally lead to higher-paid work. The pay gap, though, is very much smaller before women have children, especially for today's young women.[40] Once they do have children, a 'motherhood penalty' on pay kicks in, as women adapt their lives in the face of constrained choices and opportunities, by taking time out, working fewer hours or limiting themselves to less suitable jobs nearer to home. All of these responses affect their future wage and career progression, feeding into the gender pay gap.[41] The pandemic has forced further difficult choices on women, many of whom have been unable to carry on working or working effectively, and there is a real concern now that COVID-19 has set back women's progress in the workplace by decades.

The Scandinavian countries have got this. Their welfare states are far further ahead in providing the extensive parental leave and pre-school childcare needed to support women to participate equally as well as providing strong signals that fathers should be fully included in the entitlements. They back this up with strong legislation on closing gender pay gaps. Their economies are stronger by virtue of being able to access the skills and talents of their whole workforce on a far more equal basis, and they know this.

The time has come to address the care deficit in the UK and follow the Scandinavian countries in making care a universal service on a par with health and education. Without this, we will continue to restrict women's (and in some cases men's) ability to access opportunities in our society on anything like an equal basis. Paying for childcare or for care in old age is now becoming an overwhelming financial burden for many families; and as regards the elderly it is one that is almost impossible to plan for. This risks becoming a problem for the economy, too, if those caring for children or the elderly are increasingly unable to work because it's just not worth paying for care, or if they cannot progress their careers either because they are reliant on staying near their extended family for free care support, or because they are themselves providing care to them.

Of course, it's not all bad. Working parents in the UK are now entitled to thirty hours of free nursery care for three- or four-year-olds during term times, or at the age of two for children considered disadvantaged. The problem is that up until that point, a typical working family will find themselves on their own in the market. People who are on a low enough income to claim Universal Credit will get financial support for childcare. Everyone else will find that the average bill for a full-time nursery place for a two-year-old (or indeed a younger child) will set them back £1,040 a month or £874 after claiming tax back.[42] That is a phenomenal expense to face as the cost of returning to work, making such a huge dent in take-home pay that many women find it barely worth it.

Women appear now to be having fewer children, something that is common across many of the world's leading economies. In the UK the total fertility rate has been falling steadily since 2012 and reached one of its lowest ever levels in 2019 – 1.65 children per woman by the end of their childbearing years, down from 1.94 at the 2012 peak.[43] Preliminary estimates for the first nine months of

2020 (which are pre-pandemic conceptions) show a further sharp fall in the total fertility rate to 1.6, the lowest UK rate ever recorded, including during wartime.[44] Women in every age group up to the age of forty are now having fewer children, so there is nothing to suggest that they are just putting off childbearing for a few years.

It is hard to know how much childcare costs and an awareness of the career sacrifice involved in parenting influence this. The millennial generation also have escalating housing costs, job insecurity and the precariousness of renting to contend with. It should make us pause for thought, though. Today's children are tomorrow's taxpayers and we can ill-afford fewer of them. They are also tomorrow's carers. Unpaid care provided by adult children for their frail parents may be invisible in Whitehall but its loss will be felt keenly if more people age without ever having had children.

A pro-family policy with free or highly subsidised childcare at its core would help to mitigate these very real future risks, as indeed so would a pro-immigration policy. Who knows, if the birth rate falls further in the aftermath of COVID-19, as it very probably will (although of course that does depend on how people spent their lockdown months), politicians might wake up to this of their own accord.

Staying on the theme of lockdown, the childcare infrastructure took a pounding during COVID-19 with many nurseries being forced to close permanently as a result of the loss of income. There is now a real issue over the capacity of the sector to meet medium-term needs, particularly in more deprived areas. As family incomes have fallen and women in particular have been more likely to lose their jobs than men, there is also a real risk that there will not be enough demand for childcare in the short term to sustain the sector at its previous levels. As and when the economy picks up this will potentially become a very real problem as women struggle to find childcare – something to think about now perhaps rather than react to later.

What of Later Life?

Care in old age is now not just a huge expense, it's also a lottery. Approximately one in ten people over the age of sixty-five will, as things currently stand, face lifetime care costs of over £100,000.[45] For some, costs will be well in excess of this – residential care homes in 2019 typically charged private clients around £800 a week (adding up to over £40,000 a year), and it would be far more if nursing or medical care were needed.[46] If you own a house or have other assets and you need dementia care for a period of years, then in principle you will have to pay for your care until you only have £23,250 of your assets left. That's because dementia, unlike cancer for instance, is considered a social not a medical condition.[47] When you consider that one in five people aged 85 to 89 have dementia, that's worse odds than Russian roulette! Most people would not knowingly want to play that game. Yet we do.

Fixing the crisis in social care must deal with this unpredictable liability for private care costs that depends on which particular condition you have. Whatever solution we come up with must aim to provide social care for people based on need, not the current lottery. It will of course come at a cost which is why governments have been so reluctant to act. It might mean we have to have a social insurance tax for the over-forties to 'pool risk' so that no one finds themselves with the loaded chamber facing potentially overwhelming costs. As with any insurance policy, everyone pays into it in the knowledge that if they are the one who in the end needs help, the collective pot is there to provide it. Germany and Japan have already adopted this model, so it certainly has a pretty sound track record.

An alternative might be a mixed solution where people carry on paying for their care if they have the resources to do so but there is a cap on care costs after a certain amount has been paid out – something proposed by the Dilnot Review of social care back in 2011.[48] It may not protect all of the inheritance they want to pass on, but it will help. Or we could even set up a new, dedicated national wealth fund to pay for social care, which could then be provided, like health, free at the point of need. This could in principle be created using money from taxing wealth and inheritance more effectively. Such wealth funds are long-term investment pots that, in the case of social care, could be set up with some upfront government funding and then regularly replenished from the proceeds of wealth and inheritance taxation.[49]

But solving our social care crisis is not just about how we defray care costs for the better-off. We need to get serious about the quality of care that everybody gets, especially those who ought already to be receiving free local authority funded care. These are the people whose care needs are in many cases barely being met as social care budgets are repeatedly cut. We should also now question why we are still separating so much of our social care provision from health care instead of bringing them together to support older people within a single public service, with all the efficiencies and improvements in people's quality of life that this would bring.

All of these are very significant challenges. But they are also actually an opportunity. A report produced by the Women's Budget Group in June 2020 argued that investing in a strong care sector would create more jobs than spending the same amount of money on transport or construction projects and have a significantly less negative impact on the environment.[50] If pay and working conditions are reformed for care workers, as has been argued for years is necessary, this could offer long-term secure work to hundreds and thousands of people, particularly the many women and young people who have lost jobs in retail, hospitality and personal services during the pandemic or who have been unable to find work since leaving education. Care sector vacancies remain at high levels, with not enough applicants for the jobs available, presenting a real opportunity to recruit and train new care workers if the right measures are taken to attract them.

As we plan our post COVID-19 recovery programmes and consider what our priorities should be for restructuring our economy and our public realm, care must be accorded its rightful status as a collective responsibility in a contemporary welfare state. As the Scandinavian countries have shown, valuing and supporting families in this way produces enormous paybacks in social equity and economic performance. And – one for the old-fashioned economists here – a properly remunerated high-quality care sector also adds substantially to GDP!

PART IV
AFTER THE VIRUS: WHO DO WE WANT TO BE?

10 CASTING ASIDE THE NEOLIBERAL STATE

We begin Part IV by asking whether we are, unwittingly, being driven by a storyline with a particular view about who and what we are and whether, as a corollary of that storyline, we are accepting a particular, stylised, view of history that is not fit for purpose.

Homo Economicus and the Myth of Rationality

Neoliberal economics has at its root a beguilingly persuasive representation of what 'human nature' is and what motivates us. It is built on – and indeed promotes – the view that all humans are essentially individualistic and selfish. Its economic model is based on this foundational construct of selfish rationality, in which altruism, in its pure sense, is not compatible with how people or economies behave. This is brought to life in the figure that the nineteenth-century liberal economists conjured up for us – *Homo economicus*, or 'rational economic man' to give him his more recent formulation.

Rational economic man is certainly a pretty ludicrous character, roaming through the textbooks of economics equipped with perfect information (yes, that means omniscience!) to enable him to make instant calculations about what sort of behaviour is in his best interests. His sole objective is to maximise his happiness – or 'utility' in the technical jargon – unbothered by those around him. Presumably he has a female equivalent, although we are never told about her.

Of course, we know that this is all just a fable, one that flies in the face of the much more complex realities of the human condition, in which emotions and relationships drive everything – even the love of money for some, surely an emotion in itself. Rational economic man is a pure abstraction. This fiction may make it easier to derive mathematical representations of the economy but only because maths, unlike people, *is* fundamentally rational.

Yet for all its absurdity, this approach has achieved enormous influence over our lives. As the highly respected former governor of the Bank of England, Mark Carney, has shown at length, its implicit assumption that all value worth knowing about is reflected in market prices – and the consequent faith that markets are therefore always right – led to the 2008 financial crash.[1] It has resulted in the values that most of us view as most important in our lives but which have no price – meaning and purpose, honour and dignity, family and friendship – being systematically excluded from business decisions, something painfully visible in the lives of low-paid workers.[2]

At the start of the COVID-19 pandemic there was an extreme view vocalised by some that perhaps there was nothing we could really do other than accept nature's test of the 'survival of the fittest'. The economic historian Adam Tooze parodied the way in which 'simplistic economic logic' could also be used to argue in favour of such a position. If COVID-19 was only likely to kill the unproductive, vulnerable or older members of society – those not making any active economic contribution – while preserving the productive workforce who would eventually gain immunity, then, viewed through this particular rationalist lens we might conclude we had relatively little to worry about. It was an absurd position, but it was one that followed from a way of thinking about ourselves that in effect relies on a form of rationality that is completely abstracted from morality.

Naturally, as Tooze argues, it soon became clear that 'when matters of life and death are concerned the calculus is different'.[3] Morality re-enters the picture. As the New York mayor railed on 24 March 2020 with COVID-19 spreading like wildfire, 'My mother is not expendable and your mother is not expendable and our brothers and sisters are not expendable and we're not going to accept a premise that human life is disposable and we're not going to put a dollar figure on human life.'[4]

Less extreme, but in its own way equally misguided, is the narrative that holds that the last 200 years of the triumphant free market, driven by the supposedly benevolent forces of economic rationality, have given us a happy trajectory of progress towards universal prosperity and good health. But this is also a simplifying and misleading myth, unanchored in the evidence-based realities of history. The truth is far different. It has taken repeated episodes of contested political struggle, social movements, legal and parliamentary battles – each motivated by collectivist ideals mobilised *against* outright free-market individualism – to ensure that mere wealth accumulation by the few has been converted instead into improving health, prosperity and welfare for the majority.[5]

There is now a growing, and increasingly accepted, body of work showing how far in reality people operate differently from the abstracted assumption of a singular, selfish human rationality. The field of behavioural economics has built itself on exploring the ways in which people do not follow 'perfect rationality'. As the Nobel Prize winner Daniel Kahneman (among many others) has shown, we are subject to many cognitive biases that mean even our consciously purposeful behaviour does not align with the unswervingly 'rational man' of *Homo economicus*.[6] Moreover, there is plenty of evidence of the positive reasons for this in humans' social behaviour, such as our inequity aversion (we don't like things being unequal),[7] our significant attention to social norms (i.e. we prefer to do what other people do)[8] and our willingness to engage in pro-social behaviour,[9] as we saw when divers from around the world risked their lives in the hazardous exercise to rescue twelve boys who had become trapped in caves in Thailand in July 2018, two of whom did indeed pay the ultimate price, losing their lives to save others.[10]

What all this research – and much more besides – tells us is that the view that promotes the dominance of human selfishness is wrong – it is highly partial and limiting. None of this is to say that humans cannot be selfish, of course they can. However, humans can also be altruistic and kind for no obvious benefit to themselves. Everyone reading this can think of plenty of examples of people being selfish, altruistic and everything in between. Look at the health workers who carried on at the front line of the pandemic despite the lack of proper PPE and the known risks that they faced in treating COVID-19 patients. The key point is that humans are not, by nature, born to be purely selfish, any more than they are born with a capacity for perfect knowledge.

However, we do know that we are born to be influenced by stories, including stories about ourselves. A fascinating study of children in India has shown that their performance in tests is affected by the psychological effect of narratives about the lower intellect of children from certain castes. In the study, lower-caste and higher-caste children performed similarly on tests of intelligence *except* when asked to publicly state their surname (surnames were a clear marker of caste) before completing the test. The social narrative about the lower intellect of certain castes then kicked in and created a self-fulfilling prophecy in which they performed according to that narrative – the result of a phenomenon known as 'stereotype threat'.[11]

In the same way the view that economic behaviour is driven by unbridled selfish motivations also has the potential to be self-fulfilling, able to turn people into selfish and indi-vidualistic actors attempting to be economically 'rational'. Indeed, as Rutger Bregman points out in his recent book *Humankind*, 'When modern economists assumed that peo-ple are innately selfish, they advocated policies that fos-tered self-serving behaviour.'[12] There is even a study that shows that just studying economics – where students were taught about modelling rational human decision making – can make people behave more selfishly.[13]

What can we do about this? How can we defeat the virus of neoliberalism's myth – the morally corrosive framing of rational economic man – and tell a new and rounded story about ourselves? An important first step is to look back at our own history and the sometimes surprising insights that it affords at this moment of historic opportunity for change.

History and Morality

Major shocks and crises are often the catalyst for a re-evaluation and realignment of the 'social contract' – the agreement that has implicitly been made between the gov-ernment and the governed around the rights and duties each party has in that relationship. All citizens have ceded some of their freedoms and decision making to the state, and in return, certainly within a democracy, they expect collectively agreed benefits and protections. How these are negotiated and expressed is historically contingent as cir-cumstances and power relationships evolve.

It is often argued that there was a big resetting of the social contract in 1945 in the UK, as elsewhere, after the trauma of the Second World War. Many have suggested that there may be a '2020s moment' of similar magnitude following COVID-19. To see how and why this can occur and what it takes to precipitate such a challenge to a pre-vailing status quo, we will look back at two major episodes in modern British history, both of which saw a move away from an over-dominant individualist approach towards much more collectivist thinking and policy. On both occasions the resulting new policies had extraordinary and enduring beneficial consequences for the lives and opportunities of the majority of the population.

The later of these two episodes has just been mentioned and is very well-known – the installation of the welfare state after the Second World War, along with the central government's commitment to taking responsibility for full employment. This involved taxing business and the better-off progressively to fund universal provision for all citizens of a wide range of services previously only affordable to the paying middle classes: health care, secondary education and decent-quality housing. The acceptance of these principles of the 'post-war consensus', even by three successively elected Conservative governments (1951–64), was due in part to the widely perceived bankruptcy of the 'business as usual' free-market liberal capitalism that had been reverted to after the First World War.

The charge list was long and is well-known. It was undeniable that this had firstly caused the Wall Street Crash of 1929, secondly been supine in the face of mass unemployment, thirdly been unable to stem the reactive rise of fascism in interwar Europe, and fourthly been unable on its own sufficiently to revive the liberal democratic economies so that they could effectively defend themselves against totalitarianism. The war effort from 1939 had required a self-sacrificial collective response and state-managed mobilisation of resources sustained for years. When it ended in 1945 the central state put its supportive arms around the nation's citizens 'from the cradle to the grave' – and continued to do so for the next three decades. The new social contract had Keynesian economic theory to justify it and strengthened trade unions to balance the interests of employers.

The earlier episode is much less familiar because it is not associated with a global world war, nor led by a master-plan devised in Whitehall. It occurred in many of Britain's major provincial industrial cities during the period 1870–1914, a revolution in local government given the name 'gas and water socialism' by its detractors. It transformed the survival rates of Britain's industrial workforce. In cities such as Liverpool, Manchester or Glasgow, subject to surges of in-migrants from rural areas searching for work to feed themselves, evidence collected by the authorities in the 1830s and 1840s was showing that living conditions were so overcrowded and basic sanitation so deficient that almost one half of all infants born were failing to reach their fifth birthday – literally 'little perishers'.[14] Although a Public Health Act was passed in 1848, it was all but still-born because neither central government, wedded to laissez-faire, nor local property-owning ratepayers, wedded to their own narrow self-interest, could see it as acceptable that they should be called on to pay for the expensive remedial works of water supply and sanitary housing envisaged by the Act.[15]

However, over the decades after 1848 working men pushed for the vote and a new social movement also began to emerge among local religious leaders working with the urban poor of Birmingham. They began to preach (literally) the anti-individualist message of a different guiding light – the municipal or 'civic' gospel. They argued that:

> the churches will never be able to remedy the evil [of poverty] apart from the action of municipal authorities. ... Municipal action, not the gospel only, is necessary to improve the homes of the poor. ... The man who holds municipal or political office is a 'minister of God'.[16]

The most powerful disciple who responded to this call was one of Birmingham's leading businessmen, Joseph Chamberlain.[17] He was to be Liberal mayor of that city (1873–76) thrice-elected by the new electorate of working men created by municipal franchise reforms in 1869.[18]

Chamberlain used his business and financial acumen to negotiate a massive loan, increasing the city's debt from half a million to 2.5 million pounds to buy up the private gasworks, turning private shareholder profits into a positive river of revenue for Birmingham's residents. It returned a net £165,000 to the city in its first five years (equivalent to over £20 million today), while also cutting the price of gas to Birmingham's happy householders and businesses.[19]

Parliament had long accepted the argument that where natural monopolies were concerned there could

Image 22. Cartoon depicting the 1878 Birmingham municipal election: the Liberal caucus led by Joseph Chamberlain with his trademark monocle defending the newly constructed Council House building behind them, with their cannons proclaiming their achievements of Gas, Water and Health.
Source: Reproduced from *The Dart*, 26 October 1878, by kind permission of the Cadbury Research Library, University of Birmingham

be a legitimate case on economic grounds, even in a free market, for public ownership. Now Chamberlain, the entrepreneurial 'screw king' of Birmingham (his company later became GKN) and an employer of thousands, elevated this to a positive political and ethical philosophy of municipal collectivism, based on two principles. Firstly, 'all monopolies which are sustained in any way by the state ought to be in the hands of the representatives of the people, by whom they should be administered, and to whom their profits should go'.[20] Secondly, with their more fully representative electorates to answer to, local authorities should be constituted as 'real local parliaments, supreme in their special jurisdiction' with 'increased duties and responsibilities'.[21]

Municipal, democratically accountable, public ownership of revenue-generating utilities of all kinds to fund the improvement of Britain's industrial cities swept through the country over the next three decades, moving on to include tramways and electricity supply. And even the laissez-faire state in Westminster was prepared to play a constructive role, facilitating this flourishing of energetic local self-government. The Treasury now provided subsidised loans for an enormous range of activities seen as health-related in addition to water supply and sewers, such as baths and wash-houses, housing and street improvements, peaking at an average of £10 million loaned per year from 1896 to 1905 (equivalent to £1.25 billion per year today), compared to just one tenth that amount per year from 1860 to 1869.[22] Thus, finally, from the 1870s onwards infectious and sanitary diseases went into decline and life expectancy in these still-growing cities began a long trajectory of improvement sustained for well over a century.[23]

These two quite distinct episodes, post-1945 and post-1870, each followed periods of many decades in which a free-market approach had piled up overwhelming evidence that its untrammelled operation was the cause of widespread distress and intolerable injustice – something that we are again familiar with today. In both cases a powerful *moral* (not merely economic or social) alternative narrative of 'who we are' – as a city or nation – was developed. Key individuals and networks from within the power elite of the highly educated and well-connected were, firstly, persuaded of the moral case for action and, secondly, had to be able to formulate the practical, financially responsible means to resource the major changes envisaged.

On each occasion this could only be achieved by challenging, and to a substantial extent modifying, the orthodoxy on matters of property ownership and taxation. This of course discomforted the interests of others in the power elite, who tried to argue that these new economic arrangements were illegitimate or even dangerous.[24] In both eras, the oppressed majority on the receiving end of the harshness of the free market had acquired a new-found electoral voice, but this alone was not enough – it had to be skilfully cultivated within the political arena by people prepared to battle against the dug-in vested interests of those doing very nicely for themselves. Only then could a new proactive and caring relationship between government and the governed be forged.

It is not hard to draw contemporary parallels. Neoliberalism had by 2020 provided ample evidence of the distress caused by the years of vicious austerity, by its relentless financialisation and destabilisation of the economy and people's livelihoods, coming on the back of its long-standing reckless approach to the environment and other species. This has long provoked a social movement among ecological activists, starting with Friends of the Earth and Greenpeace's early high-profile campaign to 'Save the Whales'. The 'Occupy' and 'We are the 99%' movements emerged after the 2008 crash to protest against an unjust economic system immiserating so many; and most recently Extinction Rebellion developed as a powerful protest group galvanising the young to take on the incumbent powers, whom they saw destroying the planet and, with it, their future. Many 'school strikers' were below the voting age in their respective countries, once again raising the issue of the inclusivity of the franchise as new and important political voices were seeking to be heard.

These popular protests were joined by establishment voices arguing for a narrative reset including global titans such as David Attenborough and Bill Gates. Some of the world's most powerful organisations, from the World Economic Forum to the International Monetary Fund (IMF), began to put the case for a more socially responsible capitalism; and leading establishment thinkers including Mark Carney, governor of the Bank of England from 2013 to 2020, and Christine Lagarde, managing director of the IMF from 2011 to 2019, warned in no uncertain terms of the political and economic risks of allowing further escalations of inequality. In 2014, Carney was already arguing that inequality 'risks undermining the basic social contract of fairness', while Lagarde cautioned in the same year that the gap between rich and poor that existed in 'far too many countries' was 'not a recipe for stability and sustainability'.[25]

In May 2019, New Zealand's hugely popular prime minister, Jacinda Ardern, made history by announcing a 'well-being' budget for her country, instead of the usual growth-focused economic budget. She argued that citizens' health and life satisfaction should take priority over economic growth as the metric by which progress is measured. All new spending in the well-being budget was therefore to go towards five specific well-being goals: bolstering mental health, reducing child poverty, supporting indigenous peoples, moving to a low-carbon-emission economy, and flourishing in a digital age. Her position that GDP, alone, 'does not guarantee improvement to our living standards' and nor does it 'take into account who benefits and who is left out' challenges all political leaders – and we, the voters – to re-examine at the most basic level our approach to citizen well-being and welfare.[26]

It was a further, principled moral stance challenging the prevailing orthodoxy. And Greta Thunberg would add yet another a few months later in September 2019, when she addressed the UN Climate Action Summit in New York, saying,

> *We are in the beginning of a mass extinction. And all you can talk about is money and fairy tales of eternal economic growth.*[27]

When you think about it, exponential growth – with GDP rising at 2 per cent per year, for instance – means that an economy doubles in size every thirty-five years. And yet the world continues to aspire to achieve that, even as we see the toll it is exacting on our environment. As Kate Raworth, author of *Doughnut Economics*, so cogently argues, we do not yet seem to have accepted what exponential

Image 23. Greta Thunberg, speaking at the UN Climate Action Summit.
Source: Spencer Platt / Getty Images

growth means in a closed system planet.[28] It actually means we are driving ourselves at a brick wall, without even trying to slow down. We need to get inside the head of the driver – that is all of us, with our induced addiction to consumerism.

By July 2020, with the global pandemic raging, we saw further evidence of the changing zeitgeist as eighty-three of the world's wealthiest individuals, linked to the US Patriotic Millionaires movement, and including Abigail Disney and Jerry Greenfield, called on governments to permanently increase taxes on the wealthy, saying, 'millionaires like us have a critical role to play in healing our world'.[29] A moral case was being made that was in effect challenging the narrative and philosophy of neoliberalism. Some, at least, of the wealthy were, just as Joseph Chamberlain and his allies among the business leaders of Birmingham had been in their time, now willing to step up and lead.

Such a moralised economy is exactly what Elizabeth I brought into being when she empowered her subjects with the world's first 'welfare society', which will be the subject of the next chapter. Indeed, what should really give us hope, as we contemplate what now needs to happen, is the knowledge that the period of the last forty years of the UK's history, and its extolling of the myth of the superiority of the amoral free market, is not the norm of modern history. It is in fact only a very brief interlude in a rather different story, as we have already begun to see by looking back at the eras of municipal activism and the post-war welfare settlement.

The dominant motif throughout our long modern history has not been the extreme neoliberal one of *Homo economicus*. *Homo economicus* is an opportunist upstart who falsely claims to have always been present as 'human nature' – a concept that itself is an Enlightenment invention of the eighteenth century.[30] Since the beginning of the seventeenth century, in England at least, our story has actually been predominantly one not of detached selfish rationality, but rather one of collectivist individualism. In other words it has been characterised by a form of individualism that is facilitated by collectivist community support. Individuals' independent economic initiative is, indeed, fostered, but within an encompassing moralised system of compulsory collective provision for all those unable to support themselves.[31]

The origins of this can be seen in the facilitating welfare regime established by Elizabeth I with her epoch-making Poor Law of 1601, a world first. The resulting collectivist-individualist, nurturing society – in operation for well over 200 years – was then overturned in 1834 by the new, more reductively individualist economics and utilitarianism of the nineteenth century; but it re-emerged in part with the municipal gospel and in full with the founding of the post-war Beveridge welfare state, testament again to the nurturing power of the enabling state.

In order to understand what is possible for our future, then, let us first look at what already has been made possible repeatedly in our past.

11 THE BIRTH OF A COLLECTIVIST INDIVIDUALISM

How Elizabeth I Gave Us the World's First Welfare State

The relationship between the state and society changed radically when plague became an endemic, repeated affliction in Europe during the centuries after 1347, as we have seen in Chapter 1. Rather than relying mainly on appeal to divine intervention and prayer when disaster struck, governments in Europe, following the lead of the Italian city-states, gradually began to take action themselves to protect and, if necessary, control their citizens (for their own survival, not simply for authoritarian reasons) as they sought ways to avert widespread death and disease.

With no end to the repeated outbreaks of plague the Elizabethan state formalised its response in 1578–89 in the printed Book of Plague Orders circularised to local officials and magistrates. It set out a total of seventeen protective procedures to be implemented in every parish across the land when a new wave of infection arrived, including monitoring a regular count of the dead reported by 'searchers', keeping infected houses shut up for at least six weeks and – crucially – taxing the community to provide 'relief' to the socially isolated families.[1]

But plague incursions were by no means the only threats from nature that Elizabeth I had regularly to contend with. Harvest failure was an equally destabilising risk and the Tudor monarchs were keenly aware of the potential of food shortages to incite discontent and rebellion. The

Image 24. The 'Pelican' portrait of Elizabeth I, c.1575 by Nicholas Hilliard. The pelican symbolised her sacrificial devotion to her 'children' – the nation.
Source: The Printer Collector / Getty Images

trouble was that Henry VIII's dissolution of the monasteries after his break with Rome had rather undermined a significant part of the established system for dealing with this and all the other 'normal' problems of poverty due to illness, disability and old age. One quarter of all support for the poor, year in year out, had come from the charity dispensed by the Catholic Church.[2] So Henry VIII had given himself quite a headache, such that he and his successors now spent decades experimenting with ways to deal with the gaping hole in social provision that had been left as a result. This was, of course, a particular challenge during times of 'dearth' – harvest failures threatening hunger.[3]

Elizabeth I continued this quest, promulgating a further Book of Orders in 1586 hot on the heels of the earlier one on plagues. This directed Justices of the Peace (local magistrates) on how they should protect the poor when dearth threatened famine and starvation. As well as preserving all the grain stocks that they could find these ubiquitous local officials were also tasked with restricting its use for non-essential purposes, the brewing of beer being deemed one such unnecessary activity.

Near the end of her reign, with parliament spurred on by a series of disastrous harvests and grain riots between 1594 and 1597, Elizabeth was able to bring forward an extraordinary and comprehensive response to the problems that had worried her for so long. Elizabeth I's Poor Laws of 1598 and 1601 were the culmination of several decades of earlier efforts to devise a statutory poor law.[4] These were now crafted into a perfected version, which soon entirely superseded the episodically issued Books of Dearth Orders.[5]

The Poor Laws and Local Communities

The Poor Laws put the onus on local communities to recognise that they had permanent mutual rights and responsibilities in caring for their neighbours. Each of the country's approximately 10,000 parishes (averaging around 400 people at that time) was required by the Poor Laws to set up a continuous fund that was to be used to provide a safety net so that no one would fall into destitution, not only when the hard times of dearth hit but in all circumstances of individual misfortune. Those to be protected in this way comprised all the vulnerable and unfortunate in society: orphans, widows, the old, the infirm and the sick, those involuntarily unemployed and single mothers and their children.

Good Queen Bess, as she came to be known, was, thus, truly revolutionary. It is no exaggeration to say that the Poor Laws brought into being what was in effect the world's first universal social security and welfare system – nothing like this had existed before. As the Dutch historians van Bavel and Rijpma confirm from their comparative analysis, 'from a European perspective, the degree to which the English state succeeded in enforcing a nation-wide tax-based system of poor relief was exceptional'.[6] All local communities were required to act continuously for the collective good with every subject of the Crown in England and Wales granted an absolute entitlement to life-preserving 'relief' when in need.[7] This was typically provided in the form of payments in kind (such as food or fuel in times of need) or cash.

Moreover, the Poor Laws stipulated that each parish's fund was to be financed by a tax levied on everybody – all inhabitants and occupiers – so that in principle there was no 'us' and 'them' of poor and rich. But to be fair, the poor rate was levied in proportion to the assessed value of land held in the parish. This meant collecting from those of modest means was very limited while both landowning farmers and the better-off tenant farmers – the wealthy and the 'middling sort' – were mandated into a practice of regularly paying in to the poor fund.[8] Fair play was overseen by locally resident Justices of the Peace who were required to make sure no one was avoiding the levy and to hear appeals against the decisions of the parish-appointed 'Overseers of the Poore'. If they believed they had been wrongly denied support, the poor had the right to approach a magistrate for a judgement wherever he happened to be – 'at the justice's home or on the hunting field'.[9]

Such was the appreciation of their value that the Poor Laws were upheld and even strengthened despite two decades of disruption during the English Civil Wars and Cromwell's Protectorate (1642–59).[10] By the 1660s further statutes had clarified that each individual's legal right to relief rested in one specific parish only, their parish of 'settlement', thereby removing parishes' anxieties over potentially unlimited liability for providing relief to all incomers. In a patriarchal legal system your 'settlement' was, by default, the parish of your father's settlement, while on marriage, a female subject's settlement moved to her husband's parish.

Various commentators, including Adam Smith himself, believed that this restriction of entitlement to a single parish was a critical impediment to labour mobility. However, historians have now shown that the system was far more flexible than Smith allowed for. It was perfectly possible to have one's legal settlement reassigned to a new parish of residence once you had established employment there. Local discretion was paramount and this meant that the young were rarely discouraged from moving to parishes where there was growing demand for their labour. Individuals could also be issued with portable certificates by their 'home' parishes and this developed into a practice of non-resident relief, where payments were regularly sent across distance or groups of parishes simply settled up with each other at the end of year, keeping the claimants in the places where the jobs were available, rather than repatriating them every time they needed some temporary relief.[11] Pooling of resources between different parishes had always been envisaged as a contingency to deal with exceptional circumstances in the original Poor Law legislation and here we see how parishes were also able to develop other mutually beneficial and locally economically advantageous arrangements in discharging their responsibilities.

'Crowding-in Charity': The Charitable Uses Act

There was a second, ingenious, parallel track to Elizabeth I's approach to encouraging her subjects to organise their communities against poverty and vulnerability. In 1601 the consolidating Charitable Uses Act was also passed, to complete the reform of the purpose of charity away from spiritual reward and towards practical humane philanthropy.[12] As such it was very clearly designed to sit alongside the 'public' charity of the Poor Law. Having made it obligatory for parishes to support their poor, new voluntary charities could now be created, provided their object was also to assist the same categories of the vulnerable and unfortunate specified in the Poor Law. One might initially blink at this apparent redundancy of duplicate provision. It was in fact a masterstroke of genius in statecraft, designed to make charitable giving act in concert with the Poor Laws.

Previously there had been no reliable safety net for the poor in any community if the wealthy were disinclined to give them alms – they were then thrown back entirely on family and friends who could well also be in need in hard times. From 1601 the Poor Law was laying down an unavoidable responsibility on the prosperous to look after the less fortunate in their parish at all times. But they were also being incentivised to engage in supportive charitable activity. If those charitable enterprises were effective in actually dealing with the chronic problems of the local poor – preventing them falling into destitution – they could lessen the burden on the prosperous families of paying poor rates over the long term. It was an ingenious incentive structure that 'crowded-in' a remarkable flow of competitive philanthropy from the better-off. Plaques can be seen in almost every parish church in the country, dating from the early seventeenth century onwards, commemorating the bequests made by local families, attesting to the culture of parish philanthropy that ensued.

Over time, Elizabeth's legacy encouraged a 'welfare culture' to develop in English society, a welcome contrast to previous outbreaks of fear or rejection of the poor, which at times in the past had even culminated in accusations of witchcraft and incarceration of beggars, sometimes also depicted as in league with the devil in literature pre-dating the Poor Law.[13] With responsibilities clear, parish communities set about organising to give out payments to those in need. Many also made provision to help them more directly such as paying masters to take orphans and children of overburdened families as apprentices. This was complemented by the many acts and bequests of private charity, in particular creating schools for the poor (the main additional legitimate charitable purpose, not covered by the Poor Laws) and almshouses for the old or infirm. By the eighteenth century leading figures across England were founding voluntary subscription hospitals at a rate of one every two years during the period 1720–75, many of which are still with us in our towns and cities to this day, such as Addenbrookes in Cambridge and the Chester Royal.[14]

The best estimates we have indicate an 'explosion of giving' after the 1601 Charitable Uses Act with the value to the poor of these private benefactions more than doubling in real terms from £80,000 per decade from 1560 to 1600 to £172,000 by the 1650s.[15] Almost half of this was provided directly to the poor, over one third of the total was devoted to education, with additionally about one seventh to fund almshouses for the old and infirm.[16]

The latest research shows that meanwhile statutory poor relief expanded rapidly in geographic coverage and that real expenditure (inflation-adjusted) per head of population rocketed up at a phenomenal rate of 5.5 per cent every year for five decades from 1601. An average rate of annual growth of 2.77 per cent was sustained across the entire two centuries, from 1601 to 1800. Poor Law expenditure doubled as a percentage of GDP every fifty years from 1650 to 1800, reaching 1.84 per cent of GDP in the latter year.[17]

This combination of the Poor Laws and the Charitable Uses Act succeeded, then, in creating,

> a nationwide system of social security through a progressive community tax to fund provision at local level … predicated on the assumption that poverty is an unavoidable and common risk, which can be shared and mitigated.[18]

As the most distinguished historian of the Old Poor Law, Paul Slack, has concluded, 'it is not a total anachronism to call that institution, as it had developed by 1700, a welfare state'.[19]

This sharing and mitigating of risk by acting in the common good, as Elizabeth envisaged, was by no means all that was achieved. What no one at the time could have understood was quite how significant the Poor Laws were to be in England's rise to economic pre-eminence during the course of the seventeenth and eighteenth centuries.

The Poor Laws and Economic Growth

There is a strong case to be made that these institutions of collective responsibility directly stimulated the sustained economic growth that led to England's successful industrialisation.[20] While we are certainly not arguing that they were the only cause, they were an important and necessary facilitator. By providing the old and infirm with parish relief, the Poor Laws meant that families no longer needed to be tied either to land-holding or to the proximity of their younger generation for security and support.[21] Where landlords and more prosperous farmers sought to raise productivity by increasing farm sizes, they did not face desperate resistance from the smallholders whose farms they were absorbing because parish relief meant they would not be facing utter destitution.[22]

The young, meanwhile, were liberated to be mobile, enabling them to flock to the commercially expanding towns and cities where labour was needed.[23] They were able to act individualistically, pursuing their best employment options in a regional or even national labour market, because the system of collective provision meant their parents were safe without them and that they themselves could rely on the support of their parish of settlement if things didn't work out for them. That is why historian Roger Schofield identified early modern England as an individualist-collectivist regime.[24]

All of this was to power an economy that was driven from 1600 by a rate of urbanisation over three times faster than the rest of Europe.[25] Only constant migration from the countryside could maintain such extraordinary urban growth, because all towns suffered high rates of mortality in these centuries.[26] From a position of relative backwardness at the edge of Europe in the sixteenth century, over the next two centuries the English economy came to outperform that of the Netherlands, the most advanced, urbanised society in the world in 1600. As Figure 11 shows, the proportion of England's population living in towns and cities increased dramatically – by 350 per cent – while in the rest of Europe, including even the Netherlands and mighty France, the equivalent rate of increase was only in the range of 10–25 per cent across these two centuries. London became the world's largest city, while England's population was fed effectively despite the shrinking proportion of the labour force working on the land because of a long, sustained increase in agricultural productivity.

As a result, well before the first steam-driven factories appeared in 1790, England's urbanising economy had been developing and diversifying faster than the rest of Europe for two centuries, as each generation's young adults stopped working exclusively in the fields.[27] All-important labour power was dynamically released throughout the

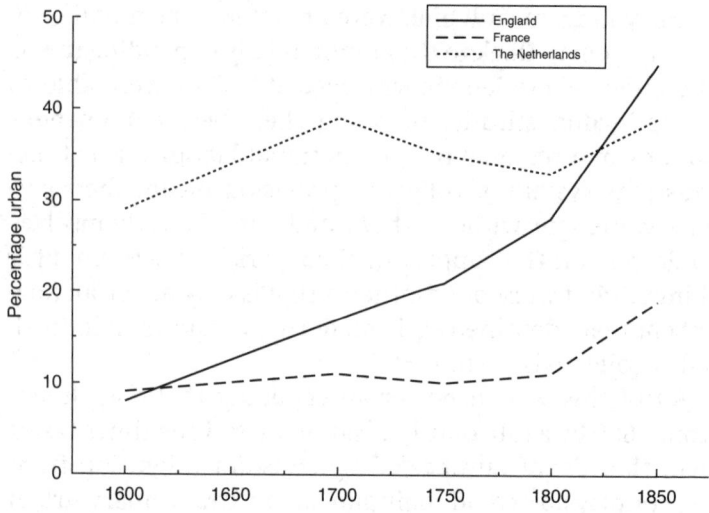

Figure 11. Urban growth in England, France and the Netherlands, 1600 to 1850.

Note: Urban population is the percentage of the total population living in towns with 5,000 or more inhabitants.

Source: Wrigley (2004), Figure 3.8, p.89

period to the economy's proliferating cottage manufacturing industries, its growing retail, professional and transport sectors, and its expanding commercial and maritime trading activities.[28]

Moreover, with the Poor Law guaranteeing relatively stable demand for grain, this sustained a continuously operating commercial agrarian economy, one that did not need to be suspended during famine, as had happened previously under the Book of Orders. This new certainty of demand could stimulate more complex and long-term planning for productive investments and commercial ventures, and England in the eighteenth century became a land of thriving provincial and country banks.[29]

Besides their role in facilitating England's economic growth, the Poor and Charitable Uses Laws were behind another record that England can claim to have notched up – the distinction of being the first nation in Europe by more than a century and a half to be free from famine and food insecurity. The last episode when actual starvation occurred in any region of England was 1622–23, when, as so often in the past, a spike in food prices followed a harvest failure, leaving some destitute and without food.[30] After that date, with the Poor Laws increasingly observed in all regions of the country, this perennial link between harvest failure, soaring grain prices and famine mortality was broken. No sign of it at all in the 1690s – a very difficult and deadly decade all across the rest of Europe – as parish relief was provided directly to those who could not afford to feed themselves. If proof were required of the Poor Laws' effectiveness in meeting parish obligations to sustain the poor through thick and thin, this is surely it.

No other country in Europe managed this feat in all its rural communities, and of course France, England's great imperial rival during the eighteenth century, lacking a universal poor law, saw social collapse and revolution. It was not that there were no poor laws on the Continent but rather that they were not universal, mostly confined to towns and especially regional centres of government where the preservation of order was the priority.[31] Peasants in the countryside were typically left to fend for themselves. Unfortunately, in periods of food shortage this encouraged mass movement of the hungry towards the towns where they knew there were grain stores. Undernourished, stressed and unwashed these unfortunate individuals would quickly contract infectious diseases, which were spread further as they moved to the towns. Inevitably mortality rates would soar.

In England, by contrast, estimates from official enquiries provide evidence that by 1696 the Poor Law funds collected and distributed annually were sufficient to support 10 per cent of the entire population for half of the year or 5 per cent for the entire year.[32] Alongside the universal entitlement to relief provided by the Poor Laws local leaders in every parish were also spurred on by the Charitable Uses Act to help the poor and sick to access education, training and medical care, and to prevent those who were most vulnerable from falling into destitution.[33] Thus England averted the disastrous consequences of famine and social breakdown seen elsewhere.

The system was not perfect by any means and it has certainly had its detractors both at the time and subsequently, notably the famous Edwardian social reformers Beatrice and Sidney Webb.[34] More recent critics have, for instance, drawn attention to the initiative from 1697 onwards to deter those in receipt of relief by attempting to compel the wearing of 'Pauper' badges, documented in several towns and parishes, though mostly only in the south of England and in the most difficult years.[35] These temporarily imposed shaming exercises had no perceptible effect on the sustained trend of rising expenditure on poor relief.[36]

Poor relief in the thousands of diverse parishes was, of course, far from a uniform experience for the poor, nor a smoothly oiled machine. There were times of tension in towns when high food prices led to protests by the poor to assert their rights.[37] The Poor Law did not magic away the harsh poverty, physical pain and loss of loved ones that many endured in eking out a living in what remained for the poor an economy of 'makeshifts'.[38] There were certainly individuals who had a hard time pleading their case for support. But the law was clear. It was a criminal offence to allow a poor person to starve and anyone destitute in a parish in England and Wales was entitled to relief.[39] The question that at times had to be resolved, though, was which parish had the responsibility – and this could be a complex legal issue. Parishes were, for instance, keen to move on single mothers with dependent children if they could prove their 'settlement' was elsewhere.

The copious surviving evidence of overseers' accounts and of settlement litigation shows that parishes could not let go of these matters and of their legal responsibilities. They would go to considerable lengths and much cost in certain cases to establish whether or not they had responsibility for a specific sojourner – travelling labourer – or pauper family. This demonstrates, above all else, how seriously these obligations were taken. While there was much local variation in practice, the evidence consistently shows the fundamental principle underlying the Poor Law statutes was ubiquitously observed and the parish's financial obligations that went with them were rigorously discharged throughout the land. All subjects knew they had an absolute entitlement to relief in their parish of settlement, which is why most made sure that each of their children was baptised and registered and that marriages and deaths were recorded;[40] and why surviving caches of letters demonstrate the poor adroitly using their rights and their bargaining power to negotiate their social security.[41]

For instance, Thomas Sokoll's publication, *Essex Pauper Letters 1731–1837,* gives a fascinating insight into how families were in practice able to secure their rights. Sokoll documents the case of David and Sarah Rivenall and their many children, who lived in London in the parish of St George in the East but received Poor Law payments from the overseers of Chelmsford, some 30 miles away. Thirty-four letters survive from the Rivenalls in the period between 1823 and 1829 (written for them in sixteen different hands!), as do the relevant overseers' records.[42] The Rivenalls, who had erratic work mostly selling oysters and who experienced increasing health problems, received a regular weekly allowance from Chelmsford. This was supplemented with additional payments on particular occasions, such as when debts were incurred in paying for a child's funeral.

Their money was handed to them by people authorised from Chelmsford, including a Mrs Nelson in Whitechapel and a coachman, Mr French, who travelled between Chelmsford and London and was entrusted with taking their money and providing information back to the overseers about the Rivenalls' situation.[43] In a desperate letter of 1826 David Rivenall threatens to return to Chelmsford with his whole family if he doesn't receive a favourable answer to his request to be advanced some money:

> Sir
>
> I am under the Necessity of informing You that I And 7 Children Are at this time in greatest distress And I have nothing to go to market with to Obtain Any relief for us there is three weeks money due on Saturday next And I hope You will bee so kind As to Advance mee a fortnite forward so that I may bee able to go to market to do my best for us if you don't think good to Comply with this whe Certainly must all Come to You Imeadietelly [sic].[44]

The Chelmsford authorities would have had no wish to see the Rivenalls returned to them, and Sokoll argues that 'their knowledge of the disadvantage of their removal to their home parish was the poor's best card' with their letters 'reveal[ing] how effectively they played this card'. Far better from the point of view of the Chelmsford overseers to send the regular payments and supplements that kept the Rivenalls in London where they at least had some prospect of 'going to market' to themselves provide for their children.[45]

The statutory Poor Laws, then, provided a sturdy and resilient backbone that was augmented by complementary philanthropic provision. In addition, all those who could continued to call upon family, friends and neighbours, following time immemorial practices of community solidarity.[46] The Poor Law deliberately encouraged such informal sources of support to continue but equally its officials realistically recognised that in many cases kin and neighbours were likely to be almost as poor as those applying for relief.

With its operation evolving across the generations, the combination of Poor Law and charitable provision developed over more than 200 years as an increasingly wide-ranging, flexible, locally diverse but effective system. In many towns, for instance, their densely settled parishes combined into 'Corporations of the Poor', pooling their resources in combination with the local charitable provisions available.[47] In the growing towns, the many philanthropic bequests by competitive, status-chasing wealthy merchants often supplied substantial support for the poor, particularly so in London, where the problems of catering for a large, mobile mass of the unsettled arriving from the provinces to seek their fortunes were always greatest. Thus, the Poor Law and Charitable Uses Acts operating together stimulated a sequence of innovative schemes, ranging for instance from the merchant Thomas Sutton's Charterhouse school and almshouse for poor boys and pensioners, which opened in 1611, to all the eighteenth-century subscription hospitals like Guy's, founded in 1721, and the Lock Hospital, offering free treatment from 1747 to the in-migrant poor who had caught a debilitating dose of the pox – venereal disease being a major menace in a capital city full of young adults looking for work.[48] It was a combined system that became more generous than anywhere else in the world; indeed, inexplicably so to some French eyes in the eighteenth century.[49]

No matter where they were in the realm and no matter what their circumstances, provided of course they were not refusing available work and had not committed a crime, the Poor Laws provided, above all else, absolute personal security from destitution to all subjects. Relief was given not only in times of food shortage but whenever they fell on hardship due to illness, accident, bereavement, frailty in old age or unemployment. Indeed, a much cited claim made by the Radical MP William Cobbett in the early nineteenth century was that 'the poor man in England is as secure from beggary as the king upon his throne, because when he makes known his distress to the parish officers, they bestow upon him, not alms but his legal dues'.[50]

At the height of the Poor Laws' operation in the hard year of 1802–3 there is evidence of year-round support being provided for fully 10–11 per cent of the population.[51] This was way beyond anything being done anywhere else at that time for the rural poor, and occurring in the most dynamic and successful economy in the world.

This collectivist-individualist society was the one into which John Locke (1632–1704) was born. The 'father of liberalism', Locke is credited with formulating the doctrine that each individual has a natural right to life, liberty and property. He came to these conclusions living in a polity that for the first time in history ubiquitously provided collectivist support for such universal individualism, free not only of feudal and monarchical but also from compelling familial and kinship constraints. Locke was describing a practical possibility that was already a reality even for many of the children of the poor in his society, thanks to its innovative Poor Law and charitable institutions.

The Turn Away from Collectivist Individualism after 1834

However, it was not to last. At the end of the eighteenth century, with protracted and expensive wars being pursued with Napoleonic France, the governing elite, influenced by new thinking stressing individual responsibility and agency, began to question the validity and expense of the Poor Laws' principle of collective provision. A new generation of liberal economists – Malthus, Ricardo and James Mill, successors to the free-market economics first championed by Adam Smith – came together in an unholy alliance with a group known as the Utilitarians. Together they argued, based on Jeremy Bentham's 'pleasure-pain' view of human nature, that workers must not be indulged into idleness but goaded and incentivised to work for whatever wages the market offered.[52] Even among the religious an evangelical turn increasingly saw the poor less as victims of misfortune to be offered the material assistance of charity and more as individual reprobates, who needed a dose of spiritual self-discipline and privation to reform themselves.[53]

A Royal Commission was set up to investigate the Poor Laws, its most influential figures being Nassau William Senior, the first professor at Oxford of the new 'science' of political economy, and Edwin Chadwick, Bentham's faithful secretary. Its selective methodology returned the verdict that the reformers wanted to hear – that the 'Old Poor Law' (as it would come to be known by historians) was too expensive and its misguided 'generosity' simply encouraged laziness – it bred 'paupers'. Chadwick then oversaw a national expansion of a new, deterrent system – the 'New' Poor Law enacted in 1834.[54]

Elizabethan 'outdoor' relief was ended, slashing in half (from approximately 2 per cent of national income to 1 per cent) funding for the country's long-standing system of social security, health and care for the aged poor within their communities.[55] It was replaced by the deliberately harsh conditions of the workhouse, into which, as Chadwick wrote, 'none will enter voluntarily'.[56] Husbands and wives were segregated in separate wings and required to undertake monotonous chores in return for meagre rations of gruel. This was to be immortalised by the hungry young Oliver holding out his bowl to the workhouse master pleading, 'Please Sir, I want some more?' in Charles Dickens' contemporary satirical novel of 1838, *Oliver Twist*.

The deterrent workhouses of the New Poor Law were also extended to Ireland in 1838, which had been incorporated into the United Kingdom in 1801. This rudimentary social security system was unfortunately not remotely up to the task of dealing with the catastrophe of the Irish potato blight fungus during 1845–51. Over a million people (about one in eight) died and a further million and a half fled as refugees (mostly to the USA) in what was the greatest microbial disaster in British history since the Black Death.

Although the Conservative prime minister Robert Peel famously split his own party by repealing the protectionist Corn Laws in 1846 (which had favoured the incomes of landowners) as part of the emergency response, which also involved dispensing 3 million soups a day at the height of the crisis in the summer of 1846, this proved to be in vain. His successors, the Whigs, who had brought in the radical Poor Law reforms in 1834, believed the crisis was over when the potato crop returned in 1847. They handed back all responsibility for the Irish poor to the workhouses, which

Image 25. Distress in Ireland: collecting limpets and seaweed for food.
Source: Universal Images Group / Getty Images

completely buckled the following year when the potato crop failed again. Suffused in the ideology of individualist political economy, the neglect of the Westminster government in leaving the Irish to their own devices at that point was responsible for the extreme loss of life that followed in the richest country on the planet.[57] The inadequacy of that response was all the more tragic and ironic for the fact that the English population had been protected from such a famine calamity for so long by the more humane Poor Laws that had been so recently replaced by the 1834 reforms.

This new ideological commitment to a cost-cutting, hands-off state with its laissez-faire free-market philosophy, which had in effect seen the Irish poor left to starve, was also damaging in other ways. The Victorian state manifestly failed to capitalise on the benefits that the Elizabethan regime of poor laws – working in harness with charity laws – had delivered in raising the quality of the nation's human capital (the economists' term for the wider health, well-being, training and education of the population). As industrialisation intensified in the nineteenth century public health went backwards in the industrial towns and cities. Workers and families made redundant both by enclosures in the countryside and by the competition of mechanised spinning and weaving crowded into the factory towns, which saw sharply rising death rates in the 1830s and 1840s, especially among those under the age of five.[58] In these same mushrooming towns literacy rates actually declined.[59]

The radical overhaul of the Poor Laws in 1834 intentionally put the working classes into a predicament of chronic vulnerability to ensure they accepted the wage rates it suited employers to offer in the 'free market'. The hated incarceral workhouses of the New Poor Laws triggered widespread protests and the grievances fed into the decades-long struggle for the vote by working men, which began with Chartism (1838–58).[60] Membership of Friendly and Burial Societies to mutually self-insure against hardships and the usage of pawnshops for credit all multiplied as families attempted to defend their security in a free-market economy of withdrawn state and parish support.[61]

During the second half of the nineteenth century Britain's manufacturing industry began to lose its world-leading place such that by the beginning of the twentieth century it had been overtaken by both the USA and Germany and then lost further ground to the USA in the interwar years. These were countries that had followed a different course as their economies industrialised. Fifty years after the Old Poor Law had been abandoned in Britain, Bismarck's Germany adopted a generous universal social insurance system for its workers during the 1880s. Primarily conceived as a measure to improve the productivity of the industrial economy, it was also for Bismarck a way of defusing workers' protests and the rise of the Social Democratic Party.[62] Meanwhile the USA was putting more than twice the public resources into educating its workforce as the UK every decade from 1850 to 1900, and led the UK by over thirty years in its commitment from 1910 to universal secondary education.[63]

Prior to 1834 Britain had been the world-leading high-wage economy, stimulating its entrepreneurs to invest in a whole sequence of famous labour-saving inventions such as the steam engine and the spinning jenny.[64] But the failure to maintain its lead in driving forward investments in human capital after the abandonment of the 'expensive' Old Poor Law held back productivity growth, squandering the enormous economic advantage that had been built up by the 1830s. As the century progressed UK productivity growth dipped to just 0.8 per cent a year between 1871 and 1911, while both Germany and the USA surged ahead with rates of 1.4 per cent and 1.5 per cent, respectively.[65] American blue-collar workers were now the world's most highly paid, stimulating American entrepreneurs to raise yet further their investment in machinery per worker to a staggering 90 per cent more than Britain's by 1900.[66]

By the end of Queen Victoria's reign – after 300 years of economic growth – Seebohm Rowntree's famous investigation into poverty shockingly found that, although children were no longer dying in their droves as in the 1840s, at any one moment 25–30 per cent of urban households were bringing up their children – the nation's future workforce – in conditions of harsh material poverty. Rowntree's research showed that life-cycle poverty in fact meant that far more than 30 per cent passed through periods of such poverty, especially at the point when they had several young children to feed and care for – exactly the kind of circumstances the Old Poor Law had been used to ameliorate before 1834.

Rowntree found that the causes of this poverty were mainly due to situations out of the control of the poor: most were poor because of low wages (52.0 per cent), some because they had very many children (22.2 per cent) and others because of the death or incapacity of the chief wage earner (20.7 per cent).[67] It was a far cry from the picture of laziness and disinclination to work painted by the economists and philosophers who had overturned the Old Poor Law in 1834.

The Boer War and the 'New Liberal' Reforms

It was war that once again began the slow process of reversing a prevailing social philosophy in Westminster. Newspapers were reporting that many working-class men brought up in poverty had to be rejected for service during the South African 'Boer' War of 1899–1902 because of their poor physical state. This had shocked many in the ruling class. It was an epiphany that ushered in a new willingness to challenge the harsh logic of the classical economic principles behind the reforms of 1834, with their focus on letting the market have free rein. No doubt rivalry with continental Germany and its formidable Prussian-officered army was also concentrating minds as the possibility of future war threatened.

With the 'New Liberal' government winning a landslide in January 1906 the next five years saw a suite of social legislation passed that introduced school meals and medical inspections (1907), old age pensions (1908), and Trade Boards (1909) to enforce minimum wages and conditions in the most exploited sectors of industry, many predominantly female, such as the chain-makers of Cradley Heath. Infant and maternity centres were also advocated and Labour Exchanges were established to help with finding work (1909). Most expensively, 'Bismarckian' national insurance was introduced for working men to protect family incomes against ill-health, accident and unemployment (1911). In 1909–11 Lloyd George pushed through his 'People's Budget' to help fund all of this, eventually overcoming entrenched House of Lords resistance to enforce a new progressive income tax on the wealthy.

Yet again a Royal Commission was set up to look at the operation of the Poor Law and its workhouses, by now mostly full of the old and the ill. The social reformer Beatrice Webb led an influential Minority Report of that commission in 1909, which argued for collective welfare support to deliver 'a national minimum of civilised life'[68] and a young researcher on that Minority Report – one William Beveridge – also published a seminal study showing that unemployment was mostly a problem generated by the economic system, not down to individuals' failings.[69]

Nevertheless, there was at that point no root and branch reform of the detested institutions of the Victorian Poor Law, which continued to operate as great hardship and poverty persisted. The interwar decades saw only modest improvement in the position of the poor overall, with

Image 26. Protest marchers on the Jarrow Crusade, March–October 1936.
Source: Keystone / Getty Images

austerity imposed from 1922 ('the Geddes Axe') instead of previous promises to build 'homes fit for heroes'. It was a period of recurrent mass unemployment, provoking the General Strike of 1926 and the many hunger marches, of which the famous Jarrow Crusade of October 1936 was only one.

The rationalist and individualist economic philosophy, now over a century old in its origins, was still militating against wholesale policies of collective support and mutual responsibility. A revolutionary new economic philosophy to bolster demand and employment, articulated by the great economist John Maynard Keynes, struggled in the 1930s to get a hearing in the corridors of power in either the Treasury or the Bank of England. Meanwhile,

British society was becoming a divisively class-ridden one, in which upper- and middle-class university students volunteered to strike-break in 1926 and those with a little property increasingly turned their backs on those without – sometimes literally. In north Oxford in 1934 a private developer built the notorious Cutteslowe Walls to keep out neighbouring council house tenants – not finally removed until 1959.[70]

Unemployment had risen in the 1920s at least in part due to the decision by the governing elite in 1925 to return to the Gold Standard and to set it at the pound's unrealistic pre-war valuation against the dollar, making British industry uncompetitive as a result. But this was as nothing to the unemployment seen in the Great Depression of the 1930s, triggered by the 1929 financial crash on Wall Street and seared into the memory of those who witnessed its unending dole queues. Indeed, it is unimaginable how much worse the effects might have been, had there been no underpinning national unemployment insurance, incomplete though it was, to mitigate the impact. How far in such circumstances might Oswald Mosley's Blackshirts have prospered politically?

Certainly, by the early stages of the Second World War the Archbishop of Canterbury, alarmed by what he had seen, endorsed the proposition that a welfare state should be understood as a democratic alternative to the fascism of a 'warfare state'. In 1942 William Beveridge published his famous – and best-selling – report setting the stage for just such a welfare state.[71]

To understand just how significant this would be we need only listen to the words of the nonagenarian Harry Smith, whose polemic memoir, *Harry's Last Stand: How the World My Generation Built Is Falling Down and What We Can Do to Save It*, was published in 2014.

Born in Barnsley in 1923 Harry describes his memory of sleeping next to his siblings on a reeking straw mattress, 'host to many insects', nevertheless a step up from the 'disease-ridden mining slum' where his older sister Marion had contracted tuberculosis. Harry recalls Marion's extreme pain as the disease 'ate away at her spine and invaded her vital organs' until, as he writes, in 1926

> *[o]n one of the last days in September my mother pawned her best dress and my father's Sunday suit and hired a man with an old dray horse and cart to come to our house and collect Marion … my dad carried Marion outside and carefully placed her into the delivery carriage where my mother was waiting for her … . I asked my dad where my sister was going and he mournfully replied: 'She's going to a better place than here.' Afterwards he put his arms around me … and we watched the horse-drawn carriage plod slowly down our road towards the workhouse infirmary.*[72]

Marion died a month later in her mother's arms and was buried in an unmarked paupers' grave, as his parents 'were too poor to afford the accoutrements of mourning'. They didn't even have a photograph to remember her by. It was an experience that was to stay with Harry for the rest of his life, inspiring his passionate campaign to protect the gains his generation had fought so hard for, as he explains in the Prologue to his book,

> *I don't have a degree in PPE from Oxbridge … But I have lived through nearly a hundred years of history. I have felt the sting of poverty, as well as the sweetness of security and success and I don't want to see everything we have worked for fall apart.*[73]

The 'Golden Age': 1945–73

In 1945 the young Harry Smith, newly returned from war, voted in a general election for the first time. It was in that epoch-defining year, following the victory in Europe over fascism, and now endowed since 1928 with universal suffrage, that the electorate, Harry among them, voted for the values of solidarity over individualism. The postwar welfare state was born, with Beveridge and Clement

Attlee – the first prime minister of a majority Labour government – its midwives.

After a 110-year absence, the collective responsibility principles of the Elizabethan (Old) Poor Law were reinstated with steeply progressive taxation once again funding universal provision of welfare, health care and now an expansion of education, too. The era's most iconic policy, the newly created National Health Service, delivered free universal health care to all from 1948. A new period of house building and slum clearance began, aiming to provide decent and affordable housing with internal hot and cold water and electricity for all (though this took decades to complete). Mothers were paid a family allowance and education was expanded with free secondary education provided for all children from 1944 and mandatory grants for university maintenance and fees established from 1962.

The post-war 'Golden Age', as it is known, lasted from 1945 to 1973. It was a period in which occupational and social mobility expanded, mass consumerism arrived, symbolised by the white goods revolution of fridges and washing machines along with fast-rising car ownership, as the economy's productivity growth fired upwards. From 1950 to 1973 UK productivity growth achieved a historic peak, averaging 2.4 per cent per annum – almost three times higher than throughout the entire period 1871–1937 and once again matching that of the USA.[74] These productivity gains were all the more impressive as they were achieved under conditions of full employment, another key government commitment that had been promised to working people when the welfare state was established.

According to official data, child poverty was varying at the low levels of 11–16 per cent from the early 1950s onwards (before the sharp rise to over double that level after 1979).[75] There was also a substantial decline in both income and wealth inequality, which had begun with

Lloyd George's progressive taxation measures and which now fell to among the lowest in the developed world.[76]

Alongside productivity, GDP grew at similarly steady and impressive rates, with uninterrupted growth that averaged 3 per cent per annum for a quarter of a century up until 1973. Keynesian policies of demand management (to prevent large rises in unemployment) ensured that there were none of the deep plunges into recession that came subsequently, as Figure 12 shows, at least, that is, until the oil price crises of the 1970s brought the era to an abrupt end.

While there were certainly many economic challenges emerging to take the shine off the Golden Age during the 1960s and early 1970s, inflation and balance of payments crises among them, neither the steady and consistent growth in GDP nor the productivity performance have been matched in the UK since that time.

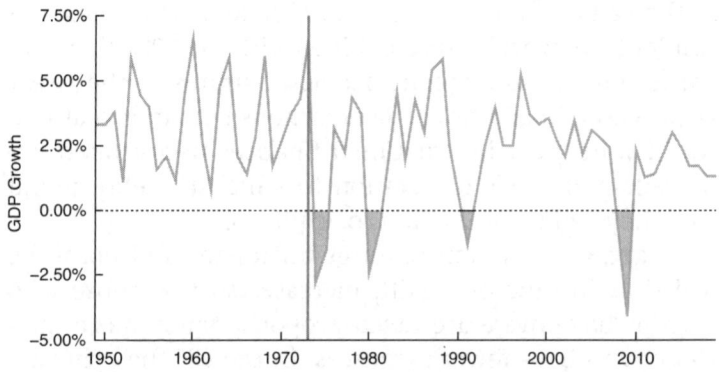

Figure 12. Gross Domestic Product, year on year growth, 1949–2019. Note: Authors' addition of shading to show periods of negative growth post-1973. Chart ends in 2019 prior to COVID-19.
Source: Office for National Statistics (2021c)

Wealth, Redistribution and Progressive Taxation

In his ground-breaking work *Capital in the Twenty-First Century*, Piketty argues that the decades after 1911 were unique in recent economic history in curtailing wealth concentrations. His analysis shows that, whereas in the years around 1910 the top decile of wealth owners in France and the UK were in command of around 90 per cent of all capital, and in the USA 80 per cent, by the early 1970s this had reduced in all three countries to around 60–65 per cent.[77] This, Piketty argued, is an exception to a general tendency of unconstrained capitalist economies to produce ever-increasing wealth inequality as the returns to simply owning wealth outpace overall growth and returns to work.[78]

Piketty's analysis shows that for several decades leading up to the 1970s a set of historically unusual circumstances coalesced to lessen wealth inequality in both Europe and the USA. This was due first of all to the severe depletion in the value of the stock of capital held by the elites as a result of two world wars combined with the 1929 financial crash and the subsequent business failures of the Great Depression. In addition, the enormous demands that two world wars placed on national finances necessitated unprecedented levels of taxation to which the elite found that they had no option but to acquiesce.

Progressive taxation requires higher rates of tax to be levied as income or wealth increases so that those who earn or have more are taxed proportionately more than those who have fewer resources. In the UK the principle of progressive taxation of inheritance, capital and income, originally established in 1911, was extended during the Second World War and then successfully retained by a post-war generation, now fully enfranchised and collectively endorsing the equitable rebuilding of their societies through a redistributionist state.

Support for much steeper taxation of income and wealth was, as Piketty shows, also strong in the USA from early on. Irving Fisher, the most highly respected economist in the USA and president of the American Economic Association, had argued in 1919 that the concentrations of wealth accumulated by robber barons like Carnegie and Rockefeller posed a threat to democracy that should be remedied by a 100 per cent tax on estates once it got to the third generation, to prevent, as he argued, the USA coming to resemble neo-aristocratic Old Europe.[79]

Although hard to believe in today's neoliberal world, for four decades from 1940 to 1980 the USA had widely supported top tax rates of between 70 and 90 per cent – applied to the highest part of income – and in the UK the top rate of income tax was 90 per cent or above for almost the entire forty-year period, as can be seen in Figure 13.

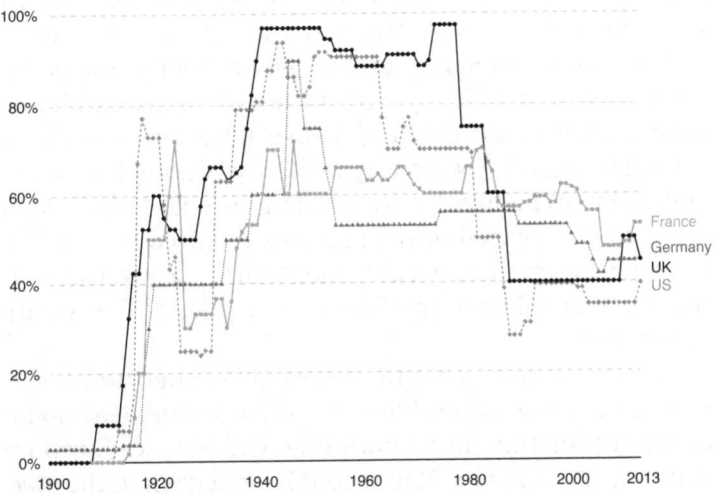

Figure 13. Comparison of top marginal income tax rates, 1900–2013 in the USA, UK, France and Germany.
Note: Chart reproduced from Our World in Data, https://ourworldindata.org/grapher/top-income-tax-rates-piketty

The US economy grew at least as strongly during the post-war period of high taxes on the wealthy as it has since, while the UK economy, as demonstrated above, experienced its highest historic rates of productivity growth during the three post-war decades of high progressive taxation. As Piketty argues, in eras of higher marginal tax rates such as this, business leaders are likely to switch from actions directed towards personal gain, in which they are no longer so invested, to decisions that focus on the longer-term productivity of their companies that deliver a wider, inclusive economic benefit. In other words high taxation of top incomes can create incentives for more beneficial economic behaviours.[80]

During this period of our history, with high marginal tax rates on the highest incomes and 'the introduction of progressive death duties and taxes on the unearned incomes from ownership of capital ... "inheritance collapsed" and in its place something more like meritocracy and upward social mobility arose'.[81] This saw the elite 10 per cent of capital owners joined by another 40 per cent of the population who were able to convert their earnings into home ownership.[82] Thus, the progressive taxation of both income and wealth – beginning with Lloyd George's People's Budget in 1911 and fully extended in the post-1945 Golden Age – saw a reversal of the previous hundred years of increasing income and wealth inequalities, a reversal that was maintained until the final two decades of the twentieth century.

Critically, these new resources also supported a sustained period of equitable investment in the health and education of the entire nation as the post-war welfare state was established. This, though, ended when the electorate returned a series of Conservative governments after 1979, whose policies dramatically reduced taxation on highest incomes and on the capital-owning elite. It led, as Piketty's analysis would predict, to a resurgence of inequality and also a significant rise in poverty, as neoliberalism took hold.

What Lessons Can We Take from History?

The lessons of the two distinct periods of impressive productivity growth in the British economy – 1601–1870 and 1951–73 – are very clear. They indicate to us something important about how the long-established characteristics of British society and culture can be best harnessed to support an inclusive and sustainable economy and society. There are six key lessons in common in both periods.[83]

Lesson 1: Embracing Collective Responsibility

Of critical importance is **a positive value of collective responsibility as expressed in Britain's indigenous invention of collectivist individualism**, dating back to institutions established from 1601. British society – and its economy – has flourished most when it has embraced both **universal social security and welfare as a legal entitlement of all citizens aimed at enhancing the positive freedoms of all those needing its support.** Such universal support contributes positively to the welfare of all by building extensive human capital (in economists' terms) to support economic productivity; and it is therefore foolish to see welfare as a burden or a supposedly unproductive cost on the economy or as something that should be begrudged to the fellow citizens who need it. The provision of collective support and security is essential for independent individualism and initiative to flourish at all levels of society, not just among the privileged.

Lesson 2: Guaranteed Freedom from Insecurity

Absolute guaranteed security for all citizens from the primary wants of food and shelter provided by the state should be a matter of national pride, not, as currently, when a miserly government has to be shamed into meeting these needs. This is not only because they are humanitarian rights that a civilised society should uphold, but also because history shows they are crucial forms of freedom for all citizens to be able to begin to act as independent economic and political agents. The true and long-term cost to the economy is not in the transfer payments that should ensure that all have food and housing security, but in the inability of those denied these functional basics to act independently; and because they are sentient humans who understand this degradation to their dignity, sources of psychic escape might be sought that are further costly to themselves and society. The now more than 2,000 food banks and the nearly 800 deaths on the streets in 2019, many linked to alcohol and drug addiction,[84] each demonstrate – as the repeated hunger marches of the interwar decades did in their different way – the current policy failure here.

Lesson 3: Maximising Labour Mobility and Individual Opportunity

Institutional and economic conditions that maximise labour mobility and access to new sources of desirable employment for the rising younger generation are crucial. This was true both in the era before 1834 when the security of poor relief enabled a rapid growth in labour mobility to towns and in the Golden Age when free educational opportunities at secondary and tertiary levels were repeatedly upgraded starting in 1944. At the same time, both geographical and social mobility were supported by a reasonably generous social security system for the mobile young and the immobile elderly, respectively; while housing opportunities for the independent young to build families were affordable across the economy.

Lesson 4: Endorsing Progressive Taxation

Contributions to public services by the more prosperous should be seen as both a responsibility that they willingly accept and a civic commitment, in which they wish to participate. The combined 1601 Acts of Elizabeth I encouraged the flowering of this dual ethos. After 1945 **the acceptance of steeply progressive taxation rates** for several decades signalled that the wealthier minority of society found it reasonable that the taxes they paid were **invested in all of their society's human capital**, and that their greater than average incomes were not just for the benefit of themselves and their own offspring. They were accepting the responsibility in particular to engage in funding health, education and training for all sections of society. This ethos needs to be fully endorsed once again.

Lesson 5: Incentivising Long-Term Behaviours

The **leaders of enterprise** were in both periods **incentivised to consider the long-term productivity of the assets under their management alongside the long-term welfare of their workforce and local communities** in which they operated. In the era of the Old Poor Law landowners and farmers in England engaged in major and often quite risky undertakings, redrawing the fields of their parishes, draining lands and innovating rotation crops, building turnpike roads and later canals and excavating mines. Little of this was a source of immediate returns and much of it required them to pay attention to the co-prosperity of the working families, for whom – through their Poor Law obligations – they could not abdicate responsibility. In Britain's late Victorian cities its leading businessmen concluded that natural monopoly services would best serve the hard-pressed community's longer-term interests by being placed in municipal hands, instead of serving the narrow interests of their own class.

In the Golden Age era, the equivalent class, the captains of both nationalised and private industry, were also constrained by the institutional and incentive structure system within which they found themselves. This meant focusing on the long-term prosperity of the businesses they ran, drawing their source of personal esteem and sense of achievement from the whole organisation's long-term performance and that of its workers, and not so much from their own salary levels – because the very high rates of marginal tax reduced their interest in such purely personal rewards. This was reflected in a shared and broad view among business leaders themselves of the corporation as being in service to its whole community.

Lesson 6: Locking in Rewards and Sanctions

A credible system of rewards, monitoring and sanctions underpins participation in the collective endeavour. In the era of the Elizabethan Poor Law small, close communities meant that all contributions to poor relief were transparent and Justices of the Peace secured compliance. Those making philanthropic contributions were publicly acknowledged in the many church plaques and civic memorials still visible today. After the Second World War, the extremely high marginal tax rates for the rich were continued even by several successive Conservative governments (1951–64), as the elite accepted the moral case for building a welfare state in the new democracy. Electoral support for the educational and health improvements secured by the post-war settlement was judged too strong to row back on. As the economy prospered, a society-wide consensus was maintained until the economic crises of the 1970s that precipitated the rise of neoliberalism, with a harsh individualist philosophy and associated weakening of sanctions against tax evasion and avoidance.

*

We will be drawing on these lessons from our history and the strong values that underpin them as we develop our proposals for the ways in which a nurturing state can build the right structures and incentives to revitalise the empowering society that is our principal historical legacy and which we need to rediscover to face the challenges of the post-viral world we are now entering.

12 A NURTURING AND EMPOWERING STATE

What Does It Mean to Have a Nurturing and Empowering State?

A nurturing state empowers its citizens by providing them with protection from vulnerabilities, with resources for all to achieve their potential, and with access to full participation in democratic institutions and decision making. It is based on an ethos of collective responsibility that values and nurtures everyone's well-being, giving this precedence over policies that tend to benefit only a privileged minority. It begins with recognising that all humans are first and foremost social and moral beings, wanting and needing to form trusting relations with others in order to thrive. They are not the desiccated, selfish, calculating machines of *Homo economicus*.

A nurturing state must legislate to create the right balance of institutions, norms and incentives to promote the practices of collectivist individualism among all its self-governing communities and families. It must start by clearly recognising the inherent tendencies and forces within a market economy that can cause imbalances and ensure that it is continually working to preserve the desirable balance, by holding the ring impartially to constrain the actions and influence of the overpowerful.

It stands in contrast to the neoliberal state of the last forty years, which under Thatcher's premiership drew to the centre as much executive political power as it could, reducing the independence of elected local government authorities and disabling as much as possible the bargaining power of trade unions. The democratic importance of these institutions was disregarded as their powers were seen as inconvenient impediments to the central government's programme. This strong-arm state was justified in the eyes of the neoliberal ideologists as being necessary to enable the free market to operate untrammelled, which they believed would supercharge the efficiency of the economy.[1] It has in its many iterations of the last forty years proved itself for too much of the time to be a severely disempowering state, in which many were excluded by poverty and lack of opportunity and in which active citizenship and participation were stifled, while overall economic performance has in fact been indifferent.

Freedom and the State

Libertarians characterise a would-be nurturing state, gathering in taxes so that it may support its more vulnerable citizens, as a 'Big Brother' threat – undesirably 'strong' in a smothering sense. Friedrich Hayek argued in 1944, for instance, that William Beveridge's plans for a welfare state would set the British on *The Road to Serfdom*. Mrs Thatcher, who idolised Hayek, invoked the image of 'the nanny state' as an interferer that prevented individuals from enjoying their freedom; and David Cameron echoed that view with the bogeyman of the 'Big State' standing in the way of his wish to see a 'Big Society' of active citizens. These anti-state political motifs appeal to what philosophers since Isaiah Berlin identify as 'negative liberty'.[2]

Negative liberty is the freedom of the individual from constraints imposed by others and most particularly by government and its officials. However, even the most committed libertarians accept, since Thomas Hobbes, that in order to benefit from living within a society there are certain laws that one has to abide by. These relate to the safety from violence of your person and your property and, as an extension of this, the payment of taxes to ensure the defence of your society. This negative liberty ideal of government was called 'the Nightwatchman state' when applied to mid-Victorian Britain.[3] It licensed the creation of county police forces all around the country from 1856 and the funding of the Royal Navy on a colossal scale, such that it could overpower the two next biggest navies in the world even if they combined together.

As the Chinese learned to their cost, that outsize navy was not merely to deter the kind of attack on the British Isles that Napoleon had planned. It was also very useful to expand Britain's 'peaceful' commercial interests all across the globe, the so-called Pax Britannica. Britain literally did rule the waves and enforced 'free trade' wherever it could, which meant concluding treaties with weaker powers giving British merchants open access – on British consular terms – to their markets. Across rural India village customs of centuries were converted by fiat of the Raj into individualist property rights and contracts. For China this infamously included the right to push opium on an industrial scale, exporting it from the Indian colony to the powerless Chinese emperor's populace. The British state was using its might to enforce free trade. It was asserting the negative liberty of British merchants to contract to sell whatever there was a market for, without interference by a would-be protective Chinese state.[4]

Here we come to a critical inconsistency for those wanting a world of negative liberty or freedom. It has to be imposed by a very powerful central state. This is not the kind of central state that provides social security, free education and health care to the poor – because that would require substantially taxing the more prosperous, another infringement of their negative freedom (to be taxed as little as possible). Instead, it is a strong state simply focused on increasing to its maximum extent the free market and to protecting through law, police and at times state-sanctioned violence the interests of property and capital. Hayek was quite open that the sanctity of private property and its negative liberty came first, democracy came second.[5] This kind of strongly state-imposed negative freedom, through exclusion and repressive control of the poor, exhibits its self-contradictory nature to the greatest extent across the USA, which has for some time incarcerated a far higher proportion of its adult citizens (about 1 in 100) than any other state on the planet, including Russia.[6]

In a world with many diverse and gross inequalities of power and resources, if we simply subscribe to the tenets of negative liberty as our touchstone for governance, we in effect agree to allow those with greater power the freedom to do pretty much as they please. History sadly confirms that time and again this helps only the minority and disempowers the majority. As R.H. Tawney put it, 'freedom for the pike is death for the minnows'.[7] So, if we really care about *all* people's freedoms, we have to turn to the principles designated by Isaiah Berlin as those of 'positive liberty'.

Positive freedoms empower all citizens in society to reach their full potential, truly nurturing what the economist Amartya Sen and the philosopher Martha Nussbaum have called their 'capabilities', to ensure all have genuine access to the opportunities available in their society.[8] They provide without fail for all classes, genders, regions and ethnicities a sufficiency of resources of quality housing, education, training, health care and social security. With an equal start in life all people can independently make their way and all have a realistic and equitable chance of choosing from a wide range of options to use their aptitudes and interests to live up to their own definition of fulfilled lives.

It is a widespread, commonly uttered clarion call by the successful, 'to follow your dreams no matter how impossible they may seem'. Lewis Hamilton said this after winning the Formula 1 championship on 4 July 2020. But without a nurturing state, this simply remains an impossible dream for most of Lewis Hamilton's fellow citizens of colour in either the UK or USA. 'We can't breathe' was the predominant feeling expressed by millions in both countries following the agonising killing of George Floyd in Minneapolis on 25 May 2020.[9]

To achieve a degree of dream-fulfilment – and basic well-being – for the vast majority of the population, including those born disadvantaged, requires a substantial amount of resources devoted to each citizen, especially while young and developing. This is the nurturing state offering positive freedoms to all. In universal suffrage democracies this has become an electorally feasible option, as was seen in the many welfare states that were created after 1945. They are funded in a variety of ways but all aim to collectively protect the populace from vulnerabilities. Though far from perfect and quite variable in their manifestations, modern welfare states have proved to be the best, empowering machines so far devised.[10]

Welfare states are also, it should be added, seen by all, bar the most extreme free-market zealots, as essential to the very viability of capitalist societies. As Professor David Garland writes in his analysis of the welfare state and its relationship to capitalism,

> Societies that allow economic life to be governed by the logic of private profit and market competition are societies at risk. They are prone to rapid undirected change; to socially-damaging concentrations of wealth and inequality; to crises of accumulation; and to periodic economic collapse – sometimes on a worldwide scale … . The chief characteristics of capitalist societies are uncertainty, insecurity [and] inequality … generat[ing] damaging consequences for our social and natural environments … . To

> *avoid self-destruction, capitalism needs a set of countervailing*
> *forces. And welfare states are the embodiment of these forces*
> *established in a functional, institutional form ... [T]he social*
> *regulation of markets, the social insurance of workers and the*
> *public provision of social services and protections ... are [the]*
> *counterweight to problem-prone capitalist economies that could*
> *not exist without them.*[11]

In other words, the pure negative liberty of unregulated capitalism would always contain the seeds of its own destruction. The experience of the last forty years suggests that the balance has now shifted far too far in the direction of the economically and socially damaging crises that Garland identifies. We need a more proactive state, committed to positive not negative freedoms, that intervenes to temper and manage these risks.

Building Collective Commitment

The virtue of a nurturing state is that everyone is provided with the social, emotional and physical resources they need to flourish. The aim is straightforward: it must be to guarantee to all citizens freedom from insecurity on the one hand, through an adequate safety net, and to ensure that they have the ability to lead a fulfilled life on the other. This must be an actively pursued objective in which engrained poverty, inequality and disadvantage are sought out and dealt with so that all can participate equally.

As Michael Marmot has emphasised, decades of experience with universalist services have shown that this requires not simple universal provision, but 'proportionate universalism'.[12] The most disadvantaged in society need additional and supplementary tailored assistance to access and benefit from their universal rights. Examples would be policies that have provided extra educational support to those at risk of falling behind through programmes such as 'Every Child a Reader', or the additional government funding provided to schools according to the number of disadvantaged children on their roll, delivered via the 'pupil premium'. Far more ambitious programmes are going to have to be designed now to set about the task of reversing widening educational inequality in the aftermath of the pandemic.

Truly universal public services must be resourced well enough and be of sufficient quality that the articulate in society will also use and – therefore – politically support them. However, all research shows that it tends to be the assertive, confident and sharp-elbowed who get the best out of such generally provided services. To actually deliver genuine equity of universal provision to people of colour, the poor, the disabled or otherwise underprivileged will require additional assistance. That means properly funded and facilitating public servants to advise, translate and guide, so that they may be empowered by receiving the same support as everybody else.

Whereas the confident middle classes tend to use their own networks for advice or perhaps go to the Citizens Advice Bureau when they know they need assistance accessing services, the less privileged need equivalent mentors within the public services to be with them from the start to build their confidence in their entitlements. In the aftermath of COVID-19's impact on the most deprived communities it will be crucial to provide this support. Building trust in the public health infrastructure, for instance, and in particular securing widespread vaccination take-up is crucial so that COVID-19 does not persist as a disease of poverty and inequality.

The nurturing state must also create an economic system within which citizens and their institutions can flourish, and which is not 'rigged' in favour of the few. Its foundation must be a commitment to a shared collective responsibility for realising its aims, in particular through high levels of progressive taxation. Contributing to the well-being of the whole of one's society, progressively pro rata to one's resources, should be an honour that all individual citizens would want to be seen to fulfil. It should be a value that all businesses are happy to be judged and measured by, and which they understand to be a higher priority than simply the maximising of profits. Indeed, the creation of a moral and civic commitment to a wider empowering society is one of the core lessons that we have drawn on from our own history. It is an essential aim of the policies and architecture of incentives that are put in place by a nurturing state.

Some of those occupying more privileged positions and holding excesses of resources will not of course find the nurturing state an attractive proposition. Those subscribing to the self-centred *Homo economicus* view of the world may choose to see the transfer of resources from themselves to others as 'handouts' to the lazy, rather than 'hand-ups' to those who will thrive from the assistance provided. That is why, with the rise of welfare states, we have seen the parallel rise of tax exiles, tax havens and an industry of tax avoidance and evasion (centred in London and the USA), which is only now becoming fully exposed to view, following the Panama Papers.[13] For the super-rich it has bred a 'Wealth Defence Industry'. Accountants, lawyers and consultants – often working within a 'family office' – support dynasties of wealth hoarders in which successive generations of the super-rich use trusts and other complex devices to pass on and shield their wealth from taxation.[14] All of these mechanisms serve wealthy individuals who have made provision to exit fiscally from the society they were born into – and which often they continue to live in for large parts of the year and continue to draw their personal wealth from – because they don't see the need to contribute to the positive freedoms of other people in their society, or at least not to the extent that the democratically elected government considers fair and just.

There should be zero tolerance for this kind of free-riding by the privileged (whether avoiding or evading). Justices of the Peace were given the role in the past of policing those not paying their Poor Law rates. Today, domestically it needs a fully staffed and respected tax inspectorate prosecuting rigorously the GAAR (the general anti-abuse rule, which is supposed to discourage highly ingenious forms of tax avoidance). This would move us on from the position we found ourselves in 2002 when the HMRC's compliance efforts were exposed as being 'in a state of virtual collapse' such that it was giving 'special favours to the largest corporate tax payers'.[15] And although already understaffed, after 2004 over four in ten officials were further removed from HMRC's workforce over the next decade.[16]

Internationally, it needs transparency. This is the principle behind Gabriel Zucman's important proposal for a worldwide register of financial wealth as the key to curtailing the abuse of tax havens, which are accurately described as secrecy jurisdictions – of value primarily to those with something to hide.[17] Several of the highly successful Scandinavian societies – Sweden, Norway and Finland – make what every citizen contributes in taxation to their society a matter of public knowledge.[18] This would be a foundational move towards instilling an ethos of pride in collective contribution among all citizens and residents of the UK.

The word 'tax', with all its pejorative associations of warring monarchs extracting payments from unwilling subjects during past centuries, should perhaps be consigned to history. Instead, the term 'civic contribution' could be adopted in its place, as providing a correct description of what this empowering transaction in fact is for today in a voting democracy committed to nurturing all its citizens.

The Case for Fair and Progressive Contributions

A common argument that is made when the case is put for higher tax contributions from those with the most income or wealth is that the number of people this would apply to would be too small to be able to raise significant extra revenue. The corollary of this position is that you need instead to focus on the amount of tax paid by the majority of the population, not the small minority of the wealthy, if a higher tax take is being sought.

This argument seems flawed from the start, when you consider the amount of current tax evasion, avoidance and offshoring by the wealthy. A robust minimum estimate is that fully 10 per cent of European citizens' financial assets were held in tax havens in 2015. Interestingly in the USA, which had far stricter regulations on tax, the figure was only 4 per cent, indicating what can be achieved solely through legal enforcement means, since nobody is suggesting that wealthy Americans liked paying their taxes more than rich Europeans.[19]

Be that as it may, the whole argument is in any case a bit of a smokescreen since it takes our attention away from the most crucial issue we should be discussing, which should not be how much can be raised from this or that group of taxpayers at any particular moment in time. Raising the tax rate on higher incomes and wealth is important not primarily because of the amounts of money raised from the wealthiest citizens. Rather it is the means to achieve consent among the middling ranks of income earners (those beneath the elite), to the fairness of the principle of everyone paying a higher rate of tax as their income goes up. Or to put it another way, it is about the need for everyone to be seen to be part of a collective endeavour in which each citizen knows that those with more wealth and income than themselves are contributing proportionately more out of those extra resources – and that this principle goes right to the top of the income and wealth pyramid. Only then can the tax system be seen as manifesting a collective system of just civic contributions.[20]

A different critique of calls for increased taxation of the better-off is that we already have a progressive income tax system since the marginal tax rate in the UK rises from 20 per cent to 40 per cent and then 45 per cent at its highest. This could just boil down, then, to an argument about the degree of progressiveness – clearly a top rate of 45 per cent is far less progressive than historic rates of 80 or 90 per cent. In fact, the argument is a lot more complex because most of the way that we tax is not progressive at all.

Many taxes are levied at a fixed percentage of purchase prices or as flat-rate contributions: VAT on goods and services, fuel tax and duties on alcohol and cigarettes, insurance tax and the BBC licence fee to name but a few. These taxes take up a bigger slice of the income of the poorest households, meaning these sorts of indirect taxes on sales are fundamentally regressive, as all economists know. National Insurance contributions, a tax in all but name, are regressive, too. Higher earners pay a lower rate – just 2 per cent – above a specified earnings threshold. On top of that, anyone who has started drawing a pension, whatever their age or income, is still liable for income tax, but becomes instantly exempt from National Insurance contributions, as are those still working over state retirement age.

Then there are all the reliefs and allowances built into our system. These in effect transfer billions of pounds each year in what amounts to a 'hidden welfare state' of tax benefits. It is a highly regressive system skewed towards wealthier households. The exemption of private homes from Capital Gains Tax, for instance, costs £25 billion a year. Subsidies for retirement savings cost even more – £40 billion a year – with tax relief on pension contributions higher for those on higher incomes, regressively rewarding those who are better-off in the first place.[21] We also forgo all of the tax revenue that we cannot collect because of private schools' historic status as charities, including VAT on school fees, despite the beneficiaries being the most privileged in our society.

All of this is amplified by the way that the tax system treats wealth. While we continue with a situation in which, in aggregate, earned income is taxed at a rate that is several multiples higher than the rate at which the proceeds from owning wealth are taxed, then we are not likely to have a progressive tax system. As Richard Murphy, Professor of Political Economy at City University, London, puts it,

> *if we treat all sources of financial gain to a household, whether from income or from increases in the value of assets as being of equal value then we have a very regressive tax system [in which] those on the lowest levels of income pay by far the highest tax rates, while those with the highest income pay at the lowest rates.*[22]

This is the inevitable consequence of not taxing wealth effectively. Hence Murphy estimates that, when earned income, unearned increases in wealth (housing, pensions etc.) and indirect taxes such as VAT are all added in, the effective tax rate for the top 10 per cent of income taxpayers is only 18 per cent. That makes it less than half the 42 per cent effective tax rate paid by the lowest earning 10 per cent of taxpayers.[23] This will surely come as quite a surprise to most fair-minded readers.

Higher marginal rates of income taxation and a reformed and fair way of taxing wealth are therefore essential if we are to achieve a genuinely progressive tax system. The case for raising income tax on the wealthy through higher marginal tax rates has also been made on the world stage by Kristalina Georgieva, the IMF's managing director, who argued in early 2020 that such a move would help close the growing gap between rich and poor, and, importantly, that it could be done without harming growth.[24] A year later the IMF was pressing for a 'solidarity tax' on pandemic winners and the wealthy. Vitor Gaspar, their head of fiscal affairs, argued that countries should be considering doing this whether or not they need to raise revenue, because it would help boost their citizens' perception 'that everybody contributes to the effort necessary for recovery from Covid-19'. Here, then, was a major international organisation promoting progressive taxation directly on grounds of social solidarity.[25]

For all that this may seem heart-warming, there are still those who object that increasing taxes may be self-defeating if it results in people working less (or businesses investing less) or just making greater efforts to get out of paying the extra taxes. This harks back to a concept known as the Laffer Curve, named after the economist Arthur Laffer, who by popular myth drew a diagram on a napkin after dinner to convince his fellow diners that raising tax rates above a certain level does not work because it will lead people to change their behaviour and, hey presto, the tax take will go down.[26]

Sitting perfectly in the neoliberal playbook as an argument for low taxation (Laffer was awarded the Presidential Medal of Freedom in 2019 by none other than that great tax-paying exemplar Donald Trump) the evidence on its applicability is thin, and estimates of any actual likely upper bound to tax rates highly variable. For instance, the respected Mirrlees Review of possible UK income tax rises in 2011 stated that 'we do not know with confidence what the revenue-maximising top tax rate is' – by which they meant the highest tax rate you can introduce before government revenues start being affected. Noting the statistical uncertainty around even pretty broad estimates of what that maximum rate might be, the review went on to focus on compliance. It argued that 'widening the income tax base – removing reliefs and clamping down on avoidance – not only raises money directly but also reduces the scope for shifting income into tax-free forms'. This would then, they conclude, 'make tax rate increases more effect-ive revenue-raisers'.[27]

Interestingly, a more recent investigation into how peo-ple might respond to potential income tax increases in the UK reported that 'it is unlikely that top taxpayers will work less hard, but it is likely they will try harder to avoid paying tax. This means tougher enforcement will be need-ed if taxes rise.'[28] In other words, given the presumption that people resist paying higher taxes, these studies are arguing that in practice it is how we resource and enforce the collection of tax that is as important in determining the amounts we can ultimately raise as the tax rate itself. As the dramatic cut in HMRC personnel over the last two decades reminds us, that is a political choice.

Higher tax rates would not mean that there would still not be plenty of people with ten or even twenty times the after-tax average of income or wealth. It just means that it would be very difficult for any individual to rack up mul-tiples of fifty or even 100 times the average, and, even if they did, then we could all be sure that they would at least have made extremely large contributions to society in doing so.

A fully progressive system of taxation can and should now be used to build social cohesion and consensus. In-stead, we have had four decades in which an increasing-ly segregated super-rich are encouraged to become ever more resentful of the taxes extracted from the wealth mountains they are obsessively heaping up, eager only to copy their mates in the game of whatever 'tax dodge' they can find next, and oblivious to the needs of the vast major-ity of others. Its amorality is perfectly captured by the Scot-tish comedian Frankie Boyle: 'If you're rich, don't look at it as tax avoidance, look at it as a children's hospital buying you a pool table.'[29]

The empowering society of positive freedoms overturns these motivations – it asks something different, something moral from those at the top of our society. Why not be proud of contributing to a children's hospital, to nurses and the NHS, care workers, social workers, police, ambulance and fire services? Why not see it as a moral duty that no one in your society should be going without food? The tragedy of the neoliberal view of taxation, endorsed by too many of the wealthy, is that something that should be viewed with pride and honour as their civic contribution has instead become something resented and divisive, as they lead their separate lives.[30] On the contrary, full and fair progressive tax contributions are the lifeblood of the healthy body of the empowering society.

Despite the fact that it has become received wisdom among journalists and politicians that what everyone wants is to pay less in tax, this flies in the face of the evidence. Gallup polls from 1978 onwards always showed support for tax cuts was falling from the beginning of Mrs Thatcher's period in office.[31] Data from the British Social Attitudes survey, which has been running every year since 1983, have consistently shown over many decades that more than 90 per cent of people do not want tax cuts that would reduce spending on education, health and social benefits (an impressive statistic curiously ignored by mainstream media and politicians).[32] Moreover, the proportion who actually support higher taxation to increase spending on public services (as opposed to just keeping tax constant) increased from 30 per cent to 60 per cent between 2010 and 2017 – driven mainly by an increase in support from Conservative voters – replicating the public level of support for such higher taxation seen throughout the 1990s.[33]

In the UK, therefore, a majority of the public agrees on the importance of supporting our public services – and doing so through a progressive income tax system. This has remained strong even during the four decades of the era of neoliberalism, at least among the general population, although owners of many newspapers and the journalists they employ consistently seem to have been fixated on the opposite story. During the post-war Golden Age in the UK there was in fact a society-wide consensus for the best part of three decades that endorsed top marginal tax rates on both income and wealth of 80 per cent and above.

We cannot afford now to fall into the dangerous position where ordinary citizens start to believe that there is 'one rule for us' and 'another rule for them' (the rich). If those with the broadest shoulders are not seen to be fair contributors to their society – even celebrating their ability to avoid doing so (as Donald Trump did in his election encounter on the subject of his tax avoidance with Hillary Clinton in 2016) – then the consensus needed to support a nurturing state will erode. Authors of Elizabeth I's Old Poor Law understood that, in their own way, and put in place strict compliance measures to ensure all were paying their dues, with complete transparency over what these were. This is a lesson from our history we would do well to replicate.

Democratic Participation and Devolved Power

Politics is always at risk in every democracy of being captured by sections of the wealthy, who seek to steer the legal and regulatory framework to serve their interests, as well as the lobbying power of the largest and most well-connected corporations, many of whom in the UK have become commercial providers of tax-funded public services. Consequently, it should not be in the least contentious that there need to be strong safeguards against this tendency and its many unseen and informal manifestations. Any society that does not have carefully policed defences and sanctions – which are themselves open to inspection and review by representatives of the public drawn from outside the worlds of politics and business – cannot function as an effective democracy.

The Freedom of Information Act put on the statute books in 2000 by New Labour gave the promise of a counterweight to this, creating a presumption in favour of more open government. Freedom of Information requests certainly played a vital role initially in empowering individual citizens and rendering government more accountable, including, famously, in enabling the MPs' expenses scandal to come to light. However, increasing delays in responding, rising rejections of requests and the operation of a clandestine 'Clearing House' in the Cabinet Office to monitor 'sensitive' Freedom of Information requests and log the names of the journalists submitting them are now revealing a worrying 'trend towards greater secrecy in central government'.[34] Contracts outsourced to private contractors for the delivery of public services are in any case not properly within the scope of the Act, putting them substantially beyond this tool of public scrutiny and leaving a glaring hole in transparency at a time of great sensitivity over government contracts.

It became clear during the pandemic just how difficult it is to disentangle the way in which public contracts are being awarded, who is benefiting from them, whether there are conflicts of interest or whether due diligence has been carried out. It seems it is often now left to the Public Accounts Committee and the National Audit Office to question the transparency, propriety and basic value for money of key areas of public contracting and delivery. All the while too little is being done to stop the 'revolving door' through which former politicians or top public servants leave to take lucrative roles in organisations seeking access to government money or lobbying influence. In fact, even former prime ministers are in on the act, as we saw with David Cameron's petitioning on behalf of his soon to be defunct employer, Greensill Capital, to get access to emergency public funding during the pandemic. Cameron did this not through formal channels, as would at least be appropriate, but via persistent messages to the Chancellor Rishi Sunak's private, and presumably normally heavily guarded, phone number, allegedly 'pleading for the [Bank of England] scheme to be amended so Greensill could qualify'.[35]

To permit privileged access to government by those with money and power is disempowering and exclusionary for ordinary citizens, for employees and their unions and for the myriad of more humble and less well-connected representatives, such as residents' associations, local traders' associations, school governing bodies and all manner of other civic associations, which are consequently unable to get their views heard in the confidential spaces where important decisions affecting their interests are made. This is democratically dangerous territory, which can have disastrous, not merely venal consequences, particularly for those most disempowered.

A particularly tragic example occurred with the Grenfell Tower fire, where the voices of local residents and their legitimate safety concerns fell on deaf ears[36]; while a myopic ideology within central government had for years seen life-preserving, health and safety regulations as just so much 'red tape' – public sector, bureaucratic impediments to money making. David Cameron boasted in 2014 of making a bonfire of unnecessary regulations.[37] The actual conflagration came three years later when seventy-two people (one an unborn child) died as flammable cladding burned up the sides of Grenfell Tower. The vast majority of those who died were people of colour, leading the lawyer representing the survivors at the subsequent inquiry to argue that it 'must not ignore' the impact of race and poverty on the disaster and the circumstances that led up to it.[38]

Without doubt our participatory democracy needs a health check. It needs to be reinvigorated in several ways, not only to make national government more transparent and accountable but also to energise local government and active civic engagement. This drive for greater democratic participation should begin by guaranteeing a stronger voice for employees in matters affecting workers' rights and for trade unions in their role as a potential key partner in national economic deliberations. Another important reform should now be to include young people far more directly in the democratic process, building from previous initiatives such as youth parliaments, which have supported in developing young people's understanding of participatory citizenship.

It is high time for a new twenty-first-century further extension of the suffrage across the whole of the UK in the age when the future of the planet is threatened – so that those aged fifteen and above, like Greta Thunberg when she began to make her impact, should now have the vote. Young people over the age of sixteen are now eligible to vote in elections to the Scottish and Welsh parliaments

Image 27. Members of the British Youth Council and Youth Parliament hold a live debate on the film set of *The Iron Lady* at Wimbledon Studios, to debate the role of women in politics on 10 April 2012. Source: Rosie Hallam / Getty Images

and this widening of the franchise should now be rolled out from the age of fifteen for all elections across the UK, where it could kickstart an activism focused on the vital (literally) interests of the rising generation.[39] It was a similar expansion of the franchise – the revolutionary inclusion of urban working-class votes in the late Victorian decades – that provided the catalyst for municipal policies that finally cleaned up the lethal industrial urban environment and transformed the life chances of the urban working classes and their children.

Accountable local government and active civic communities of all kinds have featured strongly in British history over the last four centuries, often acting in concert to support a healthily functioning society. Initiative-taking local government, from the collectivist-individualist era of the parish Poor Law, to the late Victorian policies of municipal collectivism, and the expanding range of locally provided social services by workers with a professional public service ethos in the post-war welfare state, have all played crucial roles in fostering an empowering society focused on the welfare of villages, neighbourhoods and even whole cities and regions.[40]

We need to rediscover these principles, finding innovative ways for all voices to have influence in our democracy. Citizens' assemblies are a powerful democratic mechanism that could be used to achieve this. They bring together groups with diverse views from across society to deliberate and advise on issues of national or local importance. They can be informed by expert witnesses but are not drawn from the political elite and operate outside of day-to-day political rivalries. This was used to great effect in Ireland in 2016 to provide independent advice to parliament from citizens on how to progress the referenda on gay marriage and abortion, and again in 2020 with the UK Citizens' Assembly on how to build a net zero emissions economy. It is a model that would do much to aid democratic renewal in the UK and potentially help heal some of the deep rifts of recent years manifest in the Brexit vote and the enervating sense of political disempowerment in some communities. It would be a far more constructive way forward than central government seeking to curb the rights of protestors, as they appeared to be doing in the heavy-handed legislation brought before parliament in 2021 in the form of the Police, Crime, Sentencing and Courts Bill, which was seen by many as a direct attack on democratic rights.[41]

History clearly shows that local and civic activism requires a facilitating central state to encourage those with devolved responsibilities and to grant them the discretionary resources required to improve the lot of their communities. Quite the opposite has happened in the last forty years, with independent local government being a major target of the Thatcher government and then, subsequently, a key victim of the austerity cuts of the last decade. These are cuts that local authorities are not able to recoup from raising local taxation because central government legally restricts – 'caps' – the amount by which Council Tax can be increased each year. Shrinking the budgets of local government also harms the penumbra of voluntary activities that can occur in each town and city since these often depend on subsidised facilities or on small support grants for equipment or to defray volunteers' costs.[42]

Despite these obstacles, there are several inspirational examples of contemporary municipal and civic activism that show the potential of local government to support and empower the local community. The Preston Model of 'community wealth building' is one such example. In this depressed city, which had among the highest suicide rates in the UK, the local authority has since 2011 brokered agreements among 'anchor' local employers and businesses (including hospitals, schools, the housing association that manages 6,500 homes in the city, the university, the rail station, the police) to do their utmost to source all their requirements locally so that the money they spend is recirculated in the local community. Although austerity shrank Preston Council's budget from £750 million in 2013 to £616 million in 2017, over the same period it also practised what it preached by itself focusing on local procurement. As a result the council raised the annual amount it spent directly in Preston from just £38 million to £111 million and the proportion of its budget spent in Lancashire from 39 per cent to 79 per cent of the total.[43] The Labour Group then devised a proposal for a public bank to manage a local wealth fund to support local worker co-operatives that would increase employment locally, reaping political rewards for the party as a result in the ensuing local elections.[44]

Similar virtues and outcomes have been seen in 'Marmot cities' in the UK, such as Coventry, Stoke and Newcastle, with Greater Manchester also recently signing up as a Marmot Region.[45] These work by focusing the city's policies on health and equity outcomes. Policies are formulated and their outcomes monitored in order to give every child the best start and to create healthy homes and neighbourhoods for all, in particular through a strengthening of preventative health programmes. On the economic side the emphasis is on training opportunities for all young adults and creation of quality jobs among local businesses. Local partnerships with business and civic organisations are key to the success of the project as shown by the independent report on Coventry's first six years implementing the Marmot principles. Under the difficult conditions imposed by the national government's austerity policies, Coventry defied the negative national health trends and also narrowed its health inequality gaps among the 196 small area neighbourhoods that make up the city.[46]

Further afield, Porto Alegre in Brazil initiated the practice of participatory budget setting (PBS) in 1989. A part of the city's total budget (21 per cent by 1999) was allocated according to the voting preferences of the local residents, who are free to form their own agenda and convince others of their priorities (so this is not a tick-box exercise). Different districts can be incentivised to participate in the discussion because the greater their votes, the more likely they are to see their district's priorities fulfilled. An immediate gain for Porto Alegre was a much enhanced investment in the city's overall health infrastructure once the wishes of large numbers of the poor were taken into account, interestingly just as happened in Birmingham and other British cities once the voice of the working class began to be prioritised in the late nineteenth century.[47]

The effectiveness of deliberative participation in engaging all sectors of society improves the self-confidence of the poor. Civic volunteering can also boost cross-class trust between poor communities and urban authorities. This encourages the precious resource of relationships known as linking social capital to develop and flourish.[48] While PBS has spread to many cities worldwide, it has only been used on a small scale so far in the UK, though the Scottish government has agreed to allow 1 per cent of local government budgets to be allocated in this way from 2021 through the Community Choices Fund.[49]

These are important and valuable examples, but in the current climate they are exceptions to the rule. Instead of legislation to enhance the financial resources of local authorities, austerity has of course meant the diametric opposite. As we return to a nurturing and empowering state it has to be one that devolves discretionary power and significant revenues to all democratically elected local authorities. By 2020 we had elected local mayors in many of the larger English conurbations who had a great deal of local knowledge and legitimacy, but often lacked resources to further their local agenda. New models of regional government have been proposed for years but never come to fruition. The devolved nations and the English regions will quite likely now become a flashpoint for the future assertion of democratic claims to greater power, resources and autonomy to tackle the economic and social damage of the years of neoliberalism. They will need an empowering state working alongside to support them, not a disempowering state seeking to stymie them.

The Nurturing State and Our Natural Environment

Another of the many blind spots of *Homo economicus* is his obliviousness to the exhaustibility of the natural resources he seeks to exploit for his immediate utility. To have any hope of grappling with an environmental crisis caused by two centuries of this approach, we need to start not from the premise of selfish individuals but the entirely different nurturing principle, applying it to our fellow species and to the planet's ecosystems, just as we would to our own children.

The fulfilment of our goals should be achieved by combining with other parents – (nations) to see how much, together, we can provide the help that our children (the planet's plants and animals) need. This, as we all know, is by ensuring that our children have safe and caring neighbourhoods – the sustainable natural environments – to develop, grow and healthily flourish. This is the stewardship model of international collaboration and co-operation. Once we have the right model to work with – the nurturing parent–child relationship, not the voracious 'rational economic man' – then we can begin to see how best to conduct ourselves in our local, national and international efforts to save the environment and, along with it, our actual children and grandchildren.

Neoliberalism's premise of self-interested individualism is undercut and therefore invalidated by the discovery today of our planetary resource limits. As a theory that tells us how to behave as economic agents it rests on the unspoken assumption that pursuing one's own self-inter-est – in and of itself – is a behaviour that cannot possibly do the world such irreparable harm that the players can-not continue to play the game of self-interest. Now that we have this knowledge, it is a game-changer – literally. Following one's own self-interest is no longer the best counsel, even if taken purely on its own amoral terms. Once we know that pursuing self-interest is a self-termi-nating game, it becomes highly irrational to continue to behave according to its tenets. And what is worse, we are already in the final rounds of the game. We have to stop playing now.

Fortunately, it is not the only game in town. Nor is it the only game we know. It is not even the best game we have ever played when viewed from the perspective of 90 per cent of the world's population, rather than the 10 per cent who have been the principal winners of this rigged game – mostly living in the wealthiest, ex-imperial countries. Of course some of the winners don't want to give up the game and have to be persuaded that it is now high time to play the very different game of collectivist individualism, not winner-takes-all individualism. Collective individualism is a moral and ethical game, but one that is no less sup-portive of individuals' capacity to excel and flourish, for all that. We should be good at it in the UK, because we invented it in 1601. And in fact we have been playing it for most of the last 400 years – the forty years since 1980 are something of a self-destructive aberration.

The trend to increasing inequality in many nations during these last four decades of the neoliberal ascendancy has it-self directly increased the rate of environmental destruction. It is clear that in per capita terms those responsible for the greatest volume of carbon emissions are the world's wealth-iest citizens – the top 1 per cent account for 14 per cent of annual global emissions, which is more than fifty times per person that of the entire poorest half of humanity.[50] And now their dabbling in crypto currencies such as Bitcoin is taking wealth induced environmental damage to another level. Bitcoin 'mining' is so energy hungry that it consumes more electricity per year than a country the size of Argentina.[51]

In 2019 private fortunes sitting in the world's secrecy jurisdictions were worth $28 trillion and rising.[52] What use will these piles of gold be when they and their island tax havens are all under water?[53] Far more rational to open this colossal bank of resources for investing in preserving the planet on the scale that will undoubtedly be required.

But extreme economic inequality also militates against action to tackle environmental damage because it concentrates power in the hands of corporations who are marketing the endless flow of new environmentally damaging commodities. For as long as national governments and their politicians – and we, the voting citizens – continue to believe in the promise of never-ending 'growth', the corporate elites can use their wealth and lobbying power to stealthily and behind closed doors crowd out the voices of the green lobby. In doing so they are serving the short-term interests of the shareholders and gratifying the carefully cultivated appetites of consumers, but unfortunately not the long-term interests of humanity or the planet.

The difficulty is that addressing the challenge that we now face to live within our planetary limits is a 'collective action' problem: it requires solutions that incentivise joint, co-ordinated action while preventing one group or nation from simply free-riding on the more altruistic actions of others. At the same time it also presents a 'deferred benefit' problem – meaning that those taking the action may not be the ones who directly benefit and may therefore see less reason to act.[54] Indeed, this is a point that has come into sharper relief as anxious and exasperated young

Image 28. Extinction Rebellion protest in Leeds, 15 July 2019.
Source: Ian Forsyth / Getty Images

people take to the national and international stage to put the case for their generation's future.

But these are the arguments of a world driven by a model in which self-interest reigns. On the contrary, everything involved in our adaptation to our belated appreciation of our environmental boundaries must be driven not by self-interest but by an active, nurturing state and by a business world that is acting according to collective values. We have already legislated for net zero carbon by 2050. We now need a well-designed (so as not to punish the poor) suite of rising carbon taxes to use the power of the market to encourage businesses and consumers to sell and buy products with progressively lower carbon to ensure we meet this collective goal.[55]

Again drawing fruitfully on history, Mariana Mazzucato's recently published book *Moonshot Guide* gives us an insight into another strategy to stimulate co-operative behaviours in the collective interest. The 1960s mission to land a man on the moon, accomplished by NASA within a decade of President Kennedy setting the goal, held at least partially comparable technological challenges to those needed to save earth's biosphere in the short time available to us in the 2020s. In studying how this was achieved so rapidly Mazzucato points out that it required 'partnership with purpose' where the key was for government to set the agreed goal and then to 'pick the willing' to work with from the business community – those committed primarily to reaching the collective goal, not purely dedicated to profits. Mazzucato also found that it required confident, independent-minded public officials fully capable of partnering with business – adept in leadership, risk-taking and unimpressed by the superficial salesmanship of corporate commercialism.[56]

In support of such a shift in behaviours, there is a strong argument for reforming the way we reward the highest achievements in the economics profession to embed the very different vision needed in the twenty-first century. *The Nobel Factor* has shown how the prize in Economics, invented in the 1960s, had a strong influence in raising the status of a brand of economics that favoured market liberalism over social democracy.[57] We need a revised economics and a revised prize that now focuses on recognising contributions towards sustainability – the Nobel Prize for Economic Sustainability, perhaps. This would recognise at the highest international level that the two key economic challenges we now face are counteracting global warming and protecting our natural resources and biodiversity to remain within our environmental limits.

One of the biggest barriers to the first of these – climate change mitigation – is the fact that previous technologies have taken economic development on what can now be seen as a sub-optimal path-dependent route. What this means is that, while we can agree that we no longer want to be dependent on using fossil fuel-based energy for production and consumption, our economies are structured so as to make it very hard to change. Market incentives remain strongly in favour of carbon-based development in the short term, since much of our physical energy infrastructure is reliant on it. Around 30 per cent of the market value of the FTSE 100 stock is from oil, gas and mining companies.[58] Undoing these past decisions will be costly, disruptive and potentially destabilising. The former Bank of England governor Mark Carney highlighted the possible systemic risks to the economy if the transition to a low-carbon economy is not managed smoothly and there is a too rapid fall in the value of carbon assets.[59]

All of this points to the conclusion that our response to climate change must go well beyond market solutions or market-based approaches. It requires strong government action to invest in ways that will break this path-dependent inertia.[60] Indeed, as Mariana Mazzucato has convincingly pointed out, time and time again in history this is exactly the role that states have played.[61] It is a misleading myth that the free market and private corporations have engendered any of the most important and game-changing recent innovations, which economists call GPTs (general purpose technologies). The three most recent – atomic energy, the computer and then the internet – were all largely government-sponsored creations.

What is required, then, are long-term financial commitments to uncertain technological development in support of climate adaptation. These are not generally suited to market-based investment. For that very reason, then, here too the first mover has to be the state. Once a new technological world has been opened up, private companies can then be the appropriate vehicles for its most efficient further development. With time, new technologies and engineering solutions are likely to deliver energy at lower cost than the fossil fuel-driven economy, as has clearly already been seen with the dramatic fall in offshore wind-turbine electricity costs. For the present, however, much of our investment in climate adaptation must include long-term, patient capital directed at both research and development and early stage green technology companies.[62]

Secondly, our stewardship of the environment must have at its core preserving our most precious asset – Nature – on which our economies, livelihoods and well-being all depend, as cogently set out in the 2021 Dasgupta Review of *The Economics of Biodiversity*. Among a range of recommendations, Dasgupta argues that we must reform economic models and evaluation processes to reflect the fact that the economy is actually embedded in nature. That means we need new measures of our 'economic progress' to replace the hegemony of GDP, which simply ignores damage to nature and to poor communities; and we need to reform our institutions to make wiser choices.[63]

First and foremost we need to recognise within these new models that nature is not a given, it can be – and is being – degraded. At the moment when we measure GDP all we are looking at is a flow of traded value of goods and services bought and sold without any reference to the consumption or degradation of natural resources occurring as we do this. What we need instead is a measure that fully takes into account the limited nature of the stock of finite natural resources and how to sustain them. If we don't do this – if we fail to take account of our limited environmental resources in our calculations of economic progress – then we are misleading ourselves about the true choices we have, because we are failing to correctly moderate present usage to take account of our future needs.

As Dasgupta says, GDP may be helpful as a tool for short-term macroeconomic management, although even that is debatable given how much unpaid economic activity it ignores. But it is not suitable for measuring the changes we inflict on the natural world, and for the political and economic decisions that we need to make in the light of that. For that we need a new economic grammar altogether.[64]

A team of economists from Cambridge's Bennett Institute for Public Policy is now working with the United Nations to develop an approach called 'Ecosystem Accounting' that moves beyond GDP to measure wealth and success 'with tools that recognize the value of nature and people', acknowledging, as the Institute's co-director, Diane Coyle, has said, that

> *A focus on GDP without proper regard for environmental degradation or inequality has been a disaster for global ecosystems and undermined social cohesion.*[65]

The Institute's work to progress beyond the GDP straitjacket proposes a new 'wealth economy' framework to provide 'a practical recipe for policy making for a sustainable twenty-first century'. The ingredients in their recipe are a set of assets or 'capitals' that the market economy does not currently invest in effectively, despite their critical importance. These assets include natural capital but also embrace knowledge capital, human capital and social and institutional capital. Adopting this framework would, they argue, embed concern for the future in our economic decision making, something that GDP does not do. As their report says, following COVID-19, 'Building back is not the challenge; it is Building Forward to something better.'[66]

To conclude, we must now take a long-term stewardship view that is driven by considerations of the welfare of our whole society, present, future and not yet born. This simply cannot be delivered by a state in thrall to neoliberal ideology with its dogmatic commitments to negative freedoms from regulation and to never-ending growth. It requires a nurturing state that is capable of fully taking into account the well-being of all other species and their natural habitats, which provide the sustainable biodiversity we cannot afford to lose. The measures we decide to use as we make this change will be critical in influencing how people behave because they signal what we value and what we wish to reward. This has been termed the 'performativity of measures'.[67] We have an opportunity now to embed a new set of values into these measures. These must be the values of a nurturing state that is concerned about the well-being both of its citizens and its environmental resources, and about how these are effectively curated for the future. If we don't and we keep worshipping at the totem of GDP then we may well find it will turn into our tombstone.

13 SEVEN PILLARS OF EMPOWERMENT

Wisdom has built her house, she has hewn her seven pillars.
(Proverbs 9:1)

An empowering society that nurtures its individual citizens and takes the lead in protecting our global environment needs to be built on mutually supporting pillars. We identify seven such pillars, based on the values, behaviours and policies that this book has advocated and drawn from our own history. As we build forward from the pandemic these will be crucial in creating a society that works for all, giving us the robustness and resilience that we need to face an increasingly uncertain future.

Our seven pillars are:

1. A nurturing state: Respect and inclusive support for all
2. Ethical capitalism: Working with business to redefine our values
3. Fair contributions: Full participation by the prosperous
4. Open public discourse: Enabling all voices to have an equal hearing
5. Measuring what we value: Signalling the changes we need
6. A sustainable future: Responsible stewardship of our planet's resources
7. Participatory politics: Reviving democracy and civic engagement

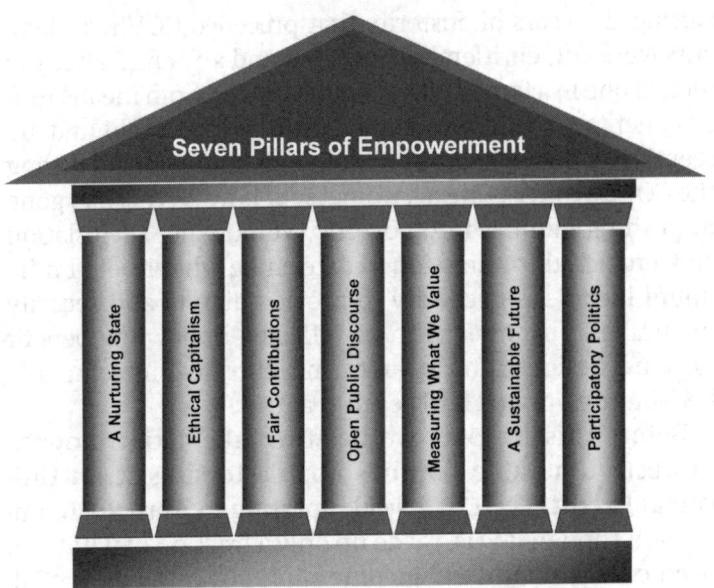

Figure 14. Seven Pillars of Empowerment.

1. A Nurturing State: Respect and Inclusive Support for All

A properly functioning welfare state should never be seen as a luxury to be cut back in times of hardship. Meeting a population's needs, which means both ensuring that no one lacks for food and shelter and investing in their capabilities – especially their health and education – benefits everyone, including the better-off, as has repeatedly been shown in our own history. Welfare investment has preceded and supported growth and prosperity, including Britain's own extraordinary economic history leading to industrialisation. It is not a discretionary afterthought and it has never worked to cut it when times are hard.

We urgently need to fix the UK's safety net to prevent an escalating crisis of child poverty and homelessness.

During the years of austerity that preceded COVID-19 benefits were cut, entitlements reduced and any child after the second one in a family was simply excluded from means-tested benefits. The unprecedented resort to food banks and unseemly rows over feeding children in school holidays during the COVID-19 crisis are a barometer of how far this had gone in pushing families into poverty. We now need legislation and a national commission to determine what level of minimum income is necessary to provide dignity and security to families. This must then be reflected in how the benefit system is designed and include a means of guaranteeing that benefits are uprated fairly each year.

Before this is done, we need to take action now to protect vulnerable families unable to subsist on Universal Credit. The £20 a week uprating in April 2020, important though it was, made up only a fraction of what had been cut from families' income since 2011. We do not advocate Universal Basic Income, which has too many drawbacks to offer a viable solution, but in the short term there is certainly an argument for an emergency Child Benefit uplift for all families as a means to target resources where they may be most needed, until longer-term changes are brought in.

We must tackle inequality and the injustices that undermine our resilience. Austerity produced widening health inequalities, increasing deaths from despair and a deeply concerning slow down in life expectancy gains. Cuts in education spending and the determination of the better-off to put a glass floor beneath their children have reduced social mobility in a system where private schools that protect privilege remain state subsidised through charitable status. We already knew from international research that inequality is strongly associated with lower growth and may also lower social cohesion, particularly damaging in a crisis, yet we have not acted to address it.

COVID-19 showed just how much poverty, inequality and structural racism combined together to expose the most deprived communities in our society to the risk of contracting and in all too many cases dying from the illness. It interacted with pre-existing health issues, overcrowded housing and insecure work, causing an encompassing syndemic. It was inequality that sapped our resilience during the pandemic and it is inequality that we must now urgently tackle to prevent it scarring future generations.

We need to restore public services that are fit for purpose. Our capacity to mount an effective response to COVID-19 was hampered by years of deliberate, calculated disinvestment in public services in accordance with neo-liberal dogma. This meant our health sector, reeling from years of damaging reorganisation, was already running at full capacity and had – whether by accident, negligence or design – no effective stockpiles of protective equipment to draw on in a pandemic, despite such an event having been identified as the leading national risk we were facing. The care sector, which had been out of sight and mind for years, was used to offload elderly patients blocking hospital beds with no proper thought for their welfare or that of care home staff as they were discharged into facilities without any requirement for COVID-19 testing.

Public sector expertise and specialist advice were both shunned in a rush to favour those private companies and individuals with contacts to the government, while transparency and competition were suspended for the duration of the emergency. Huge and costly mistakes were made during the pandemic in what should have been routine procurement; in failing, despite unbelievable expense, to build up an effective testing and tracing capacity; and in making judgements about how and when to relax restrictions or to reimpose them. The tragedy is that governments had been warned of the risks of our frayed and fragile public sector for years but were blinded by their ideological prejudices. We must now rebuild fully funded and resilient public services and end the lobbying and cronyism at the heart of government procurement.

We need to reimagine what core services mean in a twenty-first-century welfare state. As we seek to enhance investment in high-quality public services, which means not just health and education, but transport, housing and social care, we need to think carefully about what this means for current and future generations. Where access to running water and electricity may have been a measure of basic entitlement in the post-war years, it is digital access that is now key to social and economic inclusion, as became all too evident during the pandemic. Our understanding of universal services will need to expand to reflect this.

We no longer have, if we ever did, a breadwinner society in which it was primarily a male earner whose labour market needs had to be secured, with women providing unpaid care in the household, either with or without paid employment alongside. Care both for pre-school children and for the rapidly expanding older population is, arguably, the biggest unmet welfare need we face, currently accessed by most in the private market or by providing their own labour for free. The provision of care is a social benefit, yet it is one for which we currently provide no social insurance or guaranteed universal access. These are tricky issues, and we are years, if not decades, behind many other countries in addressing them. It is time we got on the front foot on this.

2. Ethical Capitalism: Working with Business to Redefine Our Values

Short-sighted 'shareholder capitalism' is not serving us well. Business leaders have too often put value extraction and pay-outs for shareholders above value creation for the economy. Incentives and bonuses designed to reward short-term risk-taking for profit instead of the long-term success of the company have created dangerously destabilising behaviour and left many companies with little resilience in a crisis. This has been compounded in a financialised economy with loose regulation and quick and easy opportunities for asset stripping and offshoring of profits. This is the amorality of the unfettered free market that an ethical capitalism must challenge, arguing instead for a new morality, as called for by the then Archbishop of Canterbury, Dr Rowan Williams, after the financial crash.[1]

The world-weary cynics writing for the mogul-owned newspapers will of course tell us that you can't change 'human nature' – corporate greed is here forever. History shows this injunction – to just stay put in your armchairs – is completely wrong. It is within our power to define the moral goals we follow. The Davos Manifesto 2020 has already set the terms for this, with its statement that 'A company is more than an economic unit generating wealth. It fulfils human and societal aspirations as part of the broader social system. Performance must be measured not only on the return to shareholders, but also on how it achieves its environmental, social and good governance objectives. Executive remuneration should reflect stakeholder responsibility.'[2]

A new vision of company purpose must, then, embrace all stakeholders. It must go beyond an exclusive focus on businesses' financial shareholders to bring employees, customers, suppliers, local communities and the natural environment within the scope of who and what a company is there to serve. Companies should focus on shared and sustained value creation both for the business and the wider economy. The primary duty of directors should be recast in law and made unequivocally the promotion of the long-term success of the company, not the maximisation of short-term 'shareholder value'.

A renewed public discourse around company purpose should also include a dialogue between business leaders, government and trade unions on how business can support common societal goals. There is no reason why this could not extend to creating a post-pandemic transformation fund. With both government and business contributing, this could be invested in mutually agreed priorities for national renewal and green investment. It has been argued that businesses could be incentivised to take an active role in this by, for instance, tying future corporation tax rates to success in achieving national transformation targets.[3]

Our economic power structures continue to give employers the upper hand. Unfair labour practices impoverish workers, notably the zero hours contracts and insecurity of work in the 'gig economy' and the exclusion of so many workers from maternity pay, parental leave, holiday and sick pay. This precarity contributed to the spread of COVID-19 because it left people unable to afford to take time off work when they had potential symptoms of the illness or had been notified that they should self-isolate.

We now need effective legislation to guarantee worker protections in all parts of the economy, prevent companies shielding behind a sham of self-employment, and restore the voice of responsible trade unions in our national conversation. This should be combined with compulsory worker-representatives on the boards of all major companies to ensure they are not taking decisions that harm their workers' interests – just as also there should be voices advocating for the green agenda.

Excessive corporate pay, pay inequalities, gender pay gaps and pay and other barriers affecting people of colour persist across the board and many companies take no action to remedy the structural inequalities within their own organisations that drive these. Many still have no employee representation or effective representation of women and people of colour on company boards and re-muneration panels, nor targets on diversity. Some of this can be addressed through industry pressure and exhorta-tion, some through legislation, for instance on genuinely diverse representation on boards or regular pay gap re-porting. There are more creative channels that could be used, too. Voters in San Francisco have approved an ad-ditional tax on businesses where the pay differential be-tween the top-paid executives in their company and the median worker in the city exceeds a certain level, one of many ways of incentivising a more equal pay distribution.[4]

Commitment to a new moral purpose requires everyone to participate. If we want to positively promote the well-being of workers instead of only the cheapness of goods to consumers or to ensure that the companies we buy from do no harm to the natural environment then we should use the many levers we have available to support this. The growth of voluntary 'ethical' consumer move-ments in both these directions – Fairtrade and sustainable sourcing – suggests that a public appetite for strengthen-ing the law may well be present. The government also has ample scope to take immediate action, including with-holding public contracts and approved supplier status from businesses that do not meet specified standards on workers' rights or environmental sustainability, and this should now become accepted practice in procurement.

Creating an ethical register can help to win hearts and minds. As an alternative to wielding the stick busi-nesses, like everyone else, should be given every encour-agement to adopt socially responsible behaviours. An ethical register, for instance, could give companies a place to report on how they pay share options and bonuses, what action they take to involve employees in company decision making and how much UK tax is paid in relation to turn-over to demonstrate they are not avoiding or evading tax.

A reformed honours system might then be designed to give public recognition to business leaders who are doing most to promote and model ethical business behaviours. At this point in our history more than ever we must reward, incentivise and commend those who work in the interests of the widest group of stakeholders, including the natural world, in the stewardship of their corporations and businesses.

3. Fair Contributions: Full Participation by the Prosperous

We are starting from a position where the scales are stacked in favour of the wealthy. Wealth holdings and assets of all kinds have risen much faster than the UK's GDP in the last thirty years without any equivalent increase in what the wealthy have been expected to contribute to society. At the same time there continues to be a bias in favour of 'unearned' income from owning capital, which is treated differently by the tax system from ordinary workers' income from employment. Corporation tax on businesses has been levied at a rate far below that of almost all other major economies, including the USA, for over a decade, with planned future increases for large businesses still barely bringing us up to the average. We have cut higher rates of income tax and created a much more regressive tax system (more regressive than most people realise) over the last forty years. Property taxation is based on Council Tax bands and valuations that have not been updated for thirty years, benefiting those whose housing wealth has grown the most.

Many of the wealthiest in our society got even richer during the pandemic. Those with capital were able to benefit from buying up assets and shares at opportune moments. Some companies were able to make super profits where their business was such that it benefited from social distancing and the switch to online platforms and home deliveries, as did shareholders in those companies.

Corporations who were in the opposite camp, facing big pandemic losses, nevertheless secured government help without any corresponding payback negotiated to deliver future environmental or job guarantees, unlike the practice in many other countries, and repeating the mistakes made after the 2008 financial crisis. Banks providing pandemic loans had few limits put on the interest they could charge, even while securing generous government protection against default.

We must now take action to secure something back from those who have either disproportionately benefited from, or received unconditional support during, the pandemic. This could be a windfall tax on super profits, or something akin to the 'solidarity tax' proposed by the IMF on high earners and firms that have directly benefited from the pandemic.

Where the government needs to intervene to support large businesses in crisis or to rescue smaller ones facing bankruptcy this should include acquiring equity stakes that can be used to benefit all of us. Over the longer term this investment should be placed in public wealth funds that can be used for social and environmental priorities. Funds of this kind can be a powerful tool in redistributing wealth more equitably across society.

There is also a strong argument for the government to do as other countries have done and withdraw any form of public support – including during emergencies such as a pandemic – from those who do not fairly pay their UK tax. The problem of non-payment should also be tackled at its root, with concerted international action to end the diversion of corporate profits and private wealth into the secrecy jurisdictions. Euphemistically termed 'tax havens', they endanger the world's democracies by depriving them of their civic resources.[5] A key early win would be to agree that multinational corporations should pay corporation tax to national governments based on their sales levels in that country, to circumvent the diversion of profits to the most advantageous jurisdiction.

A crisis of the severity of COVID-19 is not something to be 'paid off' like a household bill. The narrative that the pandemic rescue packages 'must be paid for' by the population via general tax rises, pay freezes or spending cuts must be challenged to prevent a new era of austerity again dragging the economy down (and particularly the poor and vulnerable). Economists of all political persuasions want the pandemic costs to be treated as a long-term mortgage to be added to national debt, just as war financing costs are. Any other approach will risk damaging our capacity to recover from COVID-19, as the UK government has been advised in no uncertain terms by international bodies. With interest rates so favourable, future interest payments on the debt should now be fixed at low rates over the long term, meaning that government debt should not be any more onerous to service than pre-pandemic.

Taxation of wealth and high income should be at the forefront as we focus on building a better future. Even before COVID-19 struck it was clear that there would need to be a big shift in our approach to public spending and investment in response to climate change, to the escalating health and care needs of an ageing population and to the scale of economic decline in the regions outside the South East. These pressures to increase public spending will only be intensified by the post COVID-19 health and poverty crisis and the need to restructure and rebuild our economy, retraining those who have lost their livelihoods. We can no longer afford to leave the vast resources of the wealthy outside our calculations over how we deliver the increased spending that we so clearly need. Nor should we, if those with the most to give are to contribute fully to building the nurturing state and nurtured planet that we so urgently need. It is essential for the wealthiest to demonstrate this commitment so that the rest of the population can see that what is being asked of them is also fair.

The most responsible among the wealthy are themselves increasingly calling for a conversation about how this should happen and there is no shortage of proposals on the table, ready for politicians to action. Some have already increased their philanthropic contributions, but this should not be viewed as an alternative to making full and fair contributions from wealth and income via a reformed tax system that is genuinely and fully progressive.

Now is surely the moment to recapture the sense of civic duty and mutual recognition of responsibility for public welfare that has come to the fore throughout our history – and not only at times of crisis. As that history shows, reducing inequalities and changing the way that the wealthy and those with higher incomes view their participatory and contributory role in the wider social project has previously been the spur for a far stronger economy and a more cohesive society. It has worked most effectively when combined with strong incentives and clear sanctions against those seeking to free-ride on others so that everyone is playing their part fully and equally.

4. Open Public Discourse: Enabling All Voices to Have an Equal Hearing

We need to take control of the politics of knowledge. This is essential to make sure that our ideas space is not captured by those with an interest in pushing a one-sided narrative. That means being clear about what determines why some things enter our public discourse and some things don't. The ability to control public information and set the terms of the debate is part of the democratic capture that takes place as an oligarchy of the wealthy digs itself in under neoliberal conditions of rising inequality.

Take, for instance, the corrosive myth that has been spun around tax. The notion has been continually promoted for many decades that tax is something bad and that being taxed is something that nobody wants.[6] This is often put across in a jocular manner as if it's an in-joke the whole nation can share. It implicitly legitimises the whole industry of tax avoidance, which results in the poor paying far more than their fair share through VAT and other regressive taxes. Surveys of public opinion have consistently shown, on the contrary, that the majority well understand the importance of tax in delivering strong public services and support a progressive income tax for that purpose. We must stop the media and those controlling the debate from stifling a new and serious public discourse around civic values and pride in contributing to society, including from those with the most to give.

Transparency is key to open public discourse. We need to know who is influencing public debate, who they are being funded by and why. In the autumn of 2020 think tanks on the right were publishing their research and putting out press releases to brief against policies that might ask the wealthy to contribute more. These are organisations who do not disclose their sources of funding. They are beneficiaries of 'dark money', from invisible donors guarding their privacy. They present as independent research organisations, often with charitable status, but in fact lobby and brief against new ideas that, one presumes, would be against the interests of those who finance them. Many have alarmingly close links to government ministers. There needs to be action to secure transparency and accountability from those with such levels of influence.

Just as importantly we need to ensure that the government itself is collecting and analysing data effectively. Public policy needs to be informed by objective and robust evidence and the basis for decision making made publicly available to counter the influence of the lobbyists.

Investment in the best quality of official information and a willingness to engage in open discourse about this knowledge is the wisest use of public resources in the long run. As we have seen in the pandemic an ill-informed government is doomed to stagger blindly from one error to the next. We are going to need to redouble our efforts in this direction to address the challenges of living within environmental limits as effectively as we can – with our eyes wide open to the evidence.

Control of the media and public messaging is distorting debate. A completely independent press is as vital for the health of any democracy as the integrity of its electoral system and the maintenance of its civil discourse.

There is a pressing need to reform plutocratic ownership of newspapers, and TV stations, which are currently able to project and perpetuate messages that reinforce the individualist and consumerist ideology. Politics and popular culture alike have been too much in thrall to the insidiously de-humanising language of 'winners and losers', celebrities and scroungers, and the commercial advertising industry's incessant illusory message that happiness and well-being is to be achieved through owning and using carbon-emitting and resource-using commodities. Given the elite ownership of so much of the press, independent organisations such as Open Democracy and the International Consortium of Investigative Journalists, conducting genuinely investigative research, are at the moment vital in providing this crucial service of an independent press.

With the arrival of monopolistic digital media platforms we now also have the threat of 'surveillance capitalism', so persuasively articulated by Shoshana Zuboff.[7] Private experiences are being translated into behavioural data to be used in computational processes and ultimately monetised. Regulation has not even begun to catch up with the sorts of infringements of privacy and evading of democratic accountability that this entails, and this, too, must now be an urgent priority for action.

Similarly there needs to be catch-up legislation along the lines announced in December 2020 in the EU's proposed Digital Services Act and Digital Markets Act. These are intended to provide a legal framework to ensure the safety of users online, with the aim of putting protection of fundamental rights at the forefront, while also maintaining a fair and open online platform environment.[8]

Fake news and manipulation of social media, including during elections, are also now a new enemy of open public discourse. We need to treat this as a deadly serious threat to democracy, as has been demonstrated by its role in the insurgency in Washington DC on 6 January 2021. Likewise, the methods used by organisations such as Cambridge Analytica to subvert democracy must be outlawed.

But we also need independent groups in academia, the Royal Society and the British Academy to monitor and expose fake news, and independent fact-checking organisations to publish league tables that show up those who mislead and lie. This must be combined with much stronger control of and sanctions against the practice of trolling and anonymous defamation and threats of violence, which are particularly threats against gender and ethnic equity. As the murder of Jo Cox, MP, in 2016 reminds us, maintaining the civil quality of public discourse is as precious to the lifeblood of democracy as is the universal right to vote.[9]

5. Measuring What We Value: Signalling the Changes We Need

The way things are measured dictates behaviour. It's not just that 'what gets measured gets done', but that in choosing those measures we condition behaviour – the 'performativity of measures'. That means that if we continue to use economic output as measured by Gross Domestic Product (GDP) and in particular growth in GDP as our prime measure of success, despite the environmental constraints that we are facing, then we will find it very difficult to change behaviour even where we wish to do so. So we need to think again about what we are measuring.

We need as a minimum to overhaul GDP – our current barometer of economic success. As a measure of economic performance, GDP is a recent invention and its construction has itself been radically revised several times since 1945.[10] Even on its own terms it is arguable that GDP is not measuring economic and real value and has not done so since its inception – not least in its almost complete failure (known from the outset) to count any work or economic activity that does not involve a financial payment. This may include things like DIY home improvements, but in practice a large part of what is not counted is unpaid domestic work, much of it performed by women.

The limitations of GDP are now multiplying as we think about environmental challenges or about inequality. Sustainable growth and social equity are goals that currently have no traction within our GDP measure. This means that they are given no weight in the foremost measure of national economic 'success' that we use. So they will not be able to influence behaviours as people strive to achieve that goal. The independent Dasgupta Review of *The Economics of Biodiversity*, commissioned by the UK Treasury ahead of the 15th Conference of the Parties to the Convention on Biological Diversity (COP15), has recommended that our measures of economic success be urgently revised to take account of the depletion of our natural capital.[11]

There is also the complementary approach of the Bennett Institute for Public Policy, which proposes a radical alternative to the narrowness of GDP. Their proposed wealth economy framework puts centre stage the portfolio of assets that we need for the future by giving sufficient priority to sustaining human, social and natural capital.

We should now begin a debate about defining and measuring more effectively what we value. This should start by asking whether GDP should be taking front stage at all. As the New Zealand prime minister, Jacinda Ardern, and others, have argued, there is a case for using population well-being as the primary aim of state policy rather than a simplistic, singular measure of economic output or growth. When you do that, you can specify which aspects of physical and mental well-being and equality are important to prioritise in your society and allocate resources accordingly. Or there is Bhutan's Gross National Happiness (GNH) index, which includes health, education, psychological well-being and measures of cultural and ecological diversity and resilience and good governance.

Revisiting our priorities would mean we could accord a much higher value and status to work that is nurturing, caring, teaching and rehabilitating and to all forms of green energy and natural conservation work than at present when we think about our national prosperity. That also implies that we could build in commensurate radical downgrading of activities and industries that are environmentally degrading or socially exploitative, such as tobacco, cheap cotton, cheap meat, plastics manufacture and gambling of all forms, 'noxious' industries and practices that are inflicting harm on workers, consumers and society more generally – some 'markets' are toxic, some are plain immoral.[12] This would send out signals to everyone, including businesses and CEOs, about what is important and where they should be focusing their efforts in order to align with national priorities and values.

Others, notably the economist Kate Raworth, have argued for the 'Doughnut' model of a secure and just space to drive policy. The doughnut is the place where a society is operating safely within a defined set of nine environmental boundaries that we are all constrained by, including the well-being of other species and their natural habitats, while at the same time providing all citizens with the means to live a fulfilled and just life. Its combined set of measures, based on internationally agreed indicators, offers a way to assess nation-states, regions or cities against this benchmark of a safe and just space.[13] In terms of performativity, it certainly steers behaviour in a direction that meets what we would wish to sign up to as a set of core values and sustainability objectives.

We have, therefore, a rich resource of ideas and models to draw on as we set about the task of defining our future values and how we will measure our progress in achieving them.

6. A Sustainable Future: Responsible Stewardship of Our Planet's Resources

Investing in a sustainable future is not something that can be left solely to the private sector. It must go well beyond market solutions or market-based approaches. The government must take a lead in designing and regulating the market in green technologies and taking action to create the right incentives – such as green bonds or savings accounts – for investment to come forward. The government must also itself directly invest in renewable technology now as well as providing long-term, patient capital, directed at more speculative and higher-risk, higher-reward research and development and early stage green technology companies, including for example hydrogen energy.

A recovery plan based on new green jobs should be a post-pandemic priority. This would provide work and skills for those who have permanently lost their jobs during the pandemic and should include areas that can be mobilised quickly in support of a move to zero emissions. Retrofitting of green sources of heating and insulation in homes and premises and building up the electric battery and car-charging infrastructure should be prioritised, alongside initiatives such as tree planting and peat preservation for carbon capture.

This should be combined with longer-term planning, in concert with employers and trade unions, for large-scale targeted training for the 'green-collar' jobs of the future. This would aim to ensure that the right skills are in place so that workers whose jobs are in the carbon economy can be redeployed as technologies change. Mitigating the transition risks to livelihoods and communities as the green economy emerges is crucial to gain public buy-in.

Changing values and behaviours will be essential in the move to a sustainable economy. On a practical level behavioural changes can be encouraged through targeted support such as subsidies for solar panel installation, home insulation or geothermal heating delivered in a way that makes the process of taking up the subsidies easy and barrier free, which is not always the case at present. This can be combined with advertising campaigns to nudge people's behaviour towards more sustainable ways of living. Key priorities would include eating habits, switching away from red meat and encouraging locally sourced foods, as well as changing travel habits, encouraging greater use of public transport and less air travel, and reducing levels of consumption, for instance through changing attitudes to clothing, fashion, recycling, exchanging and similar circular economy measures.[14]

David Attenborough has been doing his utmost to bring about our fuller appreciation of 'the infinitely beautiful tapestry of processes and forms that is Nature', as called for by the Dasgupta Review of *The Economics of Biodiversity*. We need to continue to support this from our children's education upwards so that people of all ages reassess their values and enable us all to 'appreciate that we are part of Nature and that Nature nurtures us'.[15]

Businesses can be similarly incentivised to take action. Public commitments to net zero targets and annual statements by businesses on their environmental sustainability and their improvement initiatives should become the norm, with those businesses not participating increasingly left out in the cold. This could for instance be required in the annual returns sent to Companies House. Public (and private) procurement and decisions by investment bodies and pension funds should have net zero commitments built in as a prerequisite. A new competitiveness to be more green than one's peers would also be no bad thing, enabling other major institutions to contribute to altering the plane of the commercial playing field against carbon-using technology. Thus, in April 2020 Oxford beat Cambridge University by six months with its announcement of divesting from all investments in fossil fuels, while in October 2020 Cambridge bested Oxford University with its plan to cut its greenhouse gas emissions to zero by 2038, more than a decade before the date set by the UK government. That is healthy competition.

Leadership at a national and international level will be crucial to delivering environmentally sustainable growth. This must include all countries being held fully accountable to international agreements and targets and their own domestic legislation to deliver on this, such as the UK's net zero targets. The 15th Conference of the Parties to the Convention on Biological Diversity (COP15), in 2021, will be seeking to adopt a new global biodiversity framework for living in harmony with nature. There will also need to be a continued focus on developing further ambitious and concrete plans to confront the climate crisis, again with all countries fully participating, including leveraging the 26th Conference of the Parties to the UN Framework Convention on Climate Change (COP26), held under the UK's presidency in 2021, to maximum effect.

Local government similarly needs to be empowered to play a full role in addressing the climate crisis. Only local government can ensure that locally relevant policies are adopted, with the participation of local citizens a priority in designing area-specific responses. There is enormous scope here for productive participatory rivalry between the nation's local authorities and their communities if they are given the appropriate information, just as occurred in the Victorian age when the General Register Office started to publish annual league tables of provincial cities' mortality. It provoked a rivalry to spend to achieve the lowest death rates, where previously they had aimed only for the lowest property rates, ignoring the health costs.[16]

7. Participatory Politics: Reviving Democracy and Civic Engagement

Politics captured by the wealthy and powerful corporations lobbying the neoliberal central state has been a disempowering and excluding experience for everybody else. This may have contributed to the general disillusionment with politics that resulted in the Leave protest vote in the EU referendum from many under-resourced communities, whose low-paid and casualised or informal sources of employment reflect the kind of labour market that most suits these global companies.

The same small set of large private corporations, such as G4S, Capita, Interserve, Sodexo, Mitie and Serco, along with the familiar consultancy firms and the now defunct Carillion, have repeatedly been awarded massive contracts by central government for front-line delivery of services or large-scale construction projects via the Private Finance Initiative (PFI), despite often indifferent and sometimes even failing performance.

This smacks of a lack of accountability and a lack of true market competition. Placing profits and the private revenue of shareholders before the quality and accountability of these tax-funded public services completely distorts their function, and in the case of PFI has demonstrably drained public money that could have been spent far more effectively. Where those at the front line of service delivery also have stringent time-constraints and quasi-commercial targets placed on them by managers so that they deliver a profitable service, there is a risk of genuine harm instead of assistance to vulnerable people.

We must therefore take action to tackle the cronyism within the Westminster political elite, which sees the wealth and corporate elites in a far too cosy relationship with politicians, promoting their own interests often without accountability or transparency.

Participatory democracy should be reinvigorated. This starts by restoring the voice of ordinary workers – as represented by trade unions – in the national conversation about our priorities. Citizens' assemblies should be convened more regularly and the conclusions of their deliberations on matters of national policy should carry a legal requirement for a parliamentary response, with a clear timeline for actions. There is evidently an appetite for greater civic activism among those fearing their voices are not being heard, as the marches both for and against Brexit showed, as does the popularity of campaigns pursued by the many large and small online petitioning organisations, such as Change.org, 38 Degrees, Avaaz and SumOfUs. There needs, too, to be room for the voices of the young in our participatory democracy with an extension of the franchise – both nationally and locally – down to age fifteen and more extensive use of, for instance, youth parliaments.

Democratic local government and local devolution of power will be a key issue. Whereas in the late nineteenth century the laissez-faire economics of central government came to be combined with a vigorous and effective role for local government in most cities, the years of austerity since the financial crash have starved local government of resources. Even so, as exemplified in Preston and Coventry, for instance, the power of local pride and energy, if well-led and guided by nurturing, participatory goals and practices, can be formidable even in the face of difficult circumstances.

But all of these initiatives would be so much more effective and generalisable if they were fuelled with the positive support of a nurturing and empowering state willing to devolve discretionary powers and the associated revenues to all democratically elected, properly accountable local authorities, in place of reliance on unaccountable profit focused private sector firms 'delivering' services under confidential contracts. This is a top priority to restore a fully participatory and vigorous local democracy, enabling it to leverage the energy of civic networks and their resources for innovative action to promote equity and sustainability in all parts of the country.

*

As an architecture for rebuilding an empowered society the seven pillars we propose are entirely practical. They are policies that we could all campaign and vote for. They are not an idealistic, unattainable utopia, any more than Elizabeth I's new welfare settlement after decades of plague and famine was, or indeed the post Second World War resetting of the social contract after so much sacrifice and suffering. They are intended to enable us to rethink our moral values so that we can chart a new way forward after the virus. More than that, they give us the foundation we need to fortify us for the challenges ahead if we are to avoid a truly dystopian alternative, as our concluding chapter argues.

14 GREATER EVEN THAN A PANDEMIC

We know without a shred of doubt that there is a crisis far greater even than a pandemic heading our way. If there is one thing we should have learned from COVID-19 it is that we are in a very fragile equilibrium with nature. What is far worse than nature 'biting back' with a deadly virus is that we now live with the disturbing knowledge that the natural world that sustains us all is liable to collapse.

COVID-19 is not a 'once in a hundred years' event that we can hope one day to confine to folklore. It is a warning shot across our bows. We now face the economic consequences of the havoc it has wrought, both in the wealthier nations where lockdowns were imposed and in poorer countries where ventilators and intensive care beds were never going to be available to most people and where there was little if any provision for income support as livelihoods were threatened. We can expect an economic 'long COVID' in many parts of the world, which will be as devastating as its health equivalent.

In October 2020 the World Bank published its latest overview of likely trends in global poverty and shared prosperity in the wake of COVID-19, estimating that potentially 150 million more people, mostly in the world's poorest countries, could as a result fall into extreme poverty in 2021, with nearly 10 per cent of the world's population living on less than $1.90 a day, the extreme poverty baseline. According to the report, global extreme poverty is expected to rise in 2020 for the first time in over 20 years as the disruption of COVID-19 compounds the forces of conflict

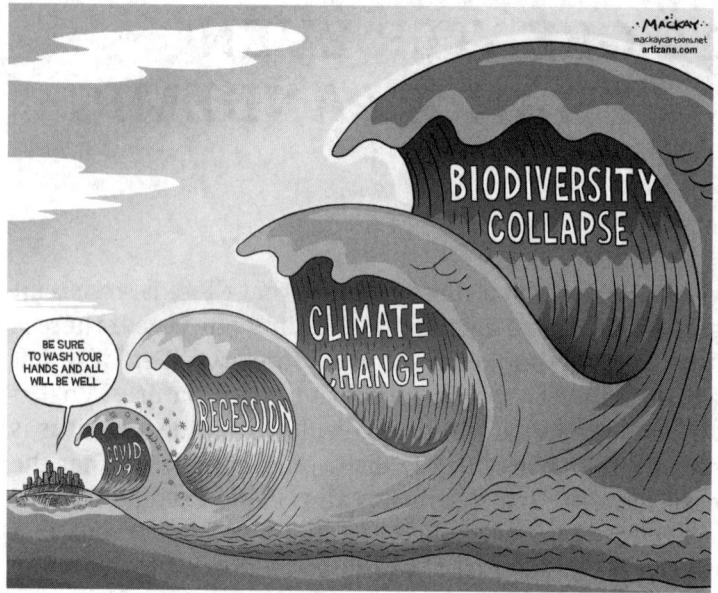

Image 29. The tsunami ahead.
Source: Graeme MacKay / Artizans

and climate change, which were already slowing poverty reduction.[1]

As the world reels under the economic fallout of COVID-19 it must of course also contend with the tsunamis of climate change and biodiversity collapse that are looming up behind it. These are crises of our own making and if we do not act with real urgency, their impact will dwarf anything in recorded human history. Indeed, they may even be the end of recorded human history.

The environmental and economic challenges this presents are profound. The risks we face include not just the future threat to our survival and that of other species, but also the very much more immediate threat of large-scale disruption as environmental disasters – including loss of food security – lead to potential conflict or mass migration, with the poorest parts of the world likely to be affected most. The United Nations' Convention on Biodiversity has clearly signalled the connection between these challenges in its first and second sets of action targets for 2030. These are, respectively, 'Reducing threats to biodiversity' and 'Meeting people's needs ... especially for the most vulnerable'.[2] This close linkage between looking after each other and looking after the planet is also clearly signalled in Pope Francis' two most recent Encyclicals, Laudato Si: 'On care of our common home' (2015), and Fratelli Tutti: 'On fraternity and social friendship' (2020) and his book, *Let Us Dream*.[3]

The world may well soon enter a new and dangerous phase in which it is in a seemingly *permanent* state of emergency. It will become ever more likely that crises will overlap and potentially reinforce each other. We have seen increasingly frequent and destabilising financial crises under the global laissez-faire regime of the last forty years. Climate change is bringing natural disasters at an intensifying pace. COVID-19, SARS, MERS and Ebola have shown us the risks of our global connectedness in a world in which we have threatened the habitats of species who can carry lethal new diseases into human populations. War, mass migrations and poverty follow from destabilised regimes and from man-made and natural disasters. When these emergencies multiply, as they are at risk of doing, they will start to coincide with increasing frequency, amplifying each other and pushing the world, if it is not prepared, into permanent reactive firefighting with unpredictable and therefore deeply worrying consequences. We will not be able to mitigate or even manage these risks within the learned helplessness (leave it all to the market, we don't need interfering states) of the neoliberal order, the washed-up 'Washington Consensus' of laissez-faire.

Perhaps COVID-19 will turn out to have been the warning that we needed. Just as an initial heart attack, once survived, may cause someone to make big changes to confront the deficiencies in their lifestyle, perhaps COVID-19 will produce an equivalent epiphany. We must hope that if anything good comes from it, it will be that we wake up to the systemic changes that we need to bring about in our approach to our fellow citizens' well-being and in challenging the wide range of at best amoral, if not frankly immoral, behaviours that we have allowed to infest our political and economic sphere for too long, and which now make us more vulnerable than ever. That vulnerability will only grow further to the extent that we continue to do nothing to redress the widening inequality that is also integral to the environmental emergency we face.

The oldest way in which humans have repeatedly learned to protect themselves in the past is by voluntarily adhering to a collective and trans-generational moral code. This teaches respect for each other as humans but also – crucially – for an entity, a force, a power – call it what you like – that is beyond our knowing as individuals. In the book of Genesis (2:15) and in the Quran, Jews, Christians and Muslims alike read that humans are entrusted with a stewardship relationship to serve the garden in which they have been placed.

One does not have to be a member of these or other religious faiths to believe there is something of infinite value in the beauty of the natural environment and in the relationships we can have with it and with our fellow species by accepting the moral calling of trans-generational stewardship. We can model how we treat the other species of our planet on the way in which we believe the relationship between parents and children ideally should be. To take this seriously leads us to an ethics and a set of goals in life as individuals and citizens that are wholly different from those of national rivalry for competitive economic growth rates and the amassing of personal, material wealth.

Conclusion

The matter of our relationship with the environment – with our planet, the earth – is an urgent one. We have no choice but to put it at the centre of an ethics that now has to go far wider than the abstracted human individual pursuing their self-interested 'utility', which is the narrow focus of the utilitarian ethics of *Homo economicus* and the neoliberal faith in markets. We should be striving to build a society in which the ethos of collective responsibility and active contributions to the greater good, not consumerist egoism, are the prevailing moral and behavioural drivers; and where citizens and voters believe in and want to bring about safe and sustainable environments for the world's children and grandchildren.

As a species we are in a relationship of collectivist individualism with the global environment, the exquisite product of 4.54 billion years of evolution. It has nurtured us throughout our short history of merely a couple of hundred thousand years. *Homo sapiens* is proving to be its most worrisome and headstrong child. Unless we each sign up to contribute in full measure – and in proportion to our means – to replenish the funds of that much larger parish, the earth, which houses us all, it will be unable to continue to support us when we need it to do so. No matter how wealthy we may make ourselves in our contemporary monetary exchange terms – as individuals or tax-shielded dynasties or corporations – we all remain vulnerable to this imminent threat. For our children and their children's children we cannot afford to shirk this collective responsibility facing us right now. We cannot hope that somehow somebody else will do the good work to maintain our community's fabric – the earth's ecosystems – while we simply carry on, attending to our own self-interests. We should certainly all continue to hope that science can prove helpful to us – like a brilliant invention to eat up all the carbon in the atmosphere – but that is not enough. Our fellow species have been going extinct in increasing numbers for some time already and a planet with only *Homo sapiens* and his latest clever app left on it is not one that will be worth living on.

It is often considered that the industrial revolution was Britain's most unique contribution to world history. However, as this book points out, that achievement emerged from a society and economy that had enjoyed unprecedented success due to its adoption since c.1600 of the policies, principles and practices of collectivist individualism, producing an inclusive form of economic growth. This turns out now to have been a more valuable British historical legacy to the world than the unbalanced, competitive individualism and unregulated free markets adopted in the course of the subsequent industrial revolution. It is a legacy that re-emerged for a generation after 1945 and which urgently needs to be rediscovered and revitalised to enable us all to find the commitment to each other needed to meet our imminent challenges.

Coexistence, anti-exploitation and nurturing are the moral codes of this collectivist-individualist ethics: nurturing of the planet, of other species, other nations, and the individuality of all other persons in our own societies, our own neighbourhoods. From where we are now, living in historically produced national polities entering the mid-twenty-first century, we need to work for, vote for and contribute to this nurturing state of positive freedoms, led by a morality of giving, not taking.

ACKNOWLEDGEMENTS

This book originated when our essay 'Incentivizing an Ethical Economics', co-authored with our son, Ben Szreter, jointly won the Institute for Public Policy Research (IPPR) Economics Prize in July 2019. This caught the eye of Jon Wood, who encouraged us to think about developing our ideas into a book for a wider audience. We are grateful for Jon's enthusiasm in acting as our agent, and we were very pleased when Michael Watson at Cambridge University Press backed our proposal to the Syndics of CUP, commissioning the book you now have in your hands.

In addition to Ben Szreter, whose contribution to the original essay, support for this new project and incisive advice and comments on the current text have been invaluable, there are many others we would like to thank for their assistance. Our first draft of 31 December 2020 benefited greatly from the comments of two anonymous readers (and a third one who commented on the original proposal). In addition, several friends and colleagues, with very diverse interests, generously read the draft and provided their extremely helpful feedback and encouragement: Jonathan Carr, Miguel Garnett, Mike Kelly, Duncan Needham and Cathy O'Neill, while Elias Nosrati and Siân Pooley read and commented on the final version. Others who provided valued advice along the way include: Kelly Davis, Ian Francis, Alastair Reid, Peter Clarke, Ha-Joon Chang and Guy Standing.

This is a book that is centred on a pivotal moment in our history, in which we – collectively – have been driven by a pandemic to reflect on what it has revealed about our society and the power relationships that are influencing it. We have titled the book *After the Virus* not because we know or believe we are yet at the point at which this can confidently be proclaimed, but because we consider it imperative that we use this moment to draw a line between what came before and what must come after COVID-19. In that sense, *After the Virus* is our challenge to readers, policy makers and the wider community to think about what this watershed moment means for each one of us, individually and as part of a local, national and worldwide community.

When we embarked on this project we were not only writing a book about a pandemic: we were also simultaneously experiencing it first hand, from the constraints of lockdown to the threats to health that it presented. Within hours of the UK's first lockdown beginning on 23rd March we were both experiencing symptoms of COVID-19, a later positive antibody test for Hilary confirming that she had indeed had the illness. After months of restrictions, the summer relaxation of rules provided us with some welcome respite before the renewed autumn and winter lockdowns confined us again. By the time of the third – 2021 – lockdown, we were fortunate to have the much welcome company of our two other children, Iridium and Zack, to sustain us.

As for so many others, technology has been our saviour, allowing access to the many stimulating policy webinars that were reporting new research and insights in 'real time' as COVID-19 unfolded. Zoom and WhatsApp also provided us with entertainment, laughter, friendship and fortitude as we stayed in touch with friends and relatives, near and far, throughout the many long winter months until vaccination gave us cautious optimism that we could see our loved ones again face to face, after a sixteen-month-long gap in the case of our close relatives (apart from those living abroad, who we will not see until travel restrictions are lifted).

There are many more people to thank. IPPR, in particular, who have been very happy for us to draw from the material in our 2019 essay. Robert Joyce at the Institute for Fiscal Studies, Jack Leslie at the Resolution Foundation, Oliver Paynel at the National Centre for Social Research and Christopher Chantrill of ukpublicspending.co.uk have all willingly supplied or given permission to use their data and original charts in the publication. Thanks are also due to Francis Bainton for preparing the bibliographic references and, again, to Ben Szreter for stepping in to provide technical support with several of the figures and images. We are grateful, too, for timely advice and help from Jon Lane, Sara Nevrkla, Cath Burns, Tone Bringa, Flavio Comin and Angels Varea; and to Beverly Jones and Sharon Goddard for allowing Hilary to step back from her collaborative work with them for the duration of this project.

We also wish to thank the production team at Cambridge University Press, who have provided us with such an efficient and speedy service throughout, starting with the cover design team who produced the image of the open door to the future. We thank in particular our content manager Ruth Boyes, our copy-editor Julene Knox, our indexer Roger Bennett, and Emily Plater and Emily Sharp for editorial assistance.

Obviously, our principal debts are to be found among all the excellent scholarly and journalistic publications listed in our references. Like all other human activity of any value, the intellectual work recorded in this publication could not have occurred without the contributions provided by this encompassing collective. For Simon this also includes the wide fraternity of the History & Policy network (www .historyandpolicy.org), whose many contributions he has learned from as its editor; colleagues in the Cambridge History faculty and co-authors of research publications of relevance to this book's themes: Keith Breckenridge, Armine Ishkanien, Graham Mooney, Kevin Siena and

Michael Woolcock; as well as others who have been helpful and encouraging: Paul Slack, Brodie Waddell, Jonathan Healey, Lorie Charlesworth, John Broad, Marjorie McIntosh, John Walter, Joanna Innes, Samantha Williams, Guido Alfani, Leigh Shaw-Taylor, Keith Snell, Bernard Harris, David Rosner, Daniel Fox, Lincoln Chen, Megan Vaughan, Sunil Amrith, Paul Warde, Philip Kreager, Danny Dorling and Roy Lowe. The Master, Fellows and staff of St John's College, Cambridge, and in particular the Health Inequalities discussion group, which has met regularly during the last six years under the wing of Ann Louise Kinmonth, Natasha Kriznik and Mike Kelly, has been a continual source of collegial support and stimulation. Finally, any tribute to intellectual influences would not be complete without reference to Tony Wrigley, Richard Smith and the late Roger Schofield and Robert Hinde.

Neither of us has ever worked on a publication in which on a daily basis news, events, data, articles and reports are changing what we know, what we can say and how we interpret the political landscape. To write a book about a continually unfolding experience is itself a salutary one. Almost every week during the first few months of 2021 new perspectives, revelations, information and books have been appearing concerning matters we originally completed writing about on 31 December 2020. The text you have before you is the product of substantial revisions and additions completed up to the spring of 2021. But we are only too well aware that we cannot freeze time and that much more will have changed before readers first have this book in front of them in the autumn of 2021. Hopefully they will make allowance for the text's temporal limitations and find value in the longer-term perspectives we are offering, which transcend – even while being informed by – the immediate experience of the pandemic.

NOTES

Introduction

1 We use the term 'people of colour' and closely related terms throughout this book to refer collectively to a range of people who are not white, if it has not been possible to be more specific about ethnicity. We recognise that selecting any single term to describe diverse groups of people is difficult and currently subject to ongoing debate.
2 Singer (2009).
3 Schwab (2019).
4 Partridge (2020).
5 The concept of *collectivist individualism* is inspired by the analysis of the historian, Roger Schofield (1989), pp.284–85, who used the term 'individualist-collectivist' to describe the distinctive principles of the late medieval and early modern English demographic regime – when most other European peasant societies were characterised by a more 'familistic' ideology.
6 Sacks (2020), pp.246–48.
7 Haidt (2012).
8 Sandel (2012), p.103.
9 Sacks (2020), p.101.

1 The Extraordinary History of Pandemic Control

1 Gates (2015).
2 Slack (1985).
3 Slack (2012), ch.2.
4 Chase-Levenson (2020).
5 Harrison (2004), p.60.
6 WHO (2019); Snowden (2019), p.7.
7 Morens, Folkers and Fauci (2009).
8 Barker (2021).
9 Slack (2012), ch.3.
10 Slack (1985), pp.218–19.

11   McMillen (2016), ch.4; Dyos and Reeder (1973).
12   Honigsbaum (2020), p.xviii.
13   Quammen (2012).
14   McNeill (1980).
15   Crosby (1972); McNeill (1976); Birn (2020), p.356.
16   Szreter (2019), pp.25–27.
17   Thomson, Kentikelenis and Stubbs (2017); Forster et al. (2020); Nosrati et al. (2021).
18   Slack (2012), p.58.
19   Martin (1995), p.101. Knighton recorded 1,480 deaths during 1349 in three of Leicester's six parishes. At the poll tax in 1377 Leicester recorded 2,380 adult taxpayers: Rigby (2010), p.415, appx I.
20   Slack (2012), p.58.
21   Slack (2012), p.73.
22   Slack (2012), p.76.
23   Heitman (2020).
24   Slack (1985), p.239.
25   Siena (2020).
26   Slack (2012), p.75.
27   Henderson (2020). See Cipolla (1979) for an intimate account of the daily fears and emotions of contemporaries during the 1630–31 plague visitation in the nearby tiny village of Monte Lupo.
28   Shaw-Taylor, Davenport and Williams (2020).
29   Slack (1985), p.211.
30   Slack (1985), p.269.
31   Shaw-Taylor et al. (2020).
32   Henderson (2020).
33   Szreter (1988); Hamlin (1998).
34   Evans (1987).
35   Durbach (2000).
36   For further details see Weaver and Parveen (2020).
37   Markel et al. (2006).
38   Bristow (2020).

2 Pandemics Are Not Random 'Black Swans'

1   Taleb (2010).
2   Public Health England Emergency Preparedness, Resilience and Response Partnership Group (2017), pp.6 and 25.
3   National Audit Office (2020b).
4   Hopkins (2020).
5   Hillier et al. (2020).
6   Lintern (2020).
7   https://twitter.com/bbcpolitics/status/1234455267322011655?lang=en
8   Booth (2020).
9   Social Care Institute for Excellence (2020).

10 Burn-Murdoch and Giles (2020).
11 Ferguson (2020).
12 Wolf (2020).
13 www.gov.uk/government/speeches/pm-speech-in-greenwich-3-february-2020
14 www.bbc.co.uk/news/av/uk-51862282
15 Henley (2020).
16 Lambert (2020).
17 Moore (2020).
18 Independent SAGE (2020a).
19 Khalaf on Twitter, 31 May 2020.
20 Mooney (2015).
21 Murphy and Marsh (2020).
22 Scientific Advisory Group for Emergencies (2020).
23 Office for Budget Responsibility (2021b), p.43.
24 Wall (2021).
25 SAGE's 'reasonable worst case planning scenario' prepared on 30th July had
    stated that as many as 85,000 people could die in a second winter wave of
    the virus (Scientific Pandemic Influenza Group on Modelling, Operational
    sub-group 2020).
26 BBC *Newsnight*, 4 August 2020, https://twitter.com/bbcnewsnight/
    status/1290779792355340288
27 View expressed during Independent Sage press conference 12 May 2020
    (Independent SAGE 2020b).
28 Baker (2020).
29 The UK's success in developing the AstraZeneca vaccine has been described
    as a case study in government led by 'mission-oriented' policy, with a clear
    strategy from early in the pandemic to secure safe vaccines at speed for
    the UK population seeing scientists, industry, government and the wider
    population co-operating to compress the timeline for vaccine development
    to under a year (Balawejder, Sampson and Stratton 2021).
30 Worldometers.info (2020).
31 Number 10 Press Briefing, 26 January 2020, including questions from
    journalists, www.youtube.com/watch?v=YWHxE0F2IoI
32 For more details see Razai, Osama and McKechnie (2021).
33 The King's Fund (2021).

3 The Fragility of the Neoliberal State

 1 The global spread occurred throughout the 1980s through the influence of
    the IMF's structural adjustment programmes imposed on scores of indebted
    countries and the similar policies of the World Bank and additionally after
    1989 the 'shock therapy' administered to the East European economies
    emerging from the Soviet yoke. The establishment of the World Trade
    Organization in 1995 symbolised the international dominance of this
    neoliberal Washington Consensus.
 2 Williamson (2020).

3   Garland (2016).

4   Shaxson (2018a), ch.2, esp.pp.58–59 on the growth of the Eurodollar market tolerated by the Bank of England.

5   Shaxson (2018a).

6   See www.inet.ox.ac.uk/news/capital-failure/; Morris and Vines (2014).

7   Drucker (1946); and see also Shaxson (2018a), p.196.

8   Mayer (2013).

9   Shaxson (2018a), p.3.

10 Pistor (2019).

11 Wood (2020a).

12 Ryan-Collins (2018); Colenutt (2020).

13 Shaxson (2018b).

14 Shaxson (2018b).

15 Piketty (2014).

16 Stewart and Syal (2020).

17 Cagé (2020).

18 Greenfield (2018).

19 Pollock and Price (2013).

20 Business, Energy and Industrial Strategy and Work and Pensions Committees (2018), p.4.

21 Business, Energy and Industrial Strategy and Work and Pensions Committees (2018), p.54.

22 Davies (2018).

23 O'Connor (2020).

24 Savage (2019).

25 Lewis (2020).

26 Monbiot (2020).

27 www.bbc.co.uk/news/uk-53672841

28 Geoghegan, Scott and Molloy (2020).

29 Geoghegan (2020); Standing (2016), ch.7 details the right-wing network spawned since 1947 by the influential Mont Pelerin Society and since 1981 by the Atlas Network, whose main fronts in the UK are those organisations, like the Institute of Economic Affairs (IEA), which have the lowest grading for non-transparency of their funds. During a Chris Cook exposé on (BBC *Newsnight*, 18 July 2018), Shanker Singham of IEA defended the anonymity of their funding on grounds that 'freedom of association and the ability of people to have their privacy protected is a very important part of a free society'. The rich thus hide behind 'privacy' while seeking to influence policy.

30 Transparify Worldwide (2018).

31 https://policyexchange.org.uk/news/matt-hancock-sets-out-vision-for-public-health/

32 For the press release opposing capital gains tax rise see www.cps.org.uk/media/press-releases/q/date/2020/11/13/capital-gains-tax-rise-will-impede-growth-and-investmen/, 13 November 2020. For the media briefing on the proposal for three-year public sector pay freeze see www.cps.org.uk/media/media-coverage/q/date/2020/11/20/a-three-year-freeze-could-save-

the-exchequer-up-to-23-b/ – report on their website on 20 November 2020 of coverage of their proposals by the *Telegraph*. For the research note recommending that the government should not increase the minimum wage see www.cps.org.uk/research/the-case-against-raising-the-minimum-wage, published 15 November 2020.

33 Warrington (2021).
34 Lawrence, F. et al. (2020).
35 Hardman (2018), ch.11.
36 Lawrence, F. et al. (2020).
37 National Audit Office (2020a), p.60.
38 National Audit Office (2020b), p.11.
39 See www.health.org.uk/news-and-comment/charts-and-infographics/health-spending-as-a-share-of-gdp-remains-at-lowest-level-in
40 Rhodes et al. (2012), fig.1.
41 Lawrence, F. et al. (2020).
42 Lawrence, F. et al. (2020).
43 See pp.8 and 41 of https://bit.ly/3vS0RWU
44 www.bbc.co.uk/news/52674073. See also the change in guidance on 16 April 2020 at https://bit.ly/3xYusQg
45 Social Care Institute for Excellence (2020).
46 Office for National Statistics (2020b), table 1.
47 Hunt (2020).
48 Starmer (2020).
49 Laing (2020); also reported in Savage (2020).
50 Savage (2020).
51 Laing (2020).
52 Altmann (2020).
53 Analysis by Chris Hatton, professor of public health and disability at Lancaster University, cited in Birrell (2020).
54 Vizard et al. (2020).
55 Birrell (2020).
56 Altmann (2020).
57 Altmann (2020).
58 Altmann (2020).
59 Ford (2020).
60 Office for National Statistics (2020a).
61 Green and Kynaston (2019), fig.2, p.5.
62 Jolly and Syal (2020).
63 Kemp (2020).
64 Garside and Smith (2020).
65 Lawrence (2020b).
66 National Audit Office (2020d).
67 Public Accounts Committee (2021).
68 Backward tracing works by identifying who gave a particular individual their infection and then tracking who else they passed it on to. It is based on the principle that most people do not transmit coronavirus, but a small number –

super-spreaders – infect a large number of people. Finding these super-spreading individuals and their contacts is more effective in containing infection than routine contact tracing applied to everyone.

69 See www.tuc.org.uk/blogs/high-rejection-rates-show-self-isolation-payment-scheme-isnt-fit-purpose

70 Smith et al. (2021).

71 NYC Health and Hospitals (2020).

72 Davies (2020).

73 www.theguardian.com/society/2020/may/07/government-gave-national-pupils-food-voucher-contract-to-small-company

74 Walker (2020).

75 Lough (2020).

76 Hill (2021).

77 Szreter (2020b).

78 www.bbc.co.uk/news/52674073

79 Horton (2020).

4 Inequality Saps Resilience

1 High Pay Centre (2021).

2 Bourquin, Joyce and Keiller (2020).

3 The Gini Coefficient ranges from 0, which is perfect income equality across all households, to 1, where all income goes to a single household.

4 For an excellent survey of poverty and inequality in Britain since 1900 putting the period since 1979 in context see Thane (2018).

5 Joyce and Xu (2019).

6 Hills (2017), pp.28–32.

7 Bangham and Leslie (2019).

8 Mandleson had said 'we are intensely relaxed about people getting filthy rich', adding, 'as long as they pay their taxes'.

9 The argument that cuts in taxes are justified not just by trickle-down notions but also by the more complex economic construct of 'optimal tax theory' has been shown to be premised on invalidating inconsistencies – see Offer and Söderberg (2016), pp.171–78.

10 https://wist.info/galbraith-john-kenneth/16956/

11 Standing (2016), ch.7, p.242.

12 Chang (2010) pp.231–41.

13 On the polluter elite see Kenner (2019); and see also Piketty (2020), p.667.

14 Stiglitz (2011).

15 Dorling (2019).

16 Office for National Statistics (2017), table 1 and fig. 3. Gross fixed capital formation in the UK was on average six percentage points lower than the OECD average over the twenty-year period from 1997 to 2017.

17 www.bbc.co.uk/news/business-51543521

18 In October 2016, Theresa May commissioned Matthew Taylor, chief executive of the Royal Society of the Arts, to conduct a review of

employment practices in the expanding informal economy, subsequently published in his report (Taylor et al. 2017). A House of Commons briefing paper over three years later was to acknowledge that 'many of the core recommendations in the Taylor Review have yet to be implemented' – see Ferguson (2020), with Taylor himself referring in February 2021 to the 'deafening silence' from the government on their promised reforms (Partington 2021).

19   Booth (2018).
20   Roberts (2019).
21   Joyce and Xu (2019).
22   Oakeshott (2012).
23   Data available in 2015 gave a figure of four in ten fit-for-work decisions being successfully appealed (Butler 2015).
24   Butler (2020a) and (2015).
25   www.bbc.co.uk/news/uk-england-nottinghamshire-55826996
26   Ishkanian and Szreter (2012).
27   HM Revenue and Customs and Department for Work and Pensions (2020), p.11.
28   Institute for Fiscal Studies (2019).
29   Bourquin et al. (2020), table 3.1.
30   The Resolution Foundation (2019).
31   Corlett (2019).
32   Office for National Statistics (2020f), fig. 1.
33   Department for Work and Pensions (2021).
34   Brewer et al. (2020), p.27.
35   Fitzpatrick et al. (2020).
36   Commons Select Committee Work and Pensions (2019).
37   Bradshaw (2020).
38   Alston (2019).
39   There is certainly much irony in the term's widespread current usage in an approving fashion, in that the sociologist who popularised the term intended it as a satire on the self-justifying self-approval of the successful Young (1958).
40   Green and Kynaston (2019), pp.11, 208 and ch.4.
41   Szreter (in press, 2021) IFS Deaton Review.
42   See Hills (2017), ch.7 for a more detailed discussion.
43   Social Mobility Commission (2019).
44   Tomlinson, J. (2020), p.530.
45   Dept of Education (1993), table A27/93A and table A27/93B, pp.178–79; Dept for Employment and Education (1999), tables 1A & 1B, pp.16–17; Dept for Employment and Education (2001); Dept for Employment and Education (2000),table 1. Ratios cited are adjusted as FTEs (full-time equivalents) for staff and pupils; independent/private schools ratio for secondary and preparatory schools combined.
46   Britton et al. (2020).
47   Britton et al. (2020).
48   Zaranko (2020), fig. 6.2, p.272.

49   Cattan et al. (2019).
50   Boushey (2019).
51   Phillips and Simpson (2018).
52   Marmot et al. (2020a).
53   Joyce and Xu (2019).
54   Ostry, Berg and Tsangarides (2014).
55   Piketty (2020), ch.16, p.4.
56   Wolf (2014a).
57   In the UK we now have a minister for suicide prevention, while Wacquant
     (2010) argues that the USA is now simply incarcerating the children of the
     poor and less educated, as a (very expensive) alternative to rehabilitation
     efforts. Furthermore, high incarceration rates exacerbate social health
     inequalities: Nosrati and Marmot (2019).
58   Wilkinson and Pickett (2009).
59   Ainsworth (1978); Cyr et al. (2010).
60   Geddes (2018).
61   Joyce and Xu (2019), p.8.
62   Zymek and Jones (2020).
63   Butler (2020d).
64   Emily Maitlis, BBC *Newsnight*, 8 April 2020.
65   Gardner, Gray and Moser (2020).
66   Financial Conduct Authority (2018).
67   Blundell et al. (2020).
68   Lawrence (2020a).
69   The Trussell Trust (2020a).
70   Blundell et al. (2020).
71   Marmot et al. (2020b).
72   Raval (2021).
73   In normal times employers cannot reclaim the cost of paying statutory sick
     pay. An exception was introduced in the pandemic allowing employers with
     fewer than 250 employees to be reimbursed for up to two weeks when an
     employee was off work with COVID-19 or self-isolating.
74   For examples for banks and teachers see: www.cityam.com/staff-at-
     british-banks-forced-to-turn-off-nhs-covid-tracing-app-at-work/ and www
     .personneltoday.com/hr/teachers-told-to-disable-nhs-contact-tracing-app-
     claims-union/
75   Sridhar (2020).
76   Mooney (2015).
77   Helm (2020).

5 The Pandemic Onslaught

1   Public Health England (2020).
2   Halliday (2021).
3   Office for National Statistics (2020a).

4   Marmot et al. (2020b), p.33.
5   Marmot et al. (2020a).
6   Office for National Statistics (2020e).
7   Butler (2020c).
8   Inman (2021).
9   Independent SAGE (2020c), p.8.
10 Independent SAGE (2020c), pp. 5, 8.
11 Independent SAGE (2020c), pp. 2, 6. See also Marmot et al. (2020b) for further amplifying evidence on the impact of indirect and direct racism.
12 Gentleman (2019).
13 Wall (2020).
14 Bell, Corlett and Handscomb (2020), p.3.
15 This rose to £331 on 1 April 2020 when the annual uprating was applied.
16 For further details see this website on European national social security systems, which can be interrogated by country: https://ec.europa.eu/social/main.jsp?catId=858&langId=en
17 Tomlinson, D. (2020), fig. 4.
18 www.gov.uk/government/news/furlough-scheme-extended-and-further-economic-support-announced
19 Office for National Statistics (2021a) and (2020g).
20 Department for Work and Pensions (2021).
21 A mortgage holiday allows monthly payments to be paused for a set period of time, although interest still accrues, and the deferred payments have to be paid back later. With the second national lockdown in November 2020 the original stipulation that banks must allow three-month mortgage holidays was increased to six months and the deadline to apply was extended. For further details see www.which.co.uk/news/2020/11/coronavirus-how-to-apply-for-a-three-month-mortgage-payment-holiday/
22 Gardiner et al. (2020).
23 Andrew et al. (2020a).
24 Britton et al. (2020), p.69.
25 Education Policy Institute (2020).
26 Crawford and Greaves (2015), p.9.
27 www.bbc.co.uk/news/uk-england-leicestershire-54423723
28 https://bit.ly/3euKycF
29 www.bbc.co.uk/newsround/54509311
30 www.bbc.co.uk/news/live/uk-54656821
31 https://bit.ly/3o6DTsy
32 See www.facebook.com/watch/?v=370432467634464
33 Buchan (2020).
34 www.bbc.co.uk/news/uk-england-54769232
35 Bell et al. (2020), p.3.
36 Scotland as a whole voted 'remain' in the 2016 Brexit referendum and calls for Scottish independence continued after the UK left the EU in early 2020. In Northern Ireland, tensions have risen following new checks on goods arriving from the UK mainland required as a result of the

Brexit deal, threatening the stability of the years since the Good Friday Agreement (1988).

6 'Too Big To Fail?' We Need a Payback This Time

1   Speech by Mervyn King to Scottish business organisations, Edinburgh, 20 October 2009 (King 2009).
2   Nao.org (2020).
3   Cribb and Johnson (2018).
4   Zaranko (2020).
5   https://tradingeconomics.com/country-list/corporate-tax-rate?continent=g20
6   Breach (2019).
7   Gardiner (2017b).
8   https://bit.ly/3o2Xeuw
9   https://bit.ly/3vT7gkt
10 Office for Budget Responsibility (2021a). Monthly Profiling data tables in embedded *Fiscal Sustainability Report and Summer Economic Update Measures*, 21 August 2020.
11 Strauss (2020).
12 Redundancies rose to 370,000 in the three months to October 2020, a record high (ONS 2020g).
13 Office for Budget Responsibility (2021b), p.124.
14 StepChange (2020).
15 Berry, Macfarlane and Nanda (2020).
16 Berry, Macfarlane and Nanda (2020), pp.20, 26.
17 Stevenson (2020).
18 UBS and PwC (2020).
19 See for instance British Airways' warning about its parent company IAG (Thicknesse 2020).
20 Luce (2020).
21 Partington (2020).
22 Needham, L. (2020).
23 Neate (2020a).
24 Wood (2020b).
25 Scotto Di Santolo (2020).
26 www.bbc.co.uk/sport/football/52120578
27 For an account of Boris Johnson's stance on fees for overseas health workers, and the mistaken figure he cited that vastly overstated the amount of money that it would cost to waive them see www.bbc.co.uk/news/uk-52750065
28 Lawrence, M. et al. (2020).
29 www.bbc.co.uk/news/business-55125802
30 For an account of the payout to Tina Green and the subsequent story of Arcadia, see Neate (2020c).
31 Lonergan and Blyth (2020b).

32 Lonergan and Blyth (2020a), p.5.
33 Lonergan and Blyth (2020a), p.2.
34 Lonergan and Blyth (2020a), p.2.
35 BBC News, 5 June 2020.
36 Measures to ban these payments for large businesses seeking government loans were announced at the end of May 2020 (www.bbc.co.uk/news/business-52719997).
37 Austrian Airlines (2020).
38 https://bit.ly/3fawQe2
39 www.bbc.co.uk/news/business-52043896
40 Berry et al. (2020), p.10.
41 Berry et al. (2020), p.9.
42 National Audit Office (2020c).
43 Wise (2020).
44 Lawrence, M. et al. (2020).
45 Corporate Leaders Group (2020).
46 In 2018 the British Academy had diagnosed this problem: that the governance of corporations had taken an errant direction over the previous decades, leaving behind their social purposes. British Academy (2018), p.14.
47 Financial Times Editorial Board (2020).
48 Schwab (2019).
49 Lawrence, M. et al. (2020).
50 Davoudi, McKenna and Olegario (2018).

7 No Time for Austerity Now

1 Office for Budget Responsibility (2021b), p.9; see also Office for Budget Responsibility (2021c) for a commentary on later ONS and OBR revisions and the differences between them.
2 Office for Budget Responsibility (2021b), pp.61–62, see paragraph 1.133 and Table 3.29.
3 https://bit.ly/3uyWtM8
4 Blyth (2013).
5 https://bit.ly/3eAie8O
6 Sparrow and Marsh (2020).
7 O'Hara (2020).
8 Office for National Statistics (2021b); for a commentary see Wolf (2014b), p.329.
9 https://bit.ly/3evom2a
10 Stirling (2019).
11 Davison (2013).
12 Royal Statistical Society (2019).
13 Royal Statistical Society (2019).
14 Royal Statistical Society (2019).
15 Reinhart and Rogoff (2010).
16 Excelgate was the term coined by the economist Mark Blyth in 2013 to describe this incident.

17   Herndon, Ash and Pollin (2013).
18   Needham (2020).
19   Office for Budget Responsibility (2021b), pp.161–62.
20   https://bit.ly/3uDQtBR
21   Slater (2018).
22   Needham (2020).
23   Institute for Fiscal Studies seminar, 'Covid-19 Deficits, Debt and Fiscal
     Strategy', 1st July. Presentation by Carl Emmerson (www.ifs.org.uk/
     publications/14913 – key point made at 26 minutes into recording).
24   New Statesman (2020).
25   https://bit.ly/3eyuyqj
26   New Statesman (2020).
27   Elliott (2020b).
28   Tooze (2020b).
29   Needham (2020).
30   There is no shortage of ideas from those with deep practical experience on
     how we might achieve continuing growth in a sustainable way. For instance,
     Gates (2021), Carney (2021), chs.11–16, Shafik (2021), ch.8.
31   Needham (2020).
32   Lightfoot (2020).
33   Goodhart and Needham (2020).
34   www.bbc.co.uk/news/uk-53207700
35   www.bbc.co.uk/news/business-53233705
36   The Resolution Foundation (2020).
37   Hutton (2020).
38   Organisation for Economic Co-operation and Development (2021).
39   Moody's Investors Service (2020).
40   Georgieva (2020); Gaspar et al (2020).
41   Office for Budget Responsibility (2021b), pp.7, 16–17.

8 Who Has the Deepest Pockets?

1   https://bit.ly/2R8yfd5
2   https://ifs.org.uk/budget-2021
3   Office for Budget Responsibility (2021b), p.18.
4   At the time of the March 2019 spring statement, the ever-active IFS director
    Paul Johnson had said 'we are now perhaps only 20 years from the moment
    when half of all state spending goes on just health, pensions and social care.
    It was 30 per cent at the turn of the century' (Johnson 2019).
5   Morgan and Harding (2018).
6   We saw a predictable start to this debate in a report from the Social Market
    Foundation in April 2020 at the start of the first lockdown suggesting
    that because the older population had been the main beneficiaries of the
    decision to close down the economy (because they were more at risk than
    other age groups) they should now be expected to step up to the plate, with
    the pension triple lock put up as the first proposed sacrifice (Corfe 2020).

7   Stewart et al. (2020).

8   Somerset Webb (2020).

9   Tax Justice UK (2020).

10 Curtice, Hudson and Montagu (eds) (2020).

11 The Treasury Select Committee did launch an inquiry, 'Tax after
    Coronavirus', in July 2020 to look at the long-term pressures on the UK tax
    system overall and what reforms might be necessary. It reported in March
    2021, making no recommendations on wealth taxation.

12 See Advani, Chamberlain and Summers (2020), p.2 for a statement on the
    funders of the Commission.

13 Advani, Chamberlain, O'Donnell and Miller (2020).

14 Dolphin (2009).

15 Roberts, Blakeley and Murphy (2018).

16 For further details of Pigou's proposal and his writings on this see www
    .madhyam.org.in/revisiting-pigous-capital-levy-in-the-time-of-covid-19/

17 Elliott (2020a).

18 Sandbu (2019). Sandbu reports the work done by Fatih Guvenen and team to
    demonstrate this (Guvenen et al. 2019).

19 Advani, Chamberlain and Summers (2020).

20 Glover and Seaford (2020).

21 Mirrlees et al. (2011), ch.20.

22 Office of Tax Simplification (2020).

23 Glover and Seaford (2020).

24 Office of Tax Simplification (2020), p.7.

25 Nanda and Parkes (2019), p.19.

26 Ryan-Collins (2020).

27 Adam et al. (2020).

28 Advani et al. (2020).

29 New Statesman (2020).

30 Szreter (2020a).

31 For a transcript of Rashford's letter in mid-June 2020 including an account of
    the poverty he experienced as a child and his conclusion that '[t]he system was
    not built for families like mine to succeed' see Rashford (2020).

32 Interview with the BBC's Laura Kuenssberg, 15 October 2020, www.bbc
    .co.uk/news/uk-politics-54549457

33 Advani, Chamberlain and Summers (2020), p.8.

34 Advani, Chamberlain and Summers (2020), p.72.

35 Advani in London School of Economics News (2020).

9 Rethinking Welfare

1   Berry (2020).

2   For a more in-depth discussion and an introduction to the idea of
    Redistributive Market Liberalism see Peter Sloman (2019) and Stewart
    Lansley (2020).

3   Ortiz et al. (2018), pp.16–17. Calculations based on income set at the poverty
    line in each country.
4   Lansley and Reed (2019); Torry (2020).
5   Lansley and Reed (2019); Torry (2020).
6   Economic Affairs Committee (2020).
7   Economic Affairs Committee (2020), p.3.
8   https://dictionary.cambridge.org/dictionary/english/welfare
9   Stephen Crabb on the *Today* programme, BBC Radio 4, 27 October 2020.
    Recording here www.facebook.com/watch/?v=1053873402102188
10 McNeil, Hochlaf and Quilter-Pinner (2019), p.2.
11 Lansley (2020).
12 Royal Commission on the Poor Laws and the Relief of Distress (1909).
13 Dorling and Szreter (2015).
14 For further details see https://bit.ly/33xH1E5
15 Savage and Ferguson (2020).
16 HM Revenue and Customs and Department for Work and Pensions (2020),
    p.11.
17 Butler (2020b).
18 Bourquain et al. (2020).
19 https://gordonandsarahbrown.com/2020/12/action-needed-to-help-forgotten-
    child-victims-of-poverty-says-gordon-brown/. The Child Poverty Action Group
    had been orchestrating similar calls for a £10 uprating of Child Benefit from
    early in the pandemic, setting out the case here: https://cpag.org.uk/news-
    blogs/news-listings/increasing-child-benefit-five-tests-five-ticks
20 Trends in pensioner poverty can be accessed via the Institute for Fiscal
    Studies' website tools www.ifs.org.uk/tools_and_resources/incomes_in_uk.
    See the data spreadsheet for pensioner poverty – less than 60 per cent of
    median income – after housing costs. Derived from Department for Work
    and Pensions Households Below Average Income (HBAI) data series.
21 McNeil et al. (2019).
22 Hudson et al. (2020), p.8.
23 Sen (1979, 1992); Comim and Nussbaum (2014).
24 Beveridge (1942).
25 Hills (2017), pp.66–67.
26 Quilter-Pinner and Hochlaf (2019).
27 Sandel (2010), pp 265–67.
28 Pendleton (2019).
29 Coote and Percy (2020).
30 Marmot (2014).
31 The Trussell Trust (2020b).
32 Andrew et al. (2020b).
33 Marçal (2015).
34 The economic historian Phyllis Deane petitioned Richard Stone, the architect
    of the measure, to include a valorisation of women's work following her
    fieldwork in Africa observing both monetised and non-monetised economic
    activity; arguments that, as we know, fell on deaf ears (Messac 2018).

35 https://bit.ly/33x8ndu
36 Roberts (2020).
37 For further details of the Dagenham machinists' long struggle beginning in 1968, the intervention of the Labour Secretary of State for Employment and Productivity, Barbara Castle, and the passing of the Equal Pay Act (1970) see https://bit.ly/3uz95mE
38 See McCarthy (2020) on married women's working lives in the 19th and 20th centuries.
39 Andrew et al. (2020b).
40 Gardiner (2017a).
41 Costa-Dias, Joyce and Parodi (2018), see esp. chart on p.10.
42 The Money Advice Service (2021).
43 Office for National Statistics (2020c).
44 Office for National Statistics (2020d).
45 Dilnot, Warner and Williams (2011), pp.12–13.
46 Care home fees vary considerably across the UK and most published average figures include both local authority places and privately (self-)funded places, although the latter can be as much as 30 per cent higher than the former. Hence it is hard to establish a typical cost except by looking at a selection of individual care homes to see what their actual charges for private clients are. *Which?* provide helpful charts with average figures (though combining charges for local authority and private places) as well as indicating the higher costs of nursing care places. There is also a tool to calculate costs for self-funders by postcode: www.which.co.uk/later-life-care/financing-care/care-home-finance/care-home-fees-akdbv8k3kwln
47 For further information on the treatment of social care and medical needs in the UK see www.kingsfund.org.uk/blog/2019/09/cancer-dementia-unfair-social-care-system. For more information on means-testing of social care see www.which.co.uk/later-life-care/financing-care/care-home-finance/local-authority-funding-for-a-care-home-arxsk9l8qzzr
48 Dilnot et al. (2011), p.14.
49 Cooper (2019); Szreter, Cooper and Szreter (2019); and Lansley, McCann and Schifferes (2018).
50 De Henau and Himmelweit (2020).

10 Casting Aside the Neoliberal State

1 Carney (2021), ch.6, esp. p.135.
2 Carney (2021), ch.2.
3 Tooze (2020a).
4 For the press conference where this point was made see https://cbsn.ws/3eySj1d
5 Szreter (2005).
6 Kahneman (2011).
7 Fehr and Schmidt (1999).

8 Schultz et al. (2007).

9 Fehr and Fischbacher (2003).

10 For a full account of the international response, the heroism of the divers and the unsung sacrifices of the local population in aiding the rescue see Bourne (2019). For the details of the divers who died see www.bbc.co.uk/news/world-asia-50931695

11 Hoff and Pandey (2006).

12 Bregman (2020).

13 Frank, Gilovich and Regan (1993).

14 General Register Office (1843, pp.50–51); and Szreter and Mooney (1998).

15 Wohl (1983); Szreter (1988), p.23.

16 Reverend Robert W. Dale (Congregationalist minister in Birmingham) cited in Hennock (1973), pp.162–63. The two other principal religious leaders were George Dawson and Henry Crosskey.

17 Marsh (1994), ch.4; Hunt (2004), ch.8.

18 Aidt, Daunton and Dutta (2010). The 1869 Municipal Franchise Act and the 1869 Assessed Rates Act were the two key reforms; they followed the 1867 Second Reform Act for parliamentary election.

19 Judd (1977), pp.61–62.

20 Marsh (1994), p.84.

21 Hunt (2004), p.250.

22 Harris and Hinde (2019), fig.10.

23 Szreter (2005), chs.6 and 7.

24 Chamberlain's opponents accused him of 'gas and water socialism' and decried 'municipal trading' – public bodies providing such services. Beveridge's Reports of 1942 and 1944 immediately provoked Hayek's conservative and libertarian counterblast, arguing that the welfare state would be *The Road to Serfdom*.

25 Cadman (2014); Giles(2014).

26 Samuel (2019).

27 A recording of Greta Thunberg's impassioned speech to the UN Climate Action Summit can be found here: https://nbcnews.to/3eAiWmu. On 'the quasi-religious adoration of growth' see Schmelzer (2016), p.6.

28 Raworth (2017), p.273, referring to John Fullerton, 'Can Financial Reform Fight Climate Change?' Interview on *The Laura Flanders Show*, 8 July 2012.

29 Neate (2020b).

30 Gaukroger (2016).

31 Schofield (1989), p.285.

11 The Birth of a Collectivist Individualism

1 Slack (1985), pp.209–10.

2 Van Bavel and Rijpma (2016), p.173.

3 Walter and Schofield (1989).

4 As McIntosh (2012) has argued, Edward VI's Poor Law of 1552, modified by Elizabeth I's further statutes of 1563 and 1572, were each important precursors.

5   Slack (1988).

6   Van Bavel and Rijpma (2016), p.165.

7   Slack (1990), p.57 explains the failure of a similar, effective parish scheme
    to develop in the course of the seventeenth century in Scotland (Ireland was
    not part of the United Kingdom until 1801).

8   Slack (1990), p.28.

9   Charlesworth (2010), p.51. To ensure fairness and consistency in the local
    application of the law, JPs' decisions were subject to review, if challenged, at
    quarterly Assize hearings in each county town, presided over by judges from the
    higher courts in London, who were appointed to the six regional circuits.

10 Hindle (2008).

11 All these various facilitations for labour mobility have been well
    documented by, for instance, Taylor (1989), Sokoll (2001) and Tadmor (2017).

12 Just as with the consolidating 1601 Poor Law, the 1601 Charitable Uses Act
    followed earlier efforts to encourage secular philanthropy, notably Acts of
    1572, 1576 and 1598 (Slack 1988, p.165).

13 On beggars compared to witches: Beier (1985), p.8; on witches: Macfarlane
    (1999).

14 Slack (1988), ch.8; Slack (1990), pp.19, 50–51.

15 Hadwin (1978), table 1, p.111. These figures are directly comparable as they
    have been adjusted for inflation effects.

16 Hadwin (1978), table 2, p.112; Slack (1988), p.164.

17 Waddell (2021), table 3 and p.28.

18 Szreter et al. (2016), p.2734.

19 Slack (1988), p.206.

20 Solar (1995, 1997); Szreter (2007).

21 Smith (1986), Solar and Smith (2003).

22 Solar (1995).

23 Schofield (1989); Smith (1996).

24 Schofield (1989), p.285.

25 Wrigley (2004), fig. 3.8.

26 Wrigley (1967).

27 The most recent estimates find sustained increase from the 1650s onwards
    in England's real per capita GDP growth rates (Broadberry et al. 2015, p.204,
    table 5.05 and fig. 5.05).

28 Shaw-Taylor, Erickson and Wrigley (2019).

29 Pressnel (1956).

30 Galloway (1988); Kelly and O'Grada (2011); Healey (2014).

31 Solar (1995).

32 Smith (2011), p.89.

33 On the extensive nature of Poor Law medical care see King (2018).

34 The Webbs examined the Poor Law and related statutes at great length,
    summarily pronouncing them to have been a 'Framework of Repression'
    (Webb and Webb 1927, p.396). Historians who have since researched the
    practical workings of the Old Poor Law have uncovered an entirely different
    reality (Slack 1988; Taylor 1989; Hitchcock, King and Sharpe 1997; Williams
    2013; Healey 2014).

35 Hindle (2004), pp.433–45, and table 6.1.
36 Waddell (2021).
37 Bohstedt (1983).
38 There is no shortage of documentation of the difficulties and tragedies faced by the poor in historians' studies of Poor Law sources. For instance: Sokoll (2001), Hindle (2004), Williams (2018), King (2019).
39 Charlesworth (2010), pp.94–98.
40 Szreter (2007).
41 Sokoll (2001); King (2019).
42 Sokoll (2001), pp.63–65.
43 Sokoll (2000), pp.26–30.
44 Sokoll (2001), p.229: Chelmsford Letter 186, 13 March 1826.
45 Sokoll (2000), pp.26–31.
46 Hindle (2004), ch.1.
47 Thompson (2014).
48 Slack (1999), p.71; many of London's largest parishes also had Poor Law infirmaries treating their settled poor extensively even for venereal diseases (Szreter and Siena 2021).
49 Smith (2011), p.83.
50 Charlesworth (2010), p.198.
51 Smith (2011), p.89.
52 Poynter (1969).
53 Hilton (1988).
54 Brundage (1978)
55 Lindert (1994), fig.14.5, p.383.
56 Checkland and Checkland (1974), p.386.
57 Gray (1999), p.331.
58 Pooley and D'Cruze (1994); Szreter and Mooney (1998).
59 Sanderson (1972).
60 Chase (2007).
61 Neave (1996); Johnson (1985).
62 Hennock (2007), pp.94–96.
63 Measured in terms of public expenditures on all levels of education as percentage of GDP at current prices (Lindert 2005, vol.2, appendix table C3, p.155).
64 Allen (2015).
65 Crafts (2014), table 2.2, p.28.
66 Kitson and Michie (2014), p.305.
67 Rowntree (1901), pp.118–21, 136–37, 301.
68 Royal Commission on the Poor Laws and the Relief of Distress (1909).
69 Beveridge (1909); and see Harris (1972), Boyer (2019), chs. 4–6.
70 Collison (1963).
71 Beveridge (1942).
72 Smith (2014), pp.33–36.
73 Smith (2014), p.xix.
74 Crafts (2014), p.28.

75 See above, Figure 2 for the period from 1961. The official measure of child poverty is children living in households below 60 per cent of median income. Recent research has been able to replicate that measure for the years 1953–54 finding a figure of 11 per cent (Gazeley et al. 2017, p.470).

76 Piketty (2014), pp.316–17 and Piketty (2020), p.195.

77 Piketty (2014), fig. 10.3, p.344, fig. 10.5, p.348.

78 This principle is expressed in Piketty's now famous inequality expression r > g. Piketty (2014), pp.25–27.

79 Piketty (2014), p.506.

80 Piketty (2014), pp.509–12.

81 Szreter (2015), p.348.

82 Piketty (2020), fig. 5.4, p.195.

83 See Szreter, Cooper and Szreter (2019) for an earlier exposition of these lessons, reprised here with kind permission from the Institute for Public Policy Research (IPPR).

84 Office for National Statistics (2019).

12 A Nurturing and Empowering State

1   Gamble (1988).

2   Berlin (1958).

3   The term *Nachtwächterstaat* was apparently coined by Ferdinand Lassalle in a speech in Berlin in 1862.

4   For a general history of Britain's expanding 'free trade' empire see Cain and Hopkins (2016); and see also Beckert (2014).

5   He first argued this in a 1966 essay, 'The Principles of a Liberal Social Order', and reiterated it in a public letter to *The Times*, 'The Dangers to Personal Liberty', published 11 July 1978, in which he also expressed his approval for Mrs Thatcher, at that time the Leader of the Opposition.

6   https://bit.ly/3eyKp7Y

7   Tawney (1964), p.164.

8   Robeyns and Byskov (2020), section 2.3 on social conversion factors and collective capabilities.

9   For the most important literary response to this event from within the US Black community see Glaude (2021).

10 Esping-Anderson (1990); Castles et al. (2010).

11 Garland (2016), pp.135–38.

12 Marmot (2014); Marmot et al. (2020).

13 Obermayer and Obermaier (2017).

14 Collins (2021).

15 Davies (2002).

16 Murphy (2014), pp.53–56, showing 92,000 officials in 2004–5 reduced to 62,000 in 2012–13 with planned further cuts to 52,000 by 2015–16.

17 Zucman (2015).

18 Marçal (2017).
19 Piketty (2020), fig.12.5, p.602.
20 Piketty (2020), p.462.
21 HM Revenue and Customs (2020).
22 Elliott (2020a).
23 Murphy (2020).
24 Elliott (2020c).
25 Giles (2021).
26 The best single account of the Laffer curve's curious political origins and subsequent history is to be found in Giraud (2014).
27 Mirrlees et al. (2011), p.110.
28 Manning (2015).
29 Shaxson (2018a), p.208.
30 Toynbee and Walker (2008) found their higher-paid interviewees had no idea of the incomes of the poor, tending to strongly overestimate them.
31 Crewe (1989), p.246.
32 Park et al. (2013).
33 Morgan and Harding (2018). Since 2017 support for tax rises to fund public spending increase has fallen back slightly but remains well above 50 per cent.
34 Amin (2020), p.5.
35 https://bit.ly/3uMWKvj
36 For further details see https://bbc.in/2SH70qD
37 Mark (2014).
38 https://bbc.in/3oeVUVH
39 Szreter (2002).
40 Ishkanian and Szreter (2012); Lambert (2021).
41 At the second reading of the bill, a Democratic Unionist Party MP, Gavin Robinson, said its drafting would 'make a dictator blush' (https://bit.ly/3ewTcHC).
42 Ishkanian and Szreter (2012), chs.2, 6–7, 9–12.
43 Chakrabortty (2018).
44 Hanna, Guinan and Bilsborough (2018).
45 The moniker refers to the public health expert Michael Marmot, who has globally championed the approach to health inequalities through analysing their social determinants.
46 Munroe (2020), pp.50–52.
47 Abers (1998).
48 Szreter and Woolcock (2004), pp.660–62.
49 Scottish Government News (2017).
50 Piketty (2020), p.666.
51 https://www.bbc.co.uk/news/technology-56012952
52 Collins (2021), p.29.
53 Shaxson (2011).
54 Zenghelis (2016).
55 Shafik (2021), pp.176–77.

56 Mazzucato (2021).
57 Offer and Söderberg (2016).
58 Van Lerven and Ryan-Collins (2017).
59 Carney (2015).
60 Zenghelis (2016).
61 Mazzucato (2013).
62 See Offer (2018) on the state's importance for 'patient' capital.
63 Dasgupta (2021), ch.13 and pp.491–92.
64 Dasgupta (2021); Pilling (2018).
65 Bennett Institute for Public Policy (2020a).
66 Bennett Institute for Public Policy (2020b), pp.10, 4.
67 Mazzucato (2018), p.xix.

13 Seven Pillars of Empowerment

1   Williams and Elliott (2010).
2   Schwab (2019).
3   For a more detailed argument see Szreter et al. (2019), p.23.
4   California's Proposition L, November 2020, 'Tax on Businesses with
    Disproportionate Executive Pay'.
5   Murphy (2015), ch.6, esp. pp.134–36.
6   Frank (2020).
7   Zuboff (2018).
8   European Commission (2020).
9   Szreter (2016).
10 Mazzucato (2018), ch.3; and see Fioramonti (2013) and Coyle (2014).
11 Dasgupta (2021).
12 Kanbur (2004); Satz (2010).
13 Raworth (2017); and see Stiglitz, Fitoussi and Durand (2020).
14 The scale of what is required to use the power of government, institutions
    and commerce to transform the 'choice architecture' is insightfully
    reviewed in Newell, Daley and Tweena (2021).
15 Dasgupta (2021), p.186.
16 Szreter (2005), ch.8.

14 Greater Even Than a Pandemic

1   Freije-Rodréguez et al. (2020).
2   United Nations Environment Programme (2020).
3   Pope Francis (2020).

REFERENCES

Abers, R. (1998), 'From Clientelism to Cooperation: Local Government, Participatory Policy and Civic Organizing in Porto Alegre, Brazil', *Politics and Society*, 26(4): pp.511–37

Adam, S., Hodge, L., Phillips, D. and Xu, X. (2020), Revaluation and Reform: Bringing Council Tax in England into the 21st Century, The Institute for Fiscal Studies, www.ifs.org.uk/publications/14761

Advani, A., Chamberlain, E., O'Donnell, G. and Miller, H. (2020), 'Is It Time for a UK Wealth Tax?', The Institute for Fiscal Studies, online seminar 2 July, www.ifs.org.uk/events/1830

Advani, A., Chamberlain, E. and Summers, A. (2020), *A Wealth Tax for the UK*, Wealth Tax Commission, www.ukwealth.tax/

Aidt, T., Daunton, M. and Dutta, J. (2010), 'The Retrenchment Hypothesis and the Extension of the Franchise in England and Wales', *Economic Journal*, 120(547): pp.990–1020

Ainsworth, M. (1978), *Patterns of Attachment: A Psychological Study of the Strange Situation*, Mahwah, NJ: Lawrence Erlbaum

Allen, R.C. (2015), 'The High Wage Economy and the Industrial Revolution: A Restatement', *Economic History Review*, 68(1): pp.1–22

Alston, P. (2019), *Visit to the United Kingdom of Great Britain and Northern Ireland: Report of the Special Rapporteur on Extreme Poverty and Human Rights*, United Nations General Assembly Human Rights Council forty-first session A/HRC/41/39, undocs.org/pdf?symbol=en/A/HRC/41/39/Add.1

Altmann, R. (2020), 'The Lesson of the Covid-19 Care Homes Tragedy: Renationalising Is No Longer Taboo', *The Guardian*, 6 July

Amin, L. (2020), *Art of Darkness: How the Government Is Undermining Freedom of Information*, Open Democracy, www.documentcloud.org/documents/20415987-art-of-darkness-opendemocracy

Andrew, A., Cattan, S., Costa-Dias, M., Farquharson, C., Kraftman, L., Krutikova, S., Phimister, A. and Sevilla, A. (2020a), Learning During the Lockdown: Real-Time Data on Children's Experiences During Home Learning, The Institute for Fiscal Studies, www.ifs.org.uk/publications/14848

Andrew, A., Cattan, S., Costa-Dias, M., Farquharson, C., Kraftman, L., Krutikova, S., Phimister, A. and Sevilla, A. (2020b), Family Time Use and Home Learning during the COVID-19 Lockdown, The Institute for Fiscal Studies, www.ifs.org.uk/publications/15038

Austrian Airlines (2020), 'Austrian Airlines Coronavirus Update: Austrian Airlines Receives Financial Aid from the Federal Government and Lufthansa', Austrian Airlines press release, June, https://bit.ly/3evBtjY

Baker, L. (2020), 'Independent SAGE Scientists Share Update as New Mutation Triggers Today's Lockdown Announcements', Healthcare Newsdesk, healthcare-newsdesk.co.uk/independent-sage-scientists-share-update-as-new-mutation-triggers-todays-lockdown-announcements/

Balawejder, F., Sampson, S. and Stratton, T. (2021), Lessons for Industrial Policy from Development of the Oxford/AstraZeneca Covid-19 Vaccine, Industrial Strategy Council

Bangham, G. and Leslie, J. (2019), 'Who Owns All the Pie? The Size and Distribution of Britain's £14.6 Trillion of Wealth', the Resolution Foundation, www.resolutionfoundation.org/publications/who-owns-all-the-pie/

Barker, H. (2021), 'Laying the Corpses to Rest: Grain, Embargoes, and *Yersinia pestis* in the Black Sea, 1346–48', *Speculum*, 96(1): pp.97–126

BBC News (2020), 'Coronavirus: Government under Fire for Cheap Loans to Big Firms', BBC News online, 5 June, www.bbc.co.uk/news/business-52934481

BBC *Newsnight* (2018), BBC Two Television, broadcast 18 July

BBC *Newsnight* (2020), BBC Two Television, broadcast 8 April

Beckert, S. (2014), *Empire of Cotton: A New History of Global Capitalism*, London: Allen Lane

Beier, A.L. (1985), *Masterless Men: The Vagrancy Problem in England 1560–1640*, York: Methuen

Bell, T., Corlett, A. and Handscomb, K. (2020), 'Death by £1000 Cuts? The History, Economics and Politics of Cutting Benefits for of Households Next April', the Resolution Foundation, https://bit.ly/3tCveiqMillions

Bennett Institute for Public Policy (2020a), 'Green Recovery Must End the Reign of GDP', 14 December, www.bennettinstitute.cam.ac.uk/news/green-recovery-must-end-reign-gdp-argue-cambridge-/

Bennett Institute for Public Policy (2020b), *Building Forward: Investing in a Resilient Recovery*, www.bennettinstitute.cam.ac.uk/publications/building-forward-investing-resilient-recovery/

Berlin, I. (1958), *Two Concepts of Liberty*, Oxford: Clarendon Press

Berry, C. (2020), 'Beyond Universal Basic Income', *IPPR Progressive Review*, 27(1): pp.48–57

Berry, C., Macfarlane, L. and Nanda, S. (2020), Who Wins and Who Pays? Rentier Power and the Covid Crisis, IPPR Centre for Economic Justice, www.ippr.org/research/publications/who-wins-and-who-pays

Beveridge, W.H. (1909), *Unemployment: A Problem of Industry*, London: Longmans, Green and Company

Beveridge, W.H. (1942), *Social Insurance and Allied Services*, London: Her Majesty's Stationery Office

Birn, A.-E. (2020), 'How to Have Narrative-Flipping History in a Pandemic: Views of/from Latin America', *Centaurus*, 62: pp.354–69

Birrell, I. (2020), 'Thousands of Care Home Residents Are Dying from Covid-19, and Staff Are on Minimum Wage', *Tortoise*, www.tortoisemedia.com/2020/05/18/coronavirus-care-homes-ian-birrell/#

Blundell, R., Costa-Dias, M., Joyce, R. and Xu, X. (2020), 'COVID-19 and Inequalities', *Fiscal Studies*, 41(2): pp.291–319

Blyth, M. (2013), *Austerity: The History of a Dangerous Idea*, Oxford:Oxford University Press

Bohstedt, J. (1983), *Riots and Community Politics in England and Wales 1790–1810*, Cambridge, MA: Harvard University Press

Booth, R. (2018), 'DPD Courier Who Was Fined for Day Off to See Doctor Dies from Diabetes', *The Guardian*, 5 February, https://bit.ly/3hbDtQ4

Booth, R. (2020), 'Agency Staff Were Spreading COVID-19 between Care Homes, PHE Found in April', *The Guardian*, 18 May, https://bit.ly/3exZyXi

Bourne, J. (2019), 'The Untold Story of the Daring Cave Divers Who Saved the Thai Soccer Team', *National Geographic*, 5 March, https://bit.ly/3o4qy3Z

Bourquin, P., Joyce, R. and Keiller, A.N. (2020), Living Standards, Poverty and Inequality in the UK: 2020, The Institute for Fiscal Studies, www.ifs.org.uk/publications/14901

Boushey, H. (2019), *Unbound: How Inequality Constricts Our Economy and What We Can Do about It*, Cambridge, MA: Harvard University Press

Boyer, G. (2019), *The Winding Road to the Welfare State. Economic Insecurity & Social Welfare Policy in Britain, Princeton*: Princeton University Press

Bradshaw, J. (2020), 'The Two-Child Limit: Impact on Abortion', Child Poverty Action Group, 6 December, https://cpag.org.uk/news-blogs/news-listings/two-child-limit-impact-abortion

Breach, A. (2019), Capital Cities: How the Planning System Creates Housing Shortages and Drives Wealth Inequality, Centre for Cities, https://bit.ly/3bcXvpG

Bregman, R. (2020), *Humankind: A Hopeful History*, London: Bloomsbury

Brewer, M., Corlett, A., Handscomb, K., McCurdy, C. and Tomlinson, D. (2020), The Living Standards Audit 2020, the Resolution Foundation, www.resolutionfoundation.org/app/uploads/2020/07/living-standards-audit.pdf

Bristow, N.K. (2020), 'What the 1918 Flu Pandemic Tells Us about Whether Social Distancing Works', *The Guardian*, 29 April

British Academy (2018), *Reforming Business for the 21st Century: A Framework for the Future of the Corporation*, London: The British Academy

Britton, J., Farquharson, C., Sibieta, L., Tahir, I. and Waltmann, B. (2020), *2020 Annual Report on Education Spending in England*, The Institute for Fiscal Studies, ifs.org.uk/uploads/R183-2020-annual-report-on-education-spending-in-England%20%281%29.pdf

Broadberry, S., Campbell, B.M.S., Klein, A., Overton, M. and van Leeuwen, B. (2015), *British Economic Growth, 1270–1870*, Cambridge: Cambridge University Press

Brundage, A. (1978), *The Making of the New Poor Law 1832–39*, London: Hutchinson

Buchan, L. (2020), 'Andy Burnham Blasts Tories for "Playing Poker with People's Lives" in Furious Speech', *Daily Mirror*, 20 October

Burn-Murdoch, J. and Giles, C. (2020), 'UK Suffers Second-Highest Death Rate from Coronavirus', *Financial Times*, 28 May

Business, Energy and Industrial Strategy and Work and Pensions Committees (2018), Carillon, HC 769 Published on 16 May, https://publications.parliament.uk/pa/cm201719/cmselect/cmworpen/769/769.pdf

Butler, P. (2015), 'Thousands Have Died after Being Found Fit for Work, DWP Figures Show', *The Guardian*, 27 August

Butler, P. (2020a), 'At Least 69 Suicides Linked to DWP's Handling of Benefit Claims', *The Guardian*, 7 February

Butler, P. (2020b), 'Two-Child Benefit Cap Influencing Women's Decisions on Abortion, Says BPAS', *The Guardian*, 3 December

Butler, P. (2020c), 'Nearly Half of BAME UK Households Are Living in Poverty', *The Guardian*, 1 July

Butler, P. (2020d), 'Child Poverty Increases in England across the North and Midlands', *The Guardian*, 14 October

Cadman, E. (2014), 'Mark Carney Warns of Dangers of Growing Inequality', *Financial Times*, 27 May

Cagé, J. (2020), *The Price of Democracy: How Money Shapes Politics and What to Do About It*, Cambridge, MA: Harvard University Press

Cain, P.J. and Hopkins, A.G. (2016), *British Imperialism 1688–2015*, London: Routledge

Carney, M. (2015), 'Breaking the Tragedy of the Horizon – Climate Change and Financial Stability', The Bank of England, www.bankofengland.co.uk/speech/2015/breaking-the-tragedy-of-the-horizon-climate-change-and-financial-stability

Carney, M. (2021), *Values(s): Building a Better World For All*, London: William Collins

Castles, F.G., Leibfried, S., Lewis, J., Obinger, H. and Pierson, C. (2010), *The Oxford Handbook of the Welfare State*, Oxford: Oxford University Press

Cattan, S., Conti, G., Farquharson, C. and Ginja, R. (2019), The Health Effects of Sure Start, The Institute for Fiscal Studies, www.ifs.org.uk/uploads/R155-The-health-effects-of-Sure-Start.pdf

Chakrabortty, A. (2018), 'In 2011 Preston Hit Rock Bottom. Then It Took Back Control', *The Guardian*, 31 January

Chang, H. (2010), *23 Things They Don't Tell You about Capitalism*, London: Allen Lane

Charlesworth, L. (2010), *Welfare's Forgotten Past: A Socio-Legal History of the Poor Law*, London: Routledge-Cavendish

Chase, M. (2007), *Chartism: A New History*, Manchester: Manchester University Press

Chase-Levenson, A. (2020), *The Yellow Flag: Quarantine and the British Mediterranean World, 1780–1860*, Cambridge: Cambridge University Press

Checkland, S. and Checkland, E. (1974), *The Poor Law Report of 1834*, Harmondsworth: Penguin

Cipolla, C. (1979), *Faith, Reason and the Plague in Seventeenth-Century Tuscany*, New York: W.W. Norton & Company

Collins, C. (2021), *The Wealth Hoarders. How Billionaires Pay Millions to Hide Trillions*, Cambridge: Polity Press

Collison, P. (1963), *The Cutteslowe Walls: A Study in Social Class*, London: Faber and Faber

Colenutt, B. (2020), *The Property Lobby. The Hidden Reality Behind the Housing Crisis*, Bristol: Policy Press

Comim, F. and Nussbaum, M. (2014), *Capabilities, Gender, Equality: Towards Fundamental Entitlements*, Cambridge: Cambridge University Press

Commons Select Committee Work and Pensions (2019), 'Universal Credit and "Survival Sex"', Department of Work and Pensions Committee, 25 October, publications.parliament.uk/pa/cm201919/cmselect/cmworpen/83/8304.htm

Cooper, H. (2019), 'Piecemeal Solutions to Britain's Care Crisis Will Not Do', *Financial Times*, 7 August

Coote, A. and Percy, A. (2020), *The Case for Universal Basic Services*, Cambridge: Polity Press

Corfe, S. (2020), Intergenerational Fairness in the Coronavirus Economy: Briefing Paper, Social Market Foundation, www.smf.co.uk/publications/intergenerational-fairness-coronavirus/

Corlett, A. (2019), *The Living Standards Outlook 2019*, the Resolution Foundation www.resolutionfoundation.org/app/uploads/2019/02/Living-Standards-Outlook-2019.pdf

Corporate Leaders Group (2020), Letter to Rt Hon Boris Johnson MP, 1 June

Costa-Dias, M., Joyce, R. and Parodi, F. (2018), *The Gender Pay Gap in the UK: Children and Experience in Work*, The Institute for Fiscal Studies, www.ifs.org.uk/publications/10356

Coyle, D. (2014), *GDP: A Brief but Affectionate History*, Princeton, NJ: Princeton University Press.

Crafts, N.F.R. (2014), 'Economic Growth during the Long Twentieth Century', in R. Floud, J. Humphries and P. Johnson (eds.), *The Cambridge Economic History of Modern Britain Volume II 1870 to the Present*, Cambridge: Cambridge University Press, pp.26–59

Crawford, C. and Greaves, E. (2015), Socio-economic, Ethnic and Gender Differences in HE Participation, Department for Business, Innovation and Skills, Research Paper 186, https://bit.ly/33uDbeX

Crewe, I. (1989), 'Values: The Crusade That Failed', in D. Kavanagh and A. Seldon (eds.), *The Thatcher Effect*, Oxford: Clarendon, pp.239–50

Cribb, J. and Johnson, P. (2018), '10 Years On – Have We Recovered from the Financial Crisis?', The Institute for Fiscal Studies, www.ifs.org.uk/publications/13302

Crosby, A.W. (1972), *The Columbian Exchange: Biological and Cultural Consequences of 1492*, Westport, CT: Greenwood Press

Curtice, J., Hudson, N. and Montagu, I. (eds.). (2020), 'Fairness and Justice in Britain', in *British Social Attitudes: The 37th Report*, National Centre for Social Research, bsa.natcen.ac.uk/latest-report/british-social-attitudes-37/fairness-and-justice-in-britain.aspx

Cyr, C., Euser, E.M., Bakermans-Kranenburg, M.J. and van Ijzendoorn, M.H. (2010), 'Attachment Security and Disorganization in Maltreating and High-Risk Families: A Series of Meta-analyses', *Developmental Psychopathology*, 22(1): pp.87–108

Dasgupta, P. (2021), *The Economics of Biodiversity: The Dasgupta Review*, London: HM Treasury

Davies, N. (2002), 'Confronting Sir Nick Montagu, Chairman of the Inland Revenue', Open Letter, *The Tax Journal*, 1 September, www.nickdavies.net/2002/09/01/open-letter-to-sir-nick-montagu-chairman-of-the-inland-revenue/

Davies, R. (2018), '"Recklessness, Hubris and Greed" – Carillion Slammed by MPs', *The Guardian*, 16 May

Davies, R. (2020), 'Government Awarded School Meal Voucher Contract without Tender', *The Guardian*, 7 May

Davison, R. (2013), 'We Were Wrong: IMF Report Details the Damage of Austerity', The Conversation, https://theconversation.com/we-were-wrong-imf-report-details-the-damage-of-austerity-1153

Davoudi, L., McKenna, C. and Olegario, R. (2018), 'The Historical Role of the Corporation in Society', *Journal of the British Academy*, 6(s1), pp.17–47 de Henau, J. and Himmelweit, S. (2020), *A Care-Led Recovery from Coronavirus: The Case for Investment in Care as a Better Post-Pandemic Economic Stimulus Than Investment in Construction*, Women's Budget Group, wbg.org.uk/analysis/reports/a-care-led-recovery-from-coronavirus/

Department for Education and Employment (1999), *Statistics of Education. Schools in England*

Department for Education and Employment (2000), *Statistics of Education: Class Sizes and Pupil:Teacher Ratios in England*

Department for Education and Employment (2001), SFR 15/2001 *Pupil:Teacher Ratios in Maintained Schools in England: January 2001*

Department for Work and Pensions (2021), *Universal Credit Statistics 29th April 2013 to 14th January 2021*, Department for Work and Pensions, 23 February, https://bit.ly/2Q35RIS

Department of Education (1993), *Statistics of Education. Schools in England*

Dilnot, A., Warner, N. and Williams, J. (2011), Fairer Care Funding: The Report of the Commission on Funding of Care and Support, The Dilnot Commission, https://webarchive.nationalarchives.gov.uk/20120713201059/http://www.dilnotcommission.dh.gov.uk/files/2011/07/Fairer-Care-Funding-Report.pdf

Dolphin, T. (2009), Time for Another People's Budget, Institute for Public Policy Research, www.ippr.org/publications/time-for-another-peoples-budget

Dorling, D. (2019), *Inequality and the 1%*, third edition, London: Verso

Dorling, D. and Szreter, S. (2015), 'The Great Constituency Swap', *Prospect*, 6 March, www.prospectmagazine.co.uk/politics/the-great-constituency-swap

Drucker, P. (1946), *The Concept of the Corporation*, New York: John Day

Durbach, N. (2000), 'They Might As Well Brand Us: Working Class Resistance to Compulsory Vaccination in Victorian England', *Social History of Medicine*, 13: pp.45–62

Dyos, H.J. and Reeder, D.A. (1973), 'Slums and Suburbs', in J.H. Dyos and M. Wolff (eds.), *The Victorian City: Images and Realities, Vol. I*, London: Routledge and Kegan Paul, pp.359–86

Economic Affairs Committee (2020), *Universal Credit Isn't Working: Proposals for Reform*, Economic Affairs Committee 2nd Report of Session 2019-21, HL Paper 105, House of Lords

Education Policy Institute (2020), Education in England: Annual Report 2020, 26 August, Education Policy Institute, https://epi.org.uk/publications-and-research/education-in-england-annual-report-2020/

Elliott, L. (2020a), 'Wealth Tax Rise Could Raise £174bn to Tackle Covid-19, Expert Says', *The Guardian*, 22 April

Elliott, L. (2020b), 'How Will Britain Dig Itself Out of a £300bn Coronavirus Hole?', *The Guardian*, 14 May

Elliott, L. (2020c), 'IMF Boss Says Raise Taxes on the Rich to Tackle Inequality', *The Guardian*, 7 January

Emmerson, C. and Stockton, I. (2020), 'Outlook for the Public Finances', Chapter 4 in P. Bourquin, A. Davenport, C. Emmerson, D. Miles, B. Nabarro, C. Schulz, I. Stockton, T. Waters and B. Zaranko, IFS Green Budget 2020, The Institute for Fiscal Studies, pp.179–224, www.ifs.org.uk/publications/15081

Esping-Andersen, G. (1990), *The Three Worlds of Welfare Capitalism*, Cambridge and Princeton, NJ: Polity Press and Princeton University Press

European Commission (2020), 'Europe Fit for the Digital Age: Commission Proposes New Rules for Digital Platforms', press release, 15 December, ec.europa.eu/commission/presscorner/detail/en/ip_20_2347

Evans, R. (1987), *Death in Hamburg: Society and Politics in the Cholera Years 1830–1910*, Oxford: Clarendon Press

Fehr, E. and Fischbacher, U. (2003), 'The Nature of Human Altruism', *Nature*, 425: pp.785–91

Fehr, E. and Schmidt, K.M. (1999), 'A Theory of Fairness, Competition, and Cooperation', *The Quarterly Journal of Economics*, 114(3): pp.817–68

Ferguson, D. (2020), *Insecure Work: The Taylor Review and the Good Work Plan*, House of Commons Library, Briefing Paper CBP 8817, commonslibrary. parliament.uk/research-briefings/cbp-8817/

Ferguson, N. (2020), Oral Evidence to the UK Science, Research and Technology Capability and Influence in Global Disease Outbreaks inquiry, 10 June, https://bit.ly/2SvWnqq

Financial Conduct Authority (2018), The Financial Lives of Consumers across the UK: Key Findings from the FCA's Financial Lives Survey 2017, Financial Conduct Authority, www.fca.org.uk/publication/research/financial-lives-consumers-across-uk.pdf

Financial Times Editorial Board (2020), 'Virus Lays Bare the Frailty of the Social Contract', *Financial Times*, 3 April

Fioramonti, L. (2013), *Gross Domestic Problems: The Politics Behind the World's Most Powerful Number*, London: Zed Books

Fitzpatrick, S., Bramley, G., Blenkinsopp, J., Wood, J., Sosenko, F., Littlewood, M., Johnsen, S., Watts, B., Treanor, M. and McIntyre, J. (2020), Destitution in the UK 2020, Joseph Rowntree Foundation, www.jrf.org .uk/report/destitution-uk-2020

Ford, J. (2020), 'Britain's Unhealthy Appetite for Financial Risk in Essential Services', *Financial Times*, 24 May

Forster, T., Kentikelenis, A.E., Stubbs, T. and King, L.P. (2020), 'Globalization and Health Equity: The Impact of Structural Adjustment Programs on Developing Countries', *Social Science and Medicine*, 267: pp.1–9

Frank, R. (2020), 'The Mother of All Cognitive Illusions', *Behavioral Scientist*, 10 February, https://behavioralscientist.org/behavioral-economics-robert-frank-taxes-mother-of-all-cognitive-illusions/

Frank, R.H., Gilovich, T. and Regan, D.T. (1993), 'Does Studying Economics Inhibit Cooperation?', *Journal of Economic Perspectives*, 7(2): pp.159–71

Freije-Rodríguez, S., Woolcock, M., Castañeda, R.A., Cojocaru, A., Howton, E., Lakner, C., Nguyen, M.C., Schoch, M., Yang, J. and Yonzan, N. (2020), Poverty and Shared Prosperity 2020: Reversals of Fortune, World Bank Group, www.worldbank.org/en/publication/poverty-and-shared-prosperity

Galloway, P. (1988), 'Basic Patterns in Annual Variations in Fertility, Nuptiality, Mortality and Prices in Pre-industrial Europe', *Population Studies*, 42(2): pp.275–303

Gamble, A. (1988), *The Free Economy and the Strong State: The Politics of Thatcherism*, London: Palgrave Macmillan

Gardiner, L. (2017a), 'Is the Gender Pay Gap on the Brink of Closure for Young Women Today?', the Resolution Foundation, www.resolution foundation.org/comment/the-gender-pay-gap-has-almost-closed-for-millennial-women-but-it-comes-shooting-back-when-they-turn-30/

Gardiner, L. (2017b), 'Homes Sweet Homes – the Rise of Multiple Property Ownership in Britain', the Resolution Foundation, www .resolutionfoundation.org/comment/homes-sweet-homes-the-rise-of-multiple-property-ownership-in-britain/

Gardiner, L., Gustafsson, M., Brewer, M., Handscomb, K., Henehan, K., Judge, L. and Rahman, F. (2020), An Intergenerational Audit for the UK, the Resolution Foundation, www.resolutionfoundation.org/publications/intergenerational-audit-uk-2020/

Garland, D.W. (2016), *The Welfare State: A Very Short Introduction*, Oxford: Oxford University Press

Gardner, J., Gray, M. and Möser, K. (2020), *Debt and Austerity. Implications of the Financial Crisis*, Cheltenham: Edward Elgar Publishing

Garside, J. and Smith, J. (2020), 'Tory-Linked Firm Involved in Testing Failure Given New £347m Covid Contract', *The Guardian*, 4 November

Gaspar, V., Mauro, P., Patillo, C. and Espinoza, R. (2020), 'Public Investment for the Recovery', IMF blog, 5 October, https://blogs.imf.org/2020/10/05/public-investment-for-the-recovery/

Gates, B. (2015), 'The Next Outbreak? We're Not Ready', TED Conferences, www.ted.com/talks/bill_gates_the_next_outbreak_we_re_not_ready?language=en#

Gates, B. (2021), *How to Avoid a Climate Disaster. The Solutions We Have and the Breakthroughs We Need*, London: Allen Lane

Gaukroger, S. (2016), *The Natural and the Human: Science and the Shaping of Modernity 1739–1841*, Oxford: Oxford University Press

Gazeley, I., Gutierrez Rufrancos, H., Newell, A., Reynolds, K., Searle, R. (2017), 'The Poor and the Poorest, 50 Years On: Evidence from British Household Expenditure Surveys of the 1950s and 1960s', *Journal of the Royal Statistical Society* A, 180, Part 2: pp.455–74

Geddes, H. (2018), 'The Links between Early Experiences and Responses in the Classroom', *International Journal of Nurture in Education*, 4(1): pp.15–21

General Register Office (1843), *The Fifth Annual Report of the Registrar-General of Births, Deaths and Marriages in England*, Parliamentary Papers 1843, Volume XXI

Gentleman, A. (2019), *The Windrush Betrayal: Exposing the Hostile Environment*, London: Guardian Books

Geoghegan, P. (2020), *Democracy for Sale: Dark Money and Dirty Politics*, London: Head of Zeus

Geoghegan, P., Scott, R. and Molloy, C. (2020), '"Failing" Serco Won Another £57m COVID Contract without Competition', Open Democracy, www.opendemocracy.net/en/dark-money-investigations/revealed-failing-serco-won-another-57m-covid-contract-without-competition/

Georgieva, K. (2020), Managing Director's Opening Remarks at United Kingdom Article IV Press Conference, speech given 29 October, International Monetary Fund, www.imf.org/en/News/Articles/2020/10/29/sp102920-united-kingdom-article-iv-press-conference

Giles, C. (2014), 'IMF Warns on Threat of Income Inequality', *Financial Times*, 19 January

Giles, C. (2021), 'IMF Proposes Solidarity Tax on Pandemic Winners and Wealthy', *Financial Times*, 7 April

Giraud, Y. (2014), 'Legitimizing Napkin Drawing: The Curious Dispersion of Laffer Curves (1978–2008)', in C. Coopmans (eds.), *Representation in Scientific Practice Revisited*, Cambridge, MA: MIT Press, pp.269–90

Glaude, E. (2021), *Begin Again: James Baldwin's America and Its Urgent Lessons for Today*, London: Chatto & Windus

Glover, B. and Seaford, C. (2020), 'A People's Budget: How the Public Would Raise Taxes', Demos, demos.co.uk/project/a-peoples-budget-how-the-public-would-raise-taxes/

Goodhart, C. and Needham, D. (2020), 'The Need to Issue Long-Dated Gilts', VOXeu, voxeu.org/article/need-issue-long-dated-gilts

Gray, P. (1999), *Famine, Land and Politics: British Government and Irish Society*, Newbridge, Co. Kildare: Irish Academic Press

Green, F. and Kynaston, D. (2019), *Engines of Privilege: Britain's Private School Problem*, London: Bloomsbury

Greenfield, P. (2018), 'No-Deal Brexit Ferry Company Owns No Ships and Has Never Run Channel Service', *The Guardian*, 30 December

Guvenen, F., Kambourov, G., Kuruscu, B., Ocampo-Diaz, S. and Chen, D. (2019), Use It or Lose It: Efficiency Gains from Wealth Taxation, National Bureau of Economic Research, www.nber.org/papers/w26284

Hadwin, J.F. (1978), 'Deflating Philanthropy', *Economic History Review*, 31(1): pp.105–17

Haidt, J. (2012), *The Righteous Mind: Why Good People Are Divided by Politics and Religion*, London: Penguin

Halliday, J. (2021), '"It's Heartbreaking": Inequality Reaps High Covid Toll in South Wales Valleys', *The Guardian*, 8 February

Hamlin, C. (1998), *Public Health and Social Justice in the Age of Chadwick. Britain, 1800–1854*, Cambridge: Cambridge University Press

Hanna, T.M., Guinan, J. and Bilsborough, J. (2018), 'The "Preston Model" and the Modern Politics of Municipal Socialism', Open Democracy, neweconomics.opendemocracy.net/preston-model-modern-politics-municipal-socialism/

Hardman, I. (2018), *Why We Get the Wrong Politicians*, London: Atlantic

Harris, B. and Hinde, A. (2019), 'Sanitary Investment and the Decline of Urban Mortality in England and Wales, 1817–1914', *The History of the Family*, 24(2): pp.339–76

Harris, J. (1972), *Unemployment and Politics: A Study in English Social Policy, 1886–1914*, Oxford: Clarendon Press

Harrison, M. (2004), *Disease and the Modern World: 1500 to the Present Day*, Cambridge: Polity Press

Hayek, F.A. (1944), *The Road to Serfdom*, London: Routledge Press

Hayek, F.A. (1966), 'The Principles of a Liberal Social Order', *Il Politico*, 31(4): pp.601–18

Healey, J. (2014), *The First Century of Welfare: Poverty and Poor Relief in Lancashire, 1620–1730*, Martlesham, Suffolk: Boydell Press

Heitman, K. (2020), 'Authority, Autonomy and the First London Bills of Mortality', *Centaurus*, 62: pp.275–84

Helm, T. (2020), 'Covid-19 Could Be Endemic in Deprived Parts of England', *The Guardian*, 5 September

Henderson, J. (2020), 'Epidemics and Society: Plague in Early Modern Italy', History & Policy, www.historyandpolicy.org/opinion-articles/articles/epidemics-and-society-plague-in-early-modern-italy

Henley, J. (2020), '"Complacent" UK Draws Global Criticism for Covid-19 Response', *The Guardian*, 6 May

Hennock, E.P. (1973), *Fit and Proper Persons: Ideal and Reality in Nineteenth Century Urban Government*, London: Edward Arnold

Hennock, E.P. (2007), *The Origin of the Welfare State in England and Germany, 1850–1914: Social Policies Compared*, Cambridge: Cambridge University Press

Herndon, T., Ash, M. and Pollin, R. (2013), 'Does High Public Debt Consistently Stifle Economic Growth? A Critique of Reinhart and Rogoff', Working Paper Series, No. 322, Political Economy Research

Institute, University of Massachusetts Amherst, www.peri.umass.edu/
images/WP322.pdf

High Pay Centre (2021), High Pay Day 2021, High Pay Centre, 5 January,
https://highpaycentre.org/high-pay-day-2021-ceos-earnings-for-2021-will-
surpass-the-median-uk-full-time-salary-today/

Hill, R. (2021), *The Full Fact Report 2021: Fighting a Pandemic Needs Good
Information*, Full Fact, fullfact.org/media/uploads/full-fact-report-2021.pdf

Hillier, M., Bacon, G., Badenoch, K., Blake, O., Clifton-Brown, G., Gillan, C.,
Grant, P., Holden, R., Jenkin, B., Mackinlay, C., Mahmood, S., Mohindra,
G., Olney, S., Phillipson, B., Smith, N. and Wild, J. (2020), Whole of
Government Response to COVID-19: Thirteenth Report of Session 2019-
21, Public Accounts Committee, House of Commons

Hills, J. (2017), *Good Times, Bad Times: The Welfare Myth of Them and Us*, Bristol:
Policy Press

Hilton, B. (1988), *The Age of Atonement: The Influence of Evangelicalism on Social
and Economic Thought 1785–1865*, Oxford: Clarendon Press

Hindle, S. (2004), *On the Parish? The Micro-Politics of Poor Relief in Rural England
c.1550–1750*, Oxford: Oxford University Press

Hindle, S. (2008), 'Dearth and the English Revolution: The Harvest Crisis of
1647–50', *Economic History Review*, 61(1): pp.64–98

Hitchcock, T., King, P. and Sharpe, P. (eds.) (1997), *Chronicling Poverty. The
Voices of the English Poor, 1640–1840*, Basingstoke: Macmillan Press

HM Revenue and Customs (2020), *Estimated Cost of Tax Reliefs*, HM Revenue
and Customs, 30 October, www.gov.uk/government/statistics/main-tax-
expenditures-and-structural-reliefs

HM Revenue and Customs and Department for Work and Pensions (2020),
Child Tax Credit and Universal Credit Claimants: Statistics Related
to the Policy to Provide Support for a Maximum of Two Children,
Official Statistics Publication, https://assets.publishing.service.gov.uk/
government/uploads/system/uploads/attachment_data/file/900788/
Two_children_and_exceptions_in_tax_credits_and_Universal_Credit_
April_2020.pdf

Hoff, K. and Pandey, P. (2006), 'Discrimination, Social Identity, and Durable
Inequalities', *American Economic Review*, 96(2): pp.206–11

Honigsbaum, M. (2020), *The Pandemic Century: A History of Global Contagion
from the Spanish Flu to Covid-19*, London: Ebury

Hopkins, N. (2020), 'Leaked Cabinet Office Briefing on UK Pandemic Threat –
the Key Points', *The Guardian*, 24 April

Horton, R. (2020), 'Coronavirus Is the Greatest Global Science Policy Failure
in a Generation', *The Guardian*, 9 April

Hudson, N., Grollman, C., Kolbas, V. and Taylor, I. (2020), 'Key Time Series:
Public Attitudes in the Context of COVID-19 and Brexit', in *British Social*

Attitudes: The 37th Report, National Centre for Social Research, www.bsa
.natcen.ac.uk/latest-report/british-social-attitudes-37/key-time-series
.aspx

Hunt, J. (2020), 'Figures Confirming Discharges of Hospital Patients into
Care Homes: Chair's Comment', Social Care Committee, UK Parliament,
https://bit.ly/3vVr1ba

Hunt, T. (2004), *Building Jerusalem: The Rise and Fall of the Victorian City*,
London: Weidenfeld & Nicolson

Hutton, G. (2020), Eat Out to Help Out Scheme, House of Commons Library,
Briefing Paper CBP 8978, https://commonslibrary.parliament.uk/
research-briefings/cbp-8978/

Independent SAGE (2020a), *The Independent SAGE Report – COVID-19: What Are
the Options for the UK? Recommendations for Government Based on an Open and
Transparent Examination of the Scientific Evidence*, Independent SAGE, www
.independentSAGE.org

Independent SAGE (2020b), Independent Sage Press Conference, 12 May,
www.youtube.com/c/indieSAGE/videos

Independent SAGE (2020c), *Disparities in the Impact of COVID-19 in Black and
Minority Ethnic Populations: Review of the Evidence and Recommendations
for Action*, Independent SAGE, www.independentsage.org/wp-content/
uploads/2020/09/Independent-SAGE-BME-Report_02July_FINAL.pdf

Inman, P. (2021), 'Black, Asian and Minority-Ethnic UK Workers Hit Worst
by Covid Job Cuts', *The Guardian*, 19 January

The Institute for Fiscal Studies (2019), 'Fiscal Facts: Public Finances', Long-
Run Public Spending Series, June 2019, The Institute for Fiscal Studies,
www.ifs.org.uk/tools_and_resources/public_finances

Ishkanian, A. and Szreter, S. (2012), *The Big Society Debate: A New Agenda for
Social Welfare?* Cheltenham: Edward Elgar Publishing

Johnson, P. (2019), 'An Effective Spending Review Is Urgently Needed', *Public
Finance,* 14 March, www.publicfinance.co.uk/opinion/2019/03/effective-
spending-review-urgently-needed

Johnson, P.A. (1985), *Saving and Spending: The Working-Class Economy in Britain
1870–1939*, Oxford: Clarendon Press

Johnson, P., Joyce, R. and Platt, L. (2021), *The IFS Deaton Review of Inequalities:
A New Year's Message*, The Institute for Fiscal Studies, www.ifs.org.uk/
inequality/the-ifs-deaton-review-of-inequalities-a-new-years-message/

Jolly, J. and Syal, R. (2020), 'Consultants' Fees "Up to £6,250 a Day" for Work
on Covid Test System', *The Guardian*, 14 October

Joyce, R. and Xu, X. (2019), *Inequalities in the Twenty-First Century: Introducing
the IFS Deaton Review*, The Institute for Fiscal Studies, www.ifs.org.uk/
inequality/chapter/briefing-note/

Judd, D. (1977), *Radical Joe: Life of Joseph Chamberlain*, London: H. Hamilton

Kahneman, D. (2011), *Thinking, Fast and Slow*, New York: Farrar, Straus & Giroux

Kanbur, R. (2004), 'On Obnoxious Markets', in S. Cullenberg and P. Pattanaik (eds.), *Globalization, Culture and the Limits of the Market: Essays in Economics and Philosophy*, New Delhi: Oxford University Press, pp.39–61

Kelly, M. and O'Grada, K. (2011), 'The Poor Law of Old England: Institutional Innovation and Demographic Regimes', *Journal of Interdisciplinary History*, 41(3): pp.339–66

Kemp, P. (2020), 'Go-between Paid £21m in Taxpayer Funds for NHS PPE', BBC News, www.bbc.co.uk/news/uk-54974373

Kenner, D. (2019), *The Polluter Elite Database*, https://whygreeneconomy.org/the-polluter-elite-database/

Khalaf, R. [her Twitter handle: @khalafroula ?] (31 May 2020). 'What the Government Will Not Say', Twitter page: https://bit.ly/3uBIgxV

King, M. (2009), Speech given by Mervyn King, Governor of the Bank of England to Scottish Business Organisations in Edinburgh, 20 October, www.bankofengland.co.uk/speech/2009/mervyn-king-speech-to-scottish-business-organisations

King, S. (2018), *Sickness, Medical Welfare and the English Poor 1750–1834*, Manchester: Manchester University Press

King, S. (2019), *Writing the Lives of the English Poor 1750s–1830s*, London: McGill-Queen's University Press

The King's Fund (2021), 'The Kings' Fund Responds to UK Covid-19 Deaths Exceeding 100,000', The Kings Fund press release, 27 January, www.kingsfund.org.uk/press/press-releases/kings-fund-responds-uk-covid-19-deaths-exceeding-100000

Kitson, M. and Michie, J. (2014), 'The De-industrial Revolution: The Rise and Fall of UK Manufacturing', in R. Floud, J. Humphries and P. Johnson (eds.), *The Cambridge Economic History of Modern Britain, Volume II, 1870 to the Present*, Cambridge University Press, pp.302–29

Laing, W. (2020), 'Covid Story', *Care Markets*, www.laingbuisson.com/wp-content/uploads/2020/07/Covid-story_v5.pdf

Lambert, H. (2020), 'Why Weren't We Ready?', *New Statesman*, 30 March

Lambert, M. (2021), 'The Virtues of Decentralisation for Health Services in Crisis', History & Policy, www.historyandpolicy.org/policy-papers/papers/the-virtues-of-decentralisation-for-health-services-in-crisis

Lansley, S. (2020), 'Review: Peter Sloman's *The Transfer State*', *IPPR Progressive Review*, 27(1): pp.39–47

Lansley, S., McCann, D. and Schifferes, S. (2018), *Remodelling Capitalism: How Social Wealth Funds Could Transform Britain*, Friends Provident Foundation, www.friendsprovidentfoundation.org/library/resources/remodelling-capitalism-social-wealth-funds-transform-britain/

Lansley, S. and Reed, H. (2019), *Basic Income for All: From Desirability to Feasibility*, Compass, www.compassonline.org.uk/

Lawrence, F. (2020a), 'UK Hunger Crisis: 1.5m People Go Whole Day without Food', *The Guardian*, 11 April

Lawrence, F. (2020b), 'Hancock's Former Neighbour Won Covid Test Kit Work after WhatsApp Message', *The Guardian*, 26 November

Lawrence, F., Garside, J., Pegg, D., Conn, D., Carrell, S. and Davies, H. (2020), 'How a Decade of Privatisation and Cuts Exposed England to Coronavirus', *The Guardian*, 31 May

Lawrence, M., Buller, A., Baines, J. and Hager, S. (2020), *Commoning the Company*, Common Wealth, www.common-wealth.co.uk/reports/commoning-the-company

Lewis, B. (2020), HC Debate, Hansard Volume 679: Col. 509, 8 September

Lightfoot, W. (2020), *Monetary Response to the Coronavirus Crisis: An Assessment*, Policy Exchange, policyexchange.org.uk/publication/monetary-response-to-the-coronavirus-crisis/

Lindert, P. (1994), 'Unequal Living Standards', in R. Floud and P. Johnson (eds.), *The Cambridge Economic History of Modern Britain, Volume I, 1700–1860*, Cambridge: Cambridge University Press, pp.357–86

Lindert, P. (2005), *Growing Public: Social Spending and Economic Growth since the Eighteenth Century*, Cambridge: Cambridge University Press

Lintern, S. (2020), 'Warning over Lack of Social Care Plans for UK Epidemic', *Independent*, 10 March

London School of Economics News (2020), 'One-Off Wealth Tax on Millionaire Couples Would Raise £260 Billion', LSE, www.lse.ac.uk/News/Latest-news-from-LSE/2020/L-December/Wealth-Commission-report

Lonergan, E. and Blyth, M. (2020a), *Beyond Bailouts*, IPPR, www.ippr.org/research/publications/beyond-bailouts

Lonergan, E. and Blyth, M. (2020b), *Angrynomics*, New York: Columbia University Press

Lough, C. (2020), 'Exclusive: Ofqual Missed A-level Private School Bonus', *Times Educational Supplement*, 14 August, www.tes.com/news/exclusive-ofqual-missed-level-private-school-bonus

Luce, E. (2020), '*Angrynomics*, by Eric Lonergan and Mark Blyth', review, *Financial Times*, 1 June

Macfarlane, A. (1999), *Witchcraft in Tudor and Stuart England: A Regional and Comparative Study*, second edition, London: Routledge

Manning, A. (2015), *Top Rate of Income Tax*, Centre for Economic Performance, London School of Economics, http://cep.lse.ac.uk/pubs/download/EA029.pdf

Marçal, K. (2015), *Who Cooked Adam Smith's Dinner? A Story about Women and Economics*, trans. S. Vogel, London: Portobello

Marçal, K. (2017), 'Sweden Shows That Pay Transparency Works', *Financial Times*, 17 July

Mark, L. (2014), 'Cameron Claims Victory in Bonfire of the Building Regulations', *Architects' Journal*, 27 January, www.architectsjournal0 co.uk/archive/cameron-claims-victory-in-bonfire-of-the-building-regulations

Markel, H., Stern A., Alexander Navarro, J., Michalsen, J., Monto, A., and DiGiovanni, C. (2006), 'Non-Pharmaceutical Influenza Mitigation Strategies, US Communities, 1918–1920 Pandemic', *Emerging Infectious Diseases*, 12(12), pp.1961–64

Marmot, M. (2014), 'Commentary: Mental Health and Public Health', *International Journal of Epidemiology*, 43(2): pp.293–96

Marmot, M., Allen, J., Boyce, T., Goldblatt, P. and Morrison, J. (2020a), *The Marmot Review 10 Years On*, The Institute of Health Equity, www.instituteofhealthequity.org/the-marmot-review-10-years-on

Marmot, M., Allen, J., Goldblatt, P., Herd, E. and Morrison, J. (2020b), *Build Back Fairer: The COVID-19 Marmot Review. The Pandemic, Socioeconomic and Health Inequalities in England*, The Institute of Health Equity

Marsh, P.T. (1994), *Joseph Chamberlain: Entrepreneur in Politics*, London: Yale University Press

Martin, G.H. (1995), *The Chronicle of Henry Knighton 1377–1396*, trans. G.H. Martin, Oxford: Clarendon Press

Mayer, C. (2013), *Firm Commitment: Why the Corporation Is Failing Us and How to Restore Trust In It*, Oxford: Oxford University Press

Mazzucato, M. (2013), *The Entrepreneurial State: Debunking Public vs. Private Sector Myths*, London: Anthem

Mazzucato, M. (2018), *The Value of Everything: Making and Taking in the Global Economy*, London: Allen Lane

Mazzucato, M. (2021), *Mission Economy: A Moonshot Guide to Changing Capitalism*, London: Allen Lane

McCarthy, H. (2020), *Double Lives: A History of Working Motherhood*, London: Bloomsbury

McIntosh, M. (2012), *Poor Relief in England 1350–1600*, Cambridge: Cambridge University Press

McMillen, C.W. (2016), *Pandemics: A Very Short Introduction*, Oxford: Oxford University Press

McNeil, C., Hochlaf, D. and Quilter-Pinner, H. (2019), *Social (In)security: Reforming the UK's Social Safety Net*, Institute for Public Policy Research, www.ippr.org/files/2019-11/social-insecurity-november19.pdf

McNeill, W.H. (1976), *Plagues and Peoples*, Garden City, NY: Anchor Press

McNeill, W.H. (1980), *The Human Condition: An Ecological and Historical View*, Princeton, NJ: Princeton University Press

Messac, L. (2018), 'Outside the Economy: Women's Work and Feminist Economics in the Construction and Critique of National Income Accounting', *The Journal of Imperial and Commonwealth History*, 46(3): pp.552–78

Mirrlees, J., Adam, S., Besley, T., Blundell, R., Bond, S., Chote, R., Gammie, M., Johnson, P., Myles, G. and Poterba, J.M. (2011), *Tax by Design,* Institute for Fiscal Studies, Oxford: Oxford University Press

Monbiot, G. (2020), 'When Secret Coronavirus Contracts Are Awarded without Competition, It's Deadly Serious', *The Guardian,* 15 July

The Money Advice Service (2021), 'Average Childcare Costs', www .moneyadviceservice.org.uk/en/articles/childcare-costs

Moody's Investors Service (2020), 'Rating Action: Moody's Downgrades the UK's Ratings to Aa3, Outlook Stable', Moody's, www.moodys.com/ research/Moodys-downgrades-the-UKs-ratings-to-Aa3-outlook-stable– PR_434172

Mooney, G. (2015), *Intrusive Interventions: Public Health, Domestic Space, and Infectious Disease Surveillance in England, 1840–1914,* Rochester: Rochester University Press

Moore, C. (2020), 'The Inflexibility of Our Lumbering NHS Is Why the Country Has Had to Shut Down', *Telegraph,* 3 April

Morens, D., Folkers D. and Fauci, A. (2009), 'What Is a Pandemic?', *The Journal of Infectious Diseases,* 200(7): 1018–21

Morgan, H. and Harding, R. (2018), *Attitudes to Tax and Spending: A Briefing,* NatCen Social Research, natcen.ac.uk/our-research/research/attitudes-to-tax-and-spending/

Morris, N. and Vines, D. (2014), *Capital Failure: Rebuilding Trust in Financial Services,* Oxford: Oxford University Press

Munroe, A. (2020), *Coventry – a Marmot City: An Evaluation of a City-Wide Approach to Reducing Health Inequalities,* Institute of Health Equity, www .instituteofhealthequity.org/resources-reports/coventry-marmot-city-evaluation-2020

Murphy, R. (2014), *The Tax Gap. Tax Evasion in 2014 and What Can Be Done About It,* London: Public and Commercial Services Union

Murphy, R. (2015), *The Joy of Tax. How a Fair Tax System Can Create a Better Society,* London: Bantam Press

Murphy, R. (2020), Written evidence submitted by Professor Richard Murphy (Director at Tax Research LLP) to Treasury Committee investigation into Tax after Coronavirus, TACO100, published 4 November, response to question 4, https://committees.parliament.uk/ writtenevidence/12911/html/

Murphy, S. and Marsh, S. (2020), 'UK Government Urged to Justify £108m Contact-Tracing Deal with Serco', *The Guardian,* 11 August

Nanda, S. and Parkes, H. (2019), *Just Tax: Reforming the Taxation of Income from Wealth and Work,* IPPR Centre for Economic Justice, www.ippr.org/ research/publications/just-tax

Nao.org (2020), 'Taxpayer Support for UK Banks: FAQs', National Audit Office Highlights, www.nao.org.uk/highlights/taxpayer-support-for-uk-banks-faqs/

National Audit Office (2020a), *Readying the NHS and Adult Social Care in England for COVID-19*, National Audit Office, www.nao.org.uk/wp-content/uploads/2020/06/Readying-the-NHS-and-adult-social-care-in-England-for-COVID-19.pdf

National Audit Office (2020b), *The Supply Of Personal Protective Equipment during the COVID-19 Pandemic*, National Audit Office, www.nao.org.uk/wp-content/uploads/2020/11/The-supply-of-personal-protective-equipment-PPE-during-the-COVID-19-pandemic.pdf

National Audit Office (2020c), *Investigation into the Bounce Back Loan Scheme*, National Audit Office, www.nao.org.uk/wp-content/uploads/2020/10/Investigation-into-the-Bounce-Back-Loan-Scheme.pdf

National Audit Office (2020d), *The Government's Approach to Test and Trace in England – Interim Report*, National Audit Office, www.nao.org.uk/wp-content/uploads/2020/12/The-governments-approach-to-test-and-trace-in-England-interim-report.pdf

Neate, R. (2020a), 'Richard Branson Facing Backlash over Plea for UK Bailout of Virgin', *The Guardian*, 12 April

Neate, R. (2020b), 'Super-Rich Call for Higher Taxes on Wealthy to Pay for Covid-19 Recovery', *The Guardian*, 13 July

Neate, R. (2020c), 'Philip Green's Wealth Has Shrunk as Arcadia's Fortunes Have Faded', *The Guardian*, 1 December

Neave, D. (1996), 'Friendly Societies in Great Britain', in M. van der Linden, M. Dreyfus, B. Gibaud and J. Lucassen (eds.), *Social Security Mutualism: The Comparative History of Mutual Benefit Societies*, Bern: Peter Lang, pp.41–64

Needham, D. (2020), 'Covid-19 and the UK National Debt in Historical Context', History & Policy, www.historyandpolicy.org/policy-papers/papers/covid-19-and-the-uk-national-debt-in-historical-context

Needham, L. (2020), 'Victoria Beckham Confirms U-turn on Staff Furlough Scheme after Fierce Backlash', *Daily Mirror*, 30 April

New Statesman (2020), 'Top Economists Warn the UK Not to Repeat Austerity after the Covid-19 Crisis', *New Statesman*, 4 May

Newell, P., Daley, F. and Tweena, M. (2021), *Changing Our Ways? Behaviour Change and the Climate Crisis*. The Report of the Cambridge Sustainability Commission on Scaling Behaviour Change, https://bit.ly/2SG7c9C and for the references in the report: https://bit.ly/3txNglZ

Nosrati, E., Dowd, J., Marmot, M. and King, L. (2021), 'Structural Adjustment Programmes and Communicable Disease Burdens: Causal Evidence from 187 Countries', Working Paper, MedRxiv/2021/253462

Nosrati, E. and Marmot, M. (2019), 'Punitive Social Policy: An Upstream Determinant of Health', *The Lancet*, 394: pp.376–77

NYC Health and Hospitals (2020), 'Test and Trace Corps: Take Care', NYC Health and Hospitals, www.nychealthandhospitals.org/test-and-trace/take-care/

Oakeshott, I. (2012), 'Idlers and Lords, Fear My Pointy Head', *The Sunday Times*, 22 January, www.thetimes.co.uk/article/idlers-and-lords-fear-my-pointy-head-zrbpqgv69tb

O'Connor, S. (2020), 'Leicester's Dark Factories Show Up a Diseased System', *Financial Times*, 3 July

O'Hara, M. (2020), *The Shame Game: Overturning the Toxic Poverty Narrative*, Bristol: Policy Press

Obermayer, B. and Obermaier, F. (2017), *The Panama Papers; Breaking the Story of How the Rich and Powerful Hide Their Money*, London: Oneworld

Offer, A. (2018), 'Patient and Impatient Capital: Time Horizons as Market Boundaries', University of Oxford Discussion Papers in Economic and Social History, No. 165, August, www.economics.ox.ac.uk/materials/working_papers/4670/165-avner-offer.pdf

Offer, A. and Söderberg, G. (2016), *The Nobel Factor: The Prize in Economics, Social Democracy, and the Market Turn*, Princeton, NJ: Princeton University Press

Office for Budget Responsibility (2021a), *Coronavirus Analysis: Coronavirus Scenarios*, Office for Budget Responsibility Coronavirus Analysis 2021, http://obr.uk/coronavirus-analysis/

Office for Budget Responsibility (2021b), *Economic and Fiscal Outlook March 2021*, Office for Budget Responsibility, https://obr.uk/efo/economic-and-fiscal-outlook-march-2021/

Office for Budget Responsibility (2021c), *Commentary on the Public Sector Finances: April 2021*, https://obr.uk/docs/dlm_uploads/April-2021-PSF-commentary.pdf

Organisation for Economic Co-operation and Development (2021), 'News Release: OECD GDP Growth Quarterly National Accounts', 18 February, Organisation for Economic Co-operation and Development, www.oecd.org/sdd/na/GDP-Growth-Q420.pdf

Office for National Statistics (2017), *An International Comparison of Gross Fixed Capital Formation*, Office for National Statistics, www.ons.gov.uk/economy/grossdomesticproductgdp/articles/aninternationalcomparisonofgrossfixedcapitalformation/2017-11-02

Office for National Statistics (2019), *Deaths of Homeless People in England and Wales: 2019 Registrations*, Office for National Statistics, https://bit.ly/2RBceng

Office for National Statistics (2020a), *Coronavirus (COVID-19) Related Deaths by Occupation, England and Wales: Deaths Registered between 9 March and 28 December 2020*, Office for National Statistics, https://bit.ly/3hdO90q

Office for National Statistics (2020b), *Analysis of Deaths Involving COVID-19 within the Care Sector: England and Wales*, Office for National Statistics, www.ons.gov.uk/peoplepopulationandcommunity/birthsdeathsand marriages/deaths/datasets/deathsinvolvingcovid19inthecaresector englandandwales

Office for National Statistics (2020c), *Births in England and Wales: 2019*, Office for National Statistics, www.ons.gov.uk/ peoplepopulationandcommunity/birthsdeathsandmarriages/livebirths/ bulletins/birthsummarytablesenglandandwales/2019

Office for National Statistics (2020d), *Provisional Births in England and Wales: 2020*, Office for National Statistics, www.ons.gov.uk/ peoplepopulationandcommunity/birthsdeathsandmarriages/livebirths/ articles/provisionalbirthsinenglandandwales/2020

Office for National Statistics (2020e) *Updating Ethnic Contrasts in Deaths Involving the Coronavirus (COVID-19), England and Wales: Deaths Occurring 2 March to 28 July 2020*, Office for National Statistics, https://bit.ly/3ewUsdO

Office for National Statistics (2020f), *Child Poverty and Education Outcomes by Ethnicity*, Office for National Statistics, https://bit.ly/3y1ldi7

Office for National Statistics (2020g), *Labour Market Overview, UK: December 2020. Estimates of Employment, Unemployment, Economic Inactivity and Other Employment-Related Statistics for the UK*, Office for National Statistics, https://bit.ly/2R0TGNs

Office for National Statistics (2021a), *Coronavirus and Redundancies in the UK Labour Market: September to November 2020*, Office for National Statistics, https://bit.ly/3hfHwe4

Office for National Statistics (2021b), *Gross Domestic Product: Quarter on Quarter Growth: CVM SA %*, Office for National Statistics, www.ons.gov .uk/economy/grossdomesticproductgdp/timeseries/ihyq/qna

Office for National Statistics (2021c), *Gross Domestic Product: Year on Year Growth: CVM SA %*, Office for National Statistics, https://www.ons.gov.uk/ economy/grossdomesticproductgdp/timeseries/ihyp/pn2

Office of Tax Simplification (2020), *Capital Gains Tax Review – First Report: Simplifying by Design*, Office of Tax Simplification, www.gov.uk/government/ publications/ots-capital-gains-tax-review-simplifying-by-design

Ortiz, I., Behrendt, C., Acuña-Ulate, A. and Quynh Anh, N. (2018), 'Universal Basic Income Proposals in Light of ILO Standards: Key Issues and Global Costing', International Labour Organization, Geneva

Ostry, J.D., Berg, A. and Tsangarides C.G. (2014), *Redistribution, Inequality and Growth*, International Monetary Fund Research Department, www.imf .org/external/pubs/ft/sdn/2014/sdn1402.pdf

Park, A., Bryson, C., Clery, E., Curtice, J., and Phillips, M. (2013), *British Social Attitudes: The 30th Report*, London: NatCen Social Research

Partington, R. (2020), 'Chemicals Firm BASF Biggest Beneficiary of UK Coronavirus Loan Scheme', *The Guardian*, 4 June

Partington, R. (2021), '"Deafening Silence": UK Government Blasted over Delays to Employment Reforms', *The Guardian*, 18 February, https://bit.ly/3o1BO0I

Partridge, J. (2020), 'World's Biggest Fund Manager Vows to Divest from Thermal Coal', *The Guardian*, 14 January

Pendleton, A. (2019), 'Imagining a New Social Contract', New Economics Foundation, 22 May, neweconomics.org/2019/05/imagining-a-new-social-contract

Phillips, D. and Simpson, P. (2018), *Changes in Councils' Adult Social Care and Overall Service Spending in England, 2009–10 to 2017–18*, Institute for Fiscal Studies, www.ifs.org.uk/publications/13066

Piketty, T. (2014), *Capital in the Twenty-First Century*, Cambridge, MA: Harvard University Press

Piketty, T. (2020), *Capital and Ideology*, Cambridge, MA: Harvard University Press

Pilling, D. (2018), *The Growth Delusion: The Wealth and Well-being of Nations*, London: Bloomsbury

Pistor, K. (2019), *The Code of Capital. How the Law Creates Wealth and Inequality*, Princeton, NJ: Princeton University Press

Pollock, A. and Price, D. (2013), 'PFI and the National Health Service in England', https://allysonpollock.com/wp-content/uploads/2013/09/AP_2013_Pollock_PFINHSEngland.pdf

Pooley, C.G. and D'Cruze, S. (1994), 'Migration and Urbanization in North-West England circa 1760–1830', *Social History*, 19(3): pp.339–58

Pope Francis and Ivereigh, A. (2020), *Let Us Dream: The Path to a Better Future*, London: Simon & Schuster

Poynter, J.R. (1969), *Society and Pauperism: English Ideas on Poor Relief 1795–1834*, London: Routledge and Kegan Paul

Pressnel, L.S. (1956), *Country Banking in the Industrial Revolution*, New York: Oxford University Press

Public Accounts Committee (2021), *COVID-19: Test, Track and Trace (Part 1)*, Forty-Seventh Report of Session 2019–21

Public Health England (2020), *Disparities in the Risk and Outcomes of COVID-19*, Public Health England, www.gov.uk/government/publications/covid-19-review-of-disparities-in-risks-and-outcomes

Public Health England Emergency Preparedness, Resilience and Response Partnership Group (2017), *Exercise Cygnus Report: Tier One Command Post Exercise Pandemic Influenza 18 to 20 October 2016*, Public Health England, https://assets.publishing.service.gov.uk/government/

uploads/system/uploads/attachment_data/file/927770/exercise-cygnus-report.pdf

Quammen, D. (2012), *Spillover: Animal Infections and the Next Human Pandemic*, New York: W.W. Norton

Quilter-Pinner, H. and Hochlaf, D. (2019), *There Is an Alternative: Ending Austerity in the UK*, IPPR Centre for Economic Justice, www.ippr.org/research/publications/there-is-an-alternative-ending-austerity-in-the-uk

Rashford, M. (2020), '"Protect the Vulnerable": Marcus Rashford's Emotional Letter to MPs', *The Guardian*, 15 June

Raval, A. (2021), 'Inside the "Covid Triangle": A Catastrophe Years in the Making', *The Financial Times Magazine*, 5 March

Raworth, K. (2017), *Doughnut Economics: Seven Ways to Think Like a 21st-Century Economist*, London: Cornerstone

Razai, M., Osama, T. and McKechnie, E. (2021), 'COVID-19 Vaccine Hesitancy among Ethnic Minority Groups', *British Medical Journal*, 372(513), www.bmj.com/content/372/bmj.n513

Reinhart, C.M. and Rogoff, K.S. (2010), 'Growth in a Time of Debt', National Bureau of Economic Research, www.nber.org/papers/w15639

The Resolution Foundation (2019), 'Conservative Manifesto Risks Child Poverty Reaching Record Highs While No Manifesto Will Reduce It', the Resolution Foundation, www.resolutionfoundation.org/press-releases/conservative-manifesto-risks-child-poverty-reaching-record-highs-while-no-manifesto-will-reduce-it/

The Resolution Foundation (2020), '£30 Billion "High Street Voucher" Scheme Could Kickstart Britain's Recovery', the Resolution Foundation, www.resolutionfoundation.org/press-releases/30-billion-high-street-voucher-scheme-could-kickstart-britains-recovery/

Rhodes, A., Ferdinande, P. Flaatten, H., Guidet, B., Metnitz, P.G. and Moreno, R.P. (2012), 'The Variability of Critical Care Bed Numbers in Europe', *Intensive Care Medicine*, 38(10): 1647–53

Rigby, S.H. (2010), 'Urban Population in Late Medieval England: The Evidence of the Lay Subsidies', *The Economic History Review*, 63(2)

Roberts, C. (2019), 'When the Next Crisis Hits, Progressives Must Be Ready to Seize the Agenda', Open Democracy, www.opendemocracy.net/en/oureconomy/when-next-crisis-hits-progressives-must-be-ready-seize-agenda/

Roberts, C., Blakeley, G. and Murphy, L. (2018), *A Wealth of Difference: Reforming the Taxation of Wealth*, IPPR Commission on Economic Justice, www.ippr.org/research/publications/a-wealth-of-difference

Roberts, J. (2020), 'The Civil Service Marriage Bar – Attitudes to Women and Work in the Mid-20th Century', Past to Present Genealogy, 16 January, pasttopresentgenealogy.co.uk/2020/01/16/the-civil-service-marriage-bar-attitudes-to-women-and-work-in-the-mid-20th-century/

Robeyns, I. and Byskov, M. (2020), 'The Capability Approach', in *The Stanford Encyclopedia of Philosophy* (Winter Edition), https://plato.stanford.edu/archives/win2020/entries/capability-approach/

Rowntree, B.S. (1901), *Poverty: A Study of Town Life*, London: Macmillan

Royal Commission on the Poor Laws and the Relief of Distress (1909), *Minority Report of the Royal Commission on the Poor Laws and the Relief of Distress*, London: Her Majesty's Stationery Office

Royal Statistical Society (2019), Royal Statistical Society Announces Its Statistic of the Decade, 23 December, Royal Statistical Society, https://rss.org.uk/RSS/media/File-library/News/Press%20release/RSS_Statistics_of_the_Decade.pdf

Ryan-Collins, J. (2018), *Why Can't You Afford a Home?* Cambridge: Polity Press

Ryan-Collins, J. (2020), 'Boris Johnson's 95% Mortgages Will Put Britain Back on Course for a House Price Crash', *The Guardian*, 8 October

Sacks, J. (2020), *Morality: Restoring the Common Good in Divided Times*, London: Hodder & Stoughton

Samuel, S. (2019), 'Forget GDP – New Zealand Is Prioritizing Gross National Well-being', Vox, www.vox.com/future-perfect/2019/6/8/18656710/new-zealand-wellbeing-budget-bhutan-happiness

Sandbu, M. (2019), 'Why a Wealth Tax Is Capitalism's Handmaiden', *Financial Times*, 20 September

Sandel, M. (2010), *Justice: What's the Right Thing to Do?* London: Penguin

Sandel, M. (2012), *What Money Can't Buy. The Moral Limits of Markets*, London: Penguin

Sanderson, M. (1972), 'Literacy and Social Mobility in the Industrial Revolution in England', *Past and Present*, 56: pp.75–104

Satz, D. (2010), *Why Some Things Should Not Be for Sale: The Moral Limits of Markets*, Oxford: Oxford University Press

Savage, M. (2019), 'Calls for Inquiry into Claims Johnson Backers Benefit from No-Deal Brexit', *Observer*, 28 September

Savage, M. (2020), 'More Than Half of England's Coronavirus-Related Deaths Will Be People from Care Homes', *The Guardian*, 7 June

Savage, M. and Ferguson, D. (2020), 'Children's Doctors Attack Tories over Free School Meals', *Observer*, 24 October

Schofield, R. (1989), 'Family Structure, Demographic Behaviour and Economic Growth', in J. Walter and R. Schofield (eds.), *Famine, Disease and the Social Order in Early Modern Society*, Cambridge: Cambridge University Press, pp.279–304

Schmelzer, M. (2016), *The Hegemony of Growth. The OECD and the Making of the Economic Growth Paradigm*, Cambridge: Cambridge University Press

Schultz, P.W., Nolan, J.M., Cialdini, R.B., Goldstein, N.J. and Griskevicius, V. (2007), 'The Constructive, Destructive, and Reconstructive Power of Social Norms', *Psychological Science*, 18(5): pp.429–34

Schwab, K. (2019), 'Davos Manifesto 2020: The Universal Purpose of a Company in the Fourth Industrial Revolution', World Economic Forum, www.weforum.org/agenda/2019/12/davos-manifesto-2020-the-universal-purpose-of-a-company-in-the-fourth-industrial-revolution/

Scientific Advisory Group for Emergencies (2020), *Summary of Effectiveness and Harms of NPIs*, UK Government, www.gov.uk/government/publications/summary-of-the-effectiveness-and-harms-of-different-non-pharmaceutical-interventions-16-september-2020

Scientific Pandemic Influenza Group on Modelling, Operational sub-group (2020), 'Reasonable Worst-Case Planning Scenario', 30 July, www.gov.uk/government/publications/spi-m-o-reasonable-worst-case-planning-scenario-30-july-2020

Scottish Government News (2017), 'More Choice for Communities', Scottish Government, www.gov.scot/news/more-choice-for-communities/

Scotto Di Santolo, A. (2020), 'Easyjet Pays Shareholders £170m While Requesting Taxpayer Help "Don't You Think It Wrong?"', *Daily Express*, 19 May, www.express.co.uk/news/uk/1257259/easyjet-news-coronavirus-latest-covid-19-johan-lundgren-uk-airlines-bankrupt-bbc

Sen, A. (1979), 'Equality of What?', in S. McMurrin (ed.), *Tanner Lectures on Human Values Volume I*, Cambridge: Cambridge University Press, pp.197–220

Sen, A. (1992), *Inequality Re-examined*, Oxford: Clarendon Press

Shafik, M. (2021), *What We Owe Each Other: A New Social Contract*, London: The Bodley Head

Shaw-Taylor, L., Erickson, A. and Wrigley, T. (2019), *The Occupational Structure of Britain c.1379–1911*, The Cambridge Group for the History of Population and Social Structure, www.campop.geog.cam.ac.uk/research/occupations/outputs/preliminary/overview_of_osb_2019.pdf

Shaw-Taylor, L., Williams, S. and Davenport, R. (2020), 'Quarantine, Lockdowns and Income Subsidies: Coping with Epidemic Disease in Early Modern England', The History of Now podcast, 6 April, https://bit.ly/2RDX8gX

Shaxson, N. (2011), *Treasure Islands: Tax Havens and the Men Who Stole the World*, London: The Bodley Head

Shaxson, N. (2018a), *The Finance Curse: How Global Finance Is Making Us All Poorer*, London: Penguin

Shaxson, N. (2018b), 'The Finance Curse: How the Outsized Power of the City of London Makes Britain Poorer', *The Guardian*, 5 October

Siena, K. (2020), 'Epidemics and Essential Work in Early Modern Europe', History & Policy, www.historyandpolicy.org/opinion-articles/articles/epidemics-and-essential-work-in-early-modern-europe

Singer, M. (2009), *Introduction to Syndemics: A Critical Systems Approach to Public and Community Health*, Hoboken, NJ: Wiley

Slack, P. (1985), *The Impact of Plague on Tudor and Stuart England*, London: Routledge

Slack, P. (1988), *Poverty and Policy in Tudor and Stuart England*, London: Longman

Slack, P. (1990), *The English Poor Law 1531–1782*, Basingstoke: Macmillan

Slack, P. (1999), *From Reformation to Improvement: Public Welfare in Early Modern England*, Oxford: Clarendon Press

Slack, P. (2012), *Plague: A Very Short Introduction*, Oxford: Oxford University Press

Slater, M. (2018), *The National Debt: A Short History*, Oxford: Oxford University Press

Sloman, P. (2019), *Transfer State: The Idea of a Guaranteed Income and the Politics of Redistribution in Modern Britain*, Oxford: Oxford University Press

Smith, H.L. (2014), *Harry's Last Stand: How the World My Generation Built Is Falling Down, and What We Can Do To Save It*, London: Icon Books

Smith, L., Potts, H., Amlot, R., Fear, N., Michie, S. and Rubin, G. (2021), 'Adherence to the Test, Trace, and Isolate System in the UK: Results from 37 Nationally Representative Surveys', *British Medical Journal*, 372(608), www.bmj.com/content/372/bmj.n608

Smith, R. (1986), 'Transfer Incomes, Risk and Security: The Roles of the Family and Collectivity in Recent Theories of Fertility Change', in D. Coleman and R. Schofield (eds.), *The State of Population Theory: Forward from Malthus*, London: Blackwell, pp.86–211

Smith, R. (1996), 'Charity, Self-Interest and Welfare: Reflections from Demographic and Family History', in M. Daunton (ed.), *Charity Self-Interest and Welfare in the English Past*, London: UCL Press, pp.23–49

Smith, R. (2011), 'Social Security as a Developmental Institution? The Relative Efficacy of Poor Relief Provisions under the English Old Poor Law', in C. Bayly, V. Rao, S. Szreter and M. Woolcock (eds.), *History, Historians and Development Policy: A Necessary Dialogue*, Manchester: Manchester University Press, pp.75–102

Snowden, F.M. (2019), *Epidemics and Society: From the Black Death to the Present*, New Haven, CT: Yale University Press

Social Care Institute for Excellence (2020), 'Commissioning and COVID-19: Advice for Social Care. Hospital discharge and Preventing Unnecessary Hospital Admissions (COVID-19)', www.scie.org.uk/care-providers/coronavirus-covid-19/commissioning/hospital-discharge-admissions

Social Mobility Commission (2019), *State of the Nation 2018–19: Social Mobility in Great Britain*, Social Mobility Commission, https://assets.publishing.service.gov.uk/government/uploads/system/uploads/attachment_data/file/798404/SMC_State_of_the_Nation_Report_2018-19.pdf

Sokoll, T. (2000), 'Negotiating a Living: Essex Pauper Letters from London, 1800–1834', *International Review of Social History*, 45: 19–46

Sokoll, T. (2001), *Essex Pauper Letters 1731–1837*, Oxford: Oxford University Press

Solar, P.M. (1995), 'Poor Relief and English Economic Development before the Industrial Revolution', *The Economic History Review*, 48(1): pp.1–22

Solar, P.M. (1997), 'Poor Relief and English Economic Development: A Renewed Plea for Comparative History', *The Economic History Review*, 50(2): pp.369–74

Solar, P.M. and Smith, R.M. (2003), 'An Old Poor Law for the New Europe? Reconciling Local Solidarity with Labour Mobility in Early Modern England', in P. David and M. Thomas (eds.), *The Economic Future in Historical Perspective*, Oxford: Oxford University Press, pp.463–77

Somerset Webb, M. (2020), 'The Pandemic and the Radical Change in Wealth Distribution to Come', *Financial Times*, 16 April

Sparrow, A. and Marsh, S. (2020), 'UK Coronavirus News', *The Guardian*, 30 April, www.theguardian.com/world/live/2020/apr/30/uk-coronavirus-live-boris-johnson-latest-updates

Sridhar, D. (2020), 'As More Local Lockdowns Begin, the Hard Truth Is There's No Return to "Normal"', *The Guardian*, 21 September

Standing, G. (2016), *The Corruption of Capitalism: Why Rentiers Thrive and Work Does Not Pay*, Hull: Biteback Publishing

Starmer, K. (2020), HC Debate, Hansard Volume 676: Col. 241, 13 May

StepChange (2020), *Coronavirus and Personal Debt: A Financial Recovery Strategy for Households*, StepChange, www.stepchange.org/policy-and-research/debt-research/post-covid-personal-debt.aspx

Stevenson, G. (2020), 'I Made a Fortune Predicting the Last Crisis. I Fear for What's about to Unfold', Open Democracy, www.Opendemocracy.Net/En/Oureconomy/I-Made-A-Fortune-From-Predicting-The-Last-Crisis-I-Fear-For-Whats-About-To-Unfold/

Stewart, H. and Syal, R. (2020), 'The Robert Jenrick Planning Row Explained', *The Guardian*, 24 June

Stewart, I., De, D., Simmons, T., Ireson, P. and Lambertson, M. (2020), *The Deloitte CFO Survey Q1 2020: Crash, Slow Recovery, Lasting Change*, Deloitte, www2.deloitte.com/uk/en/pages/finance/articles/deloitte-cfo-survey.html

Stiglitz, J. (2011), 'Of the 1%, by the 1%, for the 1%', *Vanity Fair*, www.vanityfair.com/news/2011/05/top-one-percent-201105

Stiglitz, J., Fitoussi, J-P. and Durand, M. (2020), *Measuring What Counts: The Global Movement for Well-Being*, New York: The New Press

Stirling, A. (2019), 'Austerity Is Subduing UK Economy by More Than £3,600 Per Household This Year', New Economics Foundation, 21 February, https://neweconomics.org/2019/02/austerity-is-subduing-uk-economy-by-more-than-3-600-per-household-this-year

Strauss, D. (2020), 'Rishi Sunak Is Warned That Support Scheme Will Not Stop Redundancies', *Financial Times*, 24 September, www.ft.com/content/6e6df855-470f-40e6-bc12-d0d53b55605e

Szreter, S. (1988), 'The Importance of Social Intervention in Britain's Mortality Decline c.1850–1914: A Re-interpretation of the Role of Public Health', *Social History of Medicine*, 1(1): pp.1–38

Szreter, S. (2002), 'A Central Role for Local Government? The Example of Late Victorian Britain', History & Policy, www.historyandpolicy.org/policy-papers/papers/a-central-role-for-local-government-the-example-of-late-victorian-britain

Szreter, S. (2005), *Health and Wealth: Studies in History and Policy*, Rochester, NY: Rochester University Press

Szreter, S. (2007), 'The Right of Registration: Development, Identity Registration, and Social Security – a Historical Perspective', *World Development*, 35(1): pp.67–86

Szreter, S. (2015), 'Wealth, Population, and Inequality: A Review Essay', *Population and Development Review*, 41(2): pp.343–68

Szreter, S. (2016), 'In Memoriam Jo Cox 1974–2016: Attending to the Well of Public Discourse', https://www.historyandpolicy.org/opinion-articles/articles/in-memoriam-jo-cox-1974-2016-attending-to-the-well-of-public-discourse

Szreter, S. (2019), *The Hidden Affliction: Sexually Transmitted Infections and Infertility in History*, Rochester, NY: Rochester University Press

Szreter, S. (2020a), 'Covid-19 Is Not a Black Swan: Predictable Shocks Need Fully-Funded, Resilient Public Services', History & Policy, www.historyandpolicy.org/opinion-articles/articles/covid-19-is-not-a-black-swan-predictable-shocks-need-fully-funded-resilient-public-services

Szreter, S. (2020b), 'The Cummings-Johnson Saga', Open Democracy, www.opendemocracy.net/en/opendemocracyuk/cummings-johnson-saga/

Szreter, S. (2021, in press), 'The History of Inequality – Commentary' for the IFS Deaton Review of Inequalities

Szreter, S., Cooper, H. and Szreter, B. (2019), 'Incentivising an Ethical Economics: A Radical Plan to Force a Step Change in the Quality and Quantity of the UK's Economic Growth', IPPR Economics Prize 2019, www.ippr.org/research/publications/economics-prize-winners

Szreter, S., Kinmonth, A.L., Kriznik, N.M. and Kelly, M.P. (2016), 'Health, Welfare, and the State: The Dangers of Forgetting History', *The Lancet*, 388(10061): pp.2734–35

Szreter, S. and Mooney, G. (1998), 'Urbanization, Mortality, and the Standard of Living Debate: New Estimates of the Expectation of Life at Birth in Nineteenth-Century British Cities', *The Economic History Review*, 51(1): pp.84–112

Szreter, S. and Siena, K. (2021), 'The Pox in Boswell's London: An Estimate of the Extent of Syphilis Infection in the Metropolis in the 1770s', *The Economic History Review*, 74(2): pp.372–99

Szreter, S. and Woolcock, M. (2004), 'Health by Association? Social Capital, Social Theory, and the Political Economy of Public Health', *International Journal of Epidemiology*, 33(4): pp.650–67

Tadmor, N. (2017), 'The Settlement of the Poor and the Rise of the Form in England c.1662–1780', *Past & Present*, 236: pp.43–97

Taleb, N. (2010), *The Black Swan: The Impact of the Highly Improbable*, London: Penguin

Tawney, R.H. (1964), *Equality*, fifth edition, London: George Allen and Unwin

Tax Justice UK (2020), 'YouGov Poll: Public Want Higher Taxes on Wealth and No Bailouts for Tax Haven Companies', Tax Justice UK, www .taxjustice.uk/blog/yougov-poll-public-want-higher-taxes-on-wealth-and-no-bailouts-for-tax-haven-companies

Taylor, J.S. (1989), *Poverty, Migration and Settlement in the Industrial Revolution. Sojourners' Narratives*, Palo Alto, CA: The Society for the Promotion of Science and Scholarship

Taylor, M., Marsh, G., Nicol, D. and Broadbent, P. (2017), *Good Work: The Taylor Review of Modern Working Practices*, Department for Business, Energy and Industrial Strategy, July, www.gov.uk/government/publications/good-work-the-taylor-review-of-modern-working-practices

Thane, P. (2018), *Divided Kingdom: A History of Britain, 1900 to the Present*, Cambridge: Cambridge University Press

Thicknesse, E. (2020), 'IAG Haemorrhaging Cash at £178m a Week, Says BA Boss Cruz', CityA.M., 4 June, www.cityam.com/iag-haemorrhaging-cash-at-178m-a-week-says-ba-boss-cruz/

Thompson, S.J. (2014), 'Population Growth and Corporations of the Poor, 1660–1841', in C. Briggs, P.M. Kitson and S.J. Thompson (eds.), *Population, Welfare and Economic Change in Britain 1290–1834*, Woodbridge: Boydell Press, pp.189–225

Thomson, M., Kentikelenis, A. and Stubbs, T. (2017), 'Structural Adjustment Programmes Adversely Affect Vulnerable Populations: A Systematic-Narrative Review of their Effect on Child and Maternal Health', *Public Health Reviews*, 38(13): pp.1–18

Today (2020), BBC Radio 4, 27 October, 06:00

Tomlinson, D. (2020), 'Sorting It Out – the Chancellor Moves to Fix the Job Support Scheme', the Resolution Foundation, www.resolution foundation.org/app/uploads/2020/10/sorting-it-out.pdf

Tomlinson, J. (2020), 'Social Democracy and the Problem of Equality: Economic Analysis and Political Argument in the United Kingdom', *History of Political Economy*, 52: pp.519–38

Tooze, A. (2020a), 'Coronavirus Has Shattered the Myth That the Economy Must Come First', *The Guardian*, 20 March

Tooze, A. (2020b), 'Should We Be Scared of the Coronavirus Debt Mountain?', *The Guardian*, 27 April

Torry, M. (2020), 'Evaluation of a Recovery Basic Income and of a Sustainable Revenue Neutral Citizen's Basic Income, with an Appendix Relating to Different Universal Credit Roll-out Scenarios', Euromod, Institute for Social and Economic Research, www.euromod.ac.uk/

Toynbee, P. and Walker, D. (2008), *Unjust Rewards: Exposing Greed and Inequality in Britain Today*, London: Granta

Transparify Worldwide (2018), 'Pressure Grows on UK Think Tanks That Fail to Disclose Their Funders', Transparify Worldwide, www.transparify.org/blog/2018/11/16/pressure-grows-on-uk-think-tanks-that-fail-to-disclose-their-funders

The Trussell Trust (2020a), 'New Report Reveals How Coronavirus Has Affected Food Banks Use', The Trussell Trust, 14 September, www.trusselltrust.org/2020/09/14/new-report-reveals-how-coronavirus-has-affected-food-bank-use/

The Trussell Trust (2020b), '2,600 Food Parcels Provided for Children Every Day in First Six Months of the Pandemic', The Trussell Trust, 12 November, https://bit.ly/3bfIKlE

UBS and PwC (2020), *Riding the Storm: Market Turbulence Accelerates Diverging Fortunes. Billionaires Insights 2020*, UBS and PwC, www.ubs.com/global/en/wealth-management/uhnw/billionaires-report/billionaires-insights-2020.html

United Nations Environment Programme (2020), 'Update of the Zero Draft of the Post-2020 Global Biodiversity Framework', Convention on Biological Diversity, CBD/POST2020/PREP/2/1, 17 August

van Bavel, B. and Rijpma, A. (2016), 'How Important Were Formalized Charity and Social Spending before the Rise of the Welfare State? A Long-Run Analysis of Selected Western European Cases, 1400–1850', *Economic History Review*, 69(1): pp.159–87

van Lerven, F. and Ryan-Collins, J. (2017), *Central Banks, Climate Change and the Transition to a Low-Carbon Economy*, The New Economics Foundation, neweconomics.org/2017/09/central-banks-climate-change

Vizard, P., Burchardt, T., Obolenskaya, P. and Hughes, J. (2020), 'The Conservatives' Record on Health (May 2015 to Pre-Covid 2020)', seminar slides, SPDO Social Exclusion Seminar, July, LSE, sticerd.lse.ac.uk/seminarpapers/ses22072020.pdf

Wacquant, L. (2010), 'Class, Race & Hyperincarceration in Revanchist America', *Daedalus*, 139(3): pp.74–90

Waddell, B. (2021), 'The Rise of the Parish Welfare State in England, c.1600–1800', *Past and Present*, online pre-print

Walker, P. (2020), 'Boris Johnson's Liaison Committee Appearance: What Did We Learn?', *The Guardian*, 27 May, www.theguardian.com/politics/2020/may/27/boris-johnsons-liaison-committee-appearance-what-did-we-learn

Wall, T. (2020), 'The Day Bristol Dumped Its Hated Slave Trader in the Docks and a Nation Began to Search Its Soul', *The Guardian*, 14 June

Wall, T. (2021), 'Grant Shapps Faces Fury over Mass Covid Outbreak at DVLA', *The Guardian*, 23 January

Walter, J. and Schofield, R. (1989), 'Famine, Disease and Crisis Mortality in Early Modern Society', in J. Walter and R. Schofield (eds.), *Famine, Disease and the Social Order in Early Modern Society*, Cambridge: Cambridge University Press, pp.1–73

Warrington, J. (2021), 'Richard Sharp: Who Is the Surprise New Frontrunner for the BBC Top Job?', CityA.M., 6 January, www.cityam.com/richard-sharp-who-is-the-surprise-new-frontrunner-for-the-bbc-top-job/

Weaver, M. and Parveen, N. (2020), 'Spanish Flu Survivor, 108, among Latest Victims of Coronavirus', *The Guardian*, 29 March

Webb, S. and Webb, B. (1927), *English Local Government: English Poor Law History: Part I; the Old Poor Law*, London: Longmans Green and Co.

WHO (2019), *A World at Risk – Annual Report on Global Preparedness for Health Emergencies*, WHO Global Preparedness Monitoring Board, apps.who.int/gpmb/annual_report.html

Wilkinson, R. and Pickett, K. (2009), *The Spirit Level: Why More Equal Societies Almost Always Do Better*, London: Allen Lane

Williams, R. and Elliott, L. (2010), *Crisis and Recovery. Ethics, Economics and Justice*, Basingstoke: Palgrave Macmillan

Williams, S. (2013), *Poverty, Gender and Life-Cycle under the English Poor Law, 1760–1834*, Woodbridge: Boydell Press

Williams, S. (2018), *Unmarried Motherhood in the Metropolis, 1700–1850: Pregnancy, the Poor Law and Provision*, London: Palgrave Macmillan

Williamson, A. (2020), 'Does Coronavirus Spell the End for Neoliberalism?', History & Policy, www.historyandpolicy.org/opinion-articles/articles/does-coronavirus-spell-the-end-for-neoliberalism

Wise, H. (2020), 'The Government Handed Banks over £65m of Taxpayers' Cash as Interest for Covid Business Loans in the Early Part of the Pandemic', This is Money, www.thisismoney.co.uk/money/markets/article-8896587/Government-paid-66m-banks-Covid-business-loans.html

Wohl, A. (1983), *Endangered Lives: Public Health in Victorian Britain*, Cambridge, MA: Harvard University Press

Wolf, M. (2014a), 'A More Equal Society Will Not Hinder Growth', *Financial Times*, 25 April

Wolf, M. (2014b) *The Shifts and the Shocks: What We've Learned and Have Still to Learn from the Financial Crisis*, London: Allen Lane

Wolf, M. (2020), 'The Risks of Lifting Lockdowns Prematurely Are Very Large', *Financial Times*, 4 June

Wood, Z. (2020a), 'Debenhams "Never Recovered from Private Equity Ownership"', *The Guardian*, 1 December

Wood, Z. (2020b), 'Tesco Defends £635m Dividend Payout after Coronavirus Tax Break', *The Guardian*, 8 April

Worldometers.info (2020), 'United Kingdom Coronavirus Cases', Worldmeter, www.worldometers.info/coronavirus/country/uk/

Wrigley, E.A. (1967), 'A Simple Model of London's Importance in the Changing British Society and Economy, 1650–1750', *Past and Present*, 37: pp.44–70

Wrigley, E.A. (2004), 'British Population during the "Long" Eighteenth Century 1680–1840', in R. Floud and P. Johnson (eds.), *The Cambridge Economic History of Modern Britain, Volume I, 1700–1860*, Cambridge: Cambridge University Press, pp.57–95

Young, M. (1958), *The Rise of the Meritocracy 1870–2033: An Essay on Education and Society*, London: Thames & Hudson

Zaranko, B. (2020), 'What to Look Out for in the 2020 Spending Review', Institute for Fiscal Studies, www.ifs.org.uk/publications/15177

Zenghelis, D. (2016), 'Decarbonisation: Innovation and the Economics of Climate Change', in M. Jacobs and M. Mazzucato (eds.), *Rethinking Capitalism: Economics and Policy for Sustainable and Inclusive Growth*, Chichester, West Sussex: Wiley Blackwell, pp.172–90

Zuboff, S. (2018), *The Age of Surveillance Capitalism: The Fight for a Human Future at the New Frontier of Power*, London: Profile Books

Zucman, G. (2015), *The Hidden Wealth of Nations: The Scourge of Tax Havens*, Chicago, IL: University of Chicago Press

Zymek, R. and Jones, B. (2020), *UK Regional Productivity Differences: An Evidence Review*, Industrial Strategy Council, https://bit.ly/3eAlkcW

INDEX

Introductory Note

References such as '178–79' indicate (not necessarily continuous) discussion of a topic across a range of pages. Wherever possible in the case of topics with many references, these have either been divided into sub-topics or only the most significant discussions of the topic are listed. Because the entire work is about 'COVID' and 'pandemics' the use of these terms (and certain others that occur constantly throughout the book) as entry points has been restricted. Information will be found under the corresponding detailed topics.

abortion, 112, 216, 305
absolute entitlements, 254, 263
access, 122, 124–26, 137, 139, 223, 225, 289, 291
    digital, 15, 322
    privileged, 113, 122, 303
accountability, 95, 306, 330–32, 339–40
activism, civic, 305–6, 339
adult social care *see* social care
Advani, Arun, 207
advisers, 77, 97, 206
    political, 47, 53
    professional, 292
    scientific, 49
after-shocks, 35, 194
age, 25–27, 86, 89, 115–16, 119, 228, 230–32, 296
ageing population, 15, 85, 196, 224, 328
agency workers, 47, 90

Agyapong, Mary Agyeiwaa, 128
airlines, 159, 163, 165
alcohol, 282, 296
Alcott, Louisa May, 24
allowances, 263, 296
    family, 226, 276
Alston, Philip, 112
Amazon, 158, 203
amorality, 8, 249, 299, 310, 323, 344
antibiotics, 23, 40
anti-toxins, 40
Arcadia, 161–62
Ardern, Jacinda, 247, 334
aspirations, 113, 144, 164, 171, 215
assets, 152, 163–64, 202, 205, 206, 232, 316, 326
    financial, 153, 295
AstraZeneca vaccine, 60–62
Attenborough, David, 247, 336

auditors, 77, 83
austerity, 3, 13–15, 46, 81,
        83–84, 88–90, 96–98, 109,
        115–19, 123, 143, 153,
        174–92, 213–14, 219,
        224, 246, 273, 306–8,
        320, 328, 340
    vogue, 176–80
Australia, 56

babies, 30, 41, 128, 217
backward tracing, 94
bailouts, 14, 147, 150, 158, 161,
        162, 165
BAME (Black and Minority Ethnic)
        communities *see* ethnic
        minorities and also
        people of colour
Bank of England, 123, 148, 150,
        152, 159, 166, 182,
        186–89
bankruptcy, 89, 327
    ethical, 217
banks, 122–23, 147–50, 152,
        155–59, 162, 166–67,
        182, 185
    central, 151–52, 159
        see also Bank of England
    food, 14, 107, 124, 137, 178,
        212, 282, 320
bargaining powers, 99, 263, 287
Barnard Castle, 47
BBC, 80, 213, 296
Beckham, Victoria, 160
bed capacity, 13, 45, 47, 83–86
Bell, Torsten, 185, 205
benefits, 101, 105–9, 111–14,
        135–37, 211–12, 215–19,
        221–23, 286–87
    basic, 133, 219

cap, 107
Child Benefit, 108, 211, 218, 320
five-week wait, 13, 178, 212
freezes, 109, 214, 219
housing, 107–8, 134, 137
means-tested, 107, 137, 211, 216
scroungers, 177, 213
system, 137, 214, 216, 227, 320
two-child limit, 107–9, 112,
        134, 216
unemployment, 133–34
universal, 115, 218
working age, 108, 213, 220
Bennett Institute for Public Policy,
        316, 333
Bentham, Jeremy, 267
Berlin, Isaiah, 287, 289
Berry, Christina, 209
Beveridge
    William, 16, 222–23, 250, 272,
        274–75, 287
    five giants, 222
Big Society, 107, 287
Bills of Mortality, 37
Bingham, Kate, 91
biodiversity, 11, 313, 315, 316,
        333, 336, 342–43
    collapse, 4, 342
    economics of, 11, 315, 333, 336
Birmingham, 123, 141, 243–45,
        249, 308
Birrell, Ian, 89
Bitcoin, 311
birth rate, 231
Black Death, 25–26, 33–34, 36,
        132, 268
Black Lives Matter, 5, 133, 173
Black Swan, 44
Blackpool, 59, 119
Blyth, Mark, 163–64, 168

Boer War, 271
bonuses, 72, 77, 152, 323, 325
border controls, 43, 62
Bounce Back Loans, 155, 166
Bourne, Alex, 92
Boyle, Frankie, 299
Branson, Richard, 160
Brazil, 5–6, 63, 307
breadwinner model, 15, 226–27, 322
Bregman, Rutger, 241
Brexit, 46–47, 78, 143, 192, 339
    agreement, 62
    no-deal, 46, 76, 78
    referendum, 122, 143
Bristol, 37, 133
British Youth Council, 304
Brown, Gordon, 151, 218
bubonic plague *see* plague
budget speech, 194–95
budgets
    March 2020, 123, 175
    March 2021, 156, 167, 191–2, 194
    NHS, 81–85, 93
    welfare, 105, 151, 178
Burnham, Andy, 141
burning injustices, 122–27
business failures, 149, 192, 278
business leaders, 72, 149, 249,
        280, 284, 322, 324–26
business rates, 155, 160
businesses, 72–73, 141, 154–55,
        157, 160–69, 306–7,
        322–26, 337
    local, 206, 307
buybacks, share, 161, 165, 170
buy-in, public, 9, 223, 336

Cambridge Analytica, 332
Cameron, David, 77, 122, 151,
        177, 287, 303

campaigns, 5, 215–16, 225, 246,
        275, 336, 339
Canada, 190
cancer, 10, 85, 125, 232
capabilities, 222–23, 289, 319
capacity, 46, 52, 59, 65–69, 85–86,
        90, 231, 321
capital, 70, 102, 200–1, 278, 280,
        289, 316, 326
    human, 269, 270, 281–83, 316
    natural, 316, 333
    patient, 315, 335
*Capital Failure: Rebuilding Trust in
        Financial Services*, 71
Capital Gains Tax, 80, 202, 296
Capital in the Twenty-First Century, 278
capitalism, 102, 163, 168, 242,
        290–91
    ethical, 4, 147, 318, 322–26
    exploitative, 8
    inequality-generating, 5
    rentier, 102
    residential, 74
    rigged, 77
    shareholder, 170, 322
    stakeholder, 5, 170
carbon
    emissions, 310
    net zero, 169, 305, 337
    tax, 312
care, 15, 226, 228–30, 232–34,
        267, 271, 312, 322, 328
    costs, 232–33
    medical, 30, 87, 232, 262
    social, 45, 83, 87–91, 96, 130,
        164, 196, 232–33
    unpaid, 231, 322
care homes, 13, 41, 47, 86–90, 97, 232
    deaths, 13, 49, 86–87, 130
    residents, 13, 61, 86–87, 89–90

care workers, 47, 61, 90, 130, 189, 233–34, 300
Carillion, 76–77, 338
Carney, Mark, 247, 314
Casey, Louise, 206
central banks, 151–52, 159
central government, 10, 243, 302–3, 306, 338–40
central state, 242, 288, 306, 338
Centre for Policy Studies, 79–80
Chadwick, Edwin, 267
Chamberlain, Joseph, 243–45, 249
Chancellors, 80, 133, 135–36, 151–52, 175–78, 180, 187, 189
Chang, Ha-joon, 102
charging, infrastructure, 169, 336
charitable status, 79, 113, 320, 330
Charitable Uses Act, 256, 257–58, 262
charities, 35, 107, 125, 215, 226, 253, 256, 267
Charterhouse school, 265
Chartism, 270
Chelmsford, 263–64
Cheltenham race festival, 52
Child Benefit, 108, 211, 218, 320
child poverty, 13, 109–10, 123, 178, 213–15, 218, 221, 247 276, 319
Child Poverty Act, 215, 221
childbearing, 227, 230–31
childcare, 15, 96, 172, 228–32, 233
  costs, 231
  free, 224, 228
  infrastructure, 231
children, 108–14, 138–40, 215–18, 225–26, 228–31, 263–64, 307–9, 317–20
  daily learning time, 140
  poorer, 117, 139, 226

China, 22, 32, 46, 288–89
cholera, 23, 27, 30, 39–40, 126
Christmas, 56–57, 138, 218
Christmas Carol, 218
chumocracy, 79
churches, 41, 243
Churchill, Hilda, 41
Churchill, Winston, 78–79
cities, 34, 37–39, 243–46, 257, 259, 306–8, 335, 340
citizens, 7–9, 164, 241–42, 247–48, 281–82, 289–90, 292–95, 317–18
  fellow, 34, 212, 221, 281, 344
  vulnerable, 12, 87, 89, 213, 287
  wealthiest, 295, 310
citizens' assemblies, 305, 339
civic activism, 305–6, 339
civic commitment, 283, 293
civic contributions, 294–96, 300
civic engagement, 304, 318, 338–340
civic organisations, 8, 307
civil service, 91, 97
class, 114, 271, 283–84, 289, 292
  working, 69, 122, 143, 222, 269, 271, 305, 308
Clement VI, Pope, 33–34
climate change, 4, 17, 169, 196, 313–14, 328, 337, 342–43
Clinton, Hillary, 301
closures, 41, 141
  theatre, 27, 41
coalition government, 151, 219
Cobbett, William, 265
codes, moral, 344, 346
cohesion, social, 121–22, 299, 316, 320
collective provision, 250, 259, 266
collective responsibility, 9, 70, 234, 258, 276, 286, 293, 317

collective support, 272–73
collectivism, 17
  municipal, 245, 305
collectivist individualism, 6, 16–17,
      251–85, 310, 312, 345–46
  turn away from after 1834,
      266–71
commitment, 1, 97, 165, 168, 217,
      270, 325, 329
  civic, 283, 293
communities, 16–17, 34–35,
      38, 64, 119, 251, 256,
      306
  deprived, 63, 129, 292, 321
  local, 170, 253–54, 283, 306–7,
      323
companies, 5, 14, 45, 76–77, 158,
      167, 170–72, 323–27
  private, 88, 106, 143, 314, 321
competition, 7–8, 77, 82, 92, 113,
      167, 269, 321
competitiveness, 70, 337
computers, 107, 225, 314
  free, 225
Concept of the Corporation, 72
conditionality, 14, 106, 147
consensus, 120, 121, 184, 242,
      284, 299–301
Conservatives, 79–81, 105, 107,
      151, 177–78, 193, 205–6,
      214–15
consultancy firms, 91, 338
consumerism, 103, 249, 276
consumption, 103, 314–15, 336
contact tracing *see also* test, track
      and trace, 35, 54, 82, 92
contamination, 41, 92
contracts
  government, 13, 54, 76, 78–79,
      92, 151, 172, 302

zero hours, 104, 323
contributions, 201, 282–84
  civic, 294–96, 300
  fair, 295–301, 318, 326–29
  National Insurance, 207, 211,
      227, 296
  philanthropic, 284, 329
  progressive, 295–301
COP15, 333, 337
COP26, 337
Corn Laws, 205, 268
Coronavirus Business
      Interruption Loan
      Schemes, 155, 166
Coronavirus Job Retention
      Scheme *see* furlough
corporation tax, 152, 167, 194,
      203, 324–26
corporations, 17, 72, 75, 76,
      164, 169–72, 197,
      326–27
  private, 76, 171, 314, 338
corpses, 25, 37, 43
corruption, 10, 12, 102, 171
costs, 15, 46, 89–90, 137–38,
      155–56, 183–84, 210–11,
      230–32
  housing, 100, 110, 123, 231
  living, 126, 136, 210
Council Tax, 107, 157, 203–4, 306,
      326
Coventry, 60, 307, 340
Covid Corporate Financing
      Facility, 159, 165
COVID generation, 14, 137,
      138–40
COVID-19 *see* Introductory Note
Cox, Jo, MP, 332
Coyle, Diane, 316, 165
Crabb, Stephen, 213

Cromwell's Protectorate, 255
cronyism, 10, 12, 80, 339
crowding-in, 256–58
Cummings, Dominic, 48, 52, 97
Cutteslowe Walls, 274
Cygnus, Exercise, 44–45, 90

daily learning time, 140
damage, 7, 63, 75, 121, 143, 179, 315
    long-term, 150, 155
dark money, 79, 330
Dasgupta Review, 315, 333, 336
Davis, David, 185
Davos Manifesto, 5, 170–71, 323
Day, Philippa, 107
de Mayerne, Sir Theodore, 27
death rates, 41–42, 56, 62, 128–31, 269
deaths, 12, 14, 25–27, 37, 40–41, 49–53, 59, 128
    in care homes, 13, 49, 86–87, 130
    from despair, 122, 320
    excess, 49–50, 85–86
    by local area deprivation, 129
    people of colour, 130–33
Deaton, Angus, 119
Debenhams, 73–74, 162
debt, 137, 157, 164, 175, 177–78, 181–84, 186–88, 191–94
    extra, 185, 187
    interest, 183–84, 187
    levels, 180, 184, 187
    national, 15, 150, 175, 177, 179–84, 185–87, 193–94, 328
decency, 8–9, 111
deficits, 92, 194, 198, 224
degradation, 282, 315–16

dementia, 232
democracy, 75, 76, 78, 279, 289, 301, 305, 330, 332
    capture, 75–81, 91, 329
    participatory, 303–4, 339
    reviving, 318, 338, 341
democratic institutions, 17, 80, 286
democratic participation, 10, 301–9
Denmark, 50, 134, 160, 165
Department for Education, 95
depression, 1930s, 150, 186, 274, 278
deprivation, 13–14, 64, 121, 125, 128, 218, 223
    local area, 118, 129
deprived areas, 117–18, 130, 140, 231
deprived communities, 63, 129, 292, 321
deregulation, 7, 12, 70–71, 74
Desmond, Richard, 75–76
destitution, 111, 206, 213, 253, 256, 258, 262, 265
deterrent workhouses, 2, 267
devolved power, 301–9
diabetes, 2, 104, 125, 130
Dickens, Charles, 213, 218, 267
digital exclusion, 15, 225–26, 322
dignity, 212, 221, 282, 320
Dilnot Review, 233
directors, 14, 77, 172, 323
    managing, 154, 191, 247, 297
disability, 106, 211, 218, 220, 253
discretionary powers, 10, 308, 340
disempowering state, 4, 8, 17, 287
disempowerment, 4, 8, 17, 223, 287, 289, 303, 306
Disney, Abigail, 249
disparities, 64, 104, 129–31

regional, 123, 141
distancing, social, 35, 41, 43, 48, 52, 54, 64, 73
distress, 167, 246, 264, 266–68
distrust, 40, 210
dividends, 73, 160–61, 165–66, 170
divine intervention, 11, 251
Do Not Resuscitate notices, 87
doctors, 37, 85, 131
domestic violence, 138, 139
Doughnut Economics, 248
Driver and Vehicle Licensing Agency (DVLA), 57–58
Drucker, Peter, 72
due diligence, 76, 302
Duncan Smith, Iain, 105–6, 108–9, 213
duties, 14, 34, 215, 241, 296
    primary, 171, 323

earnings, 100, 103, 133–35, 152, 179, 214, 219–21, 280
Eat Out to Help Out, 54, 189–90
Ebola, 12, 24, 29, 42–44, 343
economic fallout, 134, 188, 342
economic growth, 2, 11, 23–24, 74, 102, 120, 186, 247–48, 258–60, 271, 344, 346
amend growth, 2, 11, 23–24, 74, 102, 120, 186, 247–48, 258–60, 271, 344, 346
economic neoliberalism, 78, 237
economic performance, 2, 116, 234, 287, 333
economic progress, 24, 315
economic recovery, V-shaped, 189–90
economic system, 6–7, 157, 173, 246, 272, 292
economics, 163, 237, 241, 316, 340

of biodiversity, 11, 315, 333, 336
    profession, 184, 226, 316
economists, 167, 175, 184–85, 188, 269, 271, 316, 328
    liberal, 237, 266
economy, 9–12, 143–60, 167–69, 187–93, 229–31, 314–15, 323–26
    gig, 103–4, 126, 323
    market, 143, 286, 316
    moralised, 249
    political, 267–69
    sustainable, 281, 336
Ecosystem Accounting, 316
Edenred, 95
education, 14–15, 114–16, 164, 195, 197, 222, 224, 276
    secondary, 115–16, 223, 225, 242, 270, 276
    spending, 115–16, 140, 320
Educational Maintenance Allowance, 116
elections, 81, 122–23, 151, 174, 244, 307, 332
    general, 109, 228, 275
    local, 304, 307
electorate, 70, 244, 275, 280
elites, 181, 266, 274, 278, 280, 284, 295
    corporate, 311, 339
    political, 161, 305, 339
Elizabeth I, 2, 6, 16, 37, 213, 249–85, 340
embedded inequalities, 2, 4
emergencies, 76, 83–84, 87, 193, 196, 321, 327, 343
emissions, 165, 169, 247, 311, 335–37

employees, 135, 164, 170, 227,
       303–4, 323–25
employers, 96, 103–4, 126, 155–56,
       220, 223, 227, 242–45
employment, 223, 226–27, 273,
       276, 297, 307, 322, 326
empowering society, 285, 293,
       299–300, 305, 318, 340
empowering state, 4, 8–9, 16–17,
       308–9, 340
empowerment, 11, 17, 318–40
engagement, civic, 318, 338, 341
English Civil Wars, 255
engrained poverty, 223, 291
entitlements, 134, 208, 213, 224,
       227, 229, 255, 281, 292, 322
    absolute, 254, 263
    universal, 262
entrepreneurs, 101, 178, 201,
       270–71
environment, 29, 103, 233, 246,
       248, 309, 315, 318
    natural, 5–6, 290, 309, 323–25,
       344
environmental boundaries, 312,
       334
environmental resources, 315,
       317
environmental sustainability,
       209, 325, 337
equal pay, 227, 323
equality see also inequalities, 164,
       334
equity, 11, 163, 164, 292, 340
    ethnic, 332
    social, 11, 234, 333
    stakes, 14, 159, 327
Essex Pauper Letters, 263
ethical capitalism, 4, 147, 318,
       322–26
ethics, 172, 344–46

ethnic equity, 332
ethnic groups, 63, 110, 131
ethnic minorities see also people
       of colour, 110, 122, 125,
       131–32, 292, 332
ethnicities, 14, 125, 289
Every Child Matters, 117
evictions, 109, 138, 157
Excelgate incident, 180
excess deaths, 49–50, 85–86
exclusion, 122, 289, 323
    digital, 15, 225–26, 322
    social, 121
expertise, 44, 54, 78, 143, 321
Extinction Rebellion, 5, 246, 309
extreme poverty, 111–12, 211–12,
       341
Eyam, 22–23

failures, 12, 39, 45, 47, 58–59, 114,
       142, 148
    business, 149, 192, 278
    harvest, 251–53, 261
    policy, 49, 282
fair contributions, 295–301, 318,
       326–29
fairness, 198, 200, 202, 247, 295
fake news, 332
fallout, 175, 197, 339
    economic, 134, 188, 342
families, 107–8, 110–11, 124–25,
       135–40, 215–19, 225–27,
       269–70, 320
    working, 230, 283
family allowances, 226, 276
family incomes, 192, 231
family members, 130, 137, 156,
       226
famine, 2–3, 32, 253, 260–62, 269
farmers, 254, 283
fascism, 242, 274–75

fathers, 105, 128, 229, 275
Fauci, Anthony, 24
fees, 31, 89–90, 92–93, 276
fellow citizens, 34, 212, 221, 281, 344
fertility rate, total, 230–31
Field, Frank, 77
Finance Curse, 72
financial assets, 153, 295
financial crash, 103, 150, 153–54, 175, 177, 179, 274
    lessons, 147–55
financial crises, 4, 124, 147–50, 151–52, 158, 164, 180–83, 186
financial sector, 71–72, 74, 77, 150, 170, 177
Financial Times, 50, 53, 120, 159, 169, 197
financialisation, 12, 72, 89, 246
Finland, 294
First World War, 28, 41, 186, 200, 242
fiscal drag, 194
fiscal rules, 174, 193
fit-for-purpose safety net, 15, 212, 214
flammable cladding, 77, 303
Florence, Italy, 35, 38–39, 43
Floyd, George, 5, 290
flu, 30, 40–42, 44–46, 51, 85
    Spanish, 28, 41–42
food, 124, 138–39, 213, 224, 254, 261, 268, 281–82
    banks, 14, 107, 124, 137, 178, 212, 282, 320
    poverty, 196, 213
    prices, 261, 262
    security, 225, 342
    shortages, 251, 261, 265

forecasts, 52, 109–11, 181, 192, 194–95
fossil fuels, 168, 313–14, 337
France, 35, 160, 190, 201, 259, 261, 278–80
franchise, 244, 247, 305, 339
Fratelli Tutti, 317
free market, 6, 9, 70–72, 239, 245–46, 249, 266, 269–70
free school meals, 95, 206, 215–17
free secondary education, 115, 223, 276
freedoms, 8–9, 222, 241, 282, 287–89
    negative, 17, 288–89, 291, 317
    positive, 16–17, 222, 281, 289–90, 294, 299, 346
    and state, 287–91
Friedman, Milton, 209
Friends of the Earth, 4, 246
FTSE 100, 153, 314
funerals, 38, 41, 56, 87, 263
furlough, 135–36, 141, 147, 155, 156–57, 189, 192–94, 204
    scheme, 135, 142, 155–56, 160–61, 192
future, 141–44
    sustainable, 318, 335–38

Garland, David, 71, 290–91
Gaspar, Vitor, 298
gas and water socialism/ municipalism, 243, 245
Gates, Bill, 22, 29, 247
GDP (Gross Domestic Product), 115, 178–82, 191–92, 200, 247–48, 277, 315–16, 332–33
Geddes Axe, 273
gender, 221, 228–29, 289, 323, 332
    pay gap, 122, 173, 229, 324

general elections, 109, 228, 275
Geoghegan, Peter, 79
Georgieva, Kristalina, 154, 297
Germany, 50–51, 53, 59, 77, 85,
         134–35, 190, 270, 279
gig economy, 103–4, 105, 126, 324
Gini Coefficient, 101
glass floor, 114, 320
global poverty, 341
GNH (Gross National Happiness),
         334
Golden Age, 3, 70, 275–77, 280, 284
Goldman Sachs, 80
Goodhart, Charles, 188
Gove, Michael, 79
governance, 45, 65, 76, 91, 191,
         289, 334
government, 44–51, 53–55, 95–98,
         141–49, 154–59, 163–67,
         177–80, 215–19
    central, 10, 243, 302–3, 306,
         338–40
    coalition, 151, 219
    contracts, 13, 54, 76, 78–79, 92,
         151, 172, 302
    local, 10, 75, 117, 194, 243,
         306–8, 338, 340
    support, 135, 156, 160, 165
    UK, 45, 51, 78, 80, 95, 165–68,
         328, 337
grandchildren, 309, 317
Green, Martin, 87
Green, Philip, 161
Green, Tina, 161
green-collar jobs, 336
Green New Deal, 168
green technologies, 168, 315, 335
Greenfield, Jerry, 249
Greenpeace, 4, 165, 246
Greensill Capital, 302–3

greeting etiquettes, 43
Grenfell Tower, 303
Gross Domestic Product see GDP
Gross National Happiness see GNH
growth
    economic, 2, 11, 23–24, 74,
         102, 120, 186, 247–48,
         258–60, 271, 344, 346
    productivity, 3, 270, 276, 280–81
    sustainable, 333, 337
    uninterrupted, 69, 277
    urban, 25, 260
Guarantee Credit, 219–20
guarantees, 99, 135–36, 166, 221,
         225, 291
    legal, 219, 220
guided by the science policy, 48, 55

habitats, 22, 316, 335, 343
Haldane, Andy, 123
Hamburg, 39
Hamilton, Lewis, 290
Hamlet, 27
Hanage, William, 83
Hancock, Matt, 79, 88, 92
handouts, 164, 212–13, 293
happiness, 212, 237, 331, 334
Harding, Dido, 80, 92–93, 97
hardship, 9, 41, 206–8, 221, 265,
         270, 272, 319
harvest failure, 251–53, 261
Hayek, Friedrich, 287–89
Healey, Denis, 199, 206
health, 2–3, 64, 81, 119–20,
         195–96, 223–24, 267–69,
         303
    care, 69, 233, 242, 276, 288–89
    inequalities, 118, 129, 307, 320
    infrastructure, 43, 58, 82, 292,
         308

mental, 107, 118, 121, 138–39, 224, 247
public, 21, 42, 82–83, 92, 126, 269
heart disease, 2, 125
hedge funds, 78, 89, 162
Henry VIII, 252–53
herd immunity, 51
hidden welfare state, 296
Hilliard, Nicholas, 252
Hills, John, 101
historians, 185, 238, 254, 255, 257–58, 267
history, 1, 6, 28–29, 43, 153–54, 237–39, 280–82, 312–14
lessons to be taken, 281–85
and morality, 241–50
HIV/AIDs, 30, 42
Hobbes, Thomas, 287
holidays, 46, 55–56, 104, 138, 157–58, 172, 217, 324
home deliveries, 203, 327
home ownership, 74, 122, 139, 280
homelessness, 112, 138, 206, 319
Homo economicus, 16, 237–41, 249, 286, 293, 309, 345
Horton, Richard, 48, 97
hospitalisations, 56–57, 141
hospitality, 124, 130, 136, 155, 189, 234, 335
hospitals, 47, 76, 86–87, 90, 128, 161, 306
bed capacity, 13, 45, 47, 83–86
Nightingale, 52
temporary, 50
household incomes, 110, 124, 157
household mixing, 58
households, 39, 101, 108–11, 124, 127, 139, 218, 225
housing, 7, 9, 15, 74, 75, 106, 114, 152–53

benefit, 107–8, 134, 137
costs, 100, 110, 123, 231
wealth, 74, 153
human capital, 269, 270, 281–83, 316
human nature, 237, 249, 267, 323
human rights, 112, 171
hunger, 215–16, 253
marches, 273, 282
Hunt, Jeremy, 86
hygiene, 31, 39–40

ideology, 77–78, 176–77, 180, 269, 303, 331
neoliberal, 128, 143, 169, 317
idleness, 222–23, 267
IFS (Institute for Fiscal Studies), 100–1, 110, 115–18, 120, 183–84, 195, 198, 204
IMF (International Monetary Fund), 30, 120, 154, 179, 191, 193, 247, 297, 298
immunity, 24, 31, 238
herd, 51
incentives, 201, 202, 284–86, 311, 314, 323, 326, 329
income inequality, 13, 99–101
income tax, 199, 202–3, 207–9, 211, 278–281, 296, 297, 326, 328–330
incomes, 9–10, 109–11, 119–20, 200–3, 204–5, 219–20, 276–80, 295–301
family, 192, 231
higher, 136, 295, 296, 329
household, 110, 124, 157
lower, 120, 129–31
unearned, 197, 280, 326
Universal Basic, 15, 208–11, 320

Independent SAGE , 53, 54,
        131–32
India, 27, 63, 240, 288
individualism, 17, 250, 275, 281,
        309–10, 346
    collectivist, 6, 16–17, 250–51,
        281, 286, 310, 312,
        345–46
individualist-collectivist regime,
        259
industrial revolution, 346
    fourth, 170, 208
industrialisation, 3, 258, 269, 319
inequalities, 3, 5, 99–101, 113–14,
        118–21, 247, 290–92,
        320–21, 324
    embedded, 2, 4
    health, 118, 129, 307, 320
    income, 13, 99–101
    and laissez-faire, 99–105
    of place, 142
    regional, 191, 204
    and resilience, 99–127
    rising, 5, 103, 128, 329
    wealth, 101, 115, 158, 210,
        276–78, 280
infection rates, 31, 52, 56, 141
infections, 31, 37, 42, 50–51,
        52–59, 64, 90, 94
inflation, 70, 99, 103, 108, 116–17,
        179, 186–88, 194
influenza see flu
infrastructure
    charging, 169, 336
    deficiencies, 123
    health, 43, 58, 82, 292, 308
injustices, 120, 225, 246, 320
    burning, 122–23
insecurity, 210, 213, 290–91, 323
instability, 120, 121, 143
Institute for Fiscal Studies see IFS

Institute for Public Policy
        Research see IPPR
institutions, 1, 6, 10, 65, 71–72,
        86, 286–87, 292
    democratic, 17, 80, 286
insurance, 136, 223
    companies, 185
    social, 232, 291, 322
    tax, 232, 296
    unemployment, 134, 274
interest payments, 182–84, 187, 328
interest rates, 14–15, 112, 150,
        152, 163–64, 166, 183–84,
        187–88
International Monetary Fund see
        IMF
internet, 226, 314
    access, 107, 224
investment, 9, 15, 73–74, 169,
        191, 327–28, 331, 335–37
    productive, 71, 260
    public, 15, 76, 169
IPPR (Institute for Public Policy
        Research), 104, 157, 166,
        203, 210, 214, 221
Ireland, 3, 52, 201, 205, 267–68,
        305
    Northern, 53, 55, 62, 78, 141,
        143
isolation see also self-isolation, 22,
        35, 38, 39, 53, 54, 58, 59,
        127
Italy, 34–35, 39, 50–52, 85, 190

Japan, 94, 121, 158, 182, 190, 201,
        232
Jarrow Crusade, 273
Jenrick, Robert, 75–76
Jews, 33–34, 344
Job Retention Scheme see also
        furlough, 154, 157

Job Support Scheme, 135, 156
jobs, 105–6, 134–35, 155–56,
        161–62, 189–91, 215–16,
        227–28, 233–34
    losses, 161, 168, 208, 335
Johnson, Boris, 46–47, 51–53,
        55, 61–62, 78, 80, 123,
        176–77
Johnson, Paul, 195
Joseph, Keith, 79
journalists, 51, 300–2
just in time procurement/health
        services, 13, 81–87
justice, 204, 284, 294
    social, 117, 223
Justices of the Peace (JPs) *see also*
        magistrates, 254, 284, 294

Kahneman, Daniel, 239
Keenan, Margaret, 60–61
key workers, 49, 125, 129–30, 139,
        195
Keynes, John Maynard, 227, 273
Keynesian, 175, 191, 242, 277
Khalaf, Roula, 53
King, Mervyn, 148, 162
King, David, 49, 53
King's Fund, 64
Knighton, Henry, 34
Korea, South, 42, 53, 55, 121

labour, 99, 199, 215, 255, 259, 322
Labour governments, 69, 177,
        199, 276
labour markets, 169, 259, 322, 338
Laffer Curve, 298–99
Lagarde, Christine, 247
Laing, William, 87
laissez-faire, 1–2, 168, 243, 245,
        269, 340, 343
    and inequality, 99–105

Lancet, 48, 97
landlords, 109, 157, 204, 258
Lane, Don, 104
Lansley, Stewart, 214
laptops, 139, 225
Laudato Si, 317
law, 6–8, 14, 35, 41, 77–78,
        171–72, 287–89, 323–25
laziness, 49, 267, 271, 293
leaders, 6, 16, 53, 205, 283
    business, 72, 149, 249, 280,
        284, 322, 324–26
    political, 62, 248
    world, 61, 83, 151
leadership, 12, 46, 49, 59, 313,
        337
league tables, 49, 332, 338
legislation, 81–82, 99, 157, 221,
        308, 320, 323, 332
Lehman Brothers, 147–48
Leicester, 34, 40, 77, 141
lethality, 24, 29, 43
levelling, 2, 14, 123–24, 198, 204,
        224
    up, 15, 117, 123, 176
Liberal Democrats, 81, 214, 228
liberal economists, 237, 266
liberty, negative *see* negative
        freedoms
life chances, 117, 119, 138, 224
life expectancy, 119, 122, 245, 320
life outcomes, 64, 114, 119
Lightfoot, Warwick, 187
Lilley, Peter, 70
livelihoods, 27, 35, 39, 191, 192,
        328, 336, 341
Liverpool, 141, 243
living conditions, 94, 109, 131,
        243
living costs, 126, 136, 210
Lloyd George, David, 206, 272, 276

Loach, Ken, 104, 180
loans, 14, 155–57, 159, 165–66, 182, 203, 245, 327
lobbying, 10, 75, 303, 338
   power, 301, 311
local authorities, 81, 88, 90, 117, 204, 206, 306, 308
local communities, 170, 253–54, 283, 306–7, 323
local elections, 304, 307
local government, 10, 75, 117, 194, 243, 306–8, 338, 340
local lockdowns, 138, 206
lockdowns, 47–51, 53–56, 124, 135, 139–42, 154–58, 160, 168–69
   easing, 53–54
   first, 58, 139
   local, 138, 206
   third, 56
   tier-three, 141
Locke, John, 281
London, 22, 27, 47–48, 71, 74, 263–65, 293, 297
Lonergan, Eric, 163–64, 168
long COVID, 195, 341
losers, 155–61, 331
Low-paid, low pay: 103, 105, 106, 108, 109, 111, 126, 129, 130, 133, 161, 195, 216, 238, 338
Luce, Edward, 159

magic money tree, 174–76
magistrates *see also* Justices of the Peace, 37, 254
Maitlis, Emily, 124
malaria, 30
Mallon, Mary, 31
managing directors, 154, 191, 247, 297

Manchester, 123, 141, 243, 307
Mandelson, Peter, 101
marginal income tax rates, 279
marginal tax rates, 284, 296, 301
market economy, 143, 286, 316
markets, 70, 264, 267, 271, 288, 291, 334–35, 343
   labour, 169, 259, 322, 338
Marmot, Michael, 82, 119, 130, 291, 307
Marmot cities, 307
marriage bar, 227
married women, 227
masks, 26, 41, 47, 58, 64, 84
mass unemployment, 99, 242, 273
maternity pay, 227, 324
May, Theresa, 105, 122, 132, 174
Mazzucato, Marianna, 312–14
meals
   free school, 95, 206, 215–17
   restaurant, 54, 158
means-tested benefits, 107, 137, 211, 216
media, 95, 142, 330–31
   see also newspapers
   social, 63, 332
medical care, 30, 87, 232, 262
mental health, 107, 118, 121, 138–39, 224, 247
meritocracy, 113, 280
MERS, 12, 24, 29, 42, 44, 343
Merthyr Tydfil, 129
Middlesbrough, 123, 204
Midlands, 46, 55, 123, 141–42, 204
Milan, 35–39, 43
Minimum Income Commission, 221, 320
minimum wages, 80, 90, 141, 220, 272
ministerial accountability, 97
Ministerial Code, 97

Mirrlees Review, 202, 298
mobility, social, 69, 113–14, 117,
        276, 280, 320
models, 35, 226, 232, 237, 305,
        312, 315, 326
Moody's, 190
Moonshot Guide, 312
Moore, Charles, 52
moral codes, 344, 346
moral hazard, 148–49, 162
moralised economy, 249
morality, 6–8, 218, 238, 241, 323
    and history, 241–50
Morris, Nicholas, 71
mortality, 37, 86, 131, 261, 338
mortgage payments, 138, 157
mortgages, 138, 153, 157, 182,
        185, 187, 328
Mosley, Oswald, 274
motherhood penalty, 229
mothers, 206, 216, 226, 228–29,
        239, 275–76
    single, 16, 254, 262
MPs, 45, 80, 91, 93, 217
municipal collectivism, 245, 305
municipalism, 245, 249
Murphy, Richard, 202, 297
Murray, Richard, 64
mutations, 54, 57, 59
myths, 22–23, 105, 175, 239, 249,
        314, 330
    of rationality, 237–41

NAO, *see* National Audit Office
Napoleonic era, 103, 181, 182, 288
National Audit Office, 83, 93, 302
national debt, 15, 150, 175, 177,
        179–84, 185–87, 193–94,
        328
National Health Service *see* NHS
National Insurance, contributions,

        207, 211, 227, 296
natural capital, 316, 333
natural environment, 5–6, 290,
        309–17, 323–25, 344
natural monopolies, 244, 283
natural resources, 309, 313,
        315
Needham, Duncan, 180–82, 186–88
NEF (New Economics Foundation),
        179, 224
negative freedoms, 17, 287–89,
        291, 317
neoliberal ideology, 128, 143, 169,
        317
neoliberal project, 69–74, 81, 89,
        98–99
neoliberal state, 8–9, 17, 69,
        286
    casting aside, 237–50
    fragile society, 69–98
neoliberalism, 12–13, 70–72, 77,
        81, 99, 241, 246, 249
    economic, 78, 237
    era of, 205, 300
    Thatcherite, 284
Netherlands, 259
New Economics Foundation *see*
        NEF
New Labour, 81, 109, 115–17, 215,
        220–21, 302
New Liberal reforms, 271–72
New York, 31, 94, 239, 248
New Zealand, 51, 53, 56, 247, 334
Newcastle, 37, 123, 141, 307
newspapers, 160, 169, 271, 300,
        323, 331
NHS, 12–13, 45–46, 52, 77, 81,
        83–86, 88, 131–32
    budget, 84, 93
    Test and Trace, 92–93
Nightingale hospitals, 52

no-deal Brexit, 46, 76, 78
Northern Ireland, 53, 55, 62, 78,
        141, 143
Norway, 50, 199, 294
Notification of Diseases Acts, 37,
        54, 127
nurses, 128, 131–32, 300
nurtured planet, 329, 346
nurturing environment, 17
nurturing society, 4, 250
nurturing state, 9, 17–18, 285–87,
        290–91, 293, 301, 308, 312,
        217, 319–22, 329, 340, 346
    and natural environment,
        309–17
Nussbaum, Martha, 289

obesity, 2, 118, 125, 130
O'Donnell, Gus, 198
Office for Budget Responsibility,
        56, 195
offshoring, 75, 102, 295, 323
old age, 230, 232, 253, 265
Oldham, 123
oligarchy, 12, 75, 303, 329
Olympics, 2012, 81
one-off wealth tax, 199, 201
open public discourse, 318,
        329–32
organisations, 79, 284, 302, 323,
        332
    civic, 8, 307
orphans, 16, 254, 257
Osborne, George, 105, 109, 151,
        177–80, 185, 187
outcomes, 71, 78, 129, 131, 171, 307
    life, 64, 114, 119
overcrowding, 28, 30, 58, 113, 126,
        127, 321
overseers, 254, 263–64
ownership, 130, 163, 276, 280

    public, 149, 245
Oxford, 37, 274
    University, 60–61, 267, 337

pandemic see Introductory Note
pandemic control, 11, 44, 51
    changing role of state, 32–35
    ever-present threat, 21–22
    history, 21–43
    how pandemics spread, 29–32
    learning how, 36–43
    myth of progress, 22–29
pandemic payback, 14, 162, 166,
        173
parents, 31, 106, 110, 113–14,
        117, 121, 137, 138–40
parish relief see also Poor Laws, 261
parishes, 39, 251–56, 262–63, 283,
        345
    of settlement, 259, 263
participation, 17, 284–87, 318,
        326, 338
    deliberative, 308
    democratic, 10, 301–9
participatory budget setting (PBS),
        307–8
participatory democracy, 303–4,
        339
participatory politics, 318,
        338–40, 341–46
Patel, Priti, 97
Paterson, Owen, 92
patient capital, 315, 335
patients, 13, 24, 47, 50–51, 85–87,
        90, 240, 321
paupers, 210, 263, 267, 275
payback, 14, 147–73, 234, 327
    pandemic, 14, 162–68, 173
PBS (participatory budget setting),
        307–8
Peel, Robert, 205, 268

pelican portrait of Elizabeth I, 252

Penrose, John, 80

Pension Credit, 219–20

pensioners, 77, 106, 219–21, 265

pensions, 105, 111, 197, 206, 213, 219–20, 227, 296
    funds, 202, 337
    pots, 101, 153, 199
    triple lock, 219–20

people of colour, 1, 55, 110, 122, 125, 130–33, 161, 173, 290, 292, 303, 324–25
    deaths, 130–33

People's Budget, 199, 280

Pepys, Samuel, 22

performance
    economic, 2, 116, 234, 287, 333
    productivity, 179, 277

performativity of measures, 317, 332, 335

personal protective equipment
    see PPE

personal services, 130, 234

pesthouses, 38

PFI (Private Finance Initiative), 76, 338–39

Pfizer, 59–61, 62

Philadelphia, 42

Pickett, Kate, 121

Pigou, A.C., 200

Piketty, Thomas, 75, 120, 278–80

Pissarides, Christopher, 184

plague, 11, 21–23, 25–27, 30, 32–38, 43, 251–53

Plague Act, 38, 94

plague orders, 37–38, 251

Poland, 123, 160

police, 5, 132, 288–89, 300, 306

Policy Exchange, 79, 188

policy failures, 49, 282

political economy, 267–69

political elite, 161, 305, 339

political power, 75, 286

politicians, 76, 147, 152, 196, 204, 205, 300, 302

politics, 121, 168–69, 188, 301, 304, 329, 338
    participatory, 318, 338–40, 341–46

Pollock, Allyson, 58

polluter elite, 103

Poor Laws, 2, 16, 250, 253–72, 276, 281–84, 301, 306
    New, 267, 269
    Old, 2, 267, 270–71, 283
    overseers, 254, 263–64
    workhouses, 213, 267–69, 272, 275
        deterrent, 2, 267

poor rates, 256, 294

Pope Clement VI, 33–34

Portes, Jonathan, 184

Porto Alegre, 307–8

positive freedoms, 16–17, 222, 281, 289–90, 294, 299, 346

potato blight, 2, 205, 268

poverty, 109–12, 121–22, 206–8, 210, 214–15, 220–22, 271–72, 320–21
    engrained, 223, 291
    extreme, 111–12, 211–12, 341
    food, 196, 213
    global, 341
    line, 111, 220
    reduction, 215, 342
    relative, 110, 123

power, 96, 99, 104–5, 168–69, 173, 209–10, 289, 339–40
    balance of, 168–69
    devolved, 301–9
    discretionary, 10, 308, 340
    lobbying, 301, 311

power (*cont.*)
    political, 75, 286
    relationships, 4, 144–47, 241
PPE (personal protective
        equipment), 12, 45, 47–49,
        78, 83–84, 90, 96, 195
prayer, 33–34, 251
precarity, 104, 323
pre-distribution, 114
Preston, 39, 307, 340
    Model, 306
prices, 8, 76, 99, 114–15, 152, 158,
        163, 219
    food, 261, 262
prime ministers *see individual names*
private contractors, 54, 302
Private Finance Initiative *see* PFI
private schools, 96, 113, 115, 122,
        297, 320
privatisation, 7, 59, 70, 81, 89–91
privileges, 114, 120, 170–72, 320
proactive state, 193–207
procurement, 45, 61, 83, 307, 321,
        337
    just in time, 13, 81, 83–84
productive investments, 71, 260
productivity, 69, 72–74, 100, 103,
        179, 270, 277, 281
    gap, 123
    growth, 3, 270, 276, 280–81
    performance, 179, 277
    puzzle, 103, 179
profits, 7–9, 72, 76, 167, 170, 203,
        323, 327
progressive contributions, 295–301
progressive taxation, 10, 16, 69,
        276–80, 283, 293, 297
Project Birch, 159
proportionate universalism, 224,
        291
prorogation of parliament, 78

prosperity, 25, 104, 239, 319
    long-term, 170, 284
protective clothing/equipment
        see also PPE, 12, 26, 45,
        47, 321
protests, 5, 40, 107, 132, 166,
        246–47, 262, 269–70
Public Accounts Committee, 45,
        93, 302
public buy-in, 9, 223, 336
public discourse, open, 318,
        329–32
public health, 21, 42, 82–83, 92,
        126, 269
Public Health England, 79, 82, 97,
        129, 132
public investment, 15, 76, 169
public opinion, 6, 24, 91, 161,
        330
public ownership, 149, 245
public sector, 54, 71, 76, 80, 303,
        322
    deficit, 194
public services, 9, 13, 15, 114–15,
        223–24, 300–2, 306,
        321–22
    universal, 9, 15, 292
public spending, 13, 70, 117, 151,
        153, 194–96, 211, 328
public sphere, 71, 144, 172, 196
public transport, 40, 129–30, 336
pubs, 54, 208
pupils, 95, 113, 115–16, 196, 225

QE (quantitative easing), 150, 152
quality of life, 233
quarantine, 11, 23, 32, 35, 38–39
    hotel-based, 62

R budget, 57, 58
R rate, 31, 53, 55, 57

racism, 121, 131–33
  structural, 131, 133, 321
Ragusa, 38
rail network, 159, 165, 175, 199, 306
Randox, 92
Rashford, Marcus, 206, 215–17
rates, business, 155, 160
rational economic man *see Homo economicus*
rationality, 250
  myth, 237–41
Raworth, Kate, 248, 334
recession, 99, 105, 138, 191, 277
recovery, 21, 151, 164, 169, 188, 190–91, 192–94
red risk, 45
red tape, 70, 303
redistribution, 120, 169, 204, 210, 278, 287
redundancies, 124, 156, 165, 192, 256
Reeves, Rachel, 77
regional inequalities, 191, 204
regions, 104, 109, 123, 203–4, 261, 289, 308–9, 328, 335
regressive taxation, 203–4, 296, 326
regulation, 17, 70, 74–75, 77–78, 89, 102, 177, 210, 291, 295, 303, 316, 323, 332
Reinhart, C.M., 180, 187
rent seeking, 74
rentier capitalism, 102
rescue packages, 147, 165
residential capitalism, 74
resilience, 1, 45, 47, 84, 124, 125, 318–21, 323
  and inequality, 99–127
Resolution Foundation, 109–10, 133, 135, 185, 201, 205

resources, 10, 242, 246, 286, 289–90, 293–95, 308–9, 340
  environmental, 315, 317
  natural, 309, 313, 315
responsibilities, 82, 96–97, 245, 253, 255–57, 262–63, 268, 283
  collective, 9, 70, 234, 258, 276, 286, 293, 317
restaurants, 54, 139, 141, 158, 208
retail, 124, 130, 136, 155, 189, 208, 234
retraining, 195, 328
retrofitting, 168, 335
revenues, 88, 155, 159, 199–200, 203, 244, 295, 308
Rhondda Cynon Taf, 129
rigged capitalism, 77
rights, 172, 227, 241, 262–63, 304, 325
  human, 112, 171
risks, 14–15, 29–30, 44–45, 55–56, 129–31, 155–57, 160–62, 342–43
  real, 64, 143, 184, 231
Rivenalls, 263–64
Roberts, Carys, 104
Rogoff, K., 180, 187
Romania, 123
Rome, 39, 50, 252
Rowntree, Seebohm, 271

Sacks, Jonathan, 8
sacrifices, 56, 122, 195, 200, 227, 231
safety, 54, 88, 288, 332
safety nets, 13, 111, 133–38, 212–13, 217, 221–23, 253
  fit-for-purpose, 15, 212, 214
SAGE (Scientific Advisory Group of Experts), 55–56, 58

sanctions, 35, 97, 106, 284, 301, 332
sanitation, 30, 39, 243
SARS, 12, 24, 29, 42, 44–46, 343
savings, 14, 45, 83, 124, 137, 204,
        211, 220
Schofield, Roger, 259
school meals, free, 95, 206, 215–17
school strikers, 247
schools, 55, 57–58, 92, 95, 113,
        115, 139–41, 225
    private, 96, 113, 115, 122, 297,
        320
    state, 113, 115–16
Schwab, Klaus, 170–71
Scientific Advisory Group of
        Experts see SAGE
scientists, 12, 31, 45, 49–50, 55,
        58–59
Scotland, 53, 116, 141, 143
Scrooge, 218
scroungers, 7, 178, 331
scrutiny, 13, 131, 302, 330
Searcher of the Dead, 37
Seattle, 41
Second World War, 3, 42, 74, 112,
        121, 181, 186, 201, 241,
        242, 274, 278, 284, 340
secondary education, 115–16, 223,
        225, 242, 270, 276
second-hand clothes, 41
secrecy jurisdictions, 294, 327
security, 3, 139, 212, 220–21, 258,
        270, 275
    food, 225, 342
self-employment, 104, 324
    support, 156, 192
self-interest, 8, 71, 243, 310, 312,
        345
selfishness, 16, 237, 239–41, 250,
        286, 309

self-isolation see also isolation, 14,
        93–95, 126, 324
Sen, Amartya, 222–23, 289
Senior, Nassau William, 267
Serco, 54, 79, 338
services, 114, 118, 214, 223–24,
        226, 292, 296, 300
    health see health, care; NHS
    personal, 130, 234
    public see public services
    transport, 2, 224
    universal, 222–26, 230, 322
settlement, 255, 262
    litigation, 263
    parishes of, 259, 263
Seven Pillars, 18, 318–40
Shakespeare, William, 27
share buybacks, 161, 165, 170
shareholder capitalism, 170, 322
shareholder value, 5, 7, 72, 323
shareholders, 14, 72, 160–63,
        164, 169–72, 311, 322,
        327
Sharp, Richard, 80
Shaxson, Nicholas, 72–74
Sheffield, 141
shocks, 70, 120, 122, 135, 144,
        186, 193, 241
shortages, 34, 329
    food, 251, 261, 265
sick pay, 47, 125–26, 172, 324
Siena, Kevin, 37
signals, 24, 229, 316, 334
Singapore, 42, 55, 152
single mothers, 16, 254, 262
Skafidas, Georgios, 51
Slack, Paul, 35, 257
Slater, Martin, 182
small businesses, 167–68
smallpox, 23, 29–30, 40

smartphones, 108, 225
Smith, Adam, 70, 255, 266
Smith, Harry, 274–75
Soames, Rupert, 79
social attitudes, 221
social breakdown, 261–62
social care, 45, 83, 87–91, 96,
    117–18, 130, 164, 232–33
social cohesion, 121–22, 299, 316,
    320
social contract, 7, 224, 241–42,
    247, 340
social distancing, 35, 41, 43, 48,
    52, 54, 64, 73
social equity, 11, 234, 333
social exclusion, 121
social insurance, 232, 291, 322
social justice, 117, 223
social media, 63, 332
social mobility, 69, 113–14, 117,
    276, 280, 320
social movements, 239, 243, 246
social security, 109, 254, 258, 263,
    267, 281, 288–89
    systems, 2, 214, 268
social wage, 114, 224
society, 6–8, 168–71, 222–24,
    281–83, 291–94, 297–300,
    316–21, 326–27
    British, 6, 17, 112, 274, 281
    empowered, 10
    empowering *see* empowering
        society
    nurturing *see* nurturing society
    unequal, 104, 114, 120–21
    welfare, 249–51
Sokoll, Thomas, 263–64
solidarity, 224, 264, 275, 298, 327
Somerset Webb, Merryn, 197
South Africa, 42, 62, 271

South Korea, 42, 53, 55, 121
Spain, 50, 99
Spanish flu, 28, 41–42
spending, 15, 116–18, 136, 140,
    185, 188, 191–96, 300
    education, 115–16, 140, 320
    public, 13, 70, 117, 151, 153,
        194–96, 211, 328
spreadsheet errors, 180
Sridhar, Devi, 127
St Patrick's Day, 52
stakeholder capitalism, 5, 170
stakeholders, 170, 323–26
starvation, 3, 205, 253, 261, 262,
    269
state
    changing role, 32–35
    diminished, 91–97
    disempowering, 4, 8, 17, 287
    empowering *see* empowering
        state
    and freedoms, 287–91
    neoliberal, 8–9, 17, 69, 237, 286
    nurturing *see* nurturing state
    proactive, 193–207
    schools, 113, 115–16
    welfare *see* welfare state
status, charitable, 79, 113, 320,
    330
Stevenson, Gary, 158
stewardship, 315, 316–18, 326,
    335–38, 344
Stiglitz, Joseph, 103
stimulus, 152, 158, 169
STIs, 42
structural racism, 131, 133, 321
subsidies, 54, 165, 189–90, 296, 336
success, 192, 275, 307, 316, 324, 333
    long-term, 14, 172, 323

suicides, 107, 138, 306
Sunak, Rishi, 154, 192–95, 202
Sunday Times, 49
super-rich, 103, 299
suppliers, 47, 170, 323
support, 139–42, 211–13, 257–59,
        279–81, 292, 300–1,
        306–7, 335–36
    collective, 272–73
    self-employment, 156, 192
surges, 64, 83, 92, 125, 243
surveillance, 11, 24, 35–36, 42,
        331
survival sex, 111
sustainability, 191, 247, 316, 335, 340
    environmental, 209, 325, 337
sustainable economy, 281, 336
sustainable future, 318, 335–38
sustainable growth, 333, 337
Sutton, Thomas, 265
Sweden, 294
Switzerland, 134–35, 166, 171,
        199, 201
syndemic, 2, 321
syphilis, 30, 40

Taiwan, 42, 55
Take Care scheme, 94
take the knee, 133
TalkTalk, 92
Tawney, R.H., 289
tax, 99–102, 194, 196, 199, 201–4,
        206, 207, 278–80, 295–96,
        299, 300
    avoidance, 202, 299, 301, 330
    Capital Gains, 80, 202–3, 296
    corporation, 152, 167, 194,
        203, 324–26
    Council, 107, 157, 203–4, 306,
        326

    cuts, 7, 177, 300
    havens, 89, 160, 293–95, 311, 327
    income, 199, 202–3, 207–9,
        211, 278–81, 296, 297,
        326, 328–30
    rates, 72, 279–80, 284, 295–301
    rises, 194, 196–98, 202, 207,
        328
    social insurance, 232
    solidarity, 298, 327
    systems, 202, 296–97, 326
    wealth, 170, 197–202, 205–7,
        278–281, 296–301,
        326–328
    windfall, 203, 327
tax, carbon, 213
taxation, 35, 75, 114, 195, 202,
        246, 294, 299–300
    progressive, 10, 16, 69, 276–80,
        283, 293, 297
taxpayers, 76, 113, 149, 231, 295,
        297
TB, 30, 40, 42, 126
Tebbit, Norman, 105
technologies, 21, 225, 337
    green, 168, 315, 335
temporary hospitals, 50
test, track and trace ,10, 12, 19,
        42, 53, 58–59, 80, 82, 83,
        92–93, 126, 154, 188, 195
testing, 47–49, 78, 86, 90, 92, 196,
        321
Thailand, 240
Thatcher, Margaret, 79, 88, 99–
        101, 109, 209, 286–87,
        300, 306
think tanks, 10, 79, 189, 330
threats, 27, 37, 45–47, 75, 82, 251,
        331–32, 342
Thunberg, Greta, 5, 248, 304

Tiny Tim, 218
too big to fail argument, 149, 159
Tooze, Adam, 185, 238
total fertility rate, 230–31
towns, 37, 105, 257, 259–62, 265,
     269, 306, 310
tracing
  backward, 94
  contact, 35, 54, 82, 92
track and trace *see* test, track and
    trace
trade unions, 10, 99, 103, 143,
     303–4, 323–24, 336,
     339
transmissibility, 24, 32
transparency, 53, 78, 294, 301–2,
     321, 330, 339
transport, 130, 233, 260, 322
  public, 40, 129–30, 336
  services, 2, 224
trickle down, 102–4
Trump, Donald, 6, 301
Trumpington, 39
Trussell Trust, 107, 125, 225
trust, 8, 63, 122, 225, 292, 308
truth, 55, 74, 189, 214, 239
two-child limit, 107–9, 112, 134,
    216
typhoid, 40, 126
Typhoid Marys, 31

UBI (Universal Basic Income), 15,
    208–11, 320
UBS (Universal Basic Services),
    158, 224
UN Special Rapporteur, 112
underlying health conditions,
    125, 130
unearned incomes, 197, 280,
    326

unemployment, 99, 105, 125, 139,
    265, 272–74, 277
  benefit, 133–34
  insurance, 134, 274
  mass, 99, 242, 273
unequal society *see also*
    inequalities, 104, 114, 121
unions *see* trade unions
Universal Basic Income *see* UBI
Universal Basic Services *see* UBS
universal benefits, 115, 218
Universal Credit, 13, 106–11,
    133–38, 142, 210, 212,
    214, 217–18, 221 *see also*
    benefits
  £20 uprating, 134, 135, 192,
    218–19, 320
  five-week wait, 13, 178, 212
universal public services, 9, 15,
    292
universal services, 222–26, 230,
    322
universalism, 211
  proportionate, 224, 291
unpaid care, 231, 322
unpreparedness, reasons for, 44–59
uprating, 80, 218, 221, 320
  emergency, 218–19
urban authorities, 34–35, 308
urban growth, 25, 260
utilitarianism, 16, 250, 267, 345
U-turns, 12, 95, 218

vaccination, 30–31, 40, 43, 62–63,
    292
  programmes, 61, 192, 195
  roll out, 12, 61–63
  scepticism, 40, 63
  take-up, 122
Vaccination Acts, 40

vaccine nationalism, 62
vaccines, 12, 41, 59–65
   AstraZeneca, 60–62
   Pfizer, 59–61, 62
Vaccine Taskforce, 61, 91
valuations, 203, 274, 326
value
   creation, 170–71, 322, 323
   extraction, 162, 171, 322
   measuring, 332–35
   for money, 91, 302
VAT, 15, 151, 189, 206–7, 296–97, 330
ventilators, 45, 85, 341
victims, 41, 73, 160, 267
Vines, David, 71
violence, 121, 138–39, 288–89, 332
voters, 7, 248, 300, 317, 323
vouchers, 95, 189
V-shaped economic recovery, 189–90
vulnerabilities, 16, 128–30, 213, 256, 269, 286, 290, 344
vulnerable citizens, 12, 87, 89, 213, 287

wages, 133, 141, 154, 210, 221, 229, 267
   minimum, 80, 90, 141, 220, 272
   real, 103, 124
   social, 114, 224
Wales, 53, 55, 129, 141, 254, 262
War of the Spanish Succession, 182
Washington Consensus, 70, 343
water, 39, 215, 244
   cholera-contaminated, 40
   supply, 243, 245
waves of infection, 41, 49, 55, 64, 127–28, 192, 251, 288

wealth, 9–11, 72–75, 101, 197–202, 204–6, 278–80, 295–301, 328–29
   common, 168, 283
   concentrations, 158, 205, 278–79, 290
   funds, 164, 233, 307, 327
   inequalities, 101, 115, 158, 210, 276–78, 280
   taxes, 170, 197–202, 205–7, 278–281, 296–301, 326–328
   one-off, 199, 201
wealth defence industry, 293
Wealth of Nations, 70
Wealth Tax Commission, 198–99, 206–7
wealthiest citizens, 295, 310
wealthy, 75–76, 197–99, 204–5, 249, 293–95, 297–300, 326, 328–30
Webb, Beatrice and Sidney, 214, 262, 272
welfare, 212–13, 221, 239, 248, 276, 281, 316–19, 321
   budget, 105, 151, 178
   culture, 257
   society, 249–51
   systems, 16, 136, 205, 254
welfare state, 15, 101, 210, 211–13, 224, 226, 274, 290–91
   breadwinner model, 15, 226–27, 322
   dynamics, 71
   hidden, 296
   post-war, 16, 69–70, 226, 249, 250, 275, 280, 306
welfare state, treatment of women, 226–32

well-being, 247, 286, 290, 316, 325, 331
WHO (World Health Organization), 24, 29, 32, 44, 82
widows, 16, 254
Wilkinson, Richard, 121
Williamson, Gavin, 96
windfall tax, 203, 327
Windrush generation, 132
winners, 155–61, 310, 331
Wolf, Martin, 120
work, 57–58, 94–96, 103–6, 110–13, 135–39, 153–54, 213–15, 226–30
worker representation, 172
workers, 126–30, 135–36, 155–56, 164–65, 178–79, 269–71, 304–6, 323–25
  care, 47, 61, 90, 130, 189, 233–34, 300
  key, 49, 125, 129–30, 139, 195
  ordinary, 100, 197, 326, 339
workforce, 16, 77, 90, 115, 229, 283
workhouses, 213, 267–69, 272, 275
  deterrent, 2, 267

working age benefits, 108, 213, 220
working class, 69, 122, 143, 222, 269, 271, 305, 308
workplaces, 53–54, 57, 96, 172, 229
World Bank, 30, 341
World Economic Forum *see also* Davos Manifesto 170–71, 247
World Health Organization *see* WHO
world leaders, 61, 83, 151
World Wars
  First, 28, 41, 186, 200
  Second, 42, 112, 121, 186, 241–42, 274, 278, 284, 340

yellow fever, 40
young adults, 138–39, 164, 259, 265, 307
youth parliaments, 304, 339

zero hours, 104, 324
zero tolerance, 171, 294
Zuboff, Shoshana, 331
Zucman, Gabriel, 294